The Darker Side of Travel

ASPECTS OF TOURISM
Series Editors: Chris Cooper, *Nottingham University Business School, UK,*
C. Michael Hall, *University of Canterbury, New Zealand* and Dallen J. Timothy,
Arizona State University, USA

Aspects of Tourism is an innovative, multifaceted series, which comprises
authoritative reference handbooks on global tourism regions, research volumes,
texts and monographs. It is designed to provide readers with the latest thinking
on tourism worldwide and to push back the frontiers of tourism knowledge.
The volumes are authoritative, readable and user-friendly, providing accessible
sources for further research. Books in the series are commissioned to probe the
relationship between tourism and cognate subject areas such as strategy,
development, retailing, sport and environmental studies.

Full details of all the books in this series and of all our other publications can be
found on http://www.channelviewpublications.com, or by writing to Channel View
Publications, St Nicholas House, 31–34 High Street, Bristol BS1 2AW, UK.

ASPECTS OF TOURISM
Series Editors: Chris Cooper, C. Michael Hall and Dallen J. Timothy

The Darker Side of Travel
The Theory and Practice of Dark Tourism

Edited by

Richard Sharpley and Philip R. Stone

CHANNEL VIEW PUBLICATIONS
Bristol • Buffalo • Toronto

This book is dedicated to the memory of

John Hugh Ashton Sharpley
(1927–2006)

and

Mary McCourt Stone
(1941–2004)

Library of Congress Cataloging in Publication Data
A catalog record for this book is available from the Library of Congress.
The Darker Side of Travel: The Theory and Practice of Dark Tourism/
Edited by Richard Sharpley and Philip Stone.
Includes bibliographical references and index.
1. Tourism. 2. War memorials. 3. Historic sites. 4. Death--Social aspects.
I. Sharpley, Richard, 1956- II. Stone, Philip (Philip R.)
G155.A1D33 2009
338.4'791–dc22 2009026026

British Library Cataloguing in Publication Data
A catalogue entry for this book is available from the British Library.

ISBN-13: 978-1-84541-115-2 (hbk)
ISBN-13: 978-1-84541-114-5 (pbk)

Channel View Publications
UK: St Nicholas House, 31–34 High Street, Bristol BS1 2AW, UK.
USA: UTP, 2250 Military Road, Tonawanda, NY 14150, USA.
Canada: UTP, 5201 Dufferin Street, North York, Ontario M3H 5T8, Canada.

The policy of Multilingual Matters/Channel View Publications is to use papers that are natural, renewable and recyclable products, made from wood grown in sustainable forests. In the manufacturing process of our books, and to further support our policy, preference is given to printers that have FSC and PEFC Chain of Custody certification. The FSC and/or PEFC logos will appear on those books where full certification has been granted to the printer concerned.

Typeset by Techset Composition Ltd., Salisbury, UK.
Printed and bound in Great Britain by Short Run Press Ltd.

Contents

Contributors vii

Part 1: Dark Tourism: Theories and Concepts

1 Shedding Light on Dark Tourism: An Introduction 3
   Richard Sharpley

2 Making Absent Death Present: Consuming Dark Tourism
   in Contemporary Society 23
   Philip R. Stone

3 Dark Tourism: Mediating Between the Dead and the Living 39
   Tony Walter

4 Dark Tourism: Morality and New Moral Spaces 56
   Philip R. Stone

Part 2: Dark Tourism: Management Implications

5 Purposeful Otherness: Approaches to the Management
   of Thanatourism 75
   Tony Seaton

6 (Re)presenting the Macabre: Interpretation, Kitschification
   and Authenticity 109
   Richard Sharpley and Philip R. Stone

7 Contested National Tragedies: An Ethical Dimension 129
   Craig Wight

8 Dark Tourism and Political Ideology: Towards
   a Governance Model 145
   Richard Sharpley

Part 3: Dark Tourism in Practice

9   'It's a Bloody Guide': Fun, Fear and a Lighter Side
     of Dark Tourism at The Dungeon Visitor Attractions, UK 167
     Philip R. Stone

10 Battlefield Tourism: Bringing Organised Violence
     Back to Life 186
     Frank Baldwin and Richard Sharpley

11 'Genocide Tourism' 207
     John Beech

12 Museums, Memorials and Plantation Houses in the Black
     Atlantic: Slavery and the Development of Dark Tourism 224
     Alan Rice

13 Life, Death and Dark Tourism: Future Research Directions
     and Concluding Comments 247
     Richard Sharpley and Philip R. Stone

References 252
Index 274

Contributors

Frank Baldwin has been guiding people around battlefields since 1987 as a guide for the British Army, the Royal British Legion, Leger Holidays, The Battlefields Trust and for Business Battlefields, his own business. He has worked in operations and marketing for the Royal British Legion's travel arm 'Poppy Travel'. Frank holds Badge Number 8 from the Guild of Battlefield Guides. He serves on the council of the Guild of Battlefield Guides and is a Trustee of the Battlefields Trust. He has a BSc in Psychology from the University of Sheffield and an MBA from the University of Warwick and served as an Army Officer, leaving the British Army as a Major.

Dr John Beech is the Head of Sport and Tourism Applied Research at Coventry University, where he was previously Head of Strategy and Applied Management, Head of Leisure, Sport and Tourism Management and Acting Head of Marketing and Leisure. He is a full-time researcher based in the Applied Research Centre for Sustainable Regeneration (SURGE) and is also a co-director of the Centre for International Business of Sport (CIBS). John's tourism research interests include not only dark tourism (both genocide tourism and slavery heritage tourism) but also heritage tourism (especially the heritage of transport and other industrial aspects of heritage) and mass tourism. He is a member of the Executive Board of ATLAS, Chair of the ATLAS Mass Tourism SIG, and a member of the national committee of SPRIG.

Dr Alan Rice is Reader in American Cultural Studies at the University of Central Lancashire in Preston His first interdisciplinary monograph *Radical Narratives of the Black Atlantic* was published in 2003. His next monograph project on *Creating Memorials, Building Identities: The Politics of Memory in the Black Atlantic* (Liverpool University Press) is currently in progress. He has published essays in the *Journal of American Studies*, *Research in African Literatures*, *Atlantic Studies*, *Patterns of Prejudice*, *Wasafiri* and *Current Writing*. He is an academic advisor to and board member of the Slave Trade Arts Memorial Project (STAMP) in Lancaster which was responsible for the commissioning and building of the first British quay-side monument to the victims of the slave trade, unveiled in Lancaster in October 2005. He has consulted on a wide range of documentaries on the Black Atlantic for the BBC, Border Television and PBS in the USA. He is an advisor to museums in Liverpool, Lancaster and Manchester. Most recently he has co-curated an exhibition *Trade and Empire: Remembering Slavery* at the Whitworth Art Gallery in Manchester which ran from June 2007–April 2008 and acted as editor-in-chief and main text contributor to the *Revealing Histories* website (www.revealinghistories.org.uk).

Tony Seaton has, since 1998, been Whitbread Professor of Tourism Behaviour and Founder Director of the International Tourism Research Centre at the University of Bedfordshire. He has a first class honours degree in the Social Sciences, a Masters in English Literature from Wadham College, Oxford and a PhD in Tourism from Strathclyde University. He has written/edited six books and published widely in journals on thana-tourism, literary tourism, travel history and tourism marketing. One of his books was presented by the Queen during a royal visit to the President of Iceland as an official gift and two of his research studies led to the establishment of Scotland's book town, Wigtown, of which he is now a patron. He has lectured, researched and consulted in over 60 countries and conducted projects for the UNWTO, ETC and EU.

Richard Sharpley is Professor of Tourism and Development at the University of Central Lancashire, Preston, UK. He has previously held positions at a number of other institutions, including the University of Northumbria (Reader in Tourism) and the University of Lincoln, where he was professor of Tourism and Head of Department, Tourism and Recreation Management. His principal research interests are within the fields of tourism and development, island tourism, rural tourism and the sociol-ogy of tourism, and his books include *Tourism and Development: Concepts and Issues* (2002), *Tourism and Development in the Developing World* (2008) and *Tourism, Tourists and Society*, 4th Edition (2008).

Philip R. Stone is a former Management Consultant within the tourism and hospitality sector, and is presently employed as a Senior Lecturer with the University of Central Lancashire (UCLan), UK. He teaches Tourism, Hospitality and Event Management at undergraduate and postgraduate level. Philip is also founder and editor of The Dark Tourism Forum, the premier online dark tourism subject resource facility and global alliance of scholars and industry practitioners (see www.dark-tourism.org.uk). His primary research interests revolve around dark tourism consumption and its relationship with contemporary society. He has published in a number of international academic journals, presented at a variety of international conferences, as well as acting as media consultant on dark tourism to both press and broadcast institutions across the world.

Tony Walter works in the Centre for Death & Society at the University of Bath, where he runs the MSc on Death and Society. He has written and lectured widely on how death in the modern world is organised, symbolised, ritualised and theorised. His books include *The Human Home: The Myth of the Sacred Environment* (1982), *Funerals – and How to Improve Them* (1990), *The Eclipse of Eternity: A Sociology of the Afterlife* (1996) and *The Mourning for Diana* (1999). He is also a qualified Blue Badge tourist guide.

Craig Wight is a Business Development Consultant in the Moffat Centre, Glasgow Caledonian University. Craig undertakes consultancy project work for a range of public and private sector tourism organisations nationally and internationally. He has undertaken academic research into visitor attractions, the role of museums and heritage in remembering human tragedy, national icons in tourism, museum interpretation and 'culinary tourism'. Recently Craig has carried out research into narratives of Lithuanian and Jewish tragedy in international tourism discourses and this research continues to underpin his evolving PhD work.

Part 1

Dark Tourism: Theories and Concepts

Chapter 1

Shedding Light on Dark Tourism: An Introduction

RICHARD SHARPLEY

Introduction

On 23 August 1930, the SS Morro Castle, named after the fortress that guards the entrance to Havana Bay, set out on her maiden voyage from New York City to Cuba. Offering luxurious, though affordable, travel as well as a Prohibition-era opportunity for the legal consumption of alcohol, the ship immediately became popular among tourists and business travellers alike and over the next four years successfully plied the route between the New York and Havana.

In the early hours of 8 September 1934, however, disaster struck. During the previous evening, as the ship was approaching the eastern seaboard of the USA on the return journey from Havana, Captain Robert Wilmott apparently suffered a heart attack and died in his bathtub and, as a consequence, command passed to the First Officer, William Warms. At 2.45 am, fire broke out in the First Class Writing Room and quickly spread, with design faults and questionable crew practices contributing to the conflagration. For a variety of reasons, including alleged indecision on the part of the captain, the SOS was not sent out until 3.25 am, by which time the ship had lost all power and was fully ablaze. Despite the ship's position close to the shore, rescue operations were slow and ineffective and the eventual death toll amounted to 137 passengers and crew out of a total of 549 people on board (Gallagher, 2003; Hicks, 2006).

The devastating fire on the SS Morro Castle remains one of America's worst and most controversial peacetime maritime disasters and at the time led to significant fire safety improvements in ship design. However, it was also notable for the fact that large numbers of people arrived to witness the aftermath of the event. Attempts to salvage the ship were unsuccessful and, driven by the wind, the smouldering wreck, with numerous victims still aboard, drifted onto the shore of New Jersey at Asbury Park (Figure 1.1).

Figure 1.1 The wreck of the SS Morro Castle
Source: http://en.wikipedia.org/wiki/SS_Morro_Castle (GNU Free Document License)

Almost immediately it became a tourist attraction. Spurred on by news-paper and radio reports and special excursion train fares from New York and Philadelphia (Hegeman, 2000), up to a quarter of a million people travelled to view the wreck and, according to press reports at the time, almost a carnival atmosphere prevailed. As Hegeman (2000) observes, 'the scene at the wreck of the *Morro Castle* was both a spontaneous public festival and a media event. Postcards were printed, souvenirs were sold, and radio broadcasts offered … firsthand accounts of the scene on board the wreck complete with lurid descriptions of charred corpses.' It was even proposed that the wreck should be permanently moored at Asbury Park as a tourist attraction, although it was eventually towed away to be sold for scrap some six months later.

   In short, the SS Morro Castle disaster was an early, while by no means the first, example of a phenomenon that has more recently come to be referred to as 'dark tourism'. Indeed, for as long as people have been able to travel, they have been drawn – purposefully or otherwise – towards sites, attractions or events that are linked in one way or another with death, suffering, violence or disaster (Stone, 2005a; Seaton, *forthcoming*). For example, the gladiatorial games of the Roman era, pilgrimages, and attendance at medieval public executions were early forms of such death-related tourism. Boorstin (1964) alleges that the first guided tour in England in 1838 was a trip by train to witness the hanging of two murderers. In the specific context of warfare, Seaton (1999) observes that death, suffering and tourism have been related for centuries (see also

Smith, 1998; Knox, 2006), citing visits to the battlefield of Waterloo from 1816 onwards as a notable 19th-century example of what he terms 'thana-tourism'. Also in the 19th century, visits to the morgue were, as MacCannell (1989) notes, a regular feature of tours of Paris – perhaps a forerunner of the 'Body Worlds' exhibitions in London, Tokyo and elsewhere that have attracted visitors in their tens of thousands since the late 1990s (www.bodyworlds.com/en.html).

As will be considered shortly, the extent to which dark tourism may be considered a historical phenomenon – that is, visiting sites or attractions that predate living memory – remains a subject of debate (Wight, 2006). It is clear, however, that visitors have long been attracted to places or events associated in one way or another with death, disaster and suffering. Equally, there can be little doubt that, over the last half century and commensurate with the remarkable growth in general tourism, dark tourism has become both widespread and diverse. In terms of supply, there has been a rapid growth in the provision of such attractions or experiences; indeed, there appears to be an increasing number of people keen to promote or profit from 'dark' events as tourist attractions, such as the Pennsylvania farmer who offered a $65 per person 'Flight 93 Tour' to the crash site of the United Airlines Flight 93 – one of the 9/11 aircraft (Bly, 2003). Moreover, dark tourism has become more widely recognised both as a form of tourism and as a promotional tool, with websites such as www.thecabinet.com listing numerous dark tourism sites around the world (Dark Destinations, 2007).

At the same time, there is evidence of a greater willingness or desire on the part of tourists to visit dark attractions and, in particular, the sites of dark events. For example, in August 2002 local residents in the small town of Soham in Cambridgeshire, UK appealed for an end to the so-called 'grief tourism' that was bringing tens of thousands of visitors to their town. Many of these visitors, travelling from all over Britain, had come to lay flowers, light candles in the local church or sign books of condolence. Others had simply come to gaze at the town – indeed, it was reported that tourist buses *en route* to Cambridge or nearby Ely Cathedral were making detours through the town (O'Neill, 2002). They had been drawn to Soham by its association with a terrible – and highly publicised – crime: the abduction and murder of two young schoolgirls. In the same year, Ground Zero in New York attracted three-and-a-half million visitors, almost double the number that annually visited the observation platform of the World Trade Center prior to 9/11 (Blair, 2002). Interestingly, echoing what had occurred at Asbury Park almost 70 years earlier, the site also attracted numerous street vendors 'selling trinkets that run the gamut of taste' (Vega, 2002); souvenirs on sale ranged from framed photographs of the burning towers to Osama Bin Laden toilet paper, his picture printed on each square (see also Lisle, 2004). More generally, evidence suggests that contemporary tourists are increasingly travelling to destinations associated with death and suffering. According to one recent report, for example, places such as Rwanda, Sierra Leone, Angola and Afghanistan are experiencing a significant upsurge in tourism demand (Rowe, 2007).

Nevertheless, despite the long history and increasing contemporary evidence of travel to sites or attractions associated with death, it is only relatively and, perhaps, surprisingly recently that academic attention has been focused upon what has collectively been referred to as 'dark tourism' (Foley & Lennon, 1996a). More specifically, the publication of Lennon and Foley's (2000) *Dark Tourism: The Attraction of Death and Disaster* introduced the term to a wider audience, stimulating a significant degree of academic interest and debate. It is interesting to note, for example, that the dark tourism academic website (www.dark-tourism.org.uk), established by one of the authors of this book, annually receives over 60,000 hits. At the same time, media interest in the concept of dark tourism continues to grow, the juxtaposition of the words 'dark' and 'tourism' undoubtedly providing an attention-grabbing headline. However, to date, the academic literature remains eclectic and theoretically fragile and, consequently, understanding of the phenomenon of dark tourism remains limited. Certainly, numerous attempts have been made to define or label death-related tourist activity, with many commentators exploring and analysing specific manifestations of dark tourism, from war museums which adopt both traditional and contemporary museology methods of (re)presentation (Wight & Lennon, 2004) to genocide commemoration visitor sites and the political ideology attached to such remembrance (Williams, 2004). Much of the literature tends to be descriptive and 'supply-side comment and analysis' (Seaton & Lennon, 2004; Stone, 2005b); conversely, a demand-side perspective has been notably lacking for the most part, although some recent work has begun to focus on demand-related issues (Preece & Price, 2005; Yuill, 2003).

As a result, a number of fundamental questions with respect to dark tourism remain unanswered, not least whether it is actually possible or justifiable to categorise collectively the experience of sites or attractions that are associated with death or suffering as 'dark tourism'. That is, such is the variety of sites, attractions and experiences now falling under the collective umbrella of dark tourism that the meaning of the term has become increasingly diluted and fuzzy. More specifically, it remains unclear whether dark tourism is tourist-demand or attraction-supply driven or, more generally, the manifestation of what has been referred to as a (post)modern propensity for 'mourning sickness' (West, 2004). Other questions are also raised, but go unanswered in the literature. For example, has there indeed been a measurable growth in 'tourist interest in recent death, disaster and atrocity ... in the late 20th and early 21st centuries' (Lennon & Foley, 2000: 3) or is there simply an ever-increasing supply of 'dark' sites and attractions? Are there degrees or 'shades' of darkness that can be related to either the nature of the attraction or the intensity of interest in death or the macabre on the part of tourists (Miles, 2002; Strange & Kempa, 2003; Stone, 2006a)? What management or ethical issues are raised by labelling sites or attractions as 'dark'? And, does the popularity of 'dark' sites result from a basic, voyeuristic interest or fascination with death, or are there more powerful motivating factors?

The overall purpose of this book is to address these and other questions, thereby advancing knowledge and understanding of the phenomenon of dark tourism. In other words, it sets out to provide a contemporary and comprehensive analysis of dark tourism that, drawing upon extant concepts and introducing new theoretical perspectives on the subject, develops a theoretically informed foundation for examining the demand for and supply of dark tourism experiences. In particular, it identifies and explores issues relevant to the development, management and interpretation of dark sites and attractions, focusing in particular on the relationship between dark tourism and the cultural condition and social institutions of contemporary societies. The first task, however, is to establish the context of the book through a review of contemporary perspectives on dark tourism. The purpose of this introductory chapter is to set the scene for the concepts, debates and challenges considered in subsequent chapters.

But Why Study Dark Tourism?

To some extent, the increasing attention paid to the phenomenon of dark tourism in recent years may arguably be symptomatic of the trend within academic circles to identify and label specific forms of tourism, or to subdivide tourism into niche products and markets (Novelli, 2005). That is, the study of dark tourism may be considered simply as an academic endeavour. Equally, it may be seen as a specific manifestation of a wider social interest or fascination in death. As suggested earlier, a combination of the words 'dark' or 'grief' with 'tourism', the latter connoting relaxation, escape, hedonism or pleasure, creates an enticing headline. Thus, dark tourism may also be considered an example of media hype responding to this presumed fascination in death and dying.

However, the study of dark tourism is both justifiable and important for a number of reasons. Generally, as the following section reveals, dark tourism sites and attractions are not only numerous but also vary enormously, from 'playful' houses of horror, through places of pilgrimage such as the graves or death sites of famous people, to the Holocaust death camps or sites of major disasters or atrocities. Nevertheless, all such sites or attractions require effective and appropriate development, management, interpretation and promotion. These in turn require a fuller understanding of the phenomenon of dark tourism within social, cultural, historical and political contexts.

More specifically, the nature of many dark sites and, in particular, the conflicts they represent or inspire, point to a number of interrelated issues that demand investigation and understanding. These include the following.

Ethical issues

One question relating to many dark sites and attractions is whether it is ethical to develop, promote or offer them for touristic consumption. For example, significant debate surrounded the construction of the viewing platform at Ground Zero, enabling casual or even voyeuristic visitors to stand alongside those mourning the loss of loved ones (Lisle, 2004). The proposed construction of a large Tsunami Memorial in the Khao Lak Lamu National Park in Thailand has also been highly controversial. Not only is its potential location in a protected area deemed inappropriate, but many question whether such a large memorial should be constructed in the first place (see also Chapter 8). More generally, the rights of those whose death is commoditised or commercialised through dark tourism represent an important ethical dimension deserving consideration.

Marketing/promotional issues

Many dark tourism sites and attractions are, in a sense, 'accidental'. That is, they have not been purposefully created or developed as tourist attractions but have become so for a variety of reasons, such as the fame (or infamy) of people concerned, the events that once occurred there or even, perhaps, the beauty of a building. Frequently, the popularity of such sites may be enhanced by the marketing and promotional activity of businesses or organisations anxious to profit through tourism; equally, the media frequently play a role in 'promoting' dark sites (Seaton, 1996). In either case, greater understanding of the relationship between the site and its marketing/promotion is required.

Interpretation issues

The interpretation of dark sites and attractions, in terms of both the manner in which they are presented and the information they convey, has long been the focus of academic attention. Inevitably, perhaps, greatest attention has been paid to the development and interpretation of Holocaust sites and the dissonance of their (re)presented history (Ashworth, 1996; Ashworth & Hartmann, 2005b). However, dark tourism sites offer the opportunity to write or rewrite the history of people's lives and deaths, or to provide particular (political) interpretations of past events. For example, Cooper (2006) explores the way in which Japan's imperial past is interpreted in the context of Japanese battlefield tourism sites (see also Siegenthaler, 2002).

Site management issues

Many dark sites and attractions are, by definition, places where indi-viduals or numbers of people met their death, by whatever means. There is, therefore, a need to manage such places appropriately based upon an understanding of and respect for the manner of the victim(s) death, the integrity of the site and, where relevant, the rights of the local community in the context of the meaning or significance of the individual(s) concerned and the place of their death to those wishing to visit. It may sometimes be necessary to control or restrict access to a site. For instance, the public are allowed to visit the house and grounds of Althorp, where Princess Diana was born and raised; however, access to her burial place on an island on the estate is not permitted (Blom, 2000). In extreme cases, more drastic action may be required, such as in the case of 25 Cromwell Street, Gloucester, England, the home of Frederick and Rosemary West and site of multiple murders by the couple. In 1996, following their trial and imprisonment, the house was demolished and the site transformed into a pathway to prevent it becoming a ghoulish shrine.

To some extent, these issues represent the basic agenda for the rest of this book. That is, subsequent chapters address these issues and related topics in more detail, exploring in particular their relevance to managing both the demand for and supply of dark tourism experiences. First, how-ever, it is important to consider the meaning of dark tourism, a question that can be addressed from both descriptive/definitional and conceptual perspectives.

Dark Tourism: Definitions and Scope

Although it is only in recent years that it has been collectively referred to as dark tourism, travel to places associated with death, disaster and destruc-tion has, as noted in the introduction to this chapter, occurred as long as people have been able to travel. In other words, it has always been an iden-tifiable form of tourism (Seaton & Lennon, 2004) and, as participation in tourism more generally has grown, particularly since the mid-20th century, so too has the demand for and supply of dark tourism experiences increased in both scale and scope. Smith (1998), for example, suggests that sites asso-ciated with war probably constitute 'the largest single category of tourist attractions in the world' (see also Henderson, 2000; Ryan, 2007). Numerous specialised tour operators such as Midas Tours and Holts Tours in the UK offer trips to battlefield sites around the world (see also Chapter 10); guide-books are available to help the tourist visit war-related sites and attrac-tions. For example, Thompson (2004a, 2004b) provides a detailed guide to the '25 Best World War II Sites' in both Europe and the Pacific.

Yet war-tourism attractions, although diverse, are a subset of the total-ity of tourist sites associated with death and suffering. Reference is frequently made either to specific destinations such as the Sixth Floor in Dallas, Texas (Foley & Lennon, 1996a) or to forms of tourism such as visits to graveyards (Seaton, 2002), holocaust tourism (Ashworth, 1996; Beech, 2000), atrocity tourism (Ashworth & Hartmann, 2005c), prison tourism (Strange & Kempa, 2003), or slavery-heritage tourism (Dann & Seaton, 2001a). However, such is the diversity of death-related attractions, from the 'Dracula Experience' in Whitby, UK or Vienna's Funeral Museum to the sites of 'famous' deaths (James Dean, Buddy Holly, Elvis Presley – see Alderman, 2002) or major disasters (e.g. Ground Zero), that a full categorisation is extremely complex.

At the same time, alternative terminology has been applied to the phenomenon. For example, Seaton (1996) refers to death-related tourist activity as 'thanatourism', while other labels include 'morbid tourism' (Blom, 2000), 'Black Spot tourism' (Rojek, 1993), 'grief tourism' (see www.grief-tourism.com) or as Dann (1994: 61) alliterates, 'milking the macabre'. More specifically, Bristow and Newman (2004: 215) introduces the term 'fright tourism' as 'a variation of dark tourism … [where] … individuals may seek a thrill or shock from the experience'. In the latter case, of course, the 'fright' element of a tourism experience may not necessarily be death related. However, as will be noted shortly, Dann (1998) suggests that 'dicing with death' – that is, seeking experiences or 'holidays in hell' (O'Rourke, 1988; Pelton, 2003) that challenge tourists or heighten their own sense of mortality – may be considered one reason for participating in dark tourism.

Nevertheless, a factor common to all these terms or forms of tourism is an association, in one form or another, between a tourism site, attraction or experience and death, disaster or suffering. Consequently, definitions of dark tourism focus on this relationship between tourism and death. Tarlow (2005: 48), for example, identifies dark tourism as 'visitations to places where tragedies or historically noteworthy death has occurred and that continue to impact our lives', a definition that aligns dark tourism somewhat narrowly to certain sites and that, perhaps, hints at particular motives. However, it excludes many dark sites and attractions related to, while not necessarily the site of, death and disaster (Miles, 2002). Therefore, for the purposes of this book, dark tourism may be defined simply and more generally as *the act of travel to sites associated with death, suffering and the seemingly macabre* (Stone, 2006a).

Of course, such a definition embraces an enormous variety of places and experiences, a consideration of which is well beyond the scope of this chapter. However, a useful overview of the scope of dark tourism can be provided by summarising by category Dann's (1998) alliterative and 'postmodernistically playful inventory' (Seaton & Lennon, 2004) of manifestations of dark tourism (Table 1.1).

It is immediately evident that numerous examples could be listed under each category; equally, it is evident that the categorisation summarised in

Table 1.1 A categorisation of dark tourism

Divisions of the dark	
Perilous places Dangerous destinations from the past and present	• towns of horror • dangerous destinations
Houses of horror Buildings associated with death and horror, either actual or represented	• dungeons of death • heinous hotels
Fields of fatality Areas/land commemorating death, fear, fame or infamy	• bloody battlegrounds • the hell of the Holocaust • cemeteries for celebrities
Tours of torment Tours/visits to attractions associated with death, murder and mayhem	• mayhem and murder • the now notorious
Themed thanatos Collections/museums themed around death and suffering	• morbid museums • monuments to morality

Source: Adapted from Dann (1998)

Table 1.1 is by no means definitive. The important point is, however, that earlier attempts to define or categorise dark tourism lacked theoretical foundations and are hence largely descriptive. That is, although pointing to the scale and breadth of the phenomenon of dark tourism, little is revealed about the nature of the demand for and supply of dark tourism experiences. In particular, limited attention has been paid to exploring why tourists may be drawn towards sites or experiences associated with death and suffering.

This is not to say that this issue has been completely overlooked. A number of 'drivers' of dark tourism have been suggested in the literature, varying from a simple morbid curiosity, through *schadenfreude* (Seaton & Lennon, 2004), to a collective sense of identity or survival 'in the face of violent disruptions of collective life routines' (Rojek, 1997: 61). More specifically, Tarlow (2005) links the attraction of dark sites with either 'reflexive' or 'restorative' nostalgia, though he too resorts to suggesting a wide variety of potential motives for dark tourism consumption. Perhaps the most comprehensive list is, again, provided by Dann (1998), who identifies eight possible factors. These include the 'fear of phantoms' (i.e. overcoming childlike fears); the search for novelty; nostalgia; the desire to celebrate crime or deviance; a more basic bloodlust; and, as noted above, 'dicing with death'. The latter might include visits to specific destinations or, more generally, when travel becomes travail as tourists place themselves in peril (often, to subsequently recount their 'survival'). However, as Dann (1998) himself observes, these categorisations are largely descriptive and may be related more to specific attractions, destinations or activities rather than the motivations of individual tourists.

Nevertheless, increasing academic interest in dark tourism in recent years has resulted in an increasingly theoretically informed perspective on the subject. This has not only enabled the deconstruction of many of the broad assumptions surrounding dark tourism, but has also provided both a framework for developing our understanding of the phenomenon and a foundation for further conceptual and empirical analysis.

Dark Tourism: Theoretical Perspectives

Reference has already been made to the origins of the term 'dark tourism', first coined by Foley and Lennon (1996a, 1996b) in a special issue of the *International Journal of Heritage Studies* and, subsequently, as the title of a book that arguably remains the most widely cited study of the phenomenon (Lennon & Foley, 2000). Their work was not, however, the first to focus upon the relationship between tourism attractions and an interest in death, whether violent, untimely or otherwise. That is, sites associated with war and atrocity have long been considered within a broader heritage tourism context, in particular from an interpretative perspective. For example, Uzzell (1989b) argues for the 'hot' interpretation of war and conflict sites (interpretation that is as intense or passionate as the site/event) as a means of conveying the 'true' significance or meaning of events to visitors, while Tunbridge and Ashworth's (1996) subsequent work on 'dissonant heritage' (see also Ashworth, 1996) develops an important conceptual framework for the management of such sites. Indeed, the challenge of heritage dissonance is perhaps most starkly evident in the context of dark tourism, particularly that associated with the heritage of atrocity (Ashworth, 1996). Dissonant heritage is concerned with the way in which the past, when interpreted or represented as a tourist attraction, may, for particular groups or stakeholders, be distorted, displaced or disinherited. As Ashworth (1996) states, 'atrocity heritage is both a highly marketable combination of education and enjoyment and a powerful instrument for the transference of political or social messages' (see also Chapter 8). Inevitably, then, conflicts arise between interested groups, representing significant challenges for the managers of atrocity-tourism sites – for Ashworth, the dramatic increase in tourism to the Kazimierz district of Kraków in Poland (importantly, directly related to the 1993 film *Schindler's List*) is a powerful example.

Though contemporaneous with Foley and Lennon's (1996) work and, indeed, addressing similar issues relating to the management and manipulation of atrocity sites, Tunbridge and Ashworth's work on dissonant heritage does not refer more broadly to dark tourism. Nevertheless, the interpretative/dissonance theme remains central to a number of studies of dark sites. For example, Wight and Lennon (2007) examine selective interpretation within particular dark heritage sites in Lithuania, suggesting that 'moral complexities' ensure that important epochs remain unchallenged and uninterpreted in the nation's collective commemoration of the past. Similarly, Muzaini *et al.* (2007), assessing historical accuracy and interpretation at the Fort Siloso visitor attraction in Singapore, argue that dark tourism privileges the 'visual' and the 'experiential' over historical rigour. Additionally, dissonance remains the central theme of Ashworth and Hartmann's (2005) recent collection on atrocity tourism.

To return to the origins and development of academic interest and research in dark tourism, the notion of dark attractions was first introduced by Rojek (1993), who considers the concept of 'Black Spots', or 'the commercial development of grave sites and sites in which celebrities or large numbers of people have met with sudden and violent death' (1993: 136) as tourist attractions. Interestingly, Rojek introduces his analysis by making reference to the hordes of sightseers flocking to the sites of disasters, such as the shores of Zeebrugge in 1987 (the capsizing of the ferry *Herald of Free Enterprise*) and Lockerbie, Scotland (the crash site of Pan Am 103) in 1988, responses similar to that following the SS Morro Castle disaster in 1934. He goes on to discuss three different examples of Black Spots – the annual pilgrimage to the place where James Dean died in a car crash in 1955, the annual candlelight vigil in memory of Elvis Presley at Graceland in Tennessee and the anniversary of JFK's assassination in Dallas, Texas. These he refers to as postmodern spectacles, repeated reconstructions that are dependent on modern audiovisual media for their continued popularity (as considered below, also a fundamental underpinning of Lennon and Foley's thesis). Other attractions, such as national and metropolitan cemeteries, are categorised as 'nostalgic' sites and it is only later that he goes on to distinguish disaster sites as being 'analytically distinct from Black Spots as sensation sites' (Rojek, 1997: 63). A similar distinction is made by Blom (2000) who defines 'morbid tourism' on the one hand as tourism that 'focuses on sudden death and which quickly attracts large numbers of people' and on the other hand as 'an attraction-focused artificial morbidity-related tourism'.

Thus, the concept of dark tourism is at once rendered more complex by a number of variables, including:

- the immediacy and spontaneity of 'sensation' tourism to dark sites of contemporary death and disaster compared with premeditated visits to organised sites or events related to near and/or distant historical occurrences;
- the distinction between purposefully constructed attractions or experiences that interpret or recreate events or acts associated with death, and 'accidental' sites (that is, sites such as churches, graveyards or memorials that have become tourist attractions 'by accident');

- the extent to which an 'interest' in death – to witness the death of others, to dice with death in dangerous places, to learn about the death of famous people and so on – is the dominant reason for visiting dark attractions; and
- why and how dark sites/experiences are produced or supplied – for example, for political purposes, for education, for entertainment or for economic gain.

These issues are considered shortly and in subsequent chapters but, to return to the work of Foley and Lennon, their use of the term 'dark tourism' relates primarily to 'the presentation and consumption (by visitors) of real and commodified death and disaster sites' (1996a), a broad definition later refined by their assertion that dark tourism is 'an intimation of post-modernity' (Lennon & Foley, 2000: 11). That is, firstly, interest in and the interpretation of events associated with death is to a great extent dependent on the ability of global communication technology to instantly report them and subsequently repeat them *ad infinitum* (hence time–space compression). Secondly, it is claimed that most dark tourism sites challenge the inherent order, rationality and progress of modernity (as does the concept of postmodernity). Thirdly, at most sites the boundaries between the message (educational, political) and their commercialisation as tourist products has become increasingly blurred. As a result of these rather strict, self-imposed parameters, attractions based on events which neither took place 'within the memories of those still alive to validate them' (Lennon & Foley, 2000: 12) nor which induce a sense of anxiety about modernity, do not qualify as dark tourism. Thus, for these authors, dark tourism is a chronologically modern (i.e. 20th century onwards), primarily western phenomenon based upon (for reasons they do not justify) non-purposeful visits due to 'serendipity, the itinerary of tour companies or the merely curious who happen to be in the vicinity' (2000: 23). As Reader (2003) suggests, this lack of attention to motivation in general and an evident reluctance to accept that tourists may positively desire 'dark' experiences overlooks an essential dimension of the study of dark tourism.

Lennon and Foley's temporal positioning of dark tourism as a modern or 'within living memory' phenomenon remains, as observed earlier, an issue of contention with the literature. For example, Ryan and Kohli's (2006) study of the 'buried village' in New Zealand – the former premier tourist village of Te Wairoa that served as a base for visiting the nearby Pink and White Terraces and that was buried in ash and mud following an eruption of Mt. Tarawera in 1886 – concurs with Lennon and Foley (2000) that dark tourism is a modern phenomenon. That is, the experiences of contemporary tourists at the site are multifaceted and not predominantly related to the disaster in 1886 (but see Smith and Croy (2005) for a counter-argument). Others, of course, assert that the phenomenon of dark tourism has a long, identifiable history; Beech (2000), for example, asserts that military buildings in particular have long been tourist attractions. To some extent, this debate is underpinned by the distinction between dark tourism supply and demand. That is, both Rojek and Lennon and Foley focus primarily on the site and contemporary methods of repeated representation whereas, as explored in later chapters in this book, visitors' experiences may not necessarily be determined by the recentness or otherwise of death-related events associated with the site.

This is certainly the position adopted by Seaton (1996), who argues that dark tourism has a long history, emerging from what he refers to as a 'thanatoptic tradition' (i.e. the contemplation of death) dating back to the Middle Ages which intensified during the Romantic period of the late 18th and early 19th centuries. He cites a number of attractions, including graves, prisons, public executions and, as mentioned earlier, the battlefield of Waterloo to which tourists flocked from 1816 onwards, as well as Pompeii, 'the greatest thanatoptic travel destination of the Romantic period' (Seaton, 1996). He goes on to argue that dark tourism is the 'travel dimension of thanatopsis' (hence thanatourism), defined as 'travel to a location wholly, or partially, motivated by the desire for actual or symbolic encounters with death, particularly, but not exclusively, violent death'. Importantly, and again challenging Lennon and Foley's position, Seaton also proposes that:

- dark tourism or thanatourism is essentially a behavioural phenomenon, defined by the tourist's motives as opposed to the particular characteristics of the attraction or destination, and
- thanatourism is not an absolute form; there exists a 'continuum of intensity' dependent upon the motive(s) for visiting a site and the extent to which the interest in death is general or person specific. Thus, visits to disaster sites such as Ground Zero are a 'purer' form of thanatourism (as long as the visitor was not related to a victim) than, say, visiting the grave of a dead relative.

Based on this behavioural perspective, Seaton suggests five categories of dark travel activities.

(1) Travel to witness public enactments of death – though public executions now occur in relatively few countries, Rojek's (1997) sensation tourism at disaster sites may fall under this heading.

(2) Travel to see the sites of individual or mass deaths after they have occurred. This embraces an enormous variety of sites, from battlefields (e.g. Gallipoli), death camps (e.g. Auschwitz) and sites of genocide (e.g. Cambodia's 'killing fields') to places where celebrities died (such as the site of James Dean's death in a car crash referred to above), the sites of publicised murders (e.g. the California house where Nicole Simpson, the estranged wife of O.J. Simpson, was found stabbed to death in 1994), or the homes of infamous murderers.

(3) Travel to memorials or internment sites, including graveyards, ceno-taphs, crypts and war memorials. The reasons for such visits are diverse, from an interest in brass rubbing or epitaph collection (see Seaton, 2002) to pilgrimages to the resting places of the famous, the Père Lachaise cemetery in Paris being an oft-quoted example.
(4) Travel to see evidence or symbolic representations of death at uncon-nected sites, such as museums containing weapons of death (e.g. the Royal Armouries in Leeds, UK) or attractions that reconstruct specific events or activities. As Dann (1998) observes, these 'morbid muse-ums' may focus on selected themes and thus be 'less concerned with historical accuracy'.
(5) Travel for re-enactments or simulation of death. As Seaton (1996) suggests, this originally took the form of plays or festivals with a reli-gious theme though, over the last century, 'secular derivations' such as the re-enactment of famous battles by groups or societies have become increasingly popular.

Seaton also confirms that, although 'thanatourism' has a long history, it has become increasingly popular over the last two centuries. Importantly, and reflecting Lennon and Foley's (2000) position, he also suggests that the role of the media has been central to this growth in tourism to sites and attractions associated with death, principally through increasing the geo-graphical specificity of murder and violent death and, more recently, through global communication technology that transmits events almost as they happen into people's homes around the world.

Generally, then, two distinct bases for its analysis are evident in the emergent work on dark tourism. On the one hand, Seaton explores dark tourism or thanatourism as a behavioural phenomenon, pointing to the existence of the 'dark tourist' or 'thanatourist'. Thus, for Seaton, thanatour-ism is a form of tourism consumption. On the other hand, significant atten-tion is paid to dark sites or attractions – the objects of dark tourism consumption – in general, and their definition, interpretation and manage-ment in particular. In either case, however, little attempt is made to delve beneath the surface of these issues, to explore differing approaches to and meanings of dark tourism's demand and supply. More specifically, dark tourism, in its numerous forms, variations and guises, is evidently a func-tion of both demand and supply (Miles, 2002). Given the complex, multidi-mensional nature of dark tourism, there is a need to consider both demand and supply, and the relationship between the two, in more detail.

Dark Tourism Demand: Towards a Typology

Developing Seaton's (1996) notion of a 'continuum of intensity', reflect-ing the extent to which an interest in death is general rather than person specific, there evidently exists an almost infinite variety of forms of consumption of dark tourism. Undoubtedly, morbid curiosity, voyeurism or *schadenfreude* may be a principal driver of tourism to certain dark sites, such as visits to Rojek's (1997) 'sensation' disaster sites. For example, Cole (1999b: 114) argues that 'there can be little doubt that an element of voyeurism is central to "holocaust tourism". It is the ultimate rubbernecker's experience of passing by and gazing at someone else's tragedy.' Conversely, at other sites, an interest in death may be minimal or nonexistent, or the association with death may be of little relevance. For example, it may be argued that the thousands of visitors who annually gaze upon William Wordsworth's grave at Grasmere in the English Lake District are more interested in his life and poetry than his death. Similarly, the draw of the Taj Mahal in India is most likely to be its iconic status rather than its function as a tomb (but see Edensor, 1998). Moreover, there may, of course, be a variety of motivations among different tourists to the same site. Therefore, there may exist different 'shades of darkness' with respect to tourists' consumer behaviour.

In developing a typology of dark tourism consumption, Sharpley (2005) draws upon Holt's (1995) earlier typology of consumption practices, in which four 'metaphors' of consumption are proposed. Applying these to dark tourism in particular, varying 'shades' of dark tourism emerge.

Dark tourism as experience

A wide variety of dark tourism consumption practices may seem to be defined by or related to the social world of the tourist; that is, dark tourism experiences may be consumed in order to give some phenomenological meaning to tourists' own social existence. Included in this category are visits to: war cemeteries/memorials; battlefields; other war-related museums or attractions, such as the Death Railway and Khwae (Kwai) Bridge at Kanchanaburi in Thailand; holocaust sites; the sites of assassinations, for example Dallas (JFK) or Sveavägen in Stockholm, where Olof Palme was shot dead in 1986; and the sites of disasters (though some time after the event). In each of these cases, it is a fascination not with the manner, but rather with the meaning or implication of individual/mass death that is fundamental to the experience. Thus, such forms of dark tourism consumption arguably fall around a central to 'darker' position on the continuum. This category also embraces implicitly paler 'fantasy' experiences, such as the 'Graveline' tour in Hollywood where the interest is more in the lifestyle (and death) of celebrities.

Dark tourism as play

Representing 'paler' experiences, consumption as play focuses upon the shared, communal consumption of dark tourism sites or experiences.

That is, although it is the death of an individual or group of people that is the initial driver, it is the collective celebration, remembrance or mourning that is the dominant factor. Thus, dark tourism becomes pilgrimage, or a journey followed by the experience of 'communitas', either at 'one-off' events such as the funeral of Princess Diana or at annual celebrations like the anniversary of Elvis Presley's death at Graceland. Such play may also be sensed rather than actual, inasmuch as an individual pilgrimage to, say, the grave of a celebrity is given extra meaning by the knowledge that many others have shared, and will share, the same experience.

Dark tourism as integration

There are two levels (and shades) of dark tourism as integration. On the one hand, and with evident links to the notion of consumption as fantasy, tourists may integrate themselves into the object of consumption, the fascination not being in death itself but in the broader context within which death occurs. Henderson (2000), for example, cites the example of the Cu Chi tunnels near Ho Chi Minh City in Vietnam, where it is possible to crawl through the tunnels used to great effect by the Viet Cong and to fire replica AK-47 rifles on a nearby firing range, enabling tourists to 'become', temporarily, a soldier. On the other hand, the darkest or most intense form of dark tourism is where tourists seek to integrate themselves with death, either through witnessing violent or untimely deaths (travelling, for example to the scene of disasters or murders) or, in the extreme perhaps, travelling in the knowledge or expectation of death. In the former case, Dann (1998) refers to tours organised to Sarajevo during the Balkan conflict, the motivation for which may have been status enhancement or, perhaps, witnessing actual death and destruction associated with war. In the latter case, the practice of terminally ill people travelling to Switzerland to take advantage of the services offered by Dignitas, an organisation that assists legal euthanasia, could be regarded as the most intense form of dark tourism (Bunyan, 2003).

Dark tourism as classification

Travel has long been a marker of social status – the history of tourism is little more than the story of how tourists have sought (and continue to seek) social status through emulating the touristic practices of others. In context of dark tourism, such status may be sought through travelling to places or undertaking forms of travel (and, in either case, surviving to tell the tale) that are dangerous for the tourist. For example, some years ago, El Salvador was considered a particularly perilous destination for backpackers, with those having been there anxious to wear 'I survived El

Salvador' T-shirts. Equally, visits to dark tourism sites or attractions in more exotic destinations, such as the 'burning ghats' at Varanasi in India or the 'killing fields' of Cambodia, may be motivated more by the potential status of having visited such locations rather than by any specific fascination with death. Thus, this form of consumption falls towards the paler end of the dark tourism continuum.

Inevitably, the above analysis is open to criticism, particularly as any dark tourism site may be consumed in different ways by different tourists. Nevertheless, it serves to demonstrate that a fascination with or interest in death may often not be the principal factor driving the consumption of such experiences. Moreover, if, as Sharpley (2005) proposes, there exists a 'continuum of purpose' of supply of dark tourism attractions or experiences, varying from 'accidental' supply (that is, places that have become tourist attractions 'by accident') to supply that is directly intended to exploit, for profit or otherwise, people's 'thanatopsis', then it becomes possible to construct a matrix of dark tourism demand and supply (Figure 1.2).

Within this matrix, dark tourism attractions or experiences are measured by the extent to which both a fascination with death is a dominant consumption factor and the supply is purposefully directed towards

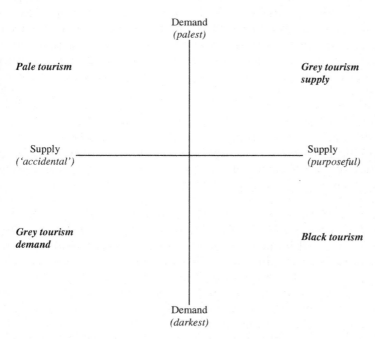

Figure 1.2 Matrix of dark tourism demand and supply

satisfying this fascination. As a result, it is possible to identify four 'shades' of dark tourism:

William Wordsworth grave

- *Pale tourism* – tourists with a minimal or limited interest in death visiting sites unintended to be tourist attractions.

Pompeii

- *Grey tourism demand* – tourists with a fascination with death visiting unintended dark tourism sites.

Death museum - UK

- *Grey tourism supply* – sites intentionally established to exploit death but attracting visitors with some, but not a dominant, interest in death.

Graveline tour

- *Black tourism* – in effect, 'pure' dark tourism, where a fascination with death is satisfied by the purposeful supply of experiences intended to satisfy this fascination.

Within these shades, it is possible to locate specific attractions or experiences. For example, the 'Flight 93' tour referred to earlier in this chapter is most appropriately placed in the 'black' quadrant, whereas visits to the graves of well known people (motivated by an interest in their lives rather than their death) would be categorised as pale tourism.

Dark Tourism: A Spectrum of Supply

Just as the consumption of dark tourism experiences may vary, particularly with respect to the intensity of interest in or meaning of the death associations, so too can it be argued that, given the diversity of dark tourism attractions, there also exist various forms of supply. In other words, as dark tourism products are multifaceted, complex in design and purpose and diverse in nature, the term 'dark' 'does not readily expose the multi-layers of dark tourism supply' (Stone, 2006a). Strange and Kempa (2003), for example, compare the design and interpretation of two former penal institutions, Alcatraz in the USA, (perhaps romanticised by movies such as 'The Birdman of Alacatraz') and South Africa's Robben Island, which held political prisoners including Nelson Mandela during the Apartheid era. They suggest that the political and cultural agendas surrounding the two sites have a profound influence on the 'memory managers' who seek to interpret the sites' respective 'dark' pasts; Alcatraz's presentation is overshadowed by commercial and entertainment values (and is hence 'lighter') whereas Robben Island is 'darker'. That is, it possesses a higher degree of political influence in its design and interpretation, promoting commemoration and education (Shackley, 2001a; Tunbridge, 2005). These issues are explored in greater detail in Chapter 8. Similarly, Miles (2002) suggests that a distinction exists between 'dark' and 'darker' tourism reflecting the temporal and spatial distinctions between sites. Thus, for Miles (2002), Auschwitz-Birkenau, a place *of* death and atrocity, is darker than Washington's Holocaust Memorial Museum, a place *associated* with death and atrocity. More generally, Ashworth and Hartmann (2005)

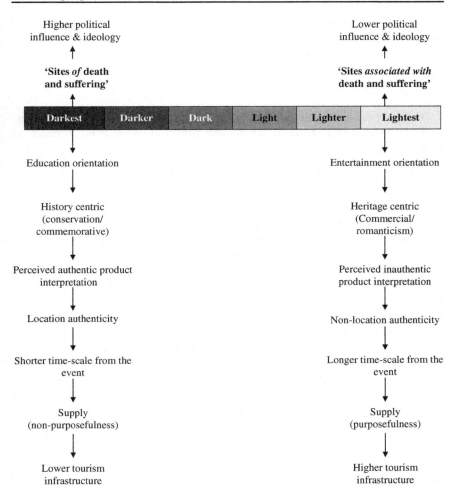

Figure 1.3 A dark tourism spectrum
Source: Stone (2006a)

provide a collection of studies into the political and cultural influences on the development and management of atrocity.

Drawing upon the issues revealed in the literature, Stone (2006a) proposes a possible 'spectrum' of dark tourism supply (Figure 1.3). Here, comparisons between, for example, location, objectives (education or entertainment), perceptions of authenticity and so on provide a basis for locating dark sites on a darkest–lightest scale. A typology of seven 'dark suppliers' is then proposed, ranging from 'Dark Fun Factories' as the lightest through to 'Dark Camps of Genocide' as the darkest. Though perhaps oversimplifying the complexity of influences on dark tourism supply, it nevertheless provides a conceptual framework for exploring different modes of dark tourism supply and, consequently, a broader base for understanding the phenomenon of dark tourism as a whole.

Conclusion

The purpose of this introductory chapter is to review 'the story so far' with respect to dark tourism, a phenomenon that has existed in practice, though not in name, for as long as people have travelled. Places associated with death, disaster or suffering have always attracted tourists; however, it is only over the last decade or so that academics and the media have turned their attention to the subject. As is evident from this chapter, there now exists a diverse and increasingly comprehensive literature on the phenomenon of dark tourism, the earlier works focusing on definitional and management issues being more recently complemented by attempts to develop conceptual frameworks for its study. Nevertheless, a fuller, theoretically informed understanding of dark tourism remains elusive, with many of the questions posed in this chapter remaining unanswered. In particular, the relationship between dark tourism and its wider socio-cultural context remains unclear, while a number of key practical issues and challenges require consideration. Above all, perhaps, questions surrounding the meaning and purpose of dark tourism as a form of touristic consumption demand attention. Why do people visit dark sites and attractions? What meanings are attached to such visits? How are visits to dark sites framed by wider socio-cultural influences? It is these and other issues that the next chapter begins to address.

Chapter 2

Making Absent Death Present: Consuming Dark Tourism in Contemporary Society[1]

PHILIP R. STONE

'Memento Mori' – Remember that you must die ...

Introduction

In May 2008, the 25th million visitor was welcomed by Gunther von Hagens' 'Body Worlds', a travelling show of anatomical donor bodies which has exhibited in 47 cities across the globe since 1996 (Institute for Plastination, 2008). Using a method for preserving putrefiable biological specimens called Plastination, whereby structural elements of cadavers are fixated, dehydrated and then, under vacuum conditions, saturated with reactive polymers such as silicone rubber, the end result is the human corpse essentially becoming *cured* for public display. A divisive exhibition experience that has inserted the post-mortal body into the cultural landscape and contemporary consciousness, Body Worlds has forever changed our notions about conception and death by provoking philosophical and religious reflection in visitors. As a modern-day Leonardo da Vinci, Gunther von Hagens positions himself as rediscovering the Renaissance mission to educate the layperson by dissecting cadavers and then adopting anatomical artistic license to exhibit preserved corpses in a variety of playful poses.

Anatomy, once the preserve of medics and health professionals, is now sold to the masses as visitors gaze at plastinated anatomical cadavers, ensuring that millions of lay people now have the opportunity to view death (and the dead body) close up. Indeed, Body Worlds and its show of anatomical awe is marketed with the strap-line *'The Original Exhibition of Real Human Bodies'*, an acknowledgement by von Hagens, perhaps, that other copycat exhibitions are tapping into the commercial value of 'death displays'. Nevertheless, despite the ethical, legal and religious concerns surrounding this 'dark exhibition' (after Stone, 2006a), diverse cultural attitudes to the event have been noted. For instance, Schulte-Sasse (2006) suggests that the intense legal, ethical and cultural controversy which surrounds the European experience of Body Worlds has not informed American discourse of the same event. Consequently, an affirmative American response to Body Worlds has conferred a new respectability on the exhibition and suppressed a critical engagement with its ethical, aesthetic, ideological and economic implications (Schulte-Sasse, 2006).

All the same, critics have been forthcoming with regard to the dignity of the body donors who now rest in plastic rather than in peace. Most notably, Burns (2007) argues that the educational objectives of the exhibition are ambiguous and that the presentation of the cadavers strips the donors of dignity. Likewise, more outspoken opponents include the Bishop of Manchester in the UK, who called the display a 'body snatch show in which exhibitions such as Body Worlds have their origins in the now long banned Victorian freak shows' (Ottewell, 2008). Additionally, debate and controversy have surrounded the source of body donors, allegedly many of them Chinese, and the potential illegal trafficking in bodies and body parts which 'supply' the various Body Worlds exhibitions across the globe (Barboza, 2006). However, despite the controversy which surrounds this dark tourism attraction, a particular reason why Body Worlds is successful – in visitor footfall at least – is because it touches upon the taboo of death. As Kriz (2007: 6) notes in the official Body Worlds catalogue, visitors 'overcome the taboos that surround human corpses ... and this transition from expecting revulsion to looking at the specimens freely and uninhibitedly amounts to a personal break with these taboos'. Similarly, where in most societies dead bodies are deemed problematic objects that are dealt with through ritual (Metcalf & Huntington, 1991), Walter (2004) suggests that Body Worlds has become a contemporary ritual which allows the dead to be transformed, taboos confronted, and for the lay person to become somewhat emotionally detached from an otherwise clinical gaze.

Similarly, Whalley (2007), who conducted empirical research at Body Worlds and explored various individuals' personal consequences of visiting the exhibition, suggests the actual exhibition had a somewhat positive effect on visitors. Indeed, Whalley notes a 'substantial proportion of visitors stated that they had been affected by the Body Worlds exhibition on fundamental questions in conjunction with their own death' (2007: 303). Likewise, the allegedly positive aspect of visiting Body Worlds is also explored by Lantermann (2007), who suggests that visitors had an enriching experience in which they became more contemplative about their own life and death and more concerned with the vulnerability of their own human body. More importantly, however, Lantermann outlines a five-phase model of a visit to the Body Worlds exhibition (see Figure 2.1), in

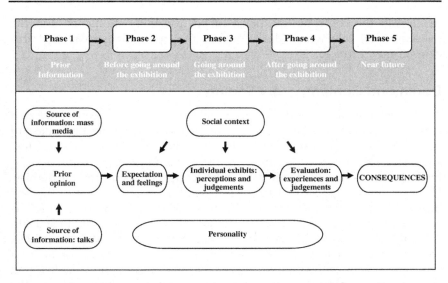

Figure 2.1 The five-phase model of a visit to a Body Worlds exhibition
Source: Lantermann (2007: 305)

which he highlights broad conditions, factors and processes that are involved in this particular dark tourism experience. Accordingly, the model which formulates visitor opinion not only presents itself as a heuristic strategy for planning and implementing a dark tourism survey but also for managing experiences and evaluations of various visitor groups.

While the exploration of specific push and pull motivating factors is beyond the scope of this chapter, the consequential aspects of the visit as suggested in Phase Five of Lantermann's model are important. In short, he proposes that the consequences of a 'dark tourism' visit, such as that to the Body Worlds exhibition, have profound implications for the visitor soon after the actual visit. In particular, Lantermann (2007) suggests that, following a visit to Body Worlds, people are likely to experience greater interest in and concerns about health and the vulnerability of the body, especially as a result of the exhibition awakening a greater interest in the juxtaposition between life and death and the ultimate demise of the human being.

Of course, while the Body Worlds exhibition is a somewhat specialist or niche example of dark tourism, it nevertheless illustrates key thanatological aspects of the wider dark tourism phenomenon. That is, it exemplifies a number of fundamental issues that revolve around mortality within western-centric societies, including the apparent taboos that surround modern-day mortality, and the consequential aspects of confronting and contemplating these 'death taboos' in the public domain. Thus, drawing upon work elsewhere by Stone and Sharpley (2008), it is these aspects of death and the confrontation of so-called 'mortality moments' and the consequential role which dark tourism may potentially play that this chapter now turns to.

Death and Contemporary Society

The establishment and evolution of sociology has been concerned almost exclusively with the problems of life rather than with the subject of death (Mellor & Shilling, 1993). However, Berger's (1967) seminal text suggested death was an essential feature of the human condition, requiring individuals to develop mechanisms to cope with their ultimate demise. He went on to suggest that to neglect death is to ignore one of the few universal parameters in which both the collective and individual self is constructed (Berger, 1967). Hence, where death and the discussion of death within the public realm was once considered taboo (Mannino, 1997; DeSpelder & Strickland, 2002; Leming & Dickinson, 2002), or at least proclaimed to be taboo (Walter, 1991), commentators are now challenging death taboos, exploring contexts where the dead share the world with the living. In particular, Harrison (2003) examines how the dead are absorbed into the living world by graves, images, literature, architecture and monuments. Similarly, Lee (2002) reviews the disenchantment of death in modernity and concludes that death is making its way back into social consciousness, suggesting the time has come to dissect death without prejudice. He goes on to advocate that death is 'coming out of the closet to redefine our assumptions of life' (Lee, 2004: 155), thus breaking the modern silence (and taboo) on death which itself, perhaps, comprises a defence mechanism for individuals against their inevitable passing. Therefore, although the inevitability of death continues to be disavowed, particularly in contemporary society, it can never be completely denied (Tercier, 2005). Indeed, contemporary society increasingly consumes, willingly or unwillingly, both real and commodified death and suffering through audiovisual representations, popular culture and the media.

Of course, 'contemporary society', the cultural framework within which (western) individuals construct coping mechanisms to deal with human finitude, is itself a contested term, particularly within sociological discourse relating to modernity and postmodernity. According to Giddens (1990, 1991), however, it is misleading to interpret contemporary societies as evidence of a radically new type of social world, whereby the characteristics of modernity have been left behind. He suggests that social life is still being forged by essentially modern concerns, even though it is only now that the implications of these are becoming apparent. Similarly, Best and Kellner (2001: 6) note that present-day society 'is in the midst of a tempestuous period of transition and metamorphosis, propelled principally by transmutations in science, technology, and capitalism' and, perhaps more recently, by geopolitical turmoil in a post 9/11 world. Consequently, Lee (2006) suggests that contestation remains over what is meant by contemporary society, as new terms such as reflexive modernisation, liquid modernity and multiple modernities add to the diverse and often contradictory views on social theory within sociological discourse. With this in mind, the author does not seek to enter into the philosophical debate over the use of the term *contemporary society* but simply aims to acknowledge significant features of sociological discourse which relate to modernism and postmodernism theory.

Even so, a Giddensian perspective points to a significant characteristic of contemporary society that can be correlated with death and mortality, namely an individual's perceived erosion of personal meaningfulness and rational order which, in turn, is often propelled by the privatisation of meaning and sequestration of death within public space. At the same time, when discussing mortality and its contemplation, a critical feature of (western) society may be seen in the extensive desacralisation of social life which has failed to replace religious certainties with scientific certainties (Giddens, 1991). Instead, while the negation of religion and an increased belief in science may have provided people with the possibility of exerting a perceived sense of control over their lives (though, crucially, it has not conquered death), it fails to provide values to guide lives (see Weber, 1948), leaving individuals vulnerable to feelings of isolation, especially when ruminating the prospect of death and an end to life projects. Hence, that the 'secularisation of life should be accompanied by the secularisation of death should come as no surprise: to live in the modern is to die in it also' (Tercier, 2005: 13). Further to this, Giddens (1991) suggests a privatisation of meaning in contemporary society, where both experience and meaning have been relocated from public space to the privatised realms of an individual's life (see also Chapter 4). Consequently, this has served both to reduce massively the scope of the sacred and to leave increasing numbers of individuals alone with the task of establishing and maintaining values to guide them and make sense of their daily lives. Ultimately, therefore, people require a sense of order and continuity in relation to their daily social lives, which Giddens (1990, 1991) refers to as 'ontological security'.

Ontological security: Meaning and mortality

A distinctive feature of contemporary society, Giddens (1991: 156) argues, is the 'purchasing of ontological security' through various institutions and experiences that protect the individual from direct contact with madness, criminality, sexuality, nature and death. Giddens, who associates contemporary society with an 'exclusion of social life from fundamental existential issues which raise central moral dilemmas for human beings' (1991: 25), suggests that ontological security is anchored, both

emotionally and cognitively, in a 'practical consciousness of the meaningfulness' of our day-to-day actions (1991: 36). However, this sense of
meaningfulness is consistently threatened by the angst of disorder or
chaos. As Mellor (1993: 12) notes, 'this chaos signals the irreality of everyday conventions, since a person's sense of what is real is intimately associated with their sense of what is meaningful.' Giddens, drawing upon
Kierkegaard's (1944) concept of dread, argues that individuals are faced
with a seemingly ubiquitous danger of being besieged by anxieties concerning the ultimate reality and meaningfulness of daily life. Hence, contemporary society strives to address this sense of dread by 'bracketing out
of everyday life those questions which might be raised about the social
frameworks which contain human existence' (Giddens, 1991: 37–38).

Death is clearly one such issue that raises uncertainties and anxieties
and hence becomes a major issue to bracket out of everyday consciousness. It could be argued, of course, that this bracketing-out process has
resulted in the contemplation of death becoming taboo; nevertheless, as
Mellor (1993) notes, the bracketing process is not always successful.
Indeed, bracketing is continual as it is contingent upon societies to be
able to control factors which offer pertinent threats to ontological security.
This level of control will, naturally, vary from society to society, but regardless of the cultural condition of society, death is a potent challenge to the
bracketing process in *all* societies (Mellor & Shilling, 1993). Therefore, the
existential confrontation of the human demise has the potential to expose
the individual to dread, the inevitability of death causing individuals to
question the social frameworks in which they live and participate. As
Giddens (1991: 162) notes:

> Death remains the great extrinsic factor of human existence; it cannot
> as such be brought within the internally referential systems of moder-
> nity … death becomes the point zero: it is nothing more or less than
> the moment at which human control over human existence finds an
> outer limit.

Therefore, death becomes a psychological and problematic issue for both
the collective and individual self. People must face up to their inevitable
demise, yet the social systems in which they reside must allow them to
live day-to-day with some sort of commitment and thus to a certain extent
deny death (Dumont & Foss, 1972). Consequently, modern ideology
espouses a celebration of life and living, amplified by a postmodern focus
on youth, beauty and the body. As a result, thoughts of death as an inevitable event are repressed (Lee, 2004). It is perhaps for this reason that both
Giddens (1991) and, previously, Berger (1967) associate death with those
'fateful moments' and 'marginal situations' whereby individuals have to
confront problems which society has attempted to conceal from public
consciousness. As Berger (1967: 23) suggests, 'death is the most significant

factor individuals can encounter in marginal situations'. This is because death has the potential to radically undermine an individual's sense of meaningfulness and reality of social life, thus calling into question onto-logical security and even the most fundamental assumptions upon which social life is constructed (Mellor, 1993). Indeed, for Berger, death is an unavoidable characteristic of the human condition and one which all societies, contemporary or otherwise, inevitably have to address. Hence, if death and mortality are not dealt with by adequate confrontation mechanisms, not only will the individual have to face up to challenges of personal meaninglessness and a significant loss of ontological security, but the social framework as a whole becomes vulnerable to collapse into chaos. However, in a contemporary age defined by rapid technological, economic and scientific progress, a cultural milieu remains that challenges the maintenance of ontological security. In this context, death is difficult to deal with, especially when values and meanings are constantly reappraised and reflected upon, thus aiding a sequestration of death from the public realm. It is to this latter point that this chapter now turns.

The Sequestration of Death: An Absent-Present Paradox

One of the fundamental discontinuist impulses of the contemporary age is expressed by Giddens in the pervasiveness of 'reflexivity' – that is, the systematic and critical examination, monitoring and revision of all beliefs and practices in the light of changing circumstances. Similar to Schelsky's (1965) notion of *Dauerreflexion* or 'permanent reflection', con-temporary societies continuously examine and re-examine meaning and values. This continual process of systematic and potentially radical reap-praisals of contemporary life can sentence the individual to a pervasive 'radical doubt' (Giddens, 1991: 21) and a perceived reduction in their sense of ontological security. While this constant re-evaluation of social life may be profound and liberating for some, especially those with a 'narcissistic personality type' (see, e.g. Lasch, 1991), it is unclear how reflexivity can ultimately help individuals deal with the phenomenon of death. More specifically, death 'is a universal parameter within which reflexivity occurs, rather than an object to which reflexivity can be convincingly applied' (Mellor, 1993: 18). Nonetheless, it can be argued that contempo-rary societies are sufficiently culturally diverse and flexible to permit indi-viduals to draw and reflect upon a variety of cultural resources to deal with death, thus creating multiple mechanisms to confront mortality.

Even so, this diversity may compound the difficulties that individuals may experience when death (and dying) is encountered. As Mellor (1993: 19) argues, 'reflexivity may be increasingly *applied* to death in a multitude of ways, but this multiplicity of *particular* approaches to death accentuates the reality-threatening potential of death in general'. In other words, the more diverse (and reflexive) the approaches to death in contemporary societies, the more difficult it becomes to contain death within social frameworks and thus limit existential anxiety and the level of ontological security it potentially offers to the individual. This apparent cultural diversity, reflexivity and flexibility in contemporary approaches to death, Mellor argues, 'can therefore be [partly] explained as being consistent with the sequestration of death from public space into the realm of the personal' (Mellor, 1993: 19). Further to this, Mellor and Shilling (1993) conclude that public legitimisations of death are becoming increasingly *absent*, thus ensuring the challenge of death to an individual's sense of reality, personal meaningfulness and, ultimately, ontological security. This ostensible absence of death from the public realm may help explain the 'intense confusion, anxiety, and even terror which are frequently experienced by individuals before signs of their own mortality' (Giddens, 1991: 160). Thus, reviews of contributions to the sociology of death and dying have drawn attention to the (institutional) sequestration of death in contemporary society. Most notably, these contributions concentrate on the privatisation and medicalisation of death (e.g. Mellor, 1993; Mellor & Shilling, 1993; Shilling, 1993; Willmott, 2000; Winkel, 2001) whereby death, rather than being an open, communal event, is now a relatively private experience marked by an 'increased uneasiness over the boundaries between the corporeal bodies of the living and dead' (Turner, 1991: 229; Howarth, 2000, 2007a).

While a full analysis of death sequestration from public space is beyond the scope of this chapter, it is worth noting fundamental changes within contemporary society towards mortality. As Mellor and Shilling (1993: 414) point out:

> ... these changes have themselves been affected by a gradual privatisation of the organisation of death (or a decrease in the public space afforded to death); a shrinkage in the scope of the sacred in terms of the experience of death; and a fundamental shift in the corporeal boundaries, symbolic and actual, associated with the dead and living.

Hence, it is argued that the absent death thesis is conspicuous by the demise of communal and social events which, when combined into a series of ritual actions, contained death by ensuring it was open or public, yet subject to religious and social control. Nevertheless, the romanticised 'good death' of pre-contemporary society was just as or even more unpleasant than it is now (Ariès, 1974). Conversely, Ariès goes on to note that the omnipresent religious order that encompassed human finiteness appeared to ensure mortality was meaningful, thus aiding a sense of ontological security for the bereaved who would inevitably evolve into the deceased. However, it is suggested that death and the prospect of dying is now unprecedently alarming because contemporary society has deprived increasing numbers of people of an overarching, existentially meaningful ritual structure. Indeed, in relation to mortality, it can be argued that contemporary society has 'not just emptied the sky of angels, but has emptied tradition, ritual and, increasingly, virtually all overarching normative meaning structures of much of their content' (Mellor & Shilling, 1993: 428). Thus, the reflexive deconstruction of religious orders that promised post-corporeal life after death and the lack of stable replacement meaningful systems has tended to leave contemporary individuals isolated and vulnerable in the face of their inevitable end.

Augmenting this perceived sense of individualisation and privatisation of death is the increased medicalisation of the dying process. In other words, the medical professional and the hospice movement have helped relocate death away from the community and into a closed private world of doctors, nurses and specialists (Byock, 2002). As Elias (1985: 85) notes, 'never before have people died as noiselessly and hygienically as today, and never in social conditions fostering so much solitude'. Indeed, medical parlance often represents death in terms of its causes (e.g. lung cancer, cardiac arrest), so that we no longer hear or perhaps think of people 'dying of mortality' (Bauman, 1993: 5). Combined with the professionalisation of the death industry, whereby dedicated organisations provide 'à la carte' menus of funeral services, death and the management of disposal is largely relocated away from a 'front region' of the community gaze and safely into a 'back region' of death industry professionals (Mellor & Shilling, 1993). However, the cumulative effect of this institutional sequestration of death is not to resolve the problem of death by neutralising its implicit threat and sense of dread but, ironically, to leave many people uncertain and socially unsupported when it comes to dealing with mortality, as a transpersonal, existential phenomenon (Shilling, 1993; Willmott, 2000). For this reason, Walter (1991: 307) suggests that the meaning of mortality in contemporary societies 'points to death being highly problematic for the modern individual, but not at all problematic for modern society – hence the lack of ritual surrounding it today'.

Despite this, to suggest death is totally absent from the contemporary public domain is to deny the pervasiveness of death within popular culture and media output (Walter *et al.*, 1995; Durkin, 2003). Indeed, death has long been *present* within wider popular culture and the media, so much so that Geoffrey Gorer first brought society's apparent fascination with the 'pornography of death' to academic attention in the 1950s (see Gorer, 1955, 1965). He asserted that the demise of social and religious rituals surrounding death and dying resulted in mortality resurfacing in society through the seemingly obsessive 'pornographic' media coverage of death, whereby 'death became removed, abstracted, intellectualised, and depersonalised' (Walter, 1991: 295). Similarly, Tercier (2005: 234) notes that 'the televised pornography of death, with its slippages of reality and representation, is no more likely to replace the experience of the deathbed than the dirty movie is likely to replace sex'. Nevertheless, as Bryant and Shoemaker (1997: 2) observe, 'thanatological themed entertainment has been and remains a traditional pervasive cultural pattern, and has become very much a prominent and integral part of contemporary popular culture'. This is no more so than within the realms of dark tourism, but thanatological themes are also evident in television news and programming (Walter *et al.*, 1995; Merrin, 1999; McIlwain, 2005), cinema production (Mortimer, 2001), music (Wass *et al.*, 1991), print media (Trend, 2003), the arts (Davies, 1996), and through jokes often referred to as 'gallows humour' (Thorson, 1993; Sayre, 2001). Indeed, death can be traced back through popular culture to folklore, in which folklorists have maintained an interest in the cultural aspects of death for many years (Bennett & Round, 1997).

It is here that the apparent paradox of death sequestration lies. On the one hand, *absent* death through privatisation of meaning and a reduction in the scope of the sacred, the medicalisation of dying and the professionalisation of the death process is evident, yet, on the other hand, death is very much *present* within popular culture, and of course *very present* since death is the single most common factor of life. It is, perhaps, because of this paradoxical position that death appears (institutionally) hidden rather than forbidden, invisible rather than denied. Durkin (2003) offers two salient explanations of this absent–present paradox. First, he suggests that while contemporary society brackets out and insulates the individual from death, it is this very insulation that leads us to crave some degree of information and insight concerning death. Secondly, he suggests the presence of death themes in popular culture and the treatment of mortality as an entertainment commodity is simply a way of bringing death back into the social consciousness. As Durkin (2003: 47) notes, 'by rendering death into humour and entertainment, we effectively neutralise it; it becomes innocuous, and thus less threatening, through its conversion and ephemerality' in popular culture and the media. Further to this, Bryant (1989: 9) suggests that 'death, dying and the dead are traumatic and anxiety producing topics, and can be better confronted if they are socially neutralised'. It is this social neutralisation of death and the role dark tourism potentially plays that this chapter now evaluates.

Making Absent Death Present: Dark Tourism, Neutralisation and De-sequestration

The social neutralisation of death, which itself may be considered a form of bracketing dread, thus boosting personal meaningfulness and ontological security, can help to assuage the disruptive impact of death for the individual. Dark tourism, with central product features of death and dying as outlined in the Body Worlds example earlier in this chapter, is an increasingly pervasive feature in the popular cultural landscape (e.g. Atkinson, 2005; Express India, 2005; Friends of Scotland, 2006; Lonely Planet, 2007). Indeed, the dark tourism phenomenon may be considered fascinating, educational and even humorous, depending upon the social, cultural and political context (Stone, 2006a). However, while the consumption of death appears to be in inverse ratio to our declining direct experience of death itself, dark tourism, within a thanatological framework, may help explain contemporary approaches to mortality and its contemplation and vice versa.

The manner in which this may occur is summarised in the conceptual model in Figure 2.2. Drawing on the preceding death sequestration and ontological security debates, it demonstrates how dark tourism may generally provide a consequential means for confronting the inevitably of one's own death and that of others. More specifically, dark tourism allows the reconceptualisation of death and mortality into forms that stimulate something other than primordial terror and dread. Despite modern society's diminishing experience with death as a result of institutional sequestration, Tercier (2005: 22) suggests that, although people are now spectators to more deaths than any prior generation, driven by both real and represented images, 'we see death, but we do not "touch" it'. With this in mind, it is argued that individuals are left isolated in the face of death and thus have to call upon their own resources when searching for meanings to cope with the limits of individual existence (see Chapter 4). Therefore, dark tourism, in its various manifestations as outlined in Chapter 1, and with its camouflaged and repackaged 'other' death, allows individuals to (un)comfortably indulge their curiosity and fascination with thanatological concerns in a socially acceptable and indeed often sanctioned environment, thus providing them with an opportunity to construct their own contemplations of mortality. With a degree of infrastructure and normality that surround the supply of dark tourism, albeit on varying scales (Stone, 2006a), the increasingly socially acceptable gaze upon death and its reconceptualisation either for entertainment, education or memorial purposes offers both the individual and collective self a pragmatic confrontational mechanism to begin the process of neutralising the impact of mortality. This can help minimise the intrinsic threat that the inevitability of death brings. The neutralising effect is aided by dark touristic exposures to death, where the process of continued sensitisation of dying ultimately results in a sanitisation of the subject area, creating a perceived immunity from death in addition to a growing acceptance that death will ultimately arrive. Thus, both sensitising and sanitising death allows individuals to view their own death as distant, unrelated to the dark tourism product which they consume, and with a hope that their own death will be a 'good' death (see Littlewood, 1993; Hart *et al.*, 1998; Tercier, 2005).

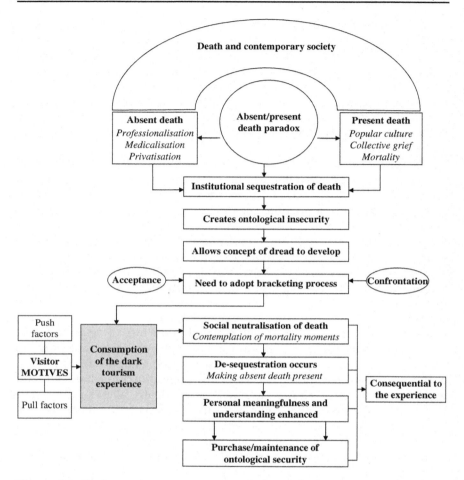

Figure 2.2 Dark tourism consumption within a thanatological framework
Source: Adapted from Stone and Sharpley (2008)

Furthermore, it can be argued that dark tourism further individualises and thus fragments the meaning of death. Indeed, while consuming the dark tourism product, people are generally exposed to the causes of death and suffering of individual people, in individual circumstances, thus perhaps encouraging the view of death as avoidable and contingent. As Bauman (1993: 6) points out, these kinds of death are 'therefore reassuring rather than threatening, since they orient people towards strategies of survival rather than making them aware of the futility of all [life] strategies in the face of mortality'.

Of course, given the enormous diversity both of dark tourism places and of the needs, experience and expectations of visitors, in addition to various socio-cultural circumstances of individuals, the potential effectiveness of dark tourism consumption as a mechanism for confronting, understanding and accepting death will vary almost infinitely. It may be argued, for example, that war cemeteries, sites of mass disasters, memorials to individual or multiple deaths/acts of personal sacrifice and so on may be a more powerful and positive means of confronting death than more 'playful' attractions, such as 'houses of horror'. Certainly, a visit to Gallipoli, where the mass graves of the fallen (including that of a young British soldier who died before reaching his 17th birthday) lie above the beaches and cliffs, is an inevitably emotive and meaningful experience, perhaps verifying the cultural and popularised representations (both visual – the Mel Gibson movie *Gallipoli* – and musical) of that tragic event. Subsequently, Hede (2008) suggests that, while Gallipoli and its commemoration through Anzac Day may have taken on quasi-religious overtones from years of Anzac myth making, the staged commemorative ceremony on the Gallipoli Peninsula does raise issues of mortality and death contemplation, especially for young participants (see also Chapter 8). Similarly, the proposed Tsunami 'Mountains of Remembrance' memorial in Khao Lak-Lam Ru National Park in Thailand may provide a focus for contemplation, mourning, hope and survival (Gerfen, 2006).

Conversely, contemporary visitors to places such as Auschwitz and other Nazi death camps, perhaps the epitome of a dark tourism destination, may come simply 'out of curiosity or because it is the thing to do' (Tarlow, 2005: 48) rather than for more meaningful purposes (but see Marcuse, 2001). Fundamentally, this latter point may result in any potential meaning of mortality within contemporary society being *consequential* to the individual. In other words, and supporting Lantermann's notion of consequence as outlined earlier in this chapter, so-called 'dark tourists' may implicitly take away meanings of mortality from their visit and subsequent experience, rather than explicitly seeking to contemplate death and dying as a primary motivation to visit any dark tourism site. That said, a diverse range of primary push and pull motivating factors will no doubt be at work with regard to 'thanatouristic demand', and these require identification and clarification (but see Rittichainuwat, 2008). Furthermore, the level of mortality meaning to the individual will no doubt depend upon their own socio-cultural background and, of course, to the varying 'intensities of darkness' perceived in any given dark tourism product and/or experience (Sharpley, 2005; Stone, 2006a).

Nevertheless, as this chapter has already suggested, the present cultural condition of contemporary (western) society calls for a revaluation of meaning systems which, in general, permit individuals to confront mortality. Hence, the reconceptualisation of death through dark tourism allows for the reconstruction of a replacement meaning system, whereby the reflexive deconstruction of religious orders are being relocated and reconstructed by the consumption of image and the pseudo. Accordingly, dark tourism may offer a revival of death within the public domain, thus de-sequestering mortality and ensuring *absent* death is made *present*, in which (private) death is turned into public discourse and a communal commodity upon which to gaze. For this reason, dark tourism may offer a new social institution whereby the functional value of death and mortality is acknowledged, its precariousness is appreciated, and efforts to assure ontological wellbeing and security become a source of not only playfulness, humour and entertainment but also education and memorial. Indeed, consuming dark tourism may allow the individual a sense of meaning and understanding of past disaster and macabre events that have perturbed life projects. This new understanding may in turn help shore up the fragility of the self's survival strategy. Thus, dark tourism can potentially transform the seemingly meaningless into the meaningful, by commodification, explanations and representations of darkness that have impacted upon the collective self. This, in turn, allows individuals to confront and contemplate their own mortality through some kind of thanatopsis by gazing upon macabre illusions and images (Seaton, 1996). Subsequently, confrontation with death and contemplation of mortality, within a socially acceptable dark tourism environment, may potentially bracket out some of the sense of dread death inevitably brings, by insulating the individual with information and potential understanding and meaning. Of course, it may be also the case where particular dark sites do not provide the sense of 'meaning' that a particular visitor may be seeking, for whatever reason, thus negating the effectiveness of the overall bracketing process and the ability to keep any 'dread threats' at bay. Nonetheless, within dark tourism, death becomes real (again) for the individual. Consequently, the real is represented so that the represented might become real. In other words, real actual death is (re)presented and commodified within dark tourism sites in order for it to become existentially valid and, therefore, inevitable for the individual who wishes to gaze upon this 'other' death.

Conclusion

Despite increasing academic attention paid to the subject, the analysis of dark tourism has to date adopted a largely descriptive, parochial perspective while questions surrounding the consumption of dark touristic experiences have for the most part been avoided. This chapter, drawing upon work elsewhere by Stone and Sharpley (2008), set out to enhance the theoretical foundations of dark tourism by considering the phenomenon within a broader thanatological perspective, exploring in particular the consequential relationship between dark tourism consumption and contemporary social responses to death and mortality. In linking the concept of dark tourism with the sociology of death, the chapter has not only developed a model that provides a conceptual basis for the further empirical study of the consumption of dark tourism, but has also contributed to a wider social scientific understanding of mechanisms for confronting death in contemporary societies.

A number of key points have emerged from the preceding discussion. Firstly, dark tourism allows death to be brought back into the public realm and discourse, thus acting as a de-sequester that allows absent death to be made present. Secondly, the consumption of dark tourism may aid the social neutralisation of death for the individual, either implicitly or explicitly, thereby reducing the potential sense of dread that death inevitably brings and permitting a search for, and a purchase of, ontological security through a new social institution. Finally, this new social institution (dark tourism) facilitates the reconstruction of a meaning system for individuals in the face of reflexivity, desacralisation and institutional sequestration, thus creating an opportunity to confront and contemplate 'mortality moments' from a perceived safe distance and environment. This in turn allows for some immunity and reassurance from the actual death or macabre event which has been (re)produced through dark tourism.

In conclusion, however, it would be naïve to suggest that the consumption of dark tourism rests solely upon a theoretical notion of providing individuals an opportunity to contemplate death and mortality. While there is some evidence that dark tourism does provide particular opportunities to confront and contemplate mortality, as outlined by the Body Worlds case earlier in the chapter, the concepts outlined by the author will, in general, require operationalisation and empirical testing in future research. This is especially so within a variety of social and cultural environments and, of course, within varying dark tourism 'products'.

Additionally, other conceptual issues undoubtedly deserve consideration, especially as dark tourism is multi-faceted, multi-tiered and exists in a variety of social, cultural, geographical and political contexts (Stone, 2006a). Thus, the demand for such products and the consequences of those experiences will no doubt be equally as diverse and fragmented, pointing to the need for further targeted empirical and theoretical analysis. In addition, dark tourists' motives will probably have varying types and intensities of meanings for various individuals within various social networks. Indeed, an awareness of mortality and the anticipation of death will differ among various social and cultural groups. It is also highly likely that dark tourism consumption will rest on numerous disparate factors, including, but not limited to, the contemplative aspects of death and dying. In particular, other aspects of the 'consumption jigsaw' may lie within grief and therapeutic discourse (Davies, 1997), conspicuous compassion and narcissism (West, 2004), media-induced emotional invigilation

(Walter *et al.*, 1995) and *schadenfreude* (Seaton & Lennon, 2004). Additionally, ethical discourse and metamorality and its impact upon dark tourism supply and demand is also suggested for consideration, as some (western) societies are propelled from a 'conventional' to a 'post-conventional' stage, where potential moral lessons are sought (and provided) from sites of (intentional) death (see Chapter 4; also Habermas, 1990). In short, the consumption of dark tourism, largely justified on the basis of untested assumptions in the extant literature, is a complex process.

Nevertheless, this chapter has commenced the interrogation of dark tourism consumption and located it within a thanatological framework for further study. In so doing, it has suggested that consuming dark tourism can help individuals within a social framework to address issues of personal meaningfulness – a key to reality, thus to life and sustaining social order, and ultimately to the maintenance and continuity of ontological security and overall wellbeing. It is with this latter point in mind that dark tourism may have more to do with life and living, rather than the dead and dying. Consequently, it is on this premise of contemporary living that the next chapter begins the task of evaluating dark tourism as a potential mediating institution between the living and the dead.

Note

1. An earlier version of part of this chapter can be found in *Annals of Tourism Research* 35 (2).

Chapter 3

Dark Tourism: Mediating Between the Dead and the Living

TONY WALTER

Introduction

Although I have written scholarly articles about tourism, including what is now termed dark tourism (Walter, 1984, 1993), I have spent most of the past two decades researching the social organisation of death, and it is there, rather than within tourism, that this chapter finds a framework in which to place dark tourism. In a sentence, dark tourism is one of a number of institutions which mediate between the living and the dead, and in this chapter I wish to introduce the reader to the family of institutions to which dark tourism belongs. Of course, dark tourism also belongs to other families – such as capitalism in general, and tourism in particular – with which readers are more likely already acquainted.

It is often argued that modern societies cut the living off from the dead. Death, along with madness and suffering, is in modern society sequestered (Giddens, 1991), hidden (Ariès, 1974), forbidden (Gorer, 1965), or denied (Becker, 1973). Stone (in Chapter 2 of this volume) and Stone and Sharpley (2008) start from this position. However, there are many channels through which even in modern societies the living encounter the dead. Harrison (2003: x) includes among these channels 'graves, homes, laws, words, images, dreams, rituals, monuments, and the archives of literature'. This chapter elaborates on this alternative position.

In psychological studies of bereavement, the dominant western 20th-century paradigm was that mourners should 'let go of the dead and move on'. Since the mid-1990s, however, this has been challenged by research demonstrating that some bereaved people successfully move on with, rather than without, the dead (Klass *et al.*, 1996); or more paradoxically, they move on both with and without the dead. The dead are not necessarily banished from the lives of individuals. Sociologists up to the 1990s have likewise written and theorised much about the absence of death and the dead from modern society, and are only just beginning to write about the channels through which death and the dead become present (e.g. Walter *et al.*, 1995; Walter, 2005; Howarth, 2007a; Mitchell, 2007). Sociologists still seem largely stuck with the idea that the dead are banished from society, producing theories in abundance about the sequestration of the dead and reactions to sequestration, but as yet little about mediations between the living and the dead. I suggest in this chapter that we need to theorise these mediations if we are to understand dark tourism. I also ask if these mediations are better understood in their own terms, rather than as a reaction by society against a presumed absence of death.

Le Rochefoucauld famously pronounced four hundred years ago: 'Death, like the sun, is not to be looked at directly.' Precisely. People need a filter. That is what mediating institutions provide. As well as Harrison's list, the many ways in which, institutionally, death has been – and is – indirectly looked at include history, archaeology, religion, medicine, the mass media and dark tourism. In an earlier article (Walter, 2005), I outlined a number of occupations that currently mediate between the recent dead and the living, arguing that the contours of their apparently diverse jobs are remarkably similar; these occupations include pathologists, coroners, funeral celebrants, registrars, obituarists and spiritualist mediums. All are contracted to produce a story about the deceased which is ritually performed in public and which in most instances goes onto public record. In this chapter, I wish to focus on those who are rather longer dead, for it is largely (though not entirely) they whom visitors encounter in dark tourism – and arguably it is they, the longer dead, to whom the sequestration theory least applies. First I identify a range of mediators, then I enquire what kind of relationships dark tourists and others have with the dead, then I enquire what kind of encounters with death are involved and, finally, I question the current trend to analyse dark tourism in terms of motives and demand. I suggest that a focus on relationships, functions and consequences may be more illuminating.

Media that Relate to the Dead

A society that did not relate to its dead would be cut off from what a modern society terms its history, and what other groups may term their ancestry. There is not necessarily any relation between how people are expected to relate to their recent dead and to the long dead. Many western industrialised societies, for example, have embraced the notion, legitimated by Freud (1984) and Bowlby (1979), that mourners should let go of their attachments to the dead; secularism denies the possibility of meaningful relationships between the living and the dead while Protestantism has for centuries been ambivalent at best about praying for the dead. This combination finds greatest force in Britain (not Ireland) and much of north-western Europe. Yet within the very same societies may be found a vibrant interest in history, a nostalgia for ways of life made redundant by technology and a proliferation of heritage tourism. The ideology of progress that relegates old people and the recent dead to the scrapheap also generates nostalgia about the past and those who inhabited it (Lowenthal, 1975; Seabrook, 2007).

What institutions mediate for us the past, and those who inhabited the past? In pre-literate societies, it is mainly the family in which stories of the ancestors are told, and even with the coming of literacy families may still have an oral tradition of their ancestry (Taylor, 1963: 85–108). A Shona friend of mine can name his forebears on the male side back over seven generations, including the great-great-grandfather who moved from Malawi to the area of Zimbabwe that the family now inhabit, and the great-grandfather whose exploits in killing an elephant led to the family name by which my friend knows he is related to anyone with that name. The spoken word links him to his ancestors through the institution of the family, providing him with a clear sense of identity unknown to me as a middle-class Briton. Ancestry in such societies is of course strongly gendered, depending on whether they are patrilineal or matrilineal; whether or not you become an ancestor depends, in part, on your gender.

In literate societies, the written word enables the possibility of history, a written record that is available to anyone, with therefore the potential for the past to become detached from personal or family identity. I can read about or visit the Colosseum in Rome with little more than an academic sense that its history is a part of who I am, and no sense of any family connection. Archaeology has added the possibility of a prehistory, whose material remains are available for anyone to view or research – precisely the point of contention between archaeology and some aboriginal groups for whom such artefacts belong to their own group, not to a world community.

Of course, postmodernist historians and archaeologists today write volumes about how history and prehistory cannot be written without being influenced by the concerns of today and, therefore, may never be objective or detached. But my point stands: history and prehistory are not attached to any one specific clan or family group. Historians and archaeologists from different societies and at different times argue with one another over the facts, which are open for all to uncover. That is not so of oral traditions about ancestors, where only in-group members may participate in the ongoing telling of the stories.

Linking ancestry and history (oral or written), for some religious groups, are pilgrimages to the shrine containing the bones of a dead saint. Religion can link the living and the dead in numerous ways, not least through prayers for the dead. This has been discouraged by Protestant Christianity (Gittings, 1984), with one notable exception, Mormonism (Davies, 2000). Mormons are concerned to provide posthumous salvation for family forebears who had not believed while alive; to this end, the Mormon church has developed extensive genealogical records, which – especially with computerisation – have greatly aided the labours of non-Mormon genealogists.

In contemporary modern societies, characterised by diasporas, bureaucratic record keeping and information technology, genealogy has become a passion for many – leading for some to personal heritage tourism (Timothy, 1997; Meethan, 2004). Given the centrality of the nation state and of ethnicity to modern self-identities, those who have migrated from other nations, especially from other continents, may have more identity work to do than those – like myself – whose known forebears all resided within the same nation. For Afro-Americans in the USA or for Caribbeans in the UK, feeling marginalised in the societies in which they reside, genealogy may be about a search for roots, and may produce ancestors of a kind (Stephenson, 2002), though not necessarily of the kind expected (Nash, 2002). For those without an international migrant history, genealogy could be about any number of things, from an obsession not dissimilar to stamp collecting (how many forebears can I collect), to a more personally meaningful way of studying history, to a search for roots. However, insofar as it relies on written documents, it seems to be a very different thing from the stories told orally within families over generations that have typified non-literate societies. For many today, I suggest that genealogy does not produce ancestors; it produces genealogy.

The modern state creates and recreates sacred ancestors, bestowing immortality on its heroes. This may occur through a state funeral, or at a later time when a changed political scene prompts the canonisation of certain figures, or even the canonisation of those previously disgraced. A century after the American Civil War, for example, the US federal government restored citizenship to the southern general, Robert E. Lee (Kearl, 1989: 305); totalitarian regimes are even more likely to create swings in which the dead shift from the status of disgraced to sanctified, or vice versa.

As well as the written word, modernity has the photograph. The still photograph is both a vivid means by which we may encounter the dead, not least our own family dead; *and*, as Barthes (1993) observed, it is a *memento mori*. Pictures of myself, 50 years ago as a child or 30 years ago as a younger man, provide a memento of my ageing, a reminder that I will never again look like that or be like that. The picture of me as a child with my now deceased uncle reminds me that I too will die. The photograph links us both with the dead, and with our own death (Beloff, 2007).

Music is a major channel through which death is present in contemporary society, linking us to the dead, primarily in the form of the crucified Christ and the deceased beloved. The requiem mass is a staple of even secular choirs (Walter, 1992), while from Wagner (*Tristan and Isolde*) via Puccini (*La Boheme*, final scene) and the Shangri Las ('Leader of the Pack') to Eric Clapton ('Tears from Heaven'), both romantic opera and pop music (Clayson, 1997) express the grief that Ariès (1974) observed is the counterpart of romantic love: how can I go on living now my beloved has died? Spirituals evoke the slave's loss of home and hope of heaven. Meanwhile, as I write, Richard Strauss's meditation on peaceful death after a long life, his exquisite *Four Last Songs*, is being broadcast live from one of the highest profile concerts of the British classical musical calendar, the first night of the Proms. As it ends, the commentator repeats the last line: 'How weary we are of journeying – is this perhaps death?' Death and loss have been central also to drama, novels and poetry, and (consider Hamlet) not only in the romantic forms of these genres.

A further institution that links the dead to the living is the law. The last will and testament, read out by the lawyer to the awaiting family, may be the first and last dramatic way in which the deceased speaks formally and publicly to the living (Drake, 2007). The millionaire who transforms his or her wealth into a philanthropic foundation may affect many lives in future generations, and – through the terms of the foundation – may indeed influence the actions of generations to come.

Clearly there are other mediators between the living and the dead. Gravestones and burial grounds have immediate relevance for some forms of dark tourism. Mourners themselves are situated between the world of the living and the world of the dead, a potentially dangerous location and hence one liable to societal policing, which I have discussed at length elsewhere (Walter, 1999).

So, archaeology, graves, genealogy, music, literature, law, the family, language (oral and written), photographs, history, these all mediate between the dead and the living. Indeed, in the period leading into modernity, more – not fewer – of these mediations have become available. But it is the last three – language, photography and history – that set the stage for two key institutions that mediate between the dead and the living in modernity: the mass media and tourism. It is often argued that religion and its rituals provided the main filter by which death could be looked at, now largely replaced by medicine, which provides both a mindset and practical measures by which death may be cheated, and in terminal illness, approached. But I have argued (Walter, 2006) that the *ideological* function of religion in mediating death, in making sense of mortality and in linking us to the dead, has in large measure in late modern society been taken on not so much by medicine as by the mass media. When there is a disaster, it is not to the priest or the doctor that we turn for information and help in making sense of what happened, but to the newspaper and the TV news. In more ordinary deaths, we record formalised sentiments in *In Memoriam* columns, and in North America obituaries are published in the local newspaper by family members (Starck, 2006). Soap operas and movies regularly highlight sudden death and consequent bereavement.

ex. Michael Jackson → news from TV

There is a close link between the media and dark tourism. I can visit Auschwitz, or I can watch a documentary about it on TV. I can visit First World War battlefields, or I can read a novel about their pity and their pain. I can visit the site of the battle of Culloden, or watch a re-enactment of it in a TV docu-drama. I do not need to dive to the bottom of the Atlantic, for I can watch the movie *Titanic*. Either, or both, or none of these pairs may touch me. A few hundred thousand attended the funeral of Princess Diana; several thousand watched it on a huge TV screen in Hyde Park; many millions around the world watched it at home on TV. Mass attendance at executions, in past centuries a popular pastime, is now anathematised, yet in the 21st century certain executions in Iraq have been watched illicitly on the web, while in the UK teenagers have disseminated pictures on their mobile phones of fellow teens being beaten up and, occasionally, murdered. If physically going to witness an execution may be labelled dark tourism, may not turning on a computer or mobile phone to witness the same execution be similarly labelled?

If so, we may then of course ask a more general question, 'Why travel, when you can see it all on the TV?' But the fact is that tourism is booming: the TV or the brochure is no substitute for the sun on your skin, the waves lapping at your feet, or photographing the Taj Mahal to show you have been there. Likewise, there may be no media substitute for squeezing yourself down Viet Cong tunnels or actually visiting Auschwitz. And for the pilgrim, as opposed to the tourist, visiting a battlefield (see Chapter 10), there is no substitute for seeing a relative's name carved in the stone on a grave or memorial (Walter, 1993). Nevertheless, the media and dark tourism are clearly in the same business: presenting and interpreting death and suffering to millions of people, and sometimes – as in witnessing an execution – the difference between the media and tourism is minimal. Sharpley is correct in Chapter 1 that the possibilities for dark tourism have been greatly increased by the advertising that the mass media can provide, but the link between dark tourism and the mass media is much closer than that. They both mediate sudden or violent death to mass audiences.

Relationships with the Dead

What kinds of relationships with the dead do the various mediating institutions enable? These too are various:

Information

Pathologists and archaeologists literally dig around the remains of the dead in order to discover information about the mode of their death, or their life, or both. This information is provided for medicine, for science or for the state. This kind of dispassionate excavation does not always sit well (in the case of pathologists) with the personal or religious needs of mourners, or (in the case of archaeologists) with ideas of ancestry held by aboriginal groups.

Intercession

At religious shrines, a major form of communication from the living to the dead is intercession: praying to the saint or spirit on behalf of the living. This is the case, for example, at Roman Catholic shrines, where the saints carry prayers from the living to God (Christian, 1971).

Guidance

At the same time, shrines are also places where the living are open to guidance from the dead. At the Yashukan War Museum at Tokyo's controversial Yasukuni shrine, visitors are greeted by Fujita Toko's (1806–1855) *Ode to the Righteous*, prominently displayed on the entrance wall:

Bodies may perish
But spirits never die
They remain in the realm
Between the heavens and Earth for all eternity
Valiantly guiding us along the path of righteousness.

Guidance from the dead may be found, of course, in all kinds of places (Marwit & Klass, 1995), but there are times and places where the lines of communication between the dead and the living are particularly clear; the reading of a will is one, spiritualist séances and shrines are others.

Care

A fourth form of communication is care for the dead. Mayumi Sekizawa, a Japanese folklorist researching French war memorials and Japanese shrines to its war dead, commented to me, 'You Europeans remember your war dead, we Japanese care for ours.' In Japan, there is the possibility of a mutual relationship of care between the living and their ancestors: the dead guide the living and the living care for the dead. The rituals at a Japanese war shrine are all about this mutual care. In a sense, it is incorrect to speak of Japanese war *memorials*: certainly acts of remembrance go on there, but that is not what they are explicitly for.

Some sociologists and anthropologists of contemporary western death practices (e.g. Francis *et al.*, 2005; Valentine, 2008) have shown that, although in the West there is no formal religion, ritual or language by which the living may care for the dead, they nevertheless do this, for example by tending graves. Behaviour at western graves may not be so dissimilar from that at Japanese household shrines, with conversations taking place with the dead, imparting the latest news from the world of the living, enquiring about life in the world of the dead and seeking guidance.

Remembrance

If there is no formal way to care for the dead, all that is left is to remember them. If a shrine is where the dead are cared for, prayed to and where guidance is sought from them, a memorial is more simply a place of memory. Memories may be internal to the individual visitor, or shared within the group, but a memorial is not designed to be a place of interaction between the living and the dead – or at least, not officially. At British war cemeteries, the formal language is not that of care for, and guidance by, the spirits of the dead; rather it is of memory: 'Lest we forget.'

> At the going down of the sun
> and in the morning
> we will remember them.

At war graves, western veterans and families come to pay respect, to remember.

In the past two decades, memory studies have become a vibrant interdisciplinary research field, involving neurologists, experimental psychologists, psychoanalysts, literary theorists, anthropologists and philosophers, to name but a few; false memory and traumatic memory have generated much debate and research. This is not the place to review a vast and rapidly changing field, but we may just sketch the different kinds of memory as the generations pass. First-generation memory refers to events, places and people that were personally experienced, though such memories are not static; they are cobbled together anew each time the memory comes to mind (Olick, 1999). Second-generation memories are those of my parents and their generation; who my parents are is shaped by what they remember, and through stories told in childhood this in turn shapes who I am, forming my understanding of how the world is. The daughter of a Holocaust survivor remembers the Holocaust in a different way from the person for whom is it just history.

By the third generation and later, the past enters our consciousness in different ways. One is history. Early 20th-century children are as likely to learn about the Second World War from history classes at school as from a grandparent, and they almost certainly learn about the First World War from books and other such media. Another is genealogy, a personal search for the history of one's own family in which forebears are researched, yet may remain essentially 'other'. A third is ancestry which, as I have suggested earlier, is rather different. Ancestors are family or group forebears who are used to frame one's current identity, as with my Zimbabwean friend or with Afro-Americans who construct an identity for themselves through their African origins, identities that have significance for everyday life.

The response of the visitor to a dark tourist site that presents deaths from several or many generations ago will depend in large measure on whether these deaths are perceived to be those of historical figures or of ancestors. I am English and have visited Dunnottar Castle, on the tourist trail in the North-East of Scotland, a visually dramatic and highly photogenic, but for me only moderately interesting, historical site. Maybe not so for some Scots, as one fictional visitor described, visiting its dungeons:

> There the Covenanting folk had screamed and died while the gentry dined and danced in their lithe, warm halls, Chris stared at the places, sick and angry and sad for those folk she could never help now, that hatred of rulers and gentry a flame in her heart, John Guthrie's [her father's] hate. Her folk and his they had been, those whose names stand graved in tragedy. (Gibbon, 1946: 101–102)

Set in 1913, events of well over two centuries previously were, for Chris Guthrie, not history but a tragedy that befell her ancestors. I have not visited the slave forts of West Africa, but were I to do so I am sure my responses as a white Englishman would not be those of a black American of slave ancestry (see also Chapter 12). Feldman (2008) argues that Israeli youth pilgrimages to concentration camps are key to how the Israeli collective identity is passed on to new generations.

The Dunnottar Castle example also shows that it is not possible to put a number on how many years or generations must pass before an event passes into history and loses its emotional and possibly traumatic hold on visitors. For many Protestants in Northern Ireland, the 1690 Battle of the Boyne remains part of their present day identity, as does the 1389 Battle of Kosovo for many Serbians today. For myself, the First World War has nothing to do with this kind of ancestry, but it holds some genealogical resonance; my Uncle Arg fell in battle in 1915 and we have some correspondence from him to my father and letters written about his death to my grandmother. The Boer War of just a few years earlier is, for me, pure history.

Remembrance is not memory (King, 1998). Remembrance entails a commemoration of those whose suffering and death one may not have personally witnessed, but is not yet history. The veteran 'remembers' all who died in his war, not just those he personally knew. The civilian 'remembers' the soldiers who died, and the trials they suffered, even though these have to be imagined, for she did not experience them. At Arg's memorial in Belgium, I can 'remember' an uncle who died 30 years before I was born.

When memory is not first hand, it turns into remembrance, or history, or genealogy, or ancestry ... and doubtless other possibilities too. These are all ways of relating to the dead and/or of contemplating their deaths. At the same dark tourist site, all may be present, for different visitors.

Education

The dead may be encountered for educational purposes. Educational visits to the dead, whether in the classroom through books or at heritage sites through educational tourism, are the basis of the teaching of history. Sometimes the dead are physically present, as in exhibitions of mummies and bog bodies.

The dead have a significant educational role in science and medicine, notably in the dissection class or autopsy in which medical students learn about the living body through a hands-on archaeology of the dead body (Hafferty, 1991). Gunther von Hagens' Body Worlds exhibition of plastinated cadavers, currently the world's most visited touring exhibition, states that it aims to educate the public about their own bodies; von Hagens does not believe only doctors should have this direct knowledge of human anatomy (Burns, 2007). At the exhibition and on its website visitors may be observed interacting intensely with both the exhibited human remains and with each other (vom Lehn, 2006).

Entertainment

Body Worlds and its imitators also have an entertainment function, to von Hagens an essential part of getting the public (especially those who are not regular museum-goers) to come and be educated, to his detractors (especially those who are regular museum-goers) proof that he is 'just a showman'. The exhibition, like all popular yet purportedly serious exhibitions, museums and heritage sites, and indeed like comparable television documentaries, is edutainment. The dead, like much else from the past, are used to educate and entertain today's masses – as they were too in 18th-century public executions.

Memento mori

Seaton (1996) has very usefully charted the decline of the medieval *memento mori*, reminding people of their mortality even as they went about their everyday lives, and its transformation (via the romantic movement) into modern dark tourism. Whether dark tourist sites actually remind visitors of their mortality varies. I have visited a number of historic cemeteries in the UK where the information leaflet reminds visitors of the cemetery's many functions – as a green lung for city dwellers, a haven for flora and fauna, a historical site, a demonstration of geology, stone carving and lettering, as a resource for genealogists – but with no mention of death or that this is a place where dead people lie! As Woodthorpe (2007) has shown, this focus on what is above ground to the exclusion of what is under the ground actually misses what it is that gives burial grounds their unique aura.

Interestingly, Body Worlds, though ostensibly edutainment, can also function as a *memento mori*. A number of visitors have commented that the exhibits bring home to them the frailty of the human body (Walter, 2004), while Body Worlds 4, currently (2008) showing in Manchester, UK, has on the walls large banners quoting Descartes, the Psalms, Nietziz, Leiniz, Seneca, Epicurus, Kant, Shakespeare and St Augustine on body and soul, life and death. On entering the exhibition, the first two big posters are 'Confrontation with death' (describing earlier times) and 'The censure of death in contemporary life'. Though all the plastinates are in lifelike poses, large banners display two of Vesalius' classic 16th-century drawings of skeletons pondering their own mortality. I have yet to see such *memento mori* displayed so prominently in the information for visitors to any historic cemetery, or for medical students approaching their first anatomy class.

So, we may encounter the dead in a way that shields us from our own mortality, or the encounter may be liberally sprinkled with *memento mori*. I may visit a historical site of medieval slaughter that makes me feel good that people don't do that kind of thing these days, or that appals me that this happened to my ancestors (and could yet happen again).

Haunting

The unquiet dead haunt individuals; they can also haunt society. Children (in the UK, e.g. Victoria Climbie in 2000 or Holly Wells and Jessica Chapman in 2002) who have died at the hands of tormenters in an otherwise civilised culture, haunt society. Those who have died in vain, in de-legitimated wars or meaningless causes, as a group of collective dead, haunt society. How can a modern society such as England incorporate Holly and Jessica into its collective narrative of itself? How did and do Jewish people incorporate the Holocaust into their collective narrative? How did the USA incorporate its Civil War (Schwartz & Schuman, 2000), how does it even now incorporate Vietnam (Wagner-Pacifici & Schwartz, 1991) into its collective sense of itself? How do Japan and Germany remember their 20th century (Schuman *et al.*, 1998)? If individuals repress memories of trauma because they are impossible to integrate into a personal narrative, collective traumas may be defined as those that cannot – or cannot at all easily – be integrated into collective narrative, even after individuals and their memories have died (Olick, 1999).

Such unquiet deaths are the very stuff both of the mass media and of dark tourism. It is precisely this traumatic, difficult-to-comprehend death and disaster that is newsworthy, providing rich pickings for national and international news (Walter, 2005). Why would the Estonia, a ferry belonging to Sweden, the safest country on the planet, sink? How can an innocent child be murdered by a young teenager? Why would anyone want to fly planes into the Twin Towers and the Pentagon? After Pearl Harbour, after 9/11, how can Americans incorporate vulnerability into their national narrative?

It is no coincidence that 9/11 is so far both the archetypal news story of the 21st century and its most visible site of dark tourism. The United States is haunted by 9/11 and by what it means. Reconstructive work entails not just rebuilding Ground Zero, not just contentious military ventures in the Middle East, but also an ongoing attempt to incorporate 9/11 into a revised narrative of America and of the West. Dark tourism and the media are central to this process of revision.

To conclude this section of the chapter, basic questions in any culture are: Where are the dead? Are they accessible? How are they accessible? From such questions follow others: Where can we meet them? Are there special places – shrines, graveyards, novels – where we can meet them? When can we meet them? Are there special times when we can meet them? (In the Christian West, All Souls Day; in Japan, the O'Bon festival.) How are we to relate to them – with care, with memory, with fear? Such questions have been asked throughout time, and dark tourism is just one particular medium through which the living may encounter the dead, and death.

I have argued that there are fundamentally different ways of relating to the dead. A shrine, for example, is not a memorial. This poses considerable linguistic problems, for there is no one word which covers both shrines and memorials. (I confronted this recently while teaching a course titled 'Funerals and Memorials'. When we got to the section on shrines, I realised with alarm that the course's very title had set students up for misunderstanding what shrines are.) Museums and heritage sites are different again. Put perhaps over-simply, shrines are where care, guidance and prayer take place; memorials are where remembrance takes place; museums and heritage sites are where edutainment takes place.

Another fundamental distinction is between relating to the past in terms of history, and relating to it in terms of ancestors, which also causes terminological problems for those mobile western individuals who have no sense of a belonging that is rooted in and justified by stories of ancestors. Such individuals may engage in the family-focused history we call genealogy, but that is not the same as belonging to a family that defines itself, and is defined by others, through its ancestors. Of course, one kind of family that does define itself ancestrally, the aristocratic family, is at the heart of many British tourist attractions.

These theoretical concepts need operationalising to see how much light they shed on the real world of dark tourism. It may be that ideal types of ancestry, history and genealogy do not help us understand the empirical realities of dark tourism. And how clear is my distinction between shrines, memorials and museums? I myself have analysed the Body Worlds exhibition as a shrine to the human body (Walter, 2004). Cooper (2006), who knows more about Japan than I do, refers to Japan's Pacific War battlefields as memorials rather than as shrines. Typologies are useful, not as if they can be found exactly in the real world, but because they shed light on complexity and change in the real world. The typologies I have developed above have not yet really been tried out.

That said, it seems likely that dark tourism can include any or all of the various kinds of relationships with the dead listed above, though there is a tendency for education and entertainment to dominate certain sites, and remembrance and haunting to dominate others. I do *not* claim that visitors to dark tourist sites are motivated by a wish for these relationships with the dead; I am simply demonstrating the kind of relationships that take place at such sites, and that they are relationships found in a range of settings as well as in dark tourism. Much of what I have written above concerns how we relate to the dead, rather than to their death – for instance, an educational visit to Stratford-upon-Avon may teach children much about Shakespeare's life but, even though his grave is visited, little or nothing about his death. This is reflected in much heritage and even cemetery tourism, in which visitors are regaled with information and stories about the lives of the cemetery's more noteworthy or interesting residents. But some of the above – notably *memento mori* and haunting – concerns not just the dead but death itself, and this is reflected in the darker varieties of dark tourism.

It is to these two issues – death itself, and motivation – that I turn in the final two sections.

Mediating Death

If there is a wide range of media through which the living may relate to both the recent and the long dead, the filters through which we perceive death itself are somewhat more limited. Traditionally, religions, their rituals and beliefs, have provided the filters. In the modern world, these have been supplemented and even replaced by medicine and the mass media. Medicine provides cures for diseases that once killed, prognoses for the terminally ill, socially legitimated accounts of why someone died, and even the tools of psychiatric medicine to help the grieving. The news media, like some religions, have a tendency to crank up fear about death, and then to provide the theodicy, or meaning system, that makes sense of what had originally been presented as unthinkable, unimaginable and senseless. The child's murderer has been arrested, the black box found, the geoscience behind the earthquake explained (Walter, 2005).

Dark tourism, as suggested earlier, has much in common with the mass media. But does it adopt the news media's strategy of first scare, then comfort? This is a question that only empirical research can answer. It seems quite likely that dark tourism will not always comfort (however, see Chapter 4). Visitors may leave Auschwitz or the Vietnam Veterans' Memorial in Washington, DC with their questions answered, or dazed and troubled, or looking for an ice cream and the next destination on the tourist trail. Even when no kith or kin are involved, such places can be profoundly troubling. Although I know no-one killed in this particular conflict, when visiting the Vietnam memorial in the late 1980s I was deeply moved by the sorrow of all wars, as indeed I was in Amsterdam's Anne Frank house. Indeed, the power of such places is precisely that the particular is made to stand for the universal – Anne Frank can represent not only all who died in the Holocaust but also all children, all civilians, everyone whose lives are destroyed by war and racism. And yet the design of such places offers some comfort. My exit from Anne Frank's house was through an exhibition that looked at the work of antiracist organisations which I was invited to join. The very design of the Vietnam memorial, and the involvement it invites alike of veterans and those against the war, itself provides some measure of healing.

That said, the deaths that dark tourism sites record are not the everyday deaths from cancer, stroke and dementia that characterise peaceful modern western societies. So, like the news report of the next disaster, dark tourism sites confront me with mortality and suffering, but not *my* mortality or suffering – unless, that is, I identify those who suffered as my group's ancestors or unless I am remarkably sensitive. I have argued elsewhere (Walter, 1994) that the reality of death today is not so much that it is taboo or denied, but that in modern medicine there is a disjuncture between the objectified, medicalised body that the medical staff treat and the me that is dying. Medicine does not model my own experience in the way that, arguably, religions can and did. So with the news media and dark tourism: they portray human suffering and mortality in some, though never anything like all, of its ghastliness, and yet this is not the death that I am likely to have to endure. Dark tourism confronts us not with human suffering and mortality, but with certain kinds of human suffering and mortality.

The deaths that the more disturbing kinds of dark tourism deal in are not those that may come to disturb me – I know of no tourist trips, for example, to the psycho-geriatric hospital wards or nursing homes where I may well end up dying. The suffering that dark tourism deals in is not the suffering of cancer or dementia, but of slavery and racism. The darker forms of dark tourism deal not in those deaths that challenge the affluent white middle class individuals who comprise the majority of visitors, but in those deaths that challenge the collective narratives of nation and of modernity. As with the media reporting of disaster (Walter, 2006), the more challenging dark tourism sites challenge not individuals, but culture. Despite the work of Bauman (1989) showing otherwise, in the popular mind the Holocaust challenges modernity's metanarratives of progress and rationality – how, we ask, could this have happened in the 20th century? Far more Americans are likely to die of cancer than of terrorist attacks, but it is Ground Zero, not cancer hospitals, to which tourists flock, for it challenges much of what Americans believe about their culture. The restorative work that has to be done, therefore, is not to comfort the individual visitor in the face of mortality, but to reconstruct the narratives of modernity, or of nation. As argued above in my discussion of haunting, this is not easily done, and loose ends are inevitably left. Hence the variety of moods in which visitors may leave.

Deficits and Motives: A Critique

We may not need a deficit model of the kind proposed by Stone in Chapter 2 to explain people's participation in dark tourism. In dark tourism, visitors encounter the dead, and in the darker varieties become aware of certain unusual kinds of death. Such encounters have been available in various forms, using various media, throughout human history. It just so happens that, in the world that citizens of affluent and peaceful societies inhabit today, one medium that offer these encounters is dark tourism. Children find themselves being taken to battlefields by teachers and parents, just as children in this and other cultures find themselves being taken to church or temple. Dark tourism is a given element of our culture, just as religion is a given element of many cultures.

The comparison with religion is instructive. Theories of religion include deficit models; for example, individuals are religious because of the lack of a father figure, or whole classes are religious because of being oppressed; religion thus provides a compensation for such lacks. But there are several other theories of religion about which scholars argue; deficit/compensation is not the only kid on the block. Likewise with dark tourism, we may not need to hypothesise that a personal or societal deficit (e.g. lack of ontological security) motivates individuals to visit such sites.

My observations suggest, though this needs to be tested empirically, that most dark tourism, like much heritage tourism, is not specifically motivated. Let me mention the chief occasions I can recall on which I myself have visited dark tourist sites. On a walking holiday in the Alps, I found myself in the resort of Zermatt on a rainy day. Having little else to do, I was window shopping on the main street and came across the town's museum; on entering, I discovered it was largely about death and disaster, its prized artefacts comprising tattered clothing, frayed ropes and broken ice axes recovered after fatal falls, not least on the nearby Matterhorn (Walter, 1984). Strolling around Amsterdam, I found myself in the vicinity of the Anne Frank house, and entered. Likewise the Vietnam memorial was for me one of a number of tourist sites to be visited on Washington's mall. I would be very surprised if many visits to Ground Zero are not similar. Many of those who laid and photographed flowers for Princess Diana at Buckingham Palace or Kensington Palace in the week after her death were tourists who were already in London; the mourning for Diana just happened to become the biggest attraction in town that week. Visits to dark tourism sites are often side trips, excursions of just a few hours within a bigger trip. Like the medieval castle, the dark tourist site is just one more site to be 'done'. Whether the site is visited or not does not depend heavily on individual motivation; rather it is contingent on whether the guide-book mentions it, whether it is chanced upon on the way to other sites, whether it fits your schedule, and so on.

A major exception is personal heritage tourism (Timothy, 1997), where there is a clear individual motive, such as genealogy, mourning or remem-brance, for visiting a site of personal significance. But even this kind of tourism rarely comprises an entire holiday, more frequently being part of a larger vacation or a side trip from a business trip. With the exception of battlefield tours and pilgrimages (Walter, 1993; Feldman, 2008), I can think of few holidays whose main *raison d'être* is dark tourism – and even with battlefields, many family or individual visits occur because the site is on the road to somewhere else.

So, individual motivation explains only a very small minority of visits to dark tourism sites. This is also true of many other forms of tourism which are not, at least initially, motivated. I was dragged up hills in the Lake District as a child, eventually discovered I liked it, and have gone on hill-walking holidays ever since. Other children go on school skiing trips; some do not take to it and never return to the slopes, while others love it and it becomes their passion. A young couple go on a city break as a change from the seaside, and get hooked. The activity comes first; the motivation may follow later. But dark tourism is not like most forms of specialised tourism. Whereas the addict may regularly take hill-walking, skiing or city break holidays, few – apart from some battlefield addicts – take an entire holiday of dark tourism, and even fewer return year after year for another week's dose of darkness. And apart from battlefield tours, dark holidays (as opposed to specific dark trips or tours as part of an otherwise light holiday) are generally not offered by the tourism industry.

It may not tell us much, therefore, to enquire into the motives of dark tourists.[1] We are likely to learn much more by carefully documenting and contextualising what they do at such sites, and how it subsequently affects them. Lantermann's (2007) model, reproduced in Chapter 2 of this book, has a significant place for consequences, but none for motives.

The trend among dark tourism scholars to emphasise motives, even in the case of Seaton (1996) to *define* dark tourism by the presence of particular motives, loses sight of the character of most dark tourism. It does not seem likely that investigating the *demand* for dark tourism will shed much light on the phenomenon. Rather, in this chapter I have suggested that considerable mileage may be gained by, firstly, investigating the kind of relationships that the living have at dark tourism sites, not just with each other but also with the dead; secondly, locating dark tourism within the large family of institutions in which the living relate to death and to the dead; and thirdly, looking at the functions such sites may hold for society as much as for individuals.

One task of social science is to make problematic the everyday, investigating why and how we do things we take for granted – that has been the calling of ethnomethodology (e.g. Garfinkel, 1967). Another task of social science is to demonstrate the normality of practices that we might have thought exotic or strange – that has been the calling of anthropology, at least in the old days when anthropologists did fieldwork with 'exotic' tribes. The dominant approach among scholars of dark tourism has been the latter – how can we explain why tourists do something so peculiar as to pay to visit a concentration camp? I am suggesting the other approach, namely to look at a range of activities we take for granted – like reading a novel, going to the movies, watching the TV news, taking a photograph, visiting a tourist site – and to suggest they all may involve things we thought modern societies didn't do, namely encounter the dead and remind people of their mortality.

So we have two different models of dark tourism and two programmes for research. Stone, Sharpley, Seaton and others, not least in the first two chapters of this book, focus on demand and motives; I suggest instead that we research what relationships are engaged in at dark tourism sites, the consequences for individuals and the functions for society. Some aspects of death certainly are sequestrated in modern society, but it is also true that there have always been institutions that link the living and the dead – even, and perhaps especially, in the modern world. Both approaches need empirical testing. I may be wrong that most dark tourism visits are typically contingent rather than motivated. Other scholars may be right that visitors to dark tourist sites come with a demonstrable sense of detachment from issues of mortality that such sites do something to remedy. We need to know.

Note

1. Not that I am against researching motives per se. In Walter (1993) I look in detail at the motives of war grave pilgrims and battlefield tour enthusiasts, but as I have noted above, in this case there is clear evidence of specific motivation.

Chapter 4

Dark Tourism: Morality and New Moral Spaces

PHILIP R. STONE

> *Everything's got a moral, if only you can find it.*
> Lewis Carroll, 1865

Introduction

The anxiety over the phenomenon of dark tourism and its subsequent moral quandaries has received increasing media attention, especially with regard to the ethical dimensions of exploiting tragic history (Lennon, 2005; Stone, 2007). Indeed, much of western media reporting of dark tourism has focused upon moral facets of visitor sites and attractions that offer a (re)presentation of death and the macabre and the individuals who visit them, so much so that Marcel (2004: 2) proclaimed in *The American Reporter* that 'death makes a holiday' and, as such, dark tourism is 'filled with moral ambiguities'. Marcel (2004: 1) goes on to state that dark tourism:

> seems to be the *dirty little secret of the tourism industry* [emphasis added]. It thrives at the Texas School Book Depository and the 'grassy knoll' in Dallas, where you can buy a coffee mug decorated with cross hair rifle-sights, at Auschwitz and in Holocaust Museums around the world, in cemeteries where celebrities are buried, and at the site of Princess Diana's tragic car crash in Paris. Tourists visit places of public executions, like the Place De La Guillotine, sites of mass death like museums and memorials like the Vietnam War Memorial in Washington, and battlefields like ancient Troy, Gettysburg, Pearl Harbor and Omaha Beach. Does it sound crazy to think of death as a niche market? Then what do you make of the 'Titanic cruises' offered by chartered companies, where tourists eat meals identical to those served on the ship, and hear music identical to the music played on the ship, as they travel to the precise spot where the ship lies at the bottom of the ocean.

While Marcel raises some valid concerns about the ethical exploitation of tragedy, more dogmatic media reports such as Avis (2007) focus upon the morality of so-called dark tourists. In particular, Avis offers a rather stark and bleak assessment of dark tourism and the individuals who consume dark experiences:

> These dark humans presumably are thrilled at witnessing killings and extreme human suffering, perhaps under the influence of the violent media-driven culture in which humanity lives. We find all this as a negative aspect of humanity and urge governments to do everything possible to abolish this sick kind of tourism. Otherwise you may find yourself in the situation that wars and misery are created for potential dark tourist benefits. And that would signify the moral end of humanity.

Accordingly, the accuracy of media reporting of tragic events and the subsequent (supposed) arrival of 'dark' or 'grief' tourists in the aftermath of tragedy has been questioned by Seaton and Lennon (2004). Specifically, they raise concerns over apparent dubious press reporting of events that followed the tragic murders of two young girls, Holly Wells and Jessica Chapman, in Soham, UK in 2002. While some individuals certainly did visit Soham in the immediate aftermath of the murders, no doubt validating media interest in the crimes, the claims that mass 'hordes of grief tourists' (O'Neill, 2002) visited the site 'turning murder into a shameful entertainment' (Masters, 2003) are perhaps somewhat unfounded. In particular, Seaton and Lennon (2004: 65) suggest 'there was little follow-up on the story [in the media], and no hard evidence about the scale and duration of Soham's status as a tourist destination'. Of course, this may simply illustrate selective and thus potentially divisive reporting by particular media institutions. While the media and its relationship with dark tourism as a mediating institution is explored further in Chapter 3, it is worth noting here that media narratives often perpetuate notions of a grief-stricken and morally barren (western) society. For instance, Halley (2004), writing in *The Sunday Independent*, reports how individuals use Soham and previously the death of Princess Diana as 'vessels to expel our own miseries' (see also Reid, 1998). Halley (2004) goes on to write:

> We now have a grief industry. Grief is the new opium of the masses and there's a diverse range available. So jump aboard the grief bandwagon, Atocha station awaits. We can all have therapeutic blubber without the debilitating side-effects of having experienced actual tragedy.

West (2004) elaborated on this theme of 'grief tourism' with his controversial monologue *Conspicuous Compassion*, in which he dismisses (western) explosions of grief and emotional hysteria as 'mourning sickness' and 'manufactured emotion' and nothing but an exercise in narcissism. However, Walter's (2007) analysis of a 'new public mourning' suggests the showing of grief in public and the consequent moral dilemmas for doing so are in fact grounded in wider historical, socio-cultural and political concerns. Consequently, the (selective) coverage of tragic events by the media and the subsequent alleged *moral panic* this causes, whereby individuals are seemingly 'emotionally invigilated' by television and newspaper reporting (Walter *et al.*, 1995), ensure the moral dimensions of dark tourism are never far from media commentary and academic discourse.

These moral dimensions often revolve around particular types of dark tourism sites, attractions or experiences. For instance, the representation of the Holocaust, perhaps the epitome of dark tourism, is regularly accused of being trivialised, merchandised and Americanised through its ephemeral touristic consumption. As a result, questions have been raised about the morality of both producing and consuming the Holocaust at various memorials and museums throughout the world and, in particular, what has been termed 'Auschwitz-land' at the former Nazi concentration camp in Poland (Cole, 1999b). For that reason, Dery (1999: 4) suggests Auschwitz-Birkenau is now a repackaged death camp resulting in the 'evisceration of history in a made-for-TV world where the past is increasingly experienced as a whirl of free-floating images, cut loose from context and complexity' (see also Stone, 2006b).

While the portrayal of the Holocaust in numerous museums and exhibitions pervades a contemporary moral consciousness, as it is a 'past that will not pass away (yet)' (Kershaw, 2003), other moral issues are often raised about the darker side of travel. For instance, the relationship between tourism, tourists and host countries that have recently experienced war has received an increasing amount of commentary. Indeed, the journalistic article by Atiyah (1999: 1) queries the ethics of tourists who visited the former Yugoslavia immediately after the Bosnian War:

> At the end of the Bosnian War, bus-loads of morbid visitors were taken into Sarajevo for the thrill of looking at bombed out buildings and of daring to tread in the footsteps of war reporters … But what kind of tourists, you may ask, would get their kicks from visiting countries on which one's own bombs have just been raining?

Atiyah may, of course, be another example of selective media reporting, and unable to substantiate the claim that 'bus-loads' of visitors did indeed visit Bosnia in the aftermath of the conflict. Nevertheless, dark tourism *has* evolved in Bosnia, with former battles and atrocities now packaged up and offered through dedicated 'war tours' in Sarajevo (Hawton, 2004; Kampschror, 2006; Zimonjic, 2006). Other dark tourism sites which have attracted 'moral criticism' include Ground Zero and the number of visitors it has received since 9/11. Blair (2002), writing in *The New York Times*, condemns the morality and subsequent ethical conduct of those sellers and sightseers at the former site of the World Trade Center in New York:

> Remember when it was just hallowed ground? Ground Zero is now one of the most popular tourism attractions in the city.... The proud can buy Twin Towers T-shirts, the angry can buy toilet paper bearing the face of Osama bin Laden and the curious can climb up the fence to take the perfect picture of what is now just a big hole. The hustle of commerce hawking to the crush of sightseers has prompted some to call it September 11 World.

Similarly, Crohn (2007) observes the 'unease' some individuals have when gazing upon Ground Zero. While he acknowledges the wider implications of identity building and mythmaking for the collective self which individuals may draw from sites such as Ground Zero (see also Chapter 6), Crohn also notes that visiting the site 'as an onlooker can be an ethically treacherous position' (2007: 2). That moral position is also replicated on the other side of the Atlantic by Wall (2004), who writes in *The Guardian* about Chernobyl, the site of the world's worst nuclear reactor accident, becoming a tourist attraction. Wall's article, provocatively entitled 'Postcard from Hell', outlines her trip to the Ukraine where Kiev-based tour operators run regular excursions into the former disaster zone. Commenting on a post-apocalyptic landscape of rusting metal and a concrete sarcophagus embedding the former nuclear reactor, and stating she feels 'uncomfortable' being photographed posing on the perimeter of the 'dead zone', Wall offers a brief insight into the undertaking of dark tourism. Even her Chernobyl tour guide suggests it was 'not a right place for tourism' and goes on to state it was 'a place of tragedy and is a place of tragedy still. Chernobyl is not a historical place. It is a sleeping lion. And when the lion is sleeping, you don't open the cage' (Wall, 2004: 3–4). Of course, the economic imperatives of the local community allied to an influx of 'curious' visitors ensured the 'Chernobyl cage' has been opened and dark tourism now flourishes in the region (Schutz, 2006).

Evidently, what these dark tourism examples illustrate, whether grieving *en masse* for murdered schoolchildren we did not know personally, or for dead celebrities with whom we had a pseudo-relationship, or consuming atrocity experiences in exhibition spaces around the world, or gazing upon sites of former disasters and tragedy, is that dark tourism in both its production and consumption generates a significant amount of moral commentary. Despite the fact much of this commentary may originate primarily from a bourgeois press and media, it remains nevertheless difficult to ignore. That said, many media 'moral comments' about the practice of dark tourism appear superficial and selective, and are seemingly based upon journalistic hunches, speculation and unfettered emotion. Of course, some of the recent moral commentary about dark tourism is inevitable when considering such a provocative (recreational) activity. This raises valid questions of whether it is right, or indeed just, to exploit and thus capitalise upon tragedy, and whether it is morally acceptable to partake in such experiences. However, while the dark tourism literature often remarks on various moral perils as an apparent consequence of these dark sites, and offers a rather parochial view of morality and ethics, it has yet to engage seriously with the broader socio-religious aspects of morality, and to clarify the potential role of dark tourism within an emotion–morality framework.

Accordingly, Uzzell and Ballantyne (1998: 152), in their critique of a 'Heritage that Hurts', contend that 'to deny the emotional side of our understanding and appreciation of the world and our relationships is to deny the very humanity that makes us part of the human race'. Similarly, within the context of tourism studies, Robinson (2005: xx) suggests that 'superficial and mechanistic studies of tourism have long given way to more penetrative analyses of what is now recognised to be a highly complex aspect of human life. Indeed, it is human life but in a temporary context, a different place, a different time; but human life all the same with all its attendant experiences and impacts, subtleties and sensitivities' (see also Fennell, 2006). Thus, it is on this very premise of attempting to understand and appreciate the emotional and moral aspects of human nature, applied within the dimensions of dark tourism and its fundamental relationships with both the individual and collective self, that an endeavour is now made to clarify moral ambiguities within dark tourism practices. In particular, the remainder of this chapter theorises how secular society has cultivated a process of individualisation, whereby the individual self feels isolated and morally confused due to the negation of dominant religious and moral frameworks. Consequently, as individuals attempt to seek (moral) meaning on their own terms and from alternative sources, the result is what Durkheim termed *collective effervescence*: the construction of new moral orders mediated by collectivities of embodied individuals who are emotionally engaged with their social world. It is these morally relative individual experiences within a collective environment, namely dark tourism, which adds to a potential resurgence of moral vitality within new contemporary spaces. Hence, it is to these issues that this chapter now turns.

Secularisation, Individualism and Moral Confusion

The issue of morality, as defined by good or bad conduct, has been subjected to increasing scrutiny by those interested in its purpose, especially within the ambivalent character of contemporary society (e.g. Selznick, 1992; Stivers, 1994, 1996; Smart, 1996). In particular, concepts such as 'postmodern ethics' (Bauman, 1993), 'dialogical democracy' (Giddens, 1994a), and 'inhumanity' (Lyotard, 1991; Tester, 1995) have all contributed to morality discourse. Subsequently, an increasing secularisation of modern (western) societies has given rise to fundamental questions of religion, morality and the moral frameworks in which we reside. A particular question revolves around the notion of religiosity and how the moral well-being of the individual self can be met within an ever fragmented world. Indeed, at the time of writing, Pope Benedict XVI, while on a visit to Australia, warned of society turning into a 'spiritual desert' as a result of increasing materialism and consumer culture (Pullella & Perry, 2008). In a rather melancholic assessment of the present day, the Pope urged individuals to reject the 'indifference, spiritual weariness and blind conformity' of the times (Eccleston, 2008), going on to state that:

> In so many of our societies, side by side with material prosperity, a spiritual desert is spreading: an interior emptiness, an unnamed fear, a quiet sense of despair ... [we require a] new age in which hope liberates us from the shallowness, apathy and self-absorption which deadens our souls and poison our relationships.

Moreover, this theme of narcissism has been capitalised on by politicians, most notably in the UK, whereby mainstream political parties warn the British electorate of a 'broken society' and 'moral neutrality', and then go on to suggest how politicians can 'mend' such societies (Cameron, 2008; Helm, 2008). Hence it appears that where religious institutions have seemingly failed, for some at least, to provide a perceived sense of moral guidance, politicians are adopting a 'politics of fear' (Furedi, 2005), where the task of morally policing secular society is built upon individuals' sense of moral confusion and ineptitude.

Consequently, as 'secularisation is an evitable outcome of social processes, which causes a realignment of the entire social fabric' (Oviedo, 2005: 359), the *sacred canopy* (after Berger, 1967) which once enveloped modern society and provided an overarching meaning system in terms of moral endeavours, has become fractionalised. However, secularisation is not a simple, one-dimensional transformation of a sacred world-view into a profane one. Instead, it is a 'complex process of reconfiguration that re-invents, translates, or cites moments of sacrality in a new concept' (Skolnick & Gordon, 2005: 7). Certainly, one key aspect of contemporary society and the secular values attached to it has been to detach individuals, or at least loosen them, from any sense of obligation which they may have felt towards traditional and organised religious institutions which previously had provided a dominant framework in which to find solace, meaning and moral guidance. Indeed, individualisation is regarded as one of the most important processes to have dramatically changed society (Beck & Beck-Gernsheim, 2002). As a result, the individual self has become free and independent from traditional, social and religious foundations. Thus, the emphasis on individual freedom lessens the control and influence of traditional institutions upon society, whereby institutional religion has become marginalised and personalised. As Halman (1996: 199) states, 'religious and moral values are no longer imposing themselves on societies'. However, individualisation should not be confused or equated with individualism; as Halman (1996: 198) points out, 'individualisation denotes a process in which traditional meaning systems and values diminish in importance in favour of personal considerations and decisions concerning values, norms and behaviours'. Individualism, meanwhile, focuses upon the individual's self-development, convictions and attitudes as the basis upon which to make decisions, whereby individual ethics are (morally) relative (Harman, 1975). However, it may be argued that increased individualism which has resulted from individualisation, combined with a reduced scope of the sacred, has resulted in moral confusion for the individual self. In other words, the lack of a consistent framework of substantive norms, values or moral principles to define and understand personal identity leaves many individuals feeling disoriented. Indeed, as the process of individualisation has made people more reliant upon themselves for moral instruction and less dependent upon traditional institutions, this raises the issue of how individuals within contemporary society seek and utilise (moral) meanings from non-traditional institutions.

Moreover, Stivers (1996: 2) suggests that 'religion is but one organised form that the collective sense of the sacred may assume'. Another organised form, of course, is tourism, especially when travel is linked with the spiritual dimensions of faith (Shackley, 2001b; Sharpley & Sundaram, 2005). In particular, Reader (2007) highlights pilgrimage growth in the modern world, where consequent meanings and implications for both the pilgrim and the actual pilgrimage site can occur. He goes on to suggest that some 'modern pilgrims appear to repudiate organised religion even while visiting sites normally associated with established religious traditions' (Reader, 2007: 210). Thus, rather than implying some form of religious revival, contemporary pilgrimage travel may, then, be viewed as evidence of an increasing turning away from traditional religion as an organised entity. The desire to discover alternative meanings, moral or otherwise, combined with the desire to escape an increasingly rationalised society, allied to the notion there is a general detachment of religious traditions has, perhaps, fuelled the growth in pilgrimage travel (Digance, 2003; Heelas & Woodhead, 2005; Reader, 2007). This growth in pilgrimage travel may also be mirrored by growth in 'dark travel'. That is, as sites of memorial, tragedy or reconstructed death increasingly enter mainstream tourism, the issue of how these 'traumascapes' can project moral meaning or why individuals may extract meaning is fundamental to understanding dark tourism as a new moral force (see also Chapter 7).

Hence, if we accept that the individual self, as a result of secular inspired individualism, is experiencing moral confusion and disorientation, then the self must begin to seek meanings and identity formulation in a complex and fragmented world. Conventional religious institutions which once provided moral space, both in the mind of the individual self and as a physical outlet for moral reflection and guidance, have largely been negated. In its place is a post-conventional society that demands 'an open identity capable of conversation with people of other perspectives in a relatively egalitarian and open communicative space' (Hyun-Sook, 2006: 1; see also Habermas, 1990 [1983]). It is these new *communicative spaces* that we must consider in framing contemporary approaches to morality. Above all, if we view dark tourism in its various manifestations as contemporary communicative spaces which interpret tragic events and, subsequently, convey morality, then we can adopt a multidimensional approach towards a morality of dark tourism. Ultimately, however, these 'new dark tourism spaces' and the ensuing ethical dilemmas which surround them result in a vitalisation and often vibrant discussion of moral concerns about the subject or event dark tourism attempts to (re)present, as well as the actual (re)presentation itself. This, in turn, could potentially inform contemporary moral instruction to the individual self. It is to this point that this chapter now turns.

Moral Spaces and Moral Panics: A Revitalisation of Morality Through Social Binding

A morality of dark tourism can greatly benefit from engaging with the philosophy of Durkheim who, in his seminal text *The Elementary Forms of Religious Life*, developed a deep concern with society as a moral, religious force which stimulated in people an effervescent 'propulsion' towards actions productive of either social cohesion or dissolution (Durkheim, 2001 [1912]; also see Bougle, 1926; Caillois, 1950; Collins, 1988). In other words, Durkheim is concerned with the asocial capabilities of the embodied individual as well as the potentialities of embodied humans at the collective level. As Shilling and Mellor (1998: 196) note, 'it is the *collective effervescence* stimulated by assembled social groups that harnesses people's passions to the symbolic order of society'. Thus, the emotional experience of these assembled social groups allows individuals to interact on the basis of shared ideas and concepts. Fundamentally, the concept of effervescence and its consequent emotional 'rush of energy' (Durkheim, 2001 [1912]: 215) permits social gatherings to infuse individuals and thus for people to become embodied and informed about particular tragic events that may have perturbed their life-world. Hence, collective effervescence has the potential to substitute the world immediately available to our perceptions for another, more moral world (Durkheim, 1984 [1893]). It is this gathering of social groups, often in socially sanctioned environments such as in the case of dark tourism sites, that a contemporary reality of *la société* is observed. In particular, the social binding of individuals in (emotional) effervescence influences and informs moral conversations about death or disaster, whereby the self can extract individualised and thus morally relative meaning about a particular tragic event (Harman, 1975). Indeed, in the case of violent events, or where communities have suffered disaster, Durkheim (2001: 302–303) suggests a collective response has implications for the individual:

> When emotions are so vivid, they may well be painful but they are not depressing. On the contrary, they indicate a state of effervescence that suggests a mobilisation of all our active forces and even an influx of external agencies. It matters little that this exaltation was provoked by a sad event; it is no less real and does not differ from the exaltation observed in joyous festivals.... Just by being collective, these ceremonies raise the vital tone of the group.... thus they are reassured, they take heart, and subjectively it is as though the rite really had repelled the dreaded danger.

Consequently, a Durkheimian perspective allows for an understanding of the construction of moral orders as mediated by collectives of embodied individuals who are both cognitively and emotionally engaged with their social world (Shilling & Mellor, 1998; Shilling, 2005). However, while Durkheim's insight of morality was an expression of what was perceived to be sacred, a contemporary application of Durkheim's work goes beyond that of the relationship between religion and morality. When applied to contemporary assembled social groups, such as those which exist within a variety of dark tourism environments, it is suggested that individual 'dark tourists' may become influenced and informed and thus embodied about the tragic event which they are consuming. This may result, in relative terms at least, in a transformation of their own emotional structure and moral order.

By way of contextualisation, a visit for many Americans to the Tribute WTC Visitor Centre, or what has been termed Ground Zero (see Figure 4.1), will no doubt collectively bind individuals not only to a loss of human life, but also to a loss of confidence and a realisation that the capitalist American Dream is not a universal 'dream' shared by all world cultures. Consequently, the atrocity on 9/11 which left thousands of people dead, begat a degree of self-reflection for many Americans. This self-reflection included the premise that secularisation as an ongoing process included competing global voices and religious forces (Habermas, 2003). Hence individuals required not only a physical outlet for memorial and commemoration of the 9/11 deceased, but also an official space to project morality and reaffirm American Christian morals and values (see Figure 4.2). Additionally, the social binding of people in emotion (that is, collective effervescence) at the Tribute WTC Visitor Centre allows the individual self to become

Tribute WTC
Visitor Center
TRIBUTE

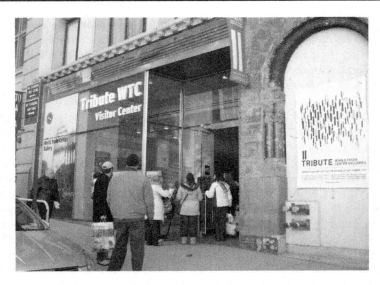

Figure 4.1 Visitors enter the (temporary) Tribute WTC Visitor Centre at Ground Zero (New York)
Photo: P.R. Stone

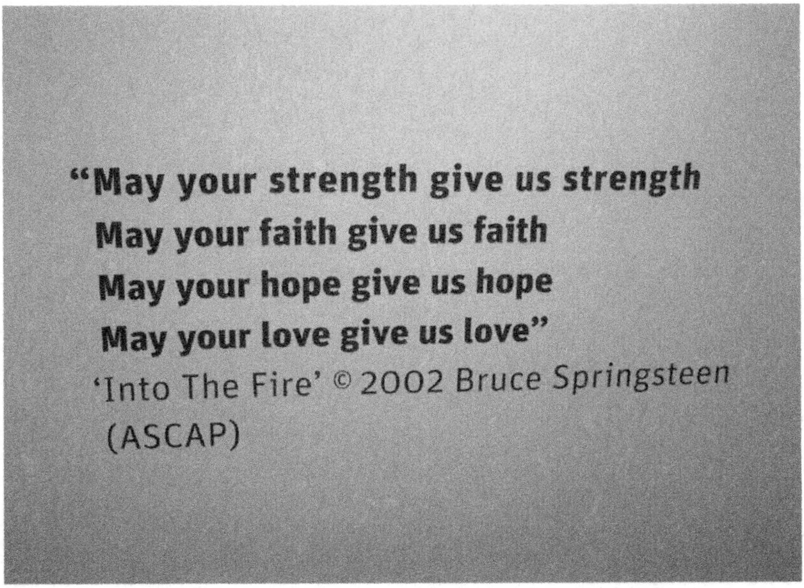
"May your strength give us strength
May your faith give us faith
May your hope give us hope
May your love give us love"
'Into The Fire' © 2002 Bruce Springsteen
(ASCAP)

Figure 4.2 A 'prayer' displayed on a wall inside the Tribute WTC Visitor Centre at Ground Zero (New York)
Photo: P.R. Stone

embodied and to formally offer its own morally relative discourse about 9/11 and its consequences. In particular, visitors are encouraged to write and record their own thoughts and emotions about the attack in a dedicated 'remembrance room' within the Tribute WTC Visitor Centre (Figure 4.3). These individual 'moral judgements' are then recorded and displayed collectively against official interpretation of tolerance and courage (Figure 4.4). It is here that sacrality and morality are reconfigured against a backdrop of political terrorism, where the physical place of the Tribute WTC Visitor Centre offers a (new) vitalised space to espouse and communicate individual moral and ethical opinion. Consequently, the formal and official interpretation offered by the 'authorities' at the Tribute WTC Visitor Centre (e.g. see Figures 4.5 and 4.6; also Chapter 6), combined with the informal and unofficial interpretation offered by individual visitors (as in Figure 4.4), ensures a *collective constitution* of a morality which is enlightened by the tragedy of 9/11. This, in turn, generates debate from the media and literature as well as among individuals themselves. Of course, this so-called 9/11 morality has wider implications for how people interact with different faiths and creeds, and the political responses to such interactions. On a more general level, however, it is here that Durkheim's concept of effervescence is revealed, as collectivities

Figure 4.3 Visitors gather to record 'moral judgments' inside the Tribute WTC Visitor Centre at Ground Zero (New York)
Photo: P.R. Stone

Figure 4.4 Visitor 'postcards of morality' inside the Tribute WTC Visitor Centre at Ground Zero (New York)
Photo: P.R. Stone

of embodied individuals are both socially and emotionally bound within a dark tourism space and, in turn, consume tragedy which may have adversely affected their intrinsic sense of morality.

Of course, the example of the Tribute WTC Visitor Centre at Ground Zero as a dark tourism case is specific to the events of 9/11 and its aftermath. Nevertheless, the principle of collective effervescence and its emotional and social binding of individuals (re)invents dark tourism places into contemporary spaces to reflect, record and interpret moral concerns. However, the incidence, intensity and scope of collective effervescence varies according to the relationship and activities characteristic of social groups (Collins, 1988). This is certainly true of dark tourism, with its diverse and eclectic mix of sites, attractions and exhibitions, and the individuals who may visit them. In particular, the perceived 'shade of darkness' (Sharpley, 2005; Stone, 2006a) within any given dark tourism experience will dictate the level of emotional (re)structuring for the individual and, of course, any subsequent moral instruction and meaning will differ invariably within different socio-cultural groups and geopolitical contexts. Furthermore, as noted by Shilling and Mellor (1998: 197), the effects of collective effervescence are, since they rooted in emotion, 'characterised by ephemerality and must be *recharged* if it is to have enduring

Figure 4.5 Audio interpretation of 9/11 from those who directly experienced events – Tribute WTC Visitor Centre at Ground Zero (New York)
Photo: P.R. Stone

social significance'. This may explain, in part at least, the exponential growth of dark tourism in its various guises as the recharging effect occurs, and different dark tourism experiences inform a broader morality framework. Even so, Durkheim warned of non-traditional institutions, or what he termed professional organisations as modern associational forms, performing the socially binding functions previously undertaken by religion (Durkheim, 1984 [1893], 1958). Consequently, the processes of effervescent vitalism within contemporary society and subsequent new moral spaces, such as those found within dark tourism, and its resultant binding effect of individuals in moral reflection can be problematic. Certainly, Graham

Figure 4.6 Visitor reading an 'official narrative' at the Tribute WTC Visitor Centre at Ground Zero (New York)
Photo: P.R. Stone

(2007) notes the ambiguity in Durkheim's theory of social effervescence and its lack of distinction between different types of social bonding. It is here that the diversity of dark tourism and its ability in both scope and generation of moral conversation is complex. For instance, a visit to Auschwitz-Birkenau will no doubt provide a more intense emotional experience and subsequent rational turn to collective moral issues than, say, a visit to a 'lighter form of dark tourism' such as the York Dungeon visitor attraction (see Chapter 9). Nevertheless, while the self may extract profound moral meanings, and indeed raise further ethical questions about the human capacity to act inhumanly, at Auschwitz-Birkenau, different but equally valid moral issues may surround the York Dungeon and the role of torture, punishment and retribution, both in the past and its ethical implications for penal justice in the present. In both examples, as with the earlier Ground Zero illustration, morality is generated, maintained, challenged or confirmed within these new vitalised contemporary spaces, albeit with varying degrees of intensity, through embodied individuals who are engaged with their life-world. In turn, this stimulates a kind of collective emotional energy, or effervescence, which socially binds individuals through their consumption of dark tourism.

Consequently, it is this, the fact that individuals collectively assemble in seemingly 'dark spaces' and gaze upon sordid human activity or collectively consume grief and tragedy that is often reported upon by the media as 'moral panic' (Seaton & Lennon, 2004). However, fundamentally, these so-called moral panics are not as unequivocal as media reporting might assume. Indeed, when examined from a Durkheimian perspective, the moral panic dark tourism seemingly provokes, both through its production and consumption, might be viewed as ethically relative to the individual but, at the collective level, has profound implications for society in its attempt to create and maintain new moral frameworks. In other words, perceived moral panic is the consequence of the process of debate generated by dark tourism. Moral panic is *not* the end result of dark tourism, but merely *a symptom* of secular society attempting to negotiate and communicate morality in new contemporary spaces. Indeed, it is against a backdrop of individualisation and construction of new secular moral orders that the communication and negotiation of 'moral meaning' within collective contemporary 'dark spaces' is often misconstrued as moral panic. There is *no* moral panic as a result of dark tourism, only talk *of* panic. It is this 'talk', frequently conveyed by media reporting of dark tourism activity, which is an integral element of the social effervescence that revitalises moral arguments which surround the consumption of death, disaster and tragedy within contemporary societies.

Conclusion

Despite an increasing ethical commentary on dark tourism, either from media reporting of specific sites or experiences or within broader academic discourse, the analysis of morality and dark tourism has to date been rather descriptive and one-dimensional. Additionally, for the most part, and in the media at least, dark tourism has largely been accused of trivialising death and exploiting tragedy for mercantile advantage or for political gain, while dark touristic experiences have often been dismissed as unethical and voyeuristic (e.g. see Garrett, 2008). This chapter, therefore, set out to enhance the theoretical foundations of the dark tourism phenomenon by considering it within a broader framework of emotion and morality. In so doing, it has not only developed a conceptual basis for the future empirical testing of ethics and morality within dark tourism practices, but has also contributed to a wider social scientific understanding of morality within contemporary societies.

Thus, a number of key issues have emerged from the preceding discussion. Firstly, secularisation and the negation of religion as a traditional dominant framework, in which meaning and moral guidance is provided, has seemingly left some individuals isolated, disoriented and morally confused. Secondly, as post-conventional societies cultivate a process of individualisation and moral confusion, individuals seek morally relative meaning on their own terms and from non-religious and non-traditional institutions, enabling dark tourism places to become contemporary communicative spaces. Thirdly, individuals collectively assemble in these new communicative (dark) spaces, resulting, potentially, in both the provision and extraction of moral meaning about a particular tragic event, which in turn allows the self to become embodied. Finally, collective effervescence and its resultant emotional energy is discharged through and by embodied individuals within these new socially sanctioned dark spaces, whereby morality is conveyed not only by official interpretation of the death or tragedy, but also by the actual presence and emotional engagement of the individual visitor. This, in turn, can be interpreted by the media and other commentators as moral panic which, to them at least, means an apparent dissolution of ethics at the collective level. In short, dark tourism may provide new spaces in which not only is immorality (re)presented for contemporary consumption, but also in which morality is communicated, reconfigured and revitalised. This reconfiguration and revitalisation of moral issues in dark tourism spaces is not moral panic, nor should it generate moral panic, but instead it should be viewed as a process of contemporary society in which we renegotiate moral boundaries and ethical principles. Therefore, it is, perhaps, the process of dark tourism which attracts individuals to consume death in new insulating spaces that generates a perceived moral panic, in addition to, or even rather than, the actual death, disaster or tragedy that dark tourism aims to represent.

In conclusion, however, it would be naïve to advocate that the process of dark tourism, both in its production and consumption, provides a defining communicative space for contemporary moral instruction. It does not. Given the extensive and complex array of dark tourism sites and experiences in a variety of social, cultural and political contexts, actual dark tourism spaces will no doubt both *provide* and *be provided with* a myriad of potential moral meanings. Nonetheless, locating dark tourism within a broader conceptual emotion – morality framework allows for moral orders and their construction within contemporary society to be interrogated. While future empirical research will no doubt test the theory of dark tourism and its potential role in the effervescent vitalisation of morality (see Chapter 9), other conceptual issues deserve attention.

In particular, issues of moral fragility and dark tourism as a source of moral communication require further scrutiny. While the author has located dark tourism as a source of morality in *society*'s collective engagement with the emotional capacities of people, the 'sequestration of morality' as advocated by Giddens (1991, 1994b) may augment any theory of dark tourism and morality. In particular, Giddens argues that moral questions have been sequestered into the back-regions of life, and that 'direct contact with events and situations which link the individual lifespan to broad issues of morality and finitude are rare and fleeting' (1991: 169). While dark tourism may indeed provide this direct contact, consequently, for Giddens at least, there is no 'moral impulse' or collective effervescence which stimulates moral conversations but, at most, a reflexive recognition of the limits of contemporary society and a rational turn to moral questions. While a Giddensian perspective of morality and the potential role of dark tourism may be an avenue for future academic inquiry, other conceptual issues should also be explored. For instance, the notion of an 'ethics of aesthetics', as outlined by Maffesoli (1991), perhaps has some relevance to how death and disaster is portrayed and presented within dark tourism. Likewise, the issue of moral relativism and individual's behaviour, values and emotions is a potential area for future research when considering the ethical dimensions of individual visitors at particular 'dark sites' (e.g. see Harman, 1975; Beesley, 2004). Additionally, while the author has suggested a largely positive view of effervescent gatherings and the identification of dark tourism as a spatial opportunity for this social vitalism, engaging the work of Meštrović (1991, 1993, 1997) offers a future research avenue which can explore dark tourism as an effervescent manifestation of fear and hatred. Adopting Meštrović's stance, then, it could be argued dark tourism and its potential inauthentic or sensational representation of tragedy and the macabre may actually heighten individuals' sense of fear. Nonetheless, while these research issues remain untapped, dark tourism and its relationship with contemporary morality is undoubted. As Wilson (2008: 6) aptly notes, 'society is identified, or rather identifies itself, at least as much by what it reviles as by what it embraces'. So much so, that we appear to have an innate need to formulate moral stories about ourselves that locate us in the world, and the moral stories about the world that locate us within ourselves. To that end, dark tourism sites as contemporary communicative spaces of morality, and the individuals who consume those spaces, means that dark tourism may not only act as a guardian of history in heritage terms, but also as a moral guardian of a contemporary society which appears to be in a midst of a resurgence of effervescent moral vitality. That said however, the consequences and effectiveness of dark tourism as potential new vitalised moral spaces remains to be seen.

Part 2

Dark Tourism: Management Implications

Chapter 5

Purposeful Otherness: Approaches to the Management of Thanatourism

TONY SEATON

Think often of death and it will frighten you the less.
Viking motto in Östersund Museum

Introduction

Tourism management has traditionally been seen as a pragmatic process of rational control, planning, implementation and evaluation of several functional business areas including: finance, human resources, marketing and promotion, visitor servicing and satisfaction, sustainable development and so on. There have been several general tourism texts published on the overall process in the context of heritage and attraction management (Shackley, 2001b; Swarbrooke, 2001), but little on the problems of thanatourism management in particular. The purpose of this chapter, therefore, is to examine some theoretical and practical issues that are distinctive to the management of thanatourism. To what extent is thanatourism simply one kind of tourism like any other, involving the same tourism management practices and activities? To what extent should it be regarded as qualitatively different? And, if there are differences, what are the management implications?

The chapter begins with a re-evaluation of the 'Other' and 'Othering', concepts well known in the social sciences and tourism, but less common in discussions of management. It is proposed that the Other of Death is the defining feature of thanatourism and that evoking and conserving its auratic impacts are the central tasks of management. The chapter assesses how these aims may be approached in the physical management of sites, and also in accommodating the needs and interests of different stakeholders who form the audiences and constituencies of thanatourism.

The Other

The Other in the social sciences and tourism

The concepts of the Other and Othering can be traced back to the contacts of travellers in history, mainly from Europe, with foreigners from other lands. These travellers returned from remote places with tales of societies where they had witnessed bizarre physical differences, extraordinary customs, strange judicial and religious practices – in short, with all manner of *differences* (see Seaton, 2001). And because western Europeans, although they did not invent printing, first developed it as a popular medium from the 15th century onward, they were progressively able to represent and disseminate their perceptions in books, journalism and graphics across wide sectors of the globe. 'The Other' became a term that retrospectively categorised the represented differences observed not only by travellers but later by anthropologists, comparing their own societies with those they were visiting or studying. 'The Other' typically meant 'people not like us', as Hawthorn's definition suggests:

> ... to characterise a person, group or individual as 'other' is to place them outside the system of normality or convention to which one belongs oneself. (Hawthorn, 1994: 141)

Travellers and anthropologists were often members of dominant societies observing subordinate ones whom they presumed to be inferior. The judgemental differences they drew, implicitly or explicitly, between their own societies and the observed 'Othered' societies included the following:

Own societies of the self	*Societies of the Other*
Modern evolving	Timeless, traditional
Civilised	Primitive
Superior	Inferior
Rational-scientific	Superstitious, ignorant
Humane	Savage, cruel, cannibalistic
Christian	Heathen
Worldly	Naïve, innocent
Disenchanted	Enchanted, mysterious

This did not mean that westerners were wholly unsympathetic to other cultures. Indeed, Europeans travelling, or residing as imperial occupants in alien lands, were often fascinated and drawn to study the beliefs, values and lifestyles they observed in the picturesque practices of people they defined as 'primitive'. In the writing of early anthropologists such as Fraser, Malinowski and Evans-Pritchard, despite the prevailing register of rational analysis delivered from Olympian heights of moral superiority, there is occasionally a sense of sneaking sympathy for the universe of myth, fable and 'primitive' enchantment – a world lost under the wheels of western modernity.

This anthropological conception of the Other and Othering was continued by later cultural commentators, including, most notably, Edward Said (1978) and post-colonial analysts following in his influential wake. But they brought a critical, more overtly political 'spin' to discussions of Othering, conceptualising it as a hegemonic process by which imperialistic cultures established dominance over subordinate ones, through processes of representation and discourse inscribed in, and transmitted through, a range of institutional practices – the media, education, academia, law and government. Said gave the name *Orientalism* to the product of these practices. Orientalism, he argued, was a composite, adverse view of the East constructed by imperialists who represented it as the Other of the West (i.e. its opposite), whose populations were, among other things, unreliable, dishonest, untrustworthy, infantile and passive. These negative stereotypes, Said concluded, produced a form of ideological emasculation of the East that was the flip side of the political and military domination the West had established as a colonising power.

This post-colonial paradigm of the Other and Othering has been very influential in analyses of the place imaging of small nations by larger ones, often theorised as constructions of the 'Other' through 'representation' by the powerful of the powerless. It has recently been applied to the analysis of Northern Italy's relationship with Southern Italy (Schneider, 1998; Moe, 2002).

Othering has also been a central focus by tourism academics studying the relations between tourists and indigenous populations in the host countries, particularly developing ones, they visit. Tourism has been seen as the pursuit by westerners of the Other, a motivation for temporary encounters with other cultures stimulated, consciously or unconsciously, by attributing to them extremes of imagined difference from their own. This encyclopaedia definition suggests the extent to which tourism theory has adopted post-colonial perspectives:

> Othering is the imaginary construction of different/alien people by external individuals who remain marginal (yet powerful) in that encounter with their exotic 'others'. The Othering of foreigners tends to deny these others of genuine identifications as they are conspiratorially (but often unconsciously) appropriated. The management/development practices, and the narratives of tourism, regularly further the capture/ destruction of others. (Hollinshead, in Jafari, 2000: 420)

'Capture', 'destruction', 'conspiratorially appropriated' – the words suggest the dominant *political* connotations of Othering. Tourism promoters and their audiences are seen as complicit in practices that trap and exoticise indigenous peoples in misperceptions and representations that deny their subjects voice. In so doing, they are seen to disallow or exclude the possibility of *autonomous identity* and *subjective self-definition* to indigenous populations, while notionally emancipating the tourist to make a temporary release from his/her own cultural identity through contact with the 'Othered'. This brief escape is a safe one since, like the western traveller and anthropologist in the past, the tourist, having experienced a release from everyday self into a world of temporary Otherness, returns with his/her identity confirmed and intact. Overall, according to this reading, Othering is a process orchestrated by the powerful with malign effects on subordinate groups who are effectively its victims. The tourist's quest for the Other may be seen as self-indulgence (in the literal sense of being an indulgence in *self*), an exercise in self-exploration and individuation by contrast and comparison with the perceived Otherness of indigenous populations encountered abroad, identities that have been pre-figured to the tourists by representational processes (promotion, publicity, education, media stereotyping) over which the observed have had no control.

Other Others? A critique of the conceptualisation of the Other

Though Said's work has its critics (Kennedy, 2000; Khawaja, 2007; Warraq, 2007), there has been limited comment focused explicitly on his understanding of the Other and Othering. One immediate observation that should be made is that his post-colonial reading of the Other and Othering is exclusively a *socio-political one* which focuses on inequities in power in relations between cultural groupings, and the relative freedom each has to judge and represent the Other. This is certainly one way of conceptualising the Other, but it a restricted one that may be criticised on several counts.

Firstly, it assumes that Othering is a one-way process in which a dominant culture targets members of a subordinate one, and appropriates how its people will be constructed, represented and dominated, or in tourism terms, visited and gazed upon. Such a one-way trajectory of domination conceals the truth that Othering is not just an ideological tendency within powerful cultures, but a universal one within human relations when *like* meets *unlike*.[1] Othering is a process that happens whenever one group first encounters an unfamiliar one. Human cultures and groups construct and evaluate their identity through perceptions of differences from others – those like us/those not like us; things we do/things they don't; our values/their values. In all encounters between two groups, each party may be at once Othering and Othered. Othering is ego attributing levels of difference to *people at a distance* (physically, socially or ideologically), whether or not ego has power over them. The issue is not whether Othering takes place, but inequities in the power to *represent* the perceptual end-results of the Othering process.

The historical development of guidebooks throws suggestive light on these relational aspects of Othering in a tourism context. From the late 18th and for much of the 19th centuries, guides published for visitors were not called tourist guidebooks but *'strangers' guides'*.[2] Many were written and published by local entrepreneurs in the places described, and the titles reflected the fact that the visitor was 'The Other', an alien among them who had to be de-estranged and familiarised before he/she could function. Until well into the 20th century, phrases such as 'stranger in town', 'stranger in these parts' or 'not from round here' were regularly applied by communities to outsiders with unfamiliar faces arriving among them. It was only as mass travel developed that strangers started to be hailed in guide books as 'tourists', a term that connoted greater autonomy for them as *active* agents with client power, rather than as novices whose insecurities in a new place had to be soothed. Today, the tourism industry promotes myths of the power of consumer choice, and the opportunities for meaningful interaction with indigenous populations, masking what older guidebooks let slip – the existential uncertainty of the first-time visitor who will always continue to arrive and, for the most part, leave as a 'stranger'. The stranger is a concept that may be due for reclamation as an analytical orientation to the phenomenology of tourist/host transactions. It redresses the emphasis that has been put on the power of the visitor and the hegemonic gaze of the tourist. Instead, it posits the, at least partial, isolation and uncertainty of the tourist in an unfamiliar world, not sure what to do, what to look at, how to manage. It is the host who is on 'home ground', a fact that throws into question Foucaultian approaches to tourist analysis associated with writers like Urry (2002), which imply that the host is a weak victim, subject to the visitor's imaginings. Allowing the tourist-as-stranger into the relationship means that there is at least the possibility that the tourist is as Otherly to the host, as it is claimed in post-colonial discourse that the host is rendered to the imperial observer – or tourist.

If the *reciprocal* aspects of Othering are recognised in encounters between groups and individuals from different behavioural worlds – whether ethnic, social or geographic – they cast doubt upon the one-way power model through which post-colonial theorists have treated it as a kind of perceptual pathology of imperialism, a construct used mainly to unpack the way powerful groups allegedly exoticise, infantilise or demonise subordinate ones. In contrast to this conspiratorial reading, Othering may be seen as a universal, two-way and reversible process in which, at any moment, an individual or group may interchangeably be the Othering subject and simultaneously the Othered object, with power not necessarily lying with one party.

Some commentators go further and assert that Othering is not just something found in relationships between groups, but an ongoing, essential and central psychological process in identity formation that is crucial to the development of the individual:

> The concept of 'otherness' is ... integral to the understanding of identities, as people construct roles for themselves in relation to an 'other' as part of a fluid process of *action-reaction* that is *not necessarily related with subjugation or stigmatization.* (Boskovic, 2007)

A second objection to post-colonial readings of the Other is the way it has been restricted to *representations of people*. Said's 'Orientalism' is wholly about representations of eastern peoples by western ones. Similarly, Stuart Hall's influential, edited collection on representation a generation later (Hall, 1997), which includes his own chapter, 'The spectacle of the Other', is exclusively about the way whites have portrayed blacks.

Though this emphasis in discussions of the Other on issues of racial stereotyping was both understandable and necessary in the social and political contexts of the 1970s, 1980s and, more arguably, the 1990s, it hardly serves as an adequate academic exploration of the Other in its many different manifestations. (Interestingly, neither Said or Hall attempted to provide any overarching, formal definition of the Other – they defined it implicitly by illustration.) Against this narrow focus, the Other may be seen as *perceptions* and *representations*, not only of people of other cultures, but of a potentially infinite variety of things and ideas whose impact and effects lie in their apparent difference from the phenomenological, day-to-day world of the observer, any observer. They comprise *social and cultural products* not necessarily or precisely associated with specific groups or cultures, but experienced initially as manifestations of nameless difference provoking verbal responses such as 'strange', 'unusual', 'weird' or 'fantastic'. The represented products may include artefacts, fashions, lifestyle habits, aesthetic forms (music, art, drama), gastronomic choices, decorative styles and so on. Cahoone has drawn attention to the dimensions of the potential theatre of cultural differences that may comprise the Other, seeing them as oppositional modes against which human groups define and maintain their own value systems:

> What appear to be cultural units – human beings, words, meanings, ideas, philosophical systems, social organisations – are maintained in their apparent unity only through an active process of exclusion, opposition, and hierarchisation. Other phenomena or units must be represented as foreign or 'other' through representing a hierarchical dualism in which the unit is 'privileged' or favoured, and the other is devalued in some way. (Cahoone, 1996: 15)

Yet the 'cultural units' of the Other are not necessarily 'hierarchically ordered' in the way Cahoone suggests. The 'phenomena and units of differences' may not be perceived as negative ones *against which* culturally located individuals define and assure their own behaviour, but a positive one *towards* which they are drawn *away from* their own value-system. The Other may be both attraction and repulsion, a negative benchmark against which to hold the line of the phenomenological world of self, but also a potential theatre of desire for those who fantasise or seek *release from* its constraining, mundane presence. The impulse to elude or transcend the mundane world has probably always existed. Religion, with its polarities of incarnate goodness and evil, its apocalyptic revelations and prophesies, its visions of heaven and hell, its mythic heroes and villains, has always offered one system of discursive alternatives to the mundane world. Religion, as Cannell (2007) has recently argued, may be the great neglected 'Other' in anthropological analysis. In more secular times, the Other has become a growing *consumer commodity* within western modernity, fed partly with tastes and products borrowed or bastardised from other cultures: esoteric religion and mysticism from the East; primitive art from Oceania and Africa; revolutionary musical forms like jazz, rock and rap from US Afro-Caribbean sub-cultures; and ephemeral fashions in clothing and self-presentation from many countries and continents (western fashion is almost, by definition, a perpetual quest for annual difference, often based on appropriating and recycling the geographical or historical Other).

But the Other is not just cultural imports. It is has also been a thriving feature of *domestic* production and consumption since the early 19th century, when the influence of Romanticism began to make *subjective difference* and *singularity* touchstones of identity and self-presentation. These ideas initially affected the educated middle classes, leading them to cultivate a self-expressive individualism in which a number of evaluative re-orderings of experiential meanings were adopted: priority was given to feeling over thinking; originality was prized more than rational consensus; picturesque, rural populations were preferred to urban workers at home; the past was idealised at the expense of the present; and travel to other cultures, times and places became a recreational essential to escape the banalities and aesthetic horrors of industrial society (see Halsted (1965) and Furst (1969) for concise discussions of Romanticism's revolutionary values and problematics). All these ideological themes, articulated in Romanticism by poets, essayists, novelists and artists, precipitated a crisis of belief in bourgeois culture by a large fraction of its members, and a counterveiling desire for the Other. This was to result in Otherly quests that were sometimes bravura physical journeys to foreign parts (the 19th century was the first great century of mass travel among the middle classes) and/or avid consumption of art and literature from alternative worlds of the imaginary – gothic horror, oriental myth, medieval romance, heroic imperial adventure.

This has had its legacy among mass populations today. One of the recognisable functions of the commercial entertainment industry, particularly the broadcast media, has been to transport mass audiences to a world less mundane by the supply of texts of the Other whose appeal is often articulated by its consumers as a desire to be taken out of themselves, in the same way that tourism has been seen and sold as an escape attempt, 'to get away from it all'. Seen in this broader light, the Other is not just being hooked on exotic myths of other cultures, but consumption of a vast discursive field of popular culture that provides escape from the mundane: freak shows and disaster movies; tales of the 'lower depths' and stories of 'high society'; legends of saints and sinners; portrayals of superheroes and serial killers. In its more benign forms, the Other may be all those manifestations and means of enjoyment of difference from the everyday that produce wonder, inspiration, laughter or sensual delight: an amazing guitar riff, a new hair style, a theme park ride – all manner of accentuated difference . . .

It may be that much of this pursuit of the Other is a degenerative substitute for religion and secular epiphany on demand. As a distinguished writer on religion who began her adult life as a nun has observed, 'Human beings seek ekstasis, a "stepping outside" of their normal, mundane experience. If they no longer find ecstasy in a synagogue, church or mosque, they look for it in dance, music, sport, sex or drugs' (Armstrong, 2007: 5).

The quest for the Other that was once a physical journey has been replaced by all manner of mental escapes from the everyday world. The word 'journey' has become a routine metaphor used by people to describe movements in their life scripts, rather than their kinetic biographies.

Finally, appraisal of the nature of the Other and Othering requires mention of an element that post-colonial analysts typically exclude in their socio-political conception of the effects – the Other's existence as *physical* presence. Like the unmentioned elephant in the sitting room, this is a very significant silence since, in perceptions and representations of place and travel, the impacts of fauna, flora, climate, landscape and built environment are often the most immediate and enduring aspects of difference. Imperial travel texts, historical and contemporary, abound with encounters with climatic extremes – desert wastes, ice-locked wildernesses, mosquito-infested jungles – that are often their most memorable features and, even when not, may constitute an omnipresent, atmospheric backdrop of Otherness to everything else. Yet post-colonial accounts of the Other pass over them in silence.

Summary

Othering is not just a malign way of imagining and representing other cultures, but the almost infinite play of identity with images and possibilities of *difference* that generates strong compulsions of negative and positive desire, approach as well as avoidance. The Other is part of the social imaginary of every member of every society, his or her idea of alternative social practices, aesthetic forms, religious beliefs, artefacts existing elsewhere, that are personally experienced by the individual as a theatre of potential, performative difference that may be embraced, ignored or proscribed.

Othering is not necessarily stigmatisation of minorities and subordinate cultures, though it may be. But it may also be romantic identification and a desire to reach them through contact, study and imitation, historical features of western attitudes to the East that Said largely passes over in silence, as Warraq (2007) has recently analysed to telling effect. Some quests for the Other are stimulated by factors within, not outside, one's own culture. They comprise not racist appropriations of other cultures as, for example, Torgovnick's (1990) interesting study of western responses to 'primitivism' suggests, but the consumption of both escapist popular culture and high culture that offer a wide variety of sensational escape hatches from the mundane and/or high roads to alternative planes of experience. The Other is whatever disturbs the world of the everyday. Rightly understood, it is all those representations and manifestations of the strange that may, on the one hand, create temporary religious or secular epiphanies of a greater or lesser kind and, on the other hand, produce fear and proscription. For some, the Other may be a desire for difference that takes them 'out of ourselves', a desire for a sabbatical from the everyday self and mundane society; for others, the Other is what always brings them back, an anti-structure that serves, in opposition to its perceived wrongnesss, to keep them right with their own world.

Death, the Other and Thanatourism

The discussion so far has established two essential premises: firstly, that the Other has previously been discussed in a way that is narrowly sociopolitical and, secondly, that once its broader dimensions are recognised it can be seen as a potent force not just in social relations, but in psychological development, self-recognition and enactment of individual identity. To these two may be added a third assertion: that that the Otherness of death is the most powerful of all Others and one which, as the unique element in thanatourism, distinguishes it from all other kinds of tourism.

The reasons for seeing death as a uniquely powerful Other are several. Firstly, it is the only Other that is universal, existing in all cultures as an absolute, not a construct of relative difference. The manifestations of the Other discussed earlier – in aesthetics, religion, fashion, customs and so on – derived from contrasts between the practices in the phenomenological world of one group with the represented practices of those in another. Thus, an exotic religion only appears exotic to those for whom it is an unfamiliar one in their own culture; a fashion only appears as 'Otherly' to someone whose culturally acquired idea of fashion is different. Death's Otherness, by contrast, is apprehended not as contrasted difference between one culture and another – although, of course, different cultures have different ways of responding to it religiously, ritually and symbolically which may themselves become cultural tourism attractions (Tanas, 2008a) – but as part of a *universal* opposition that transcends culture – that between life and death. Recognition of the absolute and universal character of death's Otherness to all peoples means that thanatourism has the potential to be one of the most widely shared reasons for travel internationally.

Secondly, most forms of Otherness are temporary, because their power diminishes the better the observer comes to know the objects that provoked it. Familiarity erodes the potency of the unknown, so that people and phenomena once thought 'Otherly' become tamed by time and contact. The Otherness of death resists and escapes these processes of erosion because it can never be known to the living. Along with birth and marriage, it is one of the three great rites of passage, but the one that none can ever consciously experience. Thus, it sustains its mystery, one that simultaneously repels and attracts. This double response to the Other, discussed earlier as negative and positive forms of desire, may be seen in the diverse representations of death in social practice and aesthetics through history. On the one hand, it has been depicted as terrifying and tragic, but there have been periods, particularly since the rise of Romanticism, when it has been aestheticised in new cultural forms, and in the age of Queen Victoria, celebrated exuberantly in social practice, ritual, art and literature (Morley, 1971; Curll, 2000).

Otherness as a feature of travel

The Otherness of death has been an important element in travel throughout history. Medieval pilgrimages were substantially journeys to death sites and relic viewing. Literary travellers, whose number expanded from the 17th century onwards, were frequently interested in how other cultures treated death. John Evelyn, James Boswell, William Beckford, Charles Dickens and Evelyn Waugh are only a few of the better known writers who have, in their travel books, left descriptions of burial customs and funerary practices, visits to cemeteries, catacombs and 'santo campo' sites, and even eye-witness accounts of judicial execution.

In summary, the Otherness of death is the central, distinctive and compelling element in thanatourism. The implications of this for managers are two-fold: the need to exhibit and protect this Otherness at sites where it already exists, and to orchestrate its performative features at new thanatourism developments such as dungeon attractions, ghost walks and funeral museums, like the new one in Amsterdam. Achieving these tasks involves two related domains of responsibility – administering the site, and shaping and responding to the perceptions of the visitor.

Managerial Practices and Implications

Sites

Thanatourism management as the custodianship
of sacred and auratic space

One aspect of the Otherness of thanatourism sites is that they may be perceived as sacred spaces by their visitors. 'Sacred space', a well-known concept in the sociology and anthropology of religion, has been described by Eliade (1959) somewhat tautologically as, 'an irruption of the sacred into the world'. According to his conception, sacred space was seen as separate from 'profane' space in which the business and traffic of everyday life were conducted. It included precincts, temples, sacred cities and mountains (Eliade, 1959: 43).The difficulty of exact definition stems from the fact that sacred spaces are impossible to characterise in physical terms – only in their effects. Sears (1989) has shown how the history of American tourism was significantly structured by notions of sacred space associated with national landscape.

Sacred spaces may have a numinous quality to their visitors, an auratic power, related not only to the people with whom they are associated but also to location and setting, architecture and design, furnishings and presentation. Sacred spaces are often set apart, elevated or bounded by physical features that separate them from the everyday world, and make approach or access difficult. Architecturally, they may tend towards grand styles (the soaring spectacularity of the Gothic medieval cathedrals) or to austere simplicity (the literary graves and gravestones of George Orwell and William Morris in Oxfordshire Churchyards which simply bear their names without eulogy or decoration). Their interior design may be grandiloquent and decorative (e.g. through the display of precious metals, jewels, fine paintings, sculpture or carving) or bare. Both the exteriors and interiors may be heightened with presentational effects that isolate or emphasise, such as subdued or high lighting, floodlighting, solemn music or incense.

But the auratic quality of thanatourism spaces may not always be sacred. There are other kinds of landscape and site with a negative, even unholy, aura – the Scottish battlefields of Glencoe and Culloden where it has been said that 'no birds sing', the house of a serial killer, or a mass grave on which nothing is said to grow. Indeed, it perhaps may require a new word coinage to fill a gap in the language of anthropology and cultural geography for space which is neither sacred nor profane, but which gains a powerful negative aura from connotations of menace and transgression.

Whether symbols of good or evil, the auratic force of the world's most potent thanatourism sites lies in their extreme Otherness. This is, not least, in the impression they give of *not appearing to be part of the managed, commercial tourism/leisure economy*, a 'have-a-nice-day' world normally perceived as contrived, upbeat, user-friendly and playful rather than serious. The more awesome thanatourism manifestations seem beyond contrivance in their Otherness as emblems of natural catastrophe, shrines to saints sacred and secular, or testaments to infamous crimes and atrocities.

How is such auratic Otherness to be managed? The first need is to recognise the vulnerability of Otherness to management. Auratic presence is a dwindling element in modern spaces where there is pressure to 'do something' profitable or useful with every square inch of space, and the tourism industry itself plays a key role in the erosion of the auratic, since it is often structured by strategies of development likely to render tourism spaces increasingly similar, anonymous and mundane. Air travel and hotel management almost inevitably end up as products that resemble one another because of the needs they must meet: commercial imperatives of profitable yield management; fulfilling visitor expectations; conforming to industry and governmental safety regulations, and so on. Globalisation and the widespread management practice of benchmarking – the identification and adoption of successful ideas that have emerged from comparisons of international or industry practice elsewhere – also result in tourism replication across the world. Branding and franchising inherently work to create uniformity and promote the growing similarity of everywhere. Branded thinking is now infecting major cultural institutions such as the Louvre and the Guggenheim, which have started on the slippery path of ceasing to be country-specific by franchising their names and loan collections to satellite developments in other countries. Thus, once unique cultural institutions that occupied distinctive, auratic spaces in their national cultures are in danger of diluting their impact. One of the emerging issues for thanatourism providers, as the possibility of replication of some of its forms is recognised, will be avoiding the tendency to cloning – a Body Worlds exhibition every year, a dungeon attraction in every capital, a ghost walk round every corner. Sites that avoid such replication, either by choice or because their Otherness is so distinctive that it cannot be duplicated or extinguished under the Procrustean direction of tourism planners, will always be at a premium. They will include major sites including the 34 cemeteries and tombs on the UNESCO World Heritage list (Tanas, 2006), disaster sites like Pompeii, monumental memorial sites like the Escureal Palace near Madrid, and other cultural institutions that remain true to themselves. But even at these there will be the managerial problem of how *not* to reduce their Otherness by providing modern visitor services.

Commodification and thanatourism

The need to preserve the auratic raises the question of the extent of acceptable commodification at thanatourism sites. Commodification of heritage and culture has been the subject of much academic debate. Some censor it on moral grounds because it represents profiteering from historic, aesthetic and religious sites that, it is argued, should be made freely available. This argument is difficult to sustain in capitalistic economies, driven by market forces where most other goods – including water, food, energy and land – are commodified and allocated by the price mechanism.

However, a different kind of moral criticism has been made against commercial development at certain thanatourism sites – that it is unacceptable to profit from the dead, particularly those dying through infamous acts of violence, by engaging in overtly commercial activities at spaces associated with them. This perspective has affected managerial debate at Holocaust sites, such as Auschwitz, where one of the key issues was how far to install visitor services, and at religious memorial sites, such as Westminster Abbey and other important historical cathedrals, where the decision to charge admission fees was contentious.

Commodification has three distinct dimensions. The first is whether financial transactions of any sort should be allowable at thanatourism sites or whether they should be kept free of commercial taint. The second is, if some commercialisation is allowable, who should benefit? And the third is, if commercialisation is introduced, how should it be achieved in a way that does not adversely affect the site?

The first two may be considered together. While the introduction of, for example, an entrance fee, a gift shop or catering outlets may seem crass at a historic or religious site, it becomes less so if the revenues are used to maintain it and to employ local people. Thus, in most cases, the decision to run a thanatourism site on a commercial or semi-commercial basis need not be contentious if a local community supports the development and the proceeds are seen to help maintain it and/or benefit regional communities. In South Africa, the battlefields of the Zulu and Boer Wars within KwaZulu Natal have been maintained and developed as tourism sites with the support and participation of local tourism authorities and communities (Moeller, 2005). At other thanatourism sites, such as Westminster Abbey, charging is not only a method of funding a historic building but also a form of visitor control, since the admission fee acts as a mechanism for limiting demand that might otherwise be overwhelming. In London, Highgate Cemetery charges admission to the living as well as the dead, since income is essential to reverse years of neglect that has also affected many other historic cemeteries around England. Tanas, a cultural geographer, has recently produced a book length study of historic cemeteries as tourism attractions in Poland, and the problems and opportunities they pose (Tanas, 2008b).

The second dimension involves a more pragmatic objection to the moral ones just considered. It is that the practices applied in the commercial management of most kinds of tourism tend, as we have seen, to destroy the Otherness of thanatourism. The mainstream tendencies of managed tourism development over the last two decades have been not just to exploit sites commercially, but to do so through a nexus of techniques intended to make tourism spaces more accessible, more easily understood, more user friendly and more familiar. Such techniques have included intrusive signage, interactive displays, pathway making, catering facilities and gift shops. The results can often be to tame and homogenise, since intrusive evidence of human intervention and manipulation of auratic spaces reduces their power. Otherness, as the early part of this chapter emphasised, is about *difference* from the world of work and the everyday. A reason for limiting commodification may therefore be that it erodes the aura upon which thanatourism and other kinds of heritage depend.

An example of the dilemmas created by the contradictory imperatives of managerial intervention and auratic preservation may be seen at historic cemeteries, where managers have to confront the issue of how far to cut back and tidy spaces that have become wild and overgrown, and how far to retain their untamed appearance. The aura of historic cemeteries like Highgate, Brompton and Kensall Green in London, or Pere La Chaise in Paris, is not just association with death, but often the picturesque interactions of time and nature. As Tanas (2004) has noted, it is old cemeteries, not modern ones, that attract. The two exceptions to this general phenomenon are celebrity graves and military cemeteries and memorials, where time and picturesque effects are less important. The 1500 or so military cemeteries to the fallen of World War I in France and Belgium, erected by the Imperial War Graves Commission, retain an auratic poignancy, *despite* a uniformity in which every soldier has the same, well-kept memorial stone, whatever his rank and social status. Their Otherness lies not in picturesque effects of history, but in the silent, mass testimony they offer to the scale and pathos of carnage in the Great War.

All this means that the routine practices adopted at the management of many tourism sites may need restraining as activities that may violate or destroy auratic space. The best management of thanatourism may be antimanagement, a hands-off, rather than hands-on intervention.

Functional varieties and transformations of thanatourism sites:
'Beginnings' and 'origins' analysis

Thanatourism sites may differ, not only from other tourism products but from each other, in the *functional variety* and *evolutionary dynamics* they manifest. These two attributes may again be exemplified by comparing the features of thanatourism attractions with more mainstream tourism products. The latter are typically created and designed for a pre-determined, functional purpose that does not change over time. An hotel is built to accommodate travellers, an airport is built to transport them, a theme park to entertain them through a specific portfolio of rides, sideshows and events. Once they have been developed, though all may require periodic updating, their functional identity and purpose remains unaffected, and so too the management forms necessary to operate them.

Thanatourism sites may display considerable variations from this basic pattern of homogenous and continuous, functional development. There have been several attempts to characterise and classify their diversity in inventories of thanatourism motivations and sites (Seaton, 1996; Dann, 1998; Sharpley, 2005; Stone, 2006a), but none have focused on the managerial implications. It is, however, possible to suggest an overall framework for understanding the distinctive managerial features necessitated by thanatourism's variety and dynamics. It is an analytical approach derived from a conceptual distinction first suggested in one of Edward Said's less well-known works, *Beginnings: Intention and Method* (Said, 1975), and discussed by Bilgrami (2005). In it, Said reflected on the difference between the words 'beginnings' and 'origins' in understanding the evolution of cultural and institutional formations.

Beginnings, he argued, was a word that could only be applied to the start of formations that had been deliberately brought into being for a defined purpose *by specific agencies* which had remained in control of its mission and functions. Conversely, *origins* was more appropriate to those which had been triggered *accidentally*, and/or by agencies which did not necessarily remain in control.

> As consistently as possible I use *beginning* as having the more active meaning, and *origin* the more passive one: 'X is the origin of Y' while 'the beginning A leads to B'. (Said, 1975: 6)

The *beginnings* of an institution can, therefore, according to Said, only be spoken of if it had from the start been run and maintained as a homogenous, evolving entity. It must manifest a trajectory of quantitative evolution, continuously maintaining its basic purpose and identity, and delivering its utilities to its members and clients, as evident from their acceptance and consumption over time. Conversely, it is the word *origins* that is more exact in describing formations whose start point was not willed and *chosen* by its recruits and members, but introduced externally, and where the institution called into existence later changed its character and membership-client base. Bilgrami (2005: 27) comments that: 'It is a deprivation of agency because the acts of *beginning* are excluded by the passivity inherent in the very notion of *origin*.'

The distinction, first made by Said in the context of the early history of religions, can be applied suggestively to the understanding of thanatourism as a generic tourism formation. Thanatourism comprises some tourism sites and products whose *beginnings* can be traced to single groups under whose control they have evolved continuously without significant qualitative change. Madame Tussauds, for example, had its *beginnings* as a waxwork gallery, comprising effigies of dead and living celebrities, and remains so to this day. Though it has quantitatively grown from a travelling side show to a global mega-attraction, its basic identity has not changed.

But many thanatourism sites do not have this qualitative continuity. They have either had their *origins* outside the deliberate will of a presiding agency, or have later been subject to discontinuous change which has shifted their identity, the nature of their management, and their function. There are three ways in which these transforming effects may happen.

Firstly, a thanatourism site may emerge *spontaneously*, independent of the will of tourism planners and, in some cases, of any kind of human intention. A sudden catastrophic act, natural or man-made (David, 1993), may make a previously little known or unknown location famous or notorious as an emergent thanatourism site. There have been several high-profile disasters in recent years that fall into this category: in the US, the Trade Centre bombing of 9/11 and the New Orleans hurricane of 2006; in Paris, the death of Princess Diana and Dodi Fayed in a motorway tunnel; and in Britain, serial killings in Soham and Gloucester that transformed the identity of the places in which they occurred. None were launched by destination planners to generate tourism revenues, but all the places involved began to attract visitors curious to check out scenes of death and disaster widely publicised by the media. The result was that, in addition to being sites of activity for emergency and social services, they became tourism management issues because of the problems of visitor control they presented. They illustrate thanatourism's propensity to develop suddenly at destinations, primed by media coverage, forcing public sector managers there to become tourism planners whether they want to or not.

A second kind of transformation may be less dramatic. This may happen when sites originally developed for a single functional purpose gradually, through processes of historical change, lose their client base and become obsolete or defunct. They may then be reclaimed and relaunched for other purposes, including exhibition as thanatourism sites. Instances include: obsolete military installations, such as the Allied Operations Room in Malta,[3] now converted to a tourist attraction that tells the story of Malta's role in World War II; penal institutions such as Alcatraz in the US which opened to visitors in the 1990s; and the Old Gaol in Melbourne, where judicial function has been replaced by museum status.

A third kind of transformation, observed in heritage, cultural attraction and destination management over the last three years, has been the use of thanatourism appeals as *a thematisation strategy*. In the attraction field, this has typically been adopted as a temporary exhibition strategy by 'high-end' institutions such as museums, libraries and art galleries, which have appealed, or have been thought to do so, to minority, educated visitors.

Thanatourism theming has been adopted as a way of reaching new and wider audiences and/or persuading the public to 'take a new look' at their services. They have been able to do so because great museums, libraries and galleries are pluralistic, polysemic resources whose heterogeneous collections of books, manuscripts, paintings, artefacts, specimens and relics may be thematically permutated in many ways (e.g. by subject, painter, author or period). Effective exhibition management lies in the skill with which thematic choices are made and implemented from available options that will appeal to relevant target audience segments (local, regional, international; young and old) and connect with contemporary/topical interests. This may be called the utilisation of 'purposeful Otherness', in which the auratic fascinations of death are harnessed by institutional managers to aims and objectives that derive from the core identity of their institutions, rather than seeming to be an extraneous method of 'milking the macabre' (Dann, 1998).

Two recent examples of elite cultural institutions which have reached popular audiences through thanatourism themes are the Wellcome Foundation in London and the Victoria State Library in Melbourne, Australia. In the summer of 2008, the first mounted an exhibition called *Skeletons*, while the second staged one called *War and Sport*. They are explored in the boxed case studies. The latter of these follows here and the first is presented later.

Thanatourism, National Identity and Popular Memory: The Sport and War Exhibition

State Library of Victoria, Melbourne, July–October 2008

In July 2008, the Melbourne Library staged a free travelling exhibition, jointly organised with the Australian War Memorial, on the ground floor of its great six-storey establishment which themed Sport and War. It ran concurrently with several other exhibitions on other floors of the library, focused on more traditional aspects of books (their historical importance, beauty of illustration, age, etc.). The Sport and War exhibits included photographs, narratives and artefacts of sportsmen who had fought for their country over the previous century. The exhibition was built around a central premise – that sport and war had been two key features of Australian identity over the last century (Figure 5.1).

The exhibition was accompanied by support talks and events. 'Sport in time of war: a panel discussion' was a public conversation between sports journalist, Barry Cassidy and broadcast host, Les Carlyon, author of two books on the Great War and Australia's part in it.

Special children's programmes included: guided school group tours; storytelling sessions on consecutive Sundays on aspects of war, including the Trojan War and Gallipoli; a week of interactive animation games in which children could create their own sporting DVDs; daily games of chess, 'the original game of sport and war', on large-scale sets in a 'play pod'. In addition, a librarian who was also an AFL goals umpire gave a one-hour lecture on the Library's extensive football archive.

The exhibition included a self-completion visitor questionnaire which tracked the gender, age and postcode of visitors, how long people spent at the exhibition, how they had heard of it, how many times they visited it, party size and composition. It also tracked specific

Figure 5.1 State Library of Victoria: promotional leaflet for *Sport and War* Exhibition, July–October 2008 (cover)
Photo: A.V. Seaton

elements – the quality of the exhibition, the labelling, the layout and its interest. The questionnaire also asked about usership of the library over the last year and whether the visitor intended to visit any of the other exhibitions in the library that day. At the time of writing it was not possible to assess the results.

Comments

The Exhibition had many strengths but one great weakness:

(1) It illustrated 'purposeful Otherness' by unexpectedly linking the melodrama and sensation of war to the more everyday one of sport, and articulating the linkage around the unifying theme of national identity.

(2) The exhibition strongly embodied 'collective memory' by including photographs and content of famous Australian sportsmen, many of whom had become legendary folk heroes, as well as wartime pictures that resonated with audience memory of the national past.

(3) The exhibition theme of national identity through war and sport was consistent with the institutional identity and mission of a great state library.

(4) The novelty of the exhibition was achieved alongside more orthodox exhibitions of rare books and maps staged simultaneously on other floors of the library.

(5) Like the Wellcome Skeletons exhibition, this demonstrated the synergy that can be achieved through collaborations between institutions (Victorian State Library and Australian War Memorial).

(6) The major weakness of the exhibition was that it virtually excluded women's role in either war or sport and, thus, constructed a purely masculine version of Australian identity.

The Sport and War exhibition represents a good example of managerial staging of the 'purposeful Other', where the war and sport theme was unusual and arresting, but consistent with the mission of a State Library as a repository of history that might include war and death as its legitimate subjects.

An example of thanatourism thematisation that was less inherently related to the identity of the enterprise concerned was an exhibition mounted between July 2008 and November 2008 by a small photographic enterprise, the Proud Galleries, in Camden, North London. It was called 'Forever 27', and featured portraits of rock stars who had died at the age of 27 (Brian Jones, Janice Joplin, Jim Morrison, Jimmy Hendrix and Kurt Cobain). The nominal pretext for this memorial to artists, hyped as members of a 'Parthenon of rock immortality', was 'to celebrate their talent and shed fresh light on their short lives and mysterious, untimely deaths'. The combined appeal of death + celebrity achieved media attention, including radio coverage on the BBC's flagship morning news programme (BBC, 2008), where the presenter asked whether the exhibition, in commemorating young celebrity deaths that were mainly self-inflicted or the result of excess, was not a morbid way of 'honouring the stupid club?'. The gallery spokesman accepted that there was perhaps, 'something morbid' about the exhibition, but that it also offered lessons, which were to 'stay clear of hotel rooms, drugs and prostitutes'.

It is not only cultural institutions and attractions which are able to adopt thanatourism themes. Destinations are multi-attribute locations with a diverse range of history, culture, physical features and commercial services – all of them potential tourism products – which can, by selective permutation, be themed in many kinds of ways. Whether they want to or not, destinations inevitably tell many stories about themselves because their marketing and promotion is never controlled by one organisation. Though a destination agency may seek to promote a specific image for a place, it will inevitably coexist with other images derived from private sector marketing. Many of the thanatourism narratives promoted in urban tourism in recent years have been by small entrepreneurial organisations, such as guided tours of Melbourne Cemetery, ghost tours of Edinburgh, Jack the Ripper walks in London's East End or Gothic tours of New Orleans.

These kinds of initiatives by cultural institutions and destinations initiatives tend to conflate the distinction between *origins* and *beginnings*. Though all the attractions and destinations that have adopted thanatourism thematisations on a temporary basis have not changed their basic identity, they have been able to modify their public face for a temporary period, by selectively emphasising aspects of their portfolio previously unknown or less known to the public.

In summary, beginnings and origins analysis may be used to identify four kinds of thanatourism site, each with its own distinctive managerial features. They comprise sites with two different kinds of origins and two different kinds of beginnings. Table 5.1 specifies some of their features and the managerial implications associated with each.

The people
Sacred to whom? The polysemia of thanatourism sites

The discussion has so far suggests that the Otherness of thanatourism sites is unproblematic and homogenous, an auratic presence that will be felt by all. The truth is that there is a world of difference between

Table 5.1 Origins and Beginnings analysis and managerial action in thanatourism developments

Typology of thanatourism origins/ beginnings	*Issues and management tasks*
Natural and Man-made Origins – natural disasters and human catastrophes	• No human group responsible for *origins of sites as tourism attractions* (flood, fire, major atrocity sites) • Visitor interest/demand triggered by historical record or modern news/publicity (Pompeii, Ground Zero after 9/11) • Reactive tourism management later required to control spontaneous tourism demand • May be ethical questions if commercial exploitation is introduced
Man-made Origins – sites of functional change	• Sites or locations *originate* with non-tourism functions (e.g. as military installations, gaols, catacombs, etc.) • Sites become functionally obsolete/defunct • Sites relaunched/represented as thanatourism sites • Tourism management required to effect changeover of function, possibly in consultation/collaboration with site's previous functionaries • Commercialisation likely to be adopted to launch and maintain transformed site
Man-made Beginnings 1: Created thanatourism attractions	• Entrepreneurial or corporate action initiates the beginnings/development of a site as thanatourism attraction (e.g. Madame Tussauds, London Dungeon, Dracula Restaurant) • Target markets are typically mass tourists • Managers totally responsible for products, promotions, pricing, distribution • Commercialisation not a problem, since the sites have been developed as private sector enterprises
Man-made Beginnings 2: Thanatourism as temporary thematisation strategy for cultural attractions and destinations	• Site or attraction established as cultural/heritage attractions/destinations, often by public sector, local authorities or community groups • Initial/main audience likely to be elite/educated • Managerial desire to reach broader audiences or diversify appeals of institution or destination • Thanatourism adopted as temporary thematisation strategy • Products from heritage collections or destination attributes selected, sometimes in collaboration with other institutions and enterprises, to support thanatourism positioning for short periods (e.g. human skeleton exhibitions, guided cemetery tours and ghost walks in urban centres, Ned Kelly trails in and around Melbourne, etc.)

space as it exists physically and space as it is perceived. There is wide-spread agreement among sociologists, social psychologists, social and cultural geographers, and urban planners that all spaces, probably most of all auratic spaces, do not have an absolute value but are polysemic, which is to say they may have different meanings for different audiences (Cresswell, 2004). Since this academic insight has crucial implications in thanatourism management it is worth examining in a little more detail.

It is generally agreed that space has at least four key attributes. Firstly, it exists as much *in people's imagination* as before their eyes. It is rather like the concept of 'nation', which was once famously described by Benedict Anderson (1991) not as a tangible entity that could be measured or actually observed, but as an 'imaginary community' that existed in the head of each of its members. Secondly, it is *socially constructed*, which is to say that its meaning is produced through the influence of other people (individuals, groups and cultures). Though we react individually to a battlefield, a cemetery or a display in the Chamber of Horrors at Madame Tussauds, our reactions will be strongly influenced by our acculturation. Thirdly, it is *temporal*, which means that space does not have a fixed meaning but one which may change over time. Finally, it is *attributed*, which means that it has no intrinsic significance in itself, but only a subjective one that the individual chooses, often without much reflection, to give it.

These four aspects of space all have critical bearing on thanatourism management because they invite questions that may lead to misunderstanding and conflict and that must be anticipated and managed. Whose imagination/imaginings are reflected at a thanatourism site and how have they influenced the social construction that embodies them? In KwaZulu Natal, South Africa, for example, British colonial authorities commemorated members of the British Army who had fallen in the Zulu Wars of the late 1870s on memorial stones across the battlefields, but until the 1990s no memorials were allowed for the Zulu dead (Moeller, 2005). What changes may have happened to the social valuation of a thanatourism space since it was created? Has it, like a church sold off as a bingo hall, ceased to be a sacred space at all? Or has one part of it become more sacred than another, as in the case of the grave of the rock star, Jim Morrison, in Pere La Chaise Cemetery in Paris, which attracts excessive amounts of retro-hippies from way back when. Whose attribution is attached to a Thanatourism site? Is Gracelands, Elvis Presley's home, a sacred shrine to a revered popular culture hero, or a tacky, commercial development? Should Robben Island, where Nelson Mandela was imprisoned, be seen as a shrine or a theme park (Shackley, 2001a)? Should certain thanatourism sites even exist? For descendants of Spanish partisans who fought in the Spanish Civil War the public existence of the Franco Memorial Hall outside Madrid is as much a source of resentment as the silence maintained about the slave labour used to build it. In 1998, the writer visited the great US Military Memorial Cemetery in Hawaii which commemorates the dead of several wars fought by American soldiers. All the memorials were in excellent order except one, a single Vietnam War monument that had been daubed with graffiti and excrement by dissenters who had opposed the war.

Thanatourism sites may be viewed as collective and popular memory, *ways of remembering the significant dead* at locations constructed physically to commemorate their dying or internment. They are thus material embodiments of communal mythology, versions of history a community wishes to make permanent in the same way that other kinds of discursive representation – history books, epic poems, films, art and music – may be. Gravestones, memorials and monuments are texts about the past which are read by groups in the present, but not all groups take away the same meaning from them. At battlefield sites such as Waterloo (Seaton, 1999), Gallipoli (Slade, 2003) and at war cemeteries like the 1500 across Belgium and France, reactions may vary according to the nationality of the audience, its age group and also according to the depth of knowledge of witnesses (see also Chapter 10). A study of war grave visitors in Flanders in the 1990s suggested that there were at least three different groups of visitors on the same coach tour, each of which reacted in different ways to the cemeteries (Seaton, 2002a).

Related to the previous point, although most thanatourism sites are historical ones, they are often bound up with *important issues of personal identity* for people who encounter them in the present. In the US antebellum, plantation houses in the South still provoke strong passions about slavery among those who view them (Dann & Seaton, 2001b). In modern Israel, hundreds of villages once owned by Arabs before 1948 are today imagined and remembered by Israelis and Palestinians in totally different ways, as Slyomovics (1998) has poignantly recounted.

In summary, thanatourism management may involve the anticipation and negotiation of contradiction and conflict, due to the polysemia of place. The more personally charged with meaning a space is for some groups, the less it may mean for others. All spaces – informal, public spaces and sacred spaces – are subject to social meanings, and the narratives told about them may be reverentially accepted, ignored, resisted or flatly denied.

How can managers take account of the polysemic nature of thanatourism sites and the plurality of responses that they may elicit from groups and individuals who come into contact with them?

The heritage force field

The first requirement is for a realistic assessment of what groups are likely to be actively affected by, and sensitive to, a thanatourism site and the narratives it embodies. A useful tool in making such an assessment of the groups and exploring some of the issues they might raise is through an analytical model called the heritage force field. This was first presented in relation to the analysis of slavery heritage management (Seaton, 2001). It does not seek to offer prescriptive directions, but focuses attention on the issues and conflicts that may be posed by thanatourism developments which managers should seek to avoid through consultation in initiating and maintaining thanatourism sites (see also Chapter 8).

The model predicates that:

- The functioning of a thanatourism site may be affected by the relationships between four main stakeholding groups.
- The stakeholding groups comprise: the *owners and controllers* who normally supply the management; the *represented subjects of thanatourism and/or their spokespersons*; the *spatial host communities* around the site; the *audience/visitors*.
- Relationships between the four groups will be dependent upon the way in which each sees its own interests and perspectives reflected in the narratives told at the site, and the perceived benefits and disbenefits likely to accrue to each in attracting visitors to hear and see the narratives.
- These relationships reflect inequities in power among stakeholders, but these may change over time. For example, visitors may be less important to a site if it is a publicly funded or charitable site, but more important if it is a commercial one. Spatial host stakeholders may be less influential in heavily developed, commercial areas than in those where there are significant communities of private residents, particularly if the neighbourhood is rich. And some represented subjects may start out with limited influence if they are small minorities, but may increase in size and power to change the qualitative and quantitative dimensions of their representation (or contest their non-representation) at particular sites.
- The task of management is to identify stakeholder interests and perspectives and, through consultation and participation, attempt to reconcile their interests and perspectives from inception, implementation and maintenance.

The stakeholders: Owners and controllers

All existing thanatourism sites, as spatial and physical entities, are owned by some group or individual, or have to be funded by them if they are new ones. The owners may be public sector or private sector groups and organisations or combinations of both. They will determine the broad mission and main goals of the site as a visitor attraction and set broad parameters for their implementation. In addition, thanatourism sites must be administered and controlled by delegated managers, if the people who own or sponsor them do not want to do so themselves.

Controllers include: appointed general managers; architects, interior designers and graphic artists; exhibition managers and curators; financial and accounting specialists; marketing, promotion and research executives; catering and merchandising staff; and reception and information staff. All may be employed full-time, part-time, as contractual consultants or as volunteers.

The key thing to recognise is that the goals and perspectives of the owners and controllers may differ from those of the other three stakeholders. For example, at a long established museum, curators and specialist staff may be more concerned about preserving collections than marketing them to visitors. In addition, owners and controllers may themselves differ within an organisation; the trustees of a military museum, for example, may resist populist exhibitions they deem to subvert the dignity of historic heritage.

The stakeholders: Represented subject groups

Thanatourism is a form of tourism that represents some groups of people from the past to others in the present. This means that, though it may be impossible to consult the subjects themselves, it may be important to respect the sensitivities of contemporary groups for whom the subjects were significant others. At some sites more than one group may have a stake in the stories. To take an obvious case, any narrative about Jerusalem would need to accommodate the perspectives of Jews, Christians and Muslims, all of whom see the city as a shrine. At battlefield sites there are always at least two sets of represented subjects, often several – the losers and winners – and their views of events may be quite different. Whose story is told? Who are the heroes and who are the villains? Whose voices should be heard and in what ways should they speak? Representation may thus be a political issue involving issues of power and relative influence which may change over time.

The main implication for managers is the importance of consultation, wherever possible, with stakeholder groups likely to have strong feelings about the representations of the subjects memorialised at thanatourism sites. History that has seemed settled can suddenly ignite into controversy, as happened recently in England when relative groups, descended from soldiers executed for desertion or disobedience in World War I and thus excluded from appearing on any memorial, campaigned on their behalf for commemorative recognition. (They argued that the unimaginable horrors of trench warfare had caused sustained traumatic stress which had resulted in uncharacteristic behaviour by the soldiers concerned.)

The stakeholders: Host communities

All thanatourism sites exist in geographical locations that some people regard as home. For them it may be a sacred space, not because of the pathos or historic importance of the people and events commemorated, but because it is their neighbourhood. Two conceptions of the sacred may thus compete on the same territory, and for residents thanatourism may be viewed as unwanted disruption of their living space.

It is therefore important for managers to anticipate the benefits and *dis*benefits to local communities. There are two main issue sets that need inventorying. The first are the common concerns expressed by host populations about tourism developments in their areas – problems of visitor numbers, physical degradation of the environment (litter, vandalism, noise, pollution, etc.), and social pathologies (crime, drugs, prostitution, etc.). All of these need to be monitored. They will vary widely at different sites depending on many variables, such as the size and scale of sites, the numbers of visitors, and their location.

To these well known impacts thanatourism adds a further one – its association with death and violence. In some instances the association comes, as we have seen, suddenly and traumatically through natural disaster, crime or atrocity which may make a locality into international headline news and thus a tourist magnet. In other cases, thanatourism may evolve less dramatically through a range of human interventions, such as: the introduction of signage, e.g. a plaque describing a house as the place where a famous author died; the erection of monumental sculpture to the victims of atrocity, murder or disaster; or the renovation of buildings with a 'dark' past as heritage sites for visitors. Though all these initiatives may be impeccably well-meaning and educational in their motives and aims, they are not always welcome among resident communities. Few want their backyard branded as a theatre of death, particularly if it involves historical legacies from a past they did not play any part in. This issue is one that has confronted efforts to commemorate Holocaust sites in Eastern Europe and also in Vienna in 2002, where an initiative to erect an anti-Nazi memorial in the centre was opposed by shopkeepers (see Ashworth, 1996; Tunbridge & Ashworth, 1996; Lennon & Foley, 2000; Lennon & Smith, 2003; Ashworth & Hartmann, 2005a, for wide-ranging explorations of Holocaust issues).

The stakeholders: Visitors

In thanatourism, as in any other form of tourism management, visitors are crucial stakeholders. If a site is commercially run, it must attract visitors whose numbers and aggregate expenditures generate enough revenue to enable the promoters to make a profit. For publicly funded and charitably supported enterprises such as galleries, museums and heritage sites, visitor revenues may be less crucial, though in the last two decades there has been increasing pressure on many of them worldwide to attract broader audiences (particularly children and families), to generate more of their own funding.

A good visitor experience at a thanatourism site experience may be produced managerially in a number of ways. In general terms it will do so by achieving that aura of 'purposeful Otherness', in which the macabre is harnessed to serious aims and narratives (military history, national heritage, medical progress, etc.), appropriate to the site or institution concerned. Successful management also depends upon correctly identifying target markets and making sure that what is exhibited, and the way in which it is delivered, will be of interest to them. The success of an exhibition or event may be assessed by putting in place feedback mechanisms that monitor satisfaction. These may vary from questionnaire-based visitor surveys to the use of visitor comment books that should be analysed systematically and continuously.

The Purposeful Other: Collective Memory, Identity and the Exhibition of Human Remains

The Wellcome Institute's Skeletons Exhibition, London, July–September 2008

The Wellcome Trust is the largest charity in the UK. It funds innovative biomedical research, in the UK and internationally, spending around £650 million each year to support the brightest scientists with the best ideas. The Wellcome Trust supports public debate about biomedical research and its impact on health and wellbeing. In modern times it has been part of the Wellcome's remit to stage public exhibitions of its collections, in addition to providing specialist research facilities. In 2007, a new exhibition room was launched and four exhibitions were staged in its first year.

Between July and September 2008, the Wellcome staged Skeletons, the fourth of its exhibitions in the new exhibition area. The exhibition was the result of collaboration between the Museum of London and the Wellcome. The core of the exhibition was the display of 27 skeletons which had been dug up from different sites in London spanning a historical period from Roman times to 1850. Each skeleton was featured in a glass table case with printed descriptions of its gender, age, likely cause of death and, in some cases, informed speculation about its social background (see Figures 5.2 and 5.3). The printed descriptions also identified the burial sites from which the skeletons had been recovered and on the wall each of the burial sites was described and dated by period. Adjacent to the historical descriptions of each site were specially commissioned photographs by Thomas Adank of the sites as they are today – a Pizza Hut, a block of flats, an office building – which produced a striking juxtaposition of past and present.

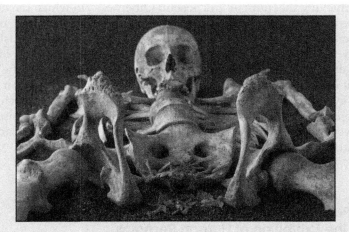

Figure 5.2 Skeletons Exhibition: Female aged 18–25, *c.* 1700–1850 (lateral view); Chelsea Old Church, Old Church Street, London SW3
Photo: Courtesy of the Museum of London/Wellcome Images

The exhibition was marketed through a website, leaflets and publicity (Figure 5.4). A small illustrated guidebook was produced which included all the information supplied in the printed descriptions for each skeleton and the details of the 11 burial sites. In addition, a children's pack was produced comprising eight postcards on the back of which were project questions. In a corner of the exhibition a video ran which focused on the dating and identification of human remains and their importance as archaeological data about different periods.

The exhibition was the most successful since the new exhibition area had been opened, achieving a higher number of visitors per day than any previous, averaging, it is thought, 300–400. On some days the visitors were so many that a queuing quota had to be imposed which

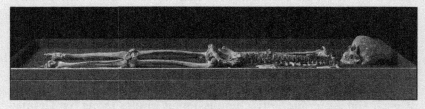

Figure 5.3 Skeletons Exhibition: Medieval female aged 25–36, *c.* 1350–1400 (lateral case view); St. Mary's Graces, Royal Mint, East Smithfield, London
Photo: Courtesy of the Museum of London/Wellcome Images

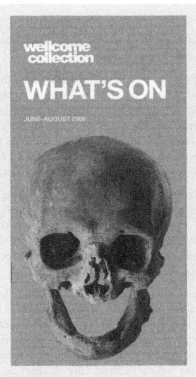

Figure 5.4 Skeletons Exhibition: programme (front cover)
Photo: Courtesy of the Museum of London/Wellcome Images

allowed people into the exhibition in sequential batches. One additional indication of the interest created was that a bookshop, Blackwells, which had an outlet adjoining the restaurant area of the Wellcome, sold a considerable number of books on skeleton analysis, the burial sites of London and human remains as archaeological evidence. Feedback provided by a visitors' comment book reflected praise for the educational value of the exhibition and the way it had provoked reflection about both the past and its comparisons with the present. Only a tiny minority questioned the ethics of displaying the dead and, in these few cases, other visitors had answered them by praising the taste and educational value of the exhibition, in addition to asking the obvious question: what, if people had qualms about such displays, were they doing visiting them? One of the Wellcome staff had also added a note that the bodies had not been specially dug up for exhibition, but had all been discovered by accident in the course of building work and road developments in London.

Comments

A number of managerial features and effects may be seen to have contributed to the exhibition's evident success:

(1) It was mounted with a *single-minded focus* on a small range of exhibits. As Ms Emily Sargent, the Wellcome Curator, noted (Sargent, 2008), from the outset the intention was to make the skeletons the primary interest, and to narrate their history and the ways in which that history could be read from the remains, using the best possible supporting materials. The design by Calum Storrie contributed to the implementation of this single-minded brief:

> 'Both the rationale and the design ... were brilliantly simple. Each skeleton was laid out in its own coffin-like display case, resting on a bed of black granules. The uniformity of the vitrines emphasised the different sizes of the skeletons, and also the equivalence in death of young and old, weak and strong, rich and poor' (Leahy, 2008: 3).

(2) The exhibition was evidently one that stemmed from the Wellcome Institute's core identity and mission as a medical foundation. It was not, therefore, seen as a sensational or exploitative excursion into the macabre. As one commentator noted, compared with the Body Worlds exhibition organised by Gunther von Hagens six years earlier, 'the ambience of Skeletons was restrained and contemplative' (Leahy, 2008: 3).

(3) Though the exhibits had undoubted impact in their Otherness and macabre appeal, this was *purposefully* anchored in an historical narrative to which visitors responded with close attention. Children in school parties, in particular, who were more numerous for this exhibition than previous ones, could be seen to be fully engaging in reading narratives, filling in the project sheets and, in some cases, anatomical sketching of the exhibits.

(4) The quality of the support materials (skeleton descriptions, site descriptions, educational materials) was excellent in both their content and the ways in which they were delivered.

(5) For Londoners, the main visitors, the use of the photographs of the modern sites at which the bodies had been recovered allowed them to make reflective links between their own identity as citizens today, and that of the populations who had preceded them. This connection cold be seen in some of the visitor comments which had a 'What must it have been like for them in those days?' 'How lucky we are today' flavour.

One of the recurrent problems with thanatourism is that of appealing to several different kinds of audience, who may have different relationships to the represented subjects whose story is being told. A particularly good example of this was the launch in 2002 of the British Empire and Commonwealth Museum in Bristol. It aimed to explore Britain's colonial past, including slavery, economic exploitation and military conquest, all of which were 'sticky subjects', as its website admitted. It was a difficult story to tell since it represented many different narratives about many different individuals and groups from many different colonised nations. The target visitors were equally diverse, since they were expected to be domestic and international, with particular interest coming from ex-colonial and colonised groups. How could colonial history be represented in a way that gave 'voice' to so many different perspectives in a way that would satisfy an equally varied range of visitors? The solution arrived at was to record video testimony from many different ex-colonial and colonised respondents from all over the world and let each tell their own story, rather than

Table 5.2 The heritage force field

Owners/controllers • Goals/interests of institution? • Goals/interests of financial backers? • Goals/interests of animators-researchers, creatives, etc? • Other groups/interests (e.g. governmental)?	**POWER** **and** **TIME**	*Host community* • Their relationship to heritage narrative and subject groups, and to owners/controllers? • Their participation in, and benefit from, heritage development? • Their acceptance of visitor numbers?
POWER **and** **TIME**	**HERITAGE** **DEVELOPMENT**	**POWER** **and** **TIME**
Subject groups • Their benefit from narrative? • Degree of participation? (Whose story? Whose blame? Whose heroic narrative? Whose exclusions/silences?	**POWER** **and** **TIME**	*Visitor groups* • Their relationship to subject narratives/ silenced narratives? • Their relationships to and with subjects, owners/ controllers. Host communities? • Their tastes – aesthetic, historical, etc?

imposing a single 'master' narrative. To complement this 'open' approach, visitors were urged to provide their own comments and feedback, including their criticisms and any omissions they wished to see corrected. After five years, the Museum is to be moved to London where it will be accessible to many more international visitors than in Bristol.

Table 5.2 is a diagrammatic summary of the stakeholder relationship.

Stakeholders: The media

In addition to these four primary stakeholders, it is worth including a fifth group, the media. Tourism in general has become far more newsworthy over the last two decades than it was previously, as evidenced by the exponential growth of travel and tourism supplements in the press, the number of documentary TV series and one-off programmes with a tourism focus, and the frequency with which tourism stories are included in general news bulletins. Thanatourism, as we have seen, may involve ethical issues, provoke conflict between different stakeholders, and have visually sensational features. The media have been, and are able, to construct 'moral panics' and righteous crusades from all these ingredients, as in the case of the Body Worlds exhibitions of Gunther von Hagens (see Chapter 3).

It is therefore good managerial practice to maintain relations with the media and keep them well briefed on the aims and objectives of particular thanatourism initiatives, including supplying them with information packs, photo exhibits and media launches that allow, if requested, interview opportunities.

Conclusion

This chapter has comprised a discussion of theoretical and practical issues in thanatourism management. It began with a re-assessment of the formulations known as the Other and Othering and proposed that Thanatourism is uniquely distinguished from other kinds of tourism since its defining feature is its association with death, the greatest and only universal Other.

It then examined the implications of this proposition in relation to *managing the spatial features* of thanatourism and the *perceptions of its main stakeholders*. Thanatourism sites were characterised as sacred/auratic spaces whose evolutionary diversity demand managerial strategies that differ from those in other kinds of tourism. Two approaches to site analysis and planning were described: Origins and Beginnings analysis, and a four-part evolutionary typology of thanatourism sites which highlighted the reactive and proactive managerial planning associated with each.

The final part of the chapter addressed the polysemia of thanatourism sites, resulting from potential differences and conflicts in the way different stakeholders perceived them. An analytical model was provided, intended to allow tourism planners to understand and attempt to harmonise stakeholder perspectives, through consultation and participation in thanatourism planning.

In conclusion, it might be said that the thanatourism manager has to be a multitasking diplomat with a versatile range of social and cultural expertise. The role requires the surefooted tact of a funeral director, the sense of the past of a historian, the educational insight of a school teacher, and sometimes the spin and showmanship of a celebrity publicist, to manage the 'Purposeful Otherness' of thanatourism in its many manifestations. Like the funeral director, the manager must tread circumspectly around issues of personal grief, albeit retrospective rather than immediate. Like the historian, s/he must cultivate awareness and knowledge of the past in order to orchestrate credible narratives about it, while constantly reviewing how the narratives 'play' to present audiences. S/he must evaluate the effects of thanatourism themes in relation to the goals and core identity of the organisation s/he represents, and make sure, on occasion, that exhibitions built around them have serious substance, in order to avoid the impression that they are an exploitative 'milking of the macabre' (Dann, 1998). And finally, since it is the Other that constitutes the main identifying element of thanatourism, it is important that the manager capitalises on this by imaginative and dramatic methods of 'performance' likely to stimulate audiences and leave them marvelling. The illustrations, particularly those for the Wellcome Skeletons Exhibition, suggest how successful presentations combine some of these values.

Notes

1. See Forman (1969) for an interesting anthology of representations by eastern peoples of 'the exotic white man', and Brotherston (1979) for a study of native American representations of the 'New World' to compare with those of the settlers.
2. Titles included:
   - Anon (1793) *Kearsley's Stranger's Guide, or Companion through London and Westminster and the Country Round: Containing a Description of the Situation, Antiquity and Curiosities of Every Place, Within the Circuit of Fourteen Miles, Together with a Map Plan, etc.* London: Kearsley.
   Planta, E. (1814) *A New Picture of Paris; or, the Stranger's Guide to the French Metropolis, to Which is Added a Description of the Environs of Paris.* London: Samuel Leigh.
   - Anon (1818) *The Picture of Glasgow, and Stranger's Guide with a Sketch of a Tour to Loch-Lomond, Loch-Ketturrin, Perth, Inverary and the Falls of Clyde.* Glasgow: R. Chapman.
   - Taylor, T. (1831) *The Picture of Liverpool, or Stranger's Guide: Containing a History of the Ancient and Present State of the Town, with a Description of its Public Works, Edifices, Literary, Scientific, and Charitable Institutions, and an Account of its Population and Commerce; with Brief Notices of the Environs. To Which is prefixed, a New and Correct Map of Liverpool.* Liverpool: Thomas Taylor.
   Anon (1837) *The Stranger's Guide to Brighton.* Brighton: W. Saunders.

- Willett, M. (1845) *The Stranger's Guide to the Banks of the Wye, Including Chepstow, Piercefield, Wyndcliff, Tintern Abbey, Raglan Castle, and Other Parts of the Welsh Borders: With Historical Topographical, and Antiquarian Remarks.* Bristol: T. Bedford.
- Grundy, J. (1845) *The Stranger's Guide to Hampton Court Palace and Gardens.* London: G. Bell.
- Anon (1848) *The Stranger's Guide through Gloucester Containing a Particular account of the Cathedral.* Gloucester: Thomas Jew.

3. This site represents a double reinvention. Before it became an Allied Control Centre in the 1940s, the underground caves in which it was located had functioned in the late Middle Ages as a centre for the Spanish Inquisition.

Chapter 6
(Re)presenting the Macabre: Interpretation, Kitschification and Authenticity

RICHARD SHARPLEY and PHILIP R. STONE

> ... *our fantasy is temperate; even in dreams, we do not experience*
> *what earlier peoples saw when awake.*
> Nietzsche, 1996 [1878]

Introduction

In December 2007, the newly renovated Grace Darling Museum, located in the small Northumberland coastal village of Bamburgh, England, opened to the public. Owned and operated by the Royal National Lifeboat Institution (RNLI), the charitable organisation that has operated the lifeboat service around Britain's coastline since 1824, the new building is the result of a two-year redevelopment of the original museum that was first opened in 1938, exactly 100 years after the event for which Grace Darling's life is commemorated. It is also, arguably, an authentic representation of heroism in the context of a maritime disaster, heroism that is afforded greater poignancy (or darkness, perhaps) by an untimely death.

Grace Darling was born in Bamburgh, Northumberland on 24 November 1815. She was the seventh child (of nine) of William Darling, the lighthouse keeper on Brownsman Island, one of the nearby Farne Islands which lie just off the Northumberland coast. William Darling lived with his family in a cottage attached to the lighthouse on Brownsman, subsequently moving to a new lighthouse on Longstone, one of the most distant of the Farne Islands, in 1826. The Farne Islands had long posed a hazard to shipping and, in the early hours of 7 September 1838, the SS Forfarshire, sailing from Hull to Dundee with some 60 passengers and crew on board, foundered on one of the islands, Big Harcar Rock, in a severe storm. Within minutes, the ship broke in two, the rear half sinking with the loss of 48 lives; nine survivors, however, managed to scramble onto the rock.

That night, only Grace and her parents were in the lighthouse. When they spotted the wreck and the survivors, Grace and her father rowed their coble (a small, flat-bottomed fishing boat) almost a mile through the storm to Big Harcar Rock, Grace then handling the boat on her own while her father helped five survivors aboard, before returning to Longstone. Her father subsequently rowed back with two of the rescued crew members to collect the remaining four survivors on Big Harcar Rock.

Within days, newspapers carried headlines of the daring rescue and both Grace and her father became national heroes. They were both also awarded medals by the Royal Humane Society and then the National Institution for the Preservation of Life (subsequently the RNLI). However, it was the bravery of 22-year old Grace that grabbed the Victorian public's imagination, as well as the attention of Queen Victoria herself who sent her £50. Sadly, however, just four years later, in April 1842, Grace Darling died from tuberculosis. She was buried in the graveyard of St Aiden's Church, Bamburgh, where a memorial to her was built in 1844 (Figure 6.1), yet she has remained the 'heroine of the Farne Islands' (Bell, 2004; also Cresswell, 1988).

The Grace Darling Museum, located close to the cottage where Grace was born, commemorates Grace's short life and her bravery in the early

Figure 6.1 The Grace Darling Memorial, Bamburgh, Northumberland, UK
Photo: R. Sharpley

hours of 7 September 1838. On display in the museum are numerous artefacts that belonged to herself and her family, including books, clothes and other personal items, as well as Grace's christening gown. A scale model of the Longhorn Lighthouse is used to describe the life of the family on the island, while the events surrounding the loss of the SS Forfarshire and the subsequent rescue by Grace and her father are depicted in detail, the centrepiece being the actual boat used for the rescue. Numerous 'Grace Darling' souvenirs produced for visitors to Bamburgh during the late 19th and early 20th centuries are also on display. Most significantly, however, from the upper floor of the museum, visitors are able to gaze out over St. Aiden's Church towards the Farne Islands in the distance, connecting the museum and its story of Grace Darling with both the site of her heroism and her final resting place.

The authenticity or reality of the Grace Darling Museum and the story it tells, or visitors' experience of it, thus derives from a number of factors: numerous genuine artefacts that belonged to Grace and her family, and items related to the famous rescue, such as original newspaper cuttings documenting the event, paintings, tourist souvenirs and, of course, the coble in which the rescue was carried out – collectively, items that are simply described as what they are; a short visual presentation, utilising sound and historical paintings, telling the story of the rescue; the location of the museum close to the houses where Grace was born and died (and marked as such); and the visual connection between the museum, the churchyard and the sea. In short, the museum presents the 'facts' (the story, verified by documentary evidence, genuine items and artefacts), which visitors may then interpret for themselves within the contemporary context of Grace Darling's life and death.

More usually, however, dark sites and attractions do not benefit from such 'completeness' in terms of location, material items and knowledge, factual accuracy and documentary or other recorded evidence of the events commemorated. In other words, the representation or commemoration of death, disaster or tragedy may frequently depend upon a particular interpretation or narrative that is created around the site, the event and the people involved. Thus, in the extreme, the representation may be far removed in time, space and reality from the original event. For example, the re-enactments of English Civil War battles by the Sealed Knot – Europe's largest re-enactment society (see www.thesealedknot.org.uk) – are based upon actual battles that occurred during the period of the war (1642–1651). However, as a playful subset of what Dann (1998) refers to as 'fields of fatality' they are, in effect, an inauthentic form of dark 'edutainment' that, despite the use of 'authentic' replica clothing and weapons, bears little relation to the events they purport to represent. As Howard (2003: 258) observes, 'the search for authenticity [in Civil war re-enactments] is completely vain unless done with seventeenth-century minds and with death on the battlefield a real possibility!' Even in an authentic setting, such as the former island prison of Alcatraz that now draws almost 1.4 million visits each year, the interpretation of the prison is overshadowed by commercial and entertainment values that arguably seek to satisfy the needs of 'Hollywood tutored visitors' rather than presenting a more accurate narrative of the island's natural and cultural significance (Strange & Kempa, 2003). Indeed, it was recently announced that the owners of the site, the US National Park Service, plan to convert part of the prison into a hotel as an 'ultimate experience in visitor access' (Elsworth, 2008), an experience that could not be further removed from that of the prison's former inmates.

Similarly, on the outskirts of Vilnius is a packaged reminder of Lithuania's repressed era under the former Soviet regime. One of many visitor sites littered throughout the Baltic states is '1984: The Survival Drama', where the brutality of a totalitarian political system is (re)presented for a tourist market (e.g. Hope, 2004; Osborn, 2006). It is, perhaps, unsurprising that this former KGB interrogation centre shares its name with George Orwell's *Nineteen Eighty-Four*, a prophetic novel of a totalitarian regime and surveillance society (Orwell, 1949). While this became reality in the former Soviet Union, the Orwellian prediction that 'there will be no curiosity, no enjoyment of the process of life' is somewhat unfounded with the 'new' 1984 visitor experience, as visitors curiously engage in mock torture and persecution. Indeed, visitors to the attraction are actively encouraged to be curious about the 'process of life' as they enter a pseudo traumascape of repression and authoritarianism (see also Chapter 7).

Consequently, depending on the nature of the interpretation employed at dark tourism sites and attractions (and, as considered later in Chapter 8, on the dominant ideology that informs the development and focus of the attraction), dark events or histories may be altered, distorted or trivialised and hence distanced from their authenticity and their meaning or significance to visitors. Of course, a similar criticism may be levelled at the interpretation of any heritage site or attraction, dark or otherwise, a debate that is reviewed in the following section. However, as Moscardo and Ballantyne (2008: 247) suggest, 'nowhere are these issues more clearly present than in the interpretation of hot topics, such as war, and dark tourism places, such as sites of massacres and prisons'. Here, the term 'hot' is used to refer to events that relate to visitors' values, beliefs, relationships, interests or memories and which 'excite a degree of emotional arousal which needs to be recognised and addressed in interpretation' (Uzzell & Ballantyne, 1998: 152). In other words, the interpretation of dark sites should ideally authenticate the events they represent or commemorate in a manner which recognises and responds to the emotions of potential visitors or visitor groups.

The purpose of this chapter is therefore to explore, within a conceptual framework of the authenticity of tourist experiences, the implications of the use of different interpretative techniques at dark tourism attractions. In particular, it relates notions of the kitsch and what will be referred to as the 'kitschification' of interpretation to the specific question of the authenticity of dark tourism experiences. In so doing, it considers the ways in which the kitsch interpretation of dark sites and events, injecting a sense of melancholy, nostalgia and perhaps even playfulness, may transform their meaning to the tourist, reducing the potential for moral panic and, as a consequence, rendering the experience of them more palatable to the visitor.

Interpretation and Dark Tourism Experiences

'Interpretation is an essential component of visitor experiences at attractions' (Moscardo & Ballantyne, 2008: 237). It provides the link between an attraction and its visitors; it is the process by which a place, an event, a history, a building, a collection of items or, more generally, what may be referred to as 'heritage' is accorded meaning which is then communicated by one means or another to the visitor. In other words, without interpretation (or, indeed, with poor or inappropriate interpretation), sites or attractions may remain meaningless to the visitor; sites of battles, disasters or other tragic events may remain 'empty', or museums may present collections of inanimate objects that, uncontextualised, have little or no significance or meaning to the visitor. As a consequence, the visitor experience may be diminished. Conversely, effective interpretation may serve to enhance the visitor experience, bringing a 'death' site or attraction 'to life'.

But what is interpretation? In a sense, heritage, whether museums, art collections, historical buildings or even dark tourism sites, have always been interpreted to the extent that factual information has, in one form or another, been provided. Thus, historical artefacts in museums have customarily been labelled to provide basic information to the viewer, battlefields or sites of disasters have been marked with a simple memorial, or the rooms or dungeons in castles have been identified by their function. In other words, the purpose of such 'interpretation' was (and frequently still is) simply to provide facts, the assumption being that the significance or meaning of the site, building, or object was/is either self-evident or, perhaps, of little relevance or interest to the viewer (Uzzell, 1998: 17). In short, traditional forms of interpretation deny or do not allow for a relationship between the place or object and the visitor. However, since the 1950s and, specifically, the seminal work of Freeman Tilden, the process of interpretation has taken on a broader, multidimensional purpose of not only informing but also connecting the site or object to the social and personal world

of the visitor. As Tilden (1977: 9) suggests in his first principle of interpretation, 'any interpretation that does not somehow relate what is being
displayed or described to something within the personality or experience
of the visitor will be sterile'.

Thus, for Tilden, interpretation is *'an educational activity which aims to
reveal meanings and relationships through the use of original objects, by firsthand
experience, and by illustrative media, rather than simply to communicate factual
information'* (Tilden, 1977: 8 – italics in original). Similarly, Moscardo and
Ballantyne (2008: 239) define interpretation as 'a set of information-focused
communication activities, designed to facilitate a rewarding visitor experience', a definition which embraces both a focus on enhancing visitors'
understanding of, and their relationship with, places or events, and a
focus on managing tourists' understanding and consequent behaviour.
Thus, Moscardo and Ballantyne (2008: 239) go on to suggest that the purpose of interpretation is to encourage 'visitors to be receptive to a management or sustainability message', a purpose that reflects the roots of
interpretation in environmentalism and conservation.

Since Tilden first introduced the concept of interpretation in the 1950s,
it has become almost universally adopted as a means of presenting, representing or explaining heritage, and of encouraging a connection with and
response to that heritage on the part of visitors. For Tilden (1977: 9), interpretation should not only inform but provoke. In short, it is a means of
enhancing visitors' understanding of heritage and how it relates to themselves and to their world. Thus, interpretation has become an essential
and recognised element of heritage management, to the extent that it has
become 'professionalised' as an activity (Uzzell, 1989a: 5; see also AHI,
2008). As a management 'tool', interpretation has also benefited, of course,
from technological advances, as the more traditional forms of interpretation such as guided tours, information signs and panels, visitor centres
and live performance are being augmented by, for example, self-directed
tours using pre-downloaded mp3-format audio-tours, like those offered
by English Heritage for some of their historic sites (see www.english-
heritage.org.uk), so-called 'talking heads', or computer-generated presentations. One problem associated with this is that the interpretation itself,
rather than the heritage it purports to interpret, becomes the attraction.
Indeed, greater use of interpretation at visitor attractions has, perhaps inevitably, attracted increasing criticism; as Uzzell (1998: 11) observes, interpretation 'has been accused of trivialising history and inculcating within
the public a reactionary, superficial and romantic view of the past'. More
specifically, Howard (2003) argues three cases against interpretation. Firstly,
interpretation encourages tourism, contributing to the negative impacts
associated with excessive visitation; secondly, by its very nature, interpretation presents selective storylines which may be politically or ideologically
biased (see Chapter 8) or may be little more than indoctrination – the

interpreter mediates between the attraction and the visitor and hence the latter's perception of the attraction and its meaning; and thirdly, those storylines may be inaccurate or inauthentic, presenting a comfortable, rose-tinted or safe, sanitised version of past events. Moreover, he suggests that interpretation should be guided by 'a moral stance of honest dealing' (Howard, 2003: 244; see also Chapter 4).

A complete review of the heritage-interpretation debate is beyond the scope of this chapter. However, in the case of dark sites and attractions, it is the potential of interpretation (or particular methods of interpretation) to trivialise, commoditise, distort, soften or depersonalise the event commemorated or represented that is of greatest concern. Additionally, according to Wight and Lennon (2007), the interpretation of historical narratives is likely to be selective. Consequently, dark sites and attractions are likely to elicit, to varying degrees, an emotional response among visitors. Such a response will be mediated by the nature of the site or attraction – for example, Uzzell and Ballantyne (1998) explore five factors, namely: time, distance, experiencing places, degree of abstraction, and management, that may influence the extent to which visitors engage emotionally with 'hot' heritage (see also Miles (2002)). Nevertheless, in order for the emotional needs of visitors to be satisfied, to enable people to confront or contemplate death, to make sense of tragedy or atrocity or to remember a loved one, there is a need for the interpretation of the site or event to recognise that emotional element, or to 'inject an affective component into its subject matter' (Uzzell & Ballantyne, 1998: 154). At the same time, the need also exists, through interpretation, to maintain the dignity of those people that the site or attraction commemorates (see Chapter 7). Thus, the interpretation of dark sites should, as far as possible, present an authentic narrative that reflects its emotive content.

Authenticity in dark tourism

The concept of authenticity in tourist experiences has been explored by commentators since the beginnings of mass tourism in the mid-1800s. In particular, as the introduction of rail travel opened up travel opportunities to greater numbers of people, distinctions came to be made between the 'traveller' and the 'tourist'. The latter became associated not only with mass forms of travel but with a particular approach to the travel experience. Thus, as Rojek (1993: 174) notes, 'high culture, the culture of the traveller, saw itself as the polar opposite of low culture, the culture of the tourist'. Implicitly, travel was seen as 'authentic', tourism as 'inauthentic'.

This distinction between travel and tourism was revisited by Boorstin (1964) who, in stimulating contemporary debates surrounding authenticity in tourism, famously argued that modern (American) society is contrived, unreal and illusory. As a consequence, modern mass tourists seek out and are satisfied with contrived, meaningless events: the tourist 'expects that the exotic and the familiar can be made to order ... expecting all this, he [sic] demands that it be supplied to him.... He has demanded that the whole world be made a stage for pseudo-events' (Boorstin, 1964: 80; see also de Botton, 2002). In contrast, MacCannell (1989) argues in his seminal work that the modern tourist recognises the inauthenticity of contemporary social life and thus becomes a secular pilgrim seeking the authentic: 'sightseeing is a kind of collective striving for a transcendence of the modern totality, a way of attempting to overcome the discontinuity of modernity' (MacCannell, 1989: 13). For MacCannell, however, the tourist's quest for authenticity is doomed to failure; authenticity is inevitably 'staged' for tourists (MacCannell, 1973).

Others, of course, argue that such failure is not inevitable. Perceptions or expectations of authenticity depend upon the needs/experience of the individual tourist, the nature of the site, attraction or event and the relationship between the two (Pearce & Moscardo, 1986). In other words, authenticity is not a given, measurable quality that can be applied to a particular place, event or experience (Wang, 1999; Olsen, 2002). Rather, when the role of the individual tourist is taken into account, the experience of authenticity and hence the extent to which tourists make sense or understand the meaning of a site or attraction within the context of their own social world becomes negotiable (Cohen, 1988). As a consequence, it has been suggested that academic attention should be focused not on the degree of authenticity of particular tourist experiences, but on the process of 'authentication' of tourist sites and attractions – that is, how and why they are deemed authentic (Xie & Wall, 2008).

MacCannell's position continues to be reflected in more recent tourism-authenticity literature (e.g. Taylor, 2001; Chhabra *et al.*, 2003) although the issue of authenticity is explored in a variety of other contexts including, for example, commoditisation (Cohen, 1988), the portrayal of indigenous populations (Ryan & Aicken, 2005), marketing (Silver, 1993) and history-heritage (Hewison, 1987, 1989). However, for the purposes of this chapter, MacCannell's concept of the tourist as pilgrim seeking to challenge the 'discontinuity of modernity' is fundamental to understanding the need for an emotive, affective or authentic component in dark heritage interpretation. That is, as argued in Chapter 2 of this book, death and mortality in contemporary society have been sequestered; the lack of social frameworks and mechanisms for confronting ones own death and the death of others reflects, perhaps, the discontinuity of modernity referred to by MacCannell (1989: 13), thereby contributing to the anomic condition of (post)modern societies. Thus, the consumption of dark tourism sites or attractions may be driven by the need not only to remember or commemorate the death/suffering of others, but also to confront and contextualise it within the individual tourist's own social world.

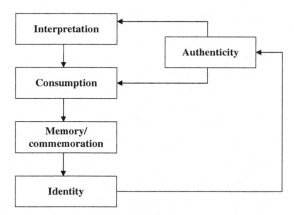

Figure 6.2 Dark tourism: Interpretation and identity

This process is conceptualised in Figure 6.2. Here, the principal issue is the link between the consumption or experience of the site and its subsequent contribution to identity creation. As considered elsewhere, the consumption of goods and services in general, and of tourism experiences in particular, is related to their social significance (Munt, 1994; Pretes, 1995; Lury, 1996; Sharpley, 2008); that is, the practice and significance of consumption is the 'active ideology that the meaning of life is to be found in buying things and pre-packed experiences' (Bocock, 1993: 50). Consumption is also considered key to postmodern identity and status creation (Miller, 1987). Thus, the consumption of dark tourism experiences has the potential to assign meaning and significance to the death of others, against which the tourist's own identity and mortality can be referenced.

Interpretation plays a key role in this process, acting as a 'filter' to emotional responses to a dark site or attraction. On the one hand, appropriate interpretation may enhance the visitor experience and fulfil the need for understanding and meaning. On the other hand, interpretation that misleads, trivialises or commercialises the experience may act as a barrier, perhaps protecting visitors from the harsh realities of the events commemorated or represented but, at the same time, denying them the opportunity to benefit spiritually from the experience. Equally, the interpretation may be ideologically influenced, conveying broader political messages beyond the immediate significance of the site, again distorting the narrative or diminishing its authenticity for the visitor.

It is to this issue that this chapter now turns. Specifically, it explores the ways in which interpretation methods may contribute successfully or otherwise to political and commemoration ideals, with a particular focus upon a kitschification of the macabre and, ultimately, the role and consequences of kitsch within the 'authentication' process of dark sites.

Dark Tourism: A Kitschification of Death and Grief

On 4 January 1903, a crowd estimated at 1500 gathered at an off-season Coney Island, a holiday resort which was famous for freak shows and fairground rides. On this occasion, however, visitors were there to witness the public execution of a circus elephant called Topsy, which had earlier killed a number of her keepers. While executions of exhibition animals were not unheard of during the 19th and early 20th centuries, what made this execution distinctive was the intervention of Thomas Edison and the demonstration of his direct current (DC) electrical system. Edison, who at the time was in a bitter battle with his rival George Westinghouse over the supremacy and safety of the DC system, used Topsy as way of demonstrating the superiority of his invention. The elephant, which had been harnessed to a series of electrodes and placed in copper-lined sandals specially constructed by Edison, was killed instantly when 6000 volts passed through her as the crowd watched (see Figure 6.3). *The New York Times* of the day reported the spectacle as 'a rather inglorious affair' (see Cross & Walton, 2005) while the headline for *The Commercial Advertiser* simply read 'Bad Elephant Killed' (Anon, 1903). This execution event would, perhaps, have been relegated to the footnotes of New York history, had it not been for the filming of Topsy's actual demise by the Edison Company, and its subsequent revival by a centenary commemoration arts exhibition in 2003 that brought the execution back into public consciousness (see Figure 6.4). In particular, artists Lee Deigaard and Gavin Heck created a memorial exhibition to Topsy at the Coney Island Museum, where visitors viewed Edison's original film through a coin-operated, hand-cranked mutoscope (a turn-of-the-century viewing medium) while standing, as Topsy the elephant did, on copper plates (BBC News, 2003). Earlier in 1999, Topsy had been 'commemorated' during the Mermaid Parade at Coney Island, in which Gavin Heck had created a 'hysterical, historical re-enactment' of Topsy using 'chicken wire, plastic pipe and lots of pink fabric' on a specially commissioned float (Vanderbilt, 2003).

Of course, the example of Topsy the elephant, at a rudimentary level at least, merely illustrates how art and artistic license can interpret a particular macabre episode in history. Indeed, the symbolic manner in which the artist/interpreter positions the viewer/visitor in pseudo 'electric sandals' and allows individuals to gaze upon the moment of death through a private mechanism, i.e. through the mutoscope but in a public place, galvanises empathy for the stricken creature. Many would argue, no doubt, that this method of commemoration is inspired, creative and well-suited to a respected museology environment. However, at a more fundamental level, equally valid arguments can be made with regard to how memorialisation, in this case simply for an elephant, is bound up in sentimental excess and irony, and where the boundaries of artistic endeavour are

Figure 6.3 Still photographs from Edison's original film of Topsy the Elephant's execution
Source: Carlson (2008)

Figure 6.4 Topsy the Elephant Memorial. Coney Island Museum, New York
Source: Heck and Deigaard (2003)

interfaced with the naïveté of kitsch. Consequently, when applied to the (dark) tourism of history, and for much more profound episodes than Topsy the elephant, the kitschification of the interpretation of dark sites has key implications for collective memory of tragic events. This point is discussed later, but firstly, an outline of kitsch and its ramifications for consumer (comfort) culture follows.

The term 'kitsch' emerged in the mid-19th century as way of describing an aesthetic that was portrayed as banal, trite, predictable and in bad taste (Calinescu, 1987). Derived from the German word *verkitschen*, meaning 'to cheapen', original connotations of the term defined it as the consequence of the mass production of consumer culture. In essence, kitsch is often associated with cost or *cheap things* that lack cultural refinement or taste. For those visitors rubbernecking at the execution of Topsy in 1903 on Coney Island, itself a place associated with low-market kitsch entertainment, and later in 2003 at the commemoration show held in Topsy's honour, the 'picture of the carnivalesque pleasures of the urban masses is utterly in keeping with the worst fears of those who saw in mass culture the portent of the end of civil society' (Hegeman, 2000: 299). However, kitsch is not exclusive to mass-produced cheap objects, or indeed restricted to perceived tastes of the so-called low market. As Calinescu (1987) suggests, while kitsch goods may be inexpensive, they are intended to suggest richness in both style and design, and can in themselves often engage individuals in a kitsch form of sentimentality and materiality. Indeed, in terms of tourism generally, Morgan and Pritchard (2005) regard tourist souvenirs as significant material objects and scrutinise how individuals use (kitsch) souvenirs as touchstones of memory, (re)creating polysensual tourism experiences, self-aware of their roles as tourists (see also Goss, 2004). Thus, kitsch is allied with social factors that accompanied postmodernity, namely the rise of mass culture, the sense of estrangement that arose from the shift from rurality to industrialisation and urbanisation, and the pervasive commodification of daily life and routine.

In terms of the prevalence of kitsch, Calinescu (1987: 237) goes on to note that 'the desire to escape from adverse or simply dull reality is perhaps the main reason for the wide appeal of kitsch'. While it is not possible to engage here in a full critique of kitsch and its interrelationship with the cultural condition of society, it is nevertheless worth noting certain distinctions of kitsch. In particular, Clement Greenberg's 1939 classic paper entitled 'Avant-Garde and Kitsch' set the parameters between art and kitsch, and suggests that:

> Kitsch is mechanical and operates by formulas. Kitsch is vicarious experience and fake sensations ... Kitsch is the epitome of all that is spurious in the life of our times. Kitsch pretends to demand nothing of its customers except their money – not even their time.

While most debates about kitsch often centre upon the distinctions between high and low culture, other debates critique kitsch as the unsophisticated and naïve taste that is associated with childhood and its culture. As Calinescu (1987: 237) notes, 'the cute culture of children's aesthetics form a continuum with the cute cultures of adult kitsch'. It is this naïveté and the seeming juvenility of kitsch, mass-produced to satisfy consumers who demand sentimentality, materiality and (childhood) nostalgia, where kitsch has been most criticised. This criticism is especially profound where tragedy has occurred and, subsequently, the (kitsch) *packaging* of tragedy for mass consumption is in evidence. For instance, Sturken (2007) highlights Ground Zero and its commodification for the (grief) tourist and singles out tourist souvenirs as a way of perpetuating kitsch forms of commemoration and interpretation. These include branded mass-produced objects such as cuddly toys, fridge magnets, key-fobs, badges, caps and book-markers (e.g. see Figure 6.5; also Hurley & Trimarco, 2004).

Sturken highlights the snow globe as a particular kitsch yet meaningful object (see Figure 6.6). The snow globe, a rather low-market souvenir found in tourist attractions throughout the world, often portrays scenes of idyll, romance and nostalgia. With regard to the Ground Zero snow globe,

Figure 6.5 Ground Zero (kitsch) tourist souvenirs, 2007
Photo: P.R. Stone

the twin towers of the World Trade Center still stand defiant as a Colossus above Lower Manhattan, depicting pre-9/11 New York and crystallising it in a safe, symbolic miniature world. Subsequently, 'the effect of the miniature is to offer a sense of containment and control over an event; the very objectness of these snow globes narrates particular stories about ... the destruction of the World Trade Center' (Sturken, 2007: 2). Of course, this snow globe and the meaning it may project is a marking of time, and captures the Twin Towers and the 'spirit' of the buildings in a mystical, animated yet temporal moment. For the tourist, the towers remain standing and unscathed and represent a 'permanent instance', which can be consumed at will, and in which time is arrested and memories provoked. Even after the romance of the shaking of the 'snow' and its animated effect upon the Twin Towers, the snow settles and the buildings remain; the *comfort* of the snow globe derives, in part at least, from 'the expectation that it returns each time to its original state' (Sturken, 2007: 3). Of course, kitsch objects such as souvenir snow globes with their prescribed emotional meaning, are often more complex than a rudimentary suggestion of bad taste or a superficial method of responding to tribute and commemoration. Indeed, the personal and personalised items left as temporal shrines in the aftermath of 9/11 in 2001 and earlier, in 1997, outside Kensington Palace after the death of Princess Diana, were objects of different but interrelated aesthetics, including teddy bears and soft toys, T-shirts, handwritten notes, posters and cards, ornaments and trinkets, candles, and of course flowers (e.g. see Figures 6.7 and 6.8; also Jorgensen-Earp & Lanzilotti, 1998). Each of these kitsch objects, as with the snow globe of

Figure 6.6 New York snow globe with the former World Trade Center Twin Towers
Photo: Svenstorm (2008)

the Twin Towers, both enhance meaning and project meaning for mass consumption. Thus, as Sturken (2007: 20) notes, 'in the context of memory and loss, kitsch can often play a much more complex role than the mass-culture critique of kitsch allows for'.

Interpreting Tragedy: Kitsch and the Commodification of Memories

The complexity of kitsch, especially with regard to dark tourism and the contemporary interpretation of grief and the macabre, is illustrated well through perspectives of melancholy and nostalgia. Consequently, Olalquiaga (1998: 291–292) suggests 'kitsch is the attempt to repossess the experience of intensity and immediacy through an object. Since this recovery can only be partial and transitory, as the fleetingness of memories well

Figure 6.7 Ground Zero temporal 'shrine' at St. Peter's fence in the days immediately after the 9/11 atrocity
Source: Mutantfrog (2005)

Figure 6.8 Diana, Princess of Wales' floral tribute and shrine after her death in 1997 above the Pont de l'Alma Tunnel in Paris
Photo: Kiwi-Lomo (2008)

testifies, kitsch objects may be considered failed commodities'. Hence, for Olalquiaga at least, *nostalgic kitsch* is a kind of remembrance that is selective and one which reforms and restructures the intensity of the experience of loss and tragedy. In other words, nostalgic kitsch interprets 'acceptable parts' of a tragic or macabre event, and consolidates them into memory that can forget, or certainly reduce, the original intensity of loss; whereas *melancholic kitsch*, in the form of souvenirs, sustains the sense of existential loss (Olalquiaga, 1998; Sturken, 2007). Certainly, the issue of nostalgic kitsch and the 'construction' of authenticity within tourist site interpretation is well documented in the literature (e.g. Jamal & Hill, 2002; Chronis, 2005). Moreover, the politicisation of nostalgic kitsch is alluded to by Hollinshead (1999), who argues that tourism is a means of production in which themes and sites are cleverly constructed narratives of past events which can manipulate individuals to become involved in configurations of political power and discourse. Consequently, kitsch conveys deliberate political communiqués which in turn generate messages of fear, hope and survival. However, within the context of dark tourism, political manipulation/interpretation will, of course, inevitably vary according to the particular shade/type of dark site (Stone, 2006a). For instance, the York Dungeon visitor attraction in the UK, with its kitsch and entertainment-laden interpretation of chronologically distant medieval torture, in addition to 'terrible tales' of the supernatural, will rarely incite historical reflection or political engagement (see also Chapter 9). Conversely, Ground Zero as a (dark) tourist attraction is constructed with narratives that are entrenched with socio-cultural and political messages. Hence, kitsch does not emerge in a political vacuum; rather it responds to particular kinds of historical events and indicates particular kinds of political acquiescence (Sturken, 2007).

Meanwhile, melancholic kitsch and the prepackaged sentimental response to death and disaster is an area that is curiously neglected within the dark tourism literature. While Sturken (2007) scrutinises the concept of kitsch as an embodiment of not only sentiment but also the conveyance of sentiments which are, or should be, universally shared, she does so within the limited confines of the American cultural response to 9/11 and the touristic consumption of Ground Zero. Nevertheless, Sturken suggests that kitsch tourist interpretation conveys a sense of comfort. Certainly, in the case of tourist souvenirs, the branding of soft 'cuddly toys' on sale at Ground Zero (see Figure 6.9) encourages visitors to feel, perhaps, a childlike comfort in survival and an accompanied sense of fortitude. However, Sturken (2007: 22–23) notes that this 'comfort cannot speak to cause; rather, it encourages visitors to feel sadness for the loss of lives in a way that discourages any discussion of the context in which those lives were lost'. That said, Sturken does not acknowledge the broader aspects of morality and collective effervescence, as discussed in Chapter 4, and how both within discourse and from new moral spaces

Figure 6.9 Branded soft toy tourist souvenir on sale at the WTC Tribute Visitor Centre, New York
Photo: P.R. Stone

such as Ground Zero, morality is allowed to be communicated, reconfigured and revitalised.

Nevertheless, 'kitsch is a central aspect of comfort culture' (Sturken, 2007: 23), and as such, the kitschification of tragic events allows the visitor to emotionally register with the period of history being commemorated/interpreted. With that emotional registration is a relationship of sentiment that is inextricably linked to political manipulation and, according to Berlant (1999: 53), 'a rhetoric of promise that a nation can be built across fields of social difference through channels of affective identification and empathy'. Thus, melancholic kitsch, which is seemingly ubiquitous in dark site interpretation, albeit to varying degrees, generates sentimentality and empathy which in turn can reduce the political complexity of a macabre event to simplified notions of tragedy. Of course, further analysis and inter-rogation is required to the suggestion that 'comfort comes as a kind of fore-closure on political engagement' (Sturken, 2007: 26). Yet there is little doubt that dark tourism, at its darkest level at least (after Stone, 2006a), revolves around the consumption of fear and the selling of comfort (see also Heller, 2005). To that end, kitsch and the kitschification process, inherent within dark site interpretation, constructs nostalgia for what has gone before, and additionally engenders a melancholic sentiment of tragedy that may have affected both the individual and collective self.

Conclusion

This chapter set out to address fundamental aspects of (re)presenting macabre and tragic episodes of history. In doing so, it highlighted broad concepts of (dark) heritage interpretation and its consequent authenticity dilemmas, including notions of selectivity, trivialisation and distortion. Of course, the paradigm of dark tourism interpretation is complex, multifac-eted, and exists within a myriad of socio-cultural and political environ-ments. As a result, a universal paradigm of dark tourism interpretation is all but beyond reach and it would, perhaps, be naïve to suggest that such a framework exists or indeed could be constructed. Nonetheless, this chapter has commenced the task of constructing a conceptual framework to begin examining dark tourism interpretation and its consequences for both projecting and extracting meaning. While this requires further con-ceptual augmentation and empirical testing, a key element appears to be the kitsch factors inherent in both the design and sentiment of dark sites. It is this kitschification and its process that is fundamental to generating empathetic feelings towards a particular tragic event. Kitsch, of course, can manifest itself in many disparate forms and techniques, although the overriding factor appears to be objects of interpretation which transmit feelings of comfort, safety and hope. Thus, when tragedy and the macabre are prepackaged and interpreted for mass consumption, melancholic sen-timents are not only engaged at the individual level but, perhaps more importantly, are politicised and rendered.

Of course, death and disaster are inevitably vulnerable to kitschifica-tion, as they require inoculation and thus rendering into *something else* that is comfortable and safe to deal with and to contemplate (see Chapter 2; also Desmond, 1999). However, concerns within dark tourism interpreta-tion remain and revolve around interrelationships between kitsch, nostal-gia and melancholy and the meanings that are consequentially projected. Even so, dark tourism, which has a sense of propinquity and, indeed, is considered relevant to the consumer, can confront traumatic memories and convert them into representational and narrative forms and, perhaps more importantly, integrate them into life stories for both the individual and collective self. Ultimately, however, kitsch interpretation of dark and tragic sites merely plays a part in conveying sentiments of empathy and nostalgia, while, at a more fundamental level, conveying narratives of redemption and a recoding of (popular) culture. It is suggested that this latter point be the focus of future research agendas.

Chapter 7

Contested National Tragedies: An Ethical Dimension

CRAIG WIGHT

Introduction

This chapter explores some of the intrinsically western ethical complexities associated with the production and consumption of dark tourism attractions, focusing specifically on contested narratives of national tragedy and disgraced monuments. As such, it addresses from an ethical perspective the issue of competing ideologies or narratives that is the subject of the following chapter. The cultural conditions which have supported the emergence of ethics and morality as discourses of international tourism are examined and the ethical implications of authorising certain narratives of national tragedy (over others) through the texts of heritage sites, monuments and visitor centres are discussed in the context of 21st-century 'moralised' tourism activity. The writings of Donald Horne and his observations about legitimating public culture through the 'dream factory' of tourism are drawn on to conceptualise the morality of selling narratives of national tragedy at heritage sites. The initial section discusses ethics and the commercialisation of dark narratives and the chapter later reflects on the application of these theories to the marketplace using Grutas Park in Lithuania as a case in point. It is argued that dark tourism may well be one strand of a contemporary discourse of 'moral tourism' and that the activity is perhaps in itself a tastefully distinct travel choice of the western tourism consumer. Some background understanding of the term 'dark tourism' is assumed.

As a preamble to the initial review of the literature, it is worth offering the suggestion that the terminologies given to tourism and heritage sites associated with tragedy and human suffering as a core theme ('dark tourism', 'thanatourism', and so on) remain perfunctory discourses of academia that seem to exist without the consent or collaboration of the tourism sector. There is the suggestion of a pejorative shade to the term 'dark tourism' and although websites and journalism articles on the topic are flourishing, these are not commercialised websites or publications and their authors are, thus far, usually commentators (with occasional input from an 'industry voice'). The author has yet to come across anything like a collaboration of war museums, memorial sites and death camp visitor centres convening and trading under the broad umbrella of 'dark tourism' (although tour operators will offer thematic trails). The terminologies remain free floating in this respect, apt to receive a number of differing meanings. Nonetheless, there remains much to say about the types of heritage sites that have so far been discussed in literature and the appetite of commentators and observers to uncover more about them will continue to fuel discussions and debate.

The Moralisation and Ethical Codes of Tourism

Among the more established and documented dilemmas of dark tourism academia are ethics and the morality of selling provocative and 'sensitive' narrative through heritage to the touring and visiting public. Some consideration of the concept of ethics is therefore a useful starting point in adding to the analysis. Ethics have been conceptualised as a set of rules and principles that claim authority to guide the actions of groups and communities (Singer, 1994). The term can, however, also refer to the systematic study of reasoning about 'how we ought to act' and finding a rational way of 'how we ought to live'. While not limited to religion (ethics exist in all human societies), ethics and morality are increasingly discussed in terms of 'religious morality'. This point, however, merits some brief acknowledgement in the context of commercial heritage but, in particular, in terms of religiously and ethnically dissonant heritage sites, such as Auschwitz Visitor Centre which is invested with narratives of Polishness, Jewishness and German, Roma and Sinti (among others) narratives of tragedy. Each of these visitor 'types' seeks to legitimate 'truth' from the same public resource.

Ethics and 'morality' suggest a stern set of duties that require subordination of natural desires in order to obey the 'moral law' (Singer, 1994). The 20th century saw philosophers approaching the question of the origin of ethics as something inaccessible. Since Charles Darwin, there has been a widely supported scientific theory that offers an explanation of the 'origin of ethics'. The attempt to draw implications from evolution has led to 'social Darwinism' (now 'unfashionable'). Ethics are not static concepts and the history of moral philosophy has involved systemising, defending, rethinking and recommending concepts of behaviour over time. Among the most publicised conceptual thinkers in the field of ethics have been (Singer, 1994: 18):

- Thrasymachus (4th century) and the thesis that ethics are imposed on the weak by the strong;

- Socrates (4th century) and the thesis that the ruler is not concerned with his own interests, but with that of the subject;
- Hobbes (17th century) and his observation that ethics give the ruler a right to command and to be obeyed;
- Nietzsche (19th century) who suggested morality is the creation of 'the herd' (led more by fear than hope).

There are numerous schools of thought, and literature on the broad subject of ethics is abundant. What is important in the context of dark tourism is suggesting a conceptual ethical framework for the analysis of selling provocative narratives of national tragedy in heritage settings. The study of the commercialisation of heritage of a 'dark' theme is concerned with two obvious elements of ethics or morality as follows (it is acknowledged that there are likely to be more):

(1) business ethics and the extent to which businesses within the heritage industry which communicate a 'dark' narrative to the visiting public consider their practices to be ethical (and inoffensive);
(2) personal morality and the extent to which these often provocative narratives are received and are acceptable according to the moral principles of visitors from widely varying cultural backgrounds.

Of relevance to this chapter is some consideration of business ethics since the topic covers the heritage industry, a collective for a number of largely commercial endeavours. The term 'business ethics' has been described at the extreme as an oxymoron in the corporate world since some argue that morality is intrinsically absent in capitalist entrepreneurial ventures (Butcher, 2003). Yet the issue of business ethics is a prominent topic attracting attention from a number of communities of interest, such as consumers, pressure groups and the media.

Corporate social responsibility is a dominant strand of the discourse of business ethics and has been coined to refer to the tacit process of communicating a legal and institutional corporate framework within which a duty of care (to people, the environment and employees among others) is implied (Crane & Matten, 2007). Dark tourism has not been fully elaborated upon in this context since there are problems in communicating the social responsibility of these types of heritage sites (particularly sites of contested heritage), such as:

- The esotericism in the scope of what is morally acceptable to various communities of interest: Is there a hierarchical order of care or responsibility that must be demonstrated? What for example is the most 'responsible' way to admit visitors to Auschwitz visitor centre and museum in compliance with the moral codes of the relatives of prisoners and victims of brutality but also with the moral codes of other visitor types such as sightseers and other transient visitors, Polish visitors, Sinti visitors, young visitors and so forth? Tunbridge and Ashworth (1996) simplify the argument to the idea that 'all heritage is someone's heritage, and therefore logically, not someone else's'. Conflicts of interest are common in heritage but more morally charged where the narrative is provocative and contested.[1]

- Can it be ethical to adopt another's national tragedy and embed it with new national discourses? Cole (1999a) discusses this in the context of the United States Holocaust Memorial Museum which he argues 'Americanises' European Jewish tragedy, repackaging 'Holocaust' for American consumption in theatre, film, tourism and heritage.
- Such sites, after all, typically serve as reminders of the consequences of social *irresponsibility*.

Discourses of corporate social responsibility are, however, present in the language of many of the operations thus far defined as being in the dark tourism business. Williams (2008: 131) remarks on this in observing the morally guided mission statements of some seven memorial museums around the world (to offer two random examples, the Hiroshima Peace Memorial Museum in Japan has the mission 'that no one else should suffer as we did', while the Terrorhaza in Budapest exists 'to research, document, educate and ensure remembrance of this Holocaust').

Ethics, viewed as an evolving discourse in thought systems, have come to the fore as a result of the disintegration of socio-cultural homogeneity (a condition of modernity) and the consequent gelatinisation of values, morals and lifestyles which together contribute to the 'postmodern condition' (Gardiner, 1996). Since the late 1970s, historiography theorists have challenged the assumption that history should be driven by the assembling of large historical truths into grand records of fact and interpretation. The progress of modernism, according to McGregor (2003), manifested itself in material progress; the production of 'things' and the development of a massive amount of objective and value-free scientific knowledge. Postmodern theory, conversely, is based upon a relativist theory of knowledge and the belief that there are no certain single truths about the world, only questions with infinite answers, each as valid as the next. The term 'postmodernism' came into popular usage after the publication of Francois Leotard's 'The Post Modern Condition' (1979) which began to challenge the veracity of monolithic systems (such as Marxism and Feminism) and meta-narratives offering overarching explanations of the world. The theory assumes that individuals conduct their own narrative, or reality, depending on different communities of knowledge. Ethics are part of this narrative and codes of morality are the governing systems of all communities of knowledge. Michel Foucault, in his later works, developed an alternative to modernist ethics defined by self-delineated (rather than externally imposed) criteria. From the perspective of a western society, 'ethical' tourism behaviour is a product of the individual decisions of tourists. Tourism consumer preference is a mark of ethical distinction (in a Bourdieusian sense) and preferences are made in opposition to the 'Other' (usually) mass tourist (see Munt, 1994).

Mass tourism has come under assault ever since Thomas Cook was accused of 'dumbing down' travel by opening up travel opportunities to an underclass imagined to be incapable of cultured behaviour (Butcher, 2003). Mass tourism continues to insult the advocates of a number of niche holiday markets united by their antipathy to the vulgar 'package tourist'. Postmodern alternatives to mass tourism are thriving and include ecotourism (considered the ultimate ethical oxymoron by critics), sustainable tourism, community tourism and adventure tourism among others (Butcher, 2003). The emergence of 'alternative tourism' (the pursuit of unusual destinations, experiences and activities) has been noted by a growing number of theorists (Wight, 2008) and is a term increasingly summoned to describe a kind of travel-catharsis among the Western 'thoughtful tourists' (Horne, 1984) who wish to feel more worldly, educated and enlightened.

Traditionally, tourism ethics are discussed in the context of tourism as a major economic engine that can wreak havoc on the environment and can negatively temper and influence host communities in destinations imagined as culturally sensitive or unenlightened. Cheong and Miller (2000) discuss tourism ethics in terms of a normalising discourse (what is acceptable or not acceptable) and an 'inspecting gaze' influenced by the manipulation of imagery in tourism marketing. Jenkins (2003: 306) develops on the power of 'image' that influences 'the inspecting gaze' in tourism:

> Texts (paintings, photographs, landscapes and words) are arranged into 'discourses' or frameworks that embrace particular combinations of narratives, concepts and ideologies that vary between cultures, classes and races.

Increasingly, western tourists turn to recollections of 'experience' and 'authentic' tourism encounters. Usually, 'alternative tourism' is understood to involve some kind of search for authenticity and there is a growing contentious debate in tourism academia over the extent to which authenticity matters (there is also no shared understanding of the concept of authenticity). The primary concern of tour operators is to market images of authentic cultures while insuring that these images will be verified during travel. As Silver (1993: 303) points out:

> ... for tourists authenticity is not necessarily determined by gaining a genuine appreciation for another culture, but rather by verifying a marketed representation of it.

The author observes that indigenous people are frequently represented in brochures as having static cultures which are largely unchanged by western colonialism, economic development and the activity of tourism itself. Entire cultural facets of nations are almost always missing from brochures presenting images of Third World countries. Since the tourist expects to see primitive indigenous cultures, industrialisation and politics are overlooked altogether, and instead a pastoral myth is presented via images and narrative. The simulation of the marketed culture is, therefore, easily realised as expectations are kept within a narrow focus, often excluding major cultural aspects of the country. These expectations are inherent in western discourse, and the images will almost always appeal to the Eurocentric (for example, Silver discusses marketing literature depicting Tahiti in which 'exotic' women are photographed in 'primitive' dress, frequently barely clothed).

The new consumer sensibility widely heralded in the business press is the 'experience economy'. This world of mediated, staged and multisensory experience (an increasingly unreal world) gives rise to a public that desires 'authentic' and 'real' experiences. Hewitt and Osbourne (1995: 28) describe the postmodern tourism space as:

> ... one in which the image-reality-representation problematic is no longer in operation, as we know reality is now hyper-real. ... Image and reality are somehow as one. ... A one-dimensional universe which is image saturated and simultaneously free floating and authentically unreal ...

Importantly, however, 'authenticity' as it is used in the language of tourism marketing must be understood as a matter of perception – a judgment made by the consumer which is linked to self-image, and the desire to purchase goods or services that are closely aligned to that self-image. Authenticity is, in this sense, simply a discourse that legitimates travel, and other consumer choices.

Dark tourism (or the intimated 'dark tourist') displays some of the traits of the 'alternative tourist', particularly because encountering 'truth' and 'reality' and the search for new (or 'rare') knowledge and experiences is central to the discursive formation of dark tourism. Donald Horne's theories of tourism as a signifier of public culture and the role of tourism in nation building lend themselves to developments in the field of tourism ethics. Horne's work would suggest that dissonant heritage products and contested memorial sites are as much about reflecting cultural discourses of the present as they are about educating visitors about the past. Horne (1984: 29) summarises this as follows:

> Anachronism is the very essence of tourism: the present is used to explain the relics of the past, then the meanings given to the past are

used to justify aspects of the present, or to justify beliefs about how things should change.

Tourism, according to Horne, takes its place among the many other ingredients of public culture, for example, 'the news' (with its 'personality cults and acts of political theatre'), the movies, paperbacks, magazines, pop music and television soaps (also referred to by Horne as 'dream factories' which create more narrative in a week than was ever available to past societies in a year or a lifetime). For Donald Horne, to walk through a museum or experience a memorial site is to gain significant exposure to contemporary narratives of the nation state. Visitors contemplate objects transformed into monuments commemorating entire social classes, events, styles and ideas which are now (according to Horne's own simile intimating the reinvestment of narrative and context into once functional artefacts) like dead coral which has been painted. The sites themselves can be legitimated by the buying of souvenirs and postcards. For Horne, monuments and museums are a source of enlightenment and it is through the 'edutainment' role of the museum that public culture is learned and interpreted to externals.

In discussing narratives of tragedy and atrocities in museum contexts, Horne observes how museums prefer to portray tragedy in particular, selective ways – for example, the portrayal of Jewish people (of the Holocaust era) as either heroes or victims. Cole (1999b) breaks down the same argument into classifications of museum interpretation by gender ('victimhood', for Cole, is feminine and 'gallantry' and heroism are masculine). For example, the evasively named 'Museum of Art in the Concentration Camp', set up in the Jewish Quarter of Prague, is a testament to the 'gallantry' of the Jews in Terezin in the Czech Republic. The sheer amount of art that was produced in the camp has remained the artefact of choice in speaking to the generations in tones of gallantry and resistance. Conversely, there are numerous other European Holocaust museums, most of which project a narrative of Jewish 'victimhood', preferring to display artefacts and photographs of incinerators and queues of victims waiting to be hanged, shot or gassed, and the consequent piles of the dead (Cole, 1999b). Horne believes, however, that Holocaust victims are (through the lens of the museum):

> ... merely innocents who were massacred. With a clear eye, one can see the concentration camp museums not as monuments to the dead, but to the sufferings of passivity ... to the tourists on a horror pilgrimage, however, all this can seem exceptional – something that ended with the Nazis. (Horne, 1984: 244)

These ideas present dilemmas for the caretakers and consumers of sites remembering national and ethnic tragedies. A common debate discussed in literature is the legitimating of 'truth' and whether or not 'truth' can be accessed when visiting dark tourism sites (or indeed when watching films themed, for example, on actual accounts of genocide). Visitor centres and museums (including those with tragedy as a core 'theme') can be considered as texts which are invested with narratives that favour particular statements (or versions) over others. Exhibits, interpretation and the organisation and displaying of artefacts and media are not culturally or politically neutral phenomena. An important observation to make here is the accessing and verification of Hollywood 'myths' in experiencing dark tourism sites. A *New Statesman* travel article discussing 'must see' sites in Cracow, Poland observes the reactions of tourists walking past the gates of the Deutsche Emailwarenfabrik (Oskar Schindler's enamelware factory). As the article's author observes:

> ... 'crocodiles' of American tourists filed past the wall where a red coated girl[2] is seen by Schindler (in the Hollywood blockbuster, *Schindler's List*) from horseback on a hilltop. Tourists wept. Here she fell! (Grant, 2006: 41)

For visitors, the Schindler tourism experience confirms a Hollywood narrative of hyper-reality that the local tourism industry is unlikely to dispute (it is more likely to legitimate such narratives through the selling of souvenirs and postcards and so forth). The *New Statesman* travel writer describes one strand of a discursive formation around Jewishness accessed by tourists in 'Jewish Cracow'. What the writer seems to have accessed (in visiting the old Jewish quarters of Cracow with a guide) is a hyper-real theme park of 'Jewishness' with restaurants offering 'traditional Jewish cuisine' and floor shows with cabaret acts performed by 'Swiss blonds' performing to parties of tourists 'dissolving into easy tears to renditions of *Mein Yiddishe Momma*'. Grant suggests of the total Jewish narrative (a blend of 'Hollywood Holocaust' and contemporary Polish Jewishness):

> They (the state) wanted to keep a simulacrum of the past alive, a holo-grammatic replica. It was as if Britain had ethnically cleansed its entire Asian population but you could still go and eat a 'genuine' balti at a Birmingham curry house run by a Welshman, and listen to sitar music played by Scottish blondes. (Grant, 2006: 41)

The 'authenticity' craved by contemporary tourists can easily be delivered, yet 'ethical' concerns come to the fore of academia and the media when the 'narrative' that is accessed through tourism encounters is a hybrid invested with other, new discourses which are accessed as 'truth'. Whether not such ethical concerns are recognised by or important to 'the tourist' remains unresearched.

As Tunbridge and Ashworth (1996) observe, a common justification for preserving surviving artefacts and sites relating to the past is the contribution these make to the construction of an accurate record of what has occurred. Authenticity is, therefore, a value judgement, and the removal or absence of 'authenticity' renders such sites and objects worthless (to the tourist). The ethical concern posited by Tunbridge and Ashworth is that while monuments and historic sites are in the custodial charge of individuals and institutions with a 'resource based' definition of their task, heritage producers use a 'demand based' definition (responding to the appetite of the consumer for 'authenticity'). Consequently, accusations of over-interpretation, triviality, dishonesty and distortion or elitism and rigidity are levied at heritage producers (Tunbridge & Ashworth, 1996). Heritage is, ultimately, a personal affair and each individual constructs heritage based on personal life experiences providing anchors of personal values and stability. Critiques of heritage are based on such personal expectations. The curiosity of people and their determination to access ever more narrative through tourism encounters has encouraged a seemingly endless supply and demand continuum of individualistic 'niche' tourism experiences often carried out in opposition to the 'Other' mass tourist.

Horne views authenticity as 'the special magic of museums'. Cole (1999a) elaborates on this 'special magic' in the context of Holocaust memorials and museums. What is important within commemorative settings in what Cole (1999a: 164) refers to as the 'Shoah Business' (the commercialisation of Holocaust narrative in museums and film and so forth) is that:

> ... it is not that this is the 'kind of' barracks that inmates at Auschwitz lived in but that that this is 'one of' the barracks that Auschwitz inmates lived in.

The author refers to a display in the United States Holocaust Memorial Museum and makes an interesting contribution to the 'ethical' debate in noting the American 'repackaging' of the Holocaust (in the Holocaust museum in Washington, DC, for example, and also in Americanised narratives of Anne Frank in film and theatre). There is something surprising, notes Cole, about this adaptation of what is someone else's history and something incongruous about American Jews (disassociated through choice with Israel, and neither survivors nor the children of survivors) talking of 'Jewishness' in terms of 'Holocaust' and 'Israel'. Yet the Holocaust Museum in Washington, DC (together, of course, with Hollywood, theatre and other 'dream factories') continues to perpetuate a competing national narrative, an adapted 'Americanised Holocaust', an atrocity that took place on foreign soil and within a European historical context. The issue throws open the debate over the esotericism in the scope of what is morally acceptable to various communities of interest.

The Washington example can be viewed in terms of ethical 'dissonance' and in particular the way in which the content of the messages contained within the interpretation of such heritage could mean recipient groups must incorporate contradictory ideas into their psychological constructs (Tunbridge & Ashworth, 1996). These contradictory ideas are explored in further detail in the final section of this chapter in an analysis of 'disgraced monuments' in Grutas Park, Lithuania as an example of a multi-ethically 'coded' heritage site with resonance for a number of visitors depending on age-group, origin and 'taste'.

Grutas Park: 'Disgraced Monuments' and Moral Panic

It has been argued (Wight & Lennon, 2007), that heritage has selective appeal to communities depending on the code of morality of host societies and their subcultures. The Vilna Gaon Jewish Museum in Vilnius, for example, reports failure in its historical attempts to attract interest (with the ultimate goal of growing visitation) from schools and other community institutions, arguing that such community groups are uncomfortable with the issues presented (Wight & Lennon, 2006). The geographic proximity of the museum to the Lithuanian 'Genocide' Museum and the fact that visitor numbers to the latter are overwhelmingly higher is an interesting observation in terms of the appeal (and contestation) of 'genocide' to visitors and also in terms of the extent to which visitors (particularly nationals) are comfortable in environments dealing with indigenous 'genocide' and those dealing with 'Jewish Holocaust'. The latter sits awkwardly in Lithuanian public culture and makes the concept of genocide a contested term in memorial sites.

Other Lithuanian dissonant heritage examples provide further useful units of analysis to contribute towards an understanding of ethics in the context of dark tourism. Grutas Park near Druskininkai, to take one such example, is a recent addition to Lithuania's 'dark' heritage landscape. This is a site that has aroused more curiosity and public controversy than any other tourist attraction in the country's touristic history (Figure 7.1). The site officially opened on 1 April 2001 (April Fools' Day) but it was in the planning stage for perhaps a year or more (Baranauskas, 2002). Word spread quickly that Grutas Park was to be the home of a number of 'disgraced' Soviet statues (including statues of Lenin, Stalin and other prominent communists). Controversy ascended throughout the nation as a number of Lithuanian nationals expressed outrage, protesting the construction on the grounds that it would 'bring back haunting memories of one of the most horrifying periods of Lithuanian history' (Baranaukas, 2002: 18) and would 'disgrace the memory' of those quarter-million Lithuanians who were arrested, killed or deported to the wastelands of Siberia under Communist rule. The controversy was further fuelled by the fact that the proposed location for Grutas Park was a site nearby Grutas Forest where Lithuanian partisans fought and lost a long and bloody war against the Red Army for a number of years.

Figure 7.1 Grutas Park can be farcical, gruelling, earnest or nostalgic

The outrage was contested as other Lithuanian communities supported the idea behind Grutas Park, arguing that it would contain a valuable historical lesson for future generations of Lithuanians. This past, as unsettling as it was, should not, according to erstwhile proponents, be abandoned. Despite the controversy and since Lithuanian law allowed the development, Viliumas Malinauskas (the Lithuanian entrepreneur behind the project whose fortune was made from selling canned mushrooms) proceeded with plans and bought a number of Soviet relics scattered throughout the country to be displayed in the heritage site.

Grutas Park has subsequently been well profiled internationally in travel magazines and on the Internet and tourists from both Lithuania and overseas continue to visit in numbers of around 700 per day (Baranauskas, 2002). Upon entering Grutas Park, a weatherproof bulletin board displays a number of letters of protest from Lithuanian locals and organisations registering disgust at the construction of 'this Stalinworld' (a parody of Disneyland and what Donald Horne might refer to as 'decorative exhilaration'). Comparisons can be made between Grutas Park and Hollinshead's (1999) description of Disney World, since in both cases the visitor enters a place of suspended reality encompassing symbols, features and structures which are considered out of context with 'real life'. Alongside these documents are listed figures of the number of Lithuanians exiled and killed at the hands of the Communists. Exhibits within the park include a cattle car (of the type used to transport deportees to the Siberian Tundra), a small zoo (with no apparent relevance to the broad 'theme' of apparently ridiculed totalitarian relics) and a collection of some 70 sculptures including the 'Totalitarian Circle' where statues of Lenin, Stalin, Marx and other are displayed together (Baranaukas, 2002: 18).

One of two Lenin statues in Grutas park captures the former leader in a pose pointing towards what used to be a KGB prison (in its original location in Lukiskiu Aikste or 'Lenin Square') and is now the Lithuanian Genocide Museum. The statue was removed after the failure of an attempted coup in Moscow, prosecuted by hardliners in 1991. It was wrenched from its pedestal using a crane which lifted and 'swung him high in the air' (Baranaukas, 2002) in a scene conjuring images of the unseating of Saddam Hussein's statue by US troops and Iraqis in 2003. Joseph Stalin's statues have also been relocated to Grutas Park. Following his death in 1953, Stalin was denounced for being responsible for the deaths of countless millions of his own people and his statues were removed. Vincas Mickevicius' statue is also displayed in Grutas Park. Mickevicius had a hand in organising the Lithuanian Communist Party and was a leader of the party in 1918.

The park's entrepreneurial founder has argued that the atmosphere allows Lithuanians to put their tragic past behind them by 'combining the charms of a Disneyland with the worst of the Soviet Gulag' (Cable News Network, 2001). Critics of the park have described it as 'tacky' and argue that such a past should not be exploited for 'cheap show business' (Cable News Network, 2001). Interestingly, the idea for the park was put to tender by the Lithuanian Ministry of Culture in 1998 (Williams, 2007), giving rise to further moral panic surrounding the Government's apparent obsession with the 'care' of such symbolic remnants of an unwished for regime.

The 'disgracing' of monuments as a cultural manifestation of moral panic is not a new gesture and similar heritage sites have been filled with disgraced monuments in Russia and Budapest (a totalitarian art museum in the latter case) and post-Apartheid Africa where monuments of erstwhile canonical icons from the Apartheid era were stockpiled in *'Boerassic Park'* (Coombes, 2003: 18). Indeed, Coombes discusses the phenomenon in detail noting:

> ... the fate of public monuments under successive regimes in the former Soviet Union and the apparently endless cycle of monumental sculptural programmes celebrating the favoured leader of the moment followed inevitably by their iconoclastic dismantling and removal ... In Russia it has always been the case that a struggle with the past was realised through a struggle with monuments.

Moscow Park has even had its own Museum of Totalitarian Art at which similar scrutiny (observed in Grutas Park) has been levelled. Williams (2007) observes how the relocation of city sculptures to parks and other suburban locations has a number of effects, not least that the monuments are 'banished' from their original locations which were chosen in order that the monuments could exert significant ideological power. A further effect may be the future perception of such sites as a form of 'reverse propaganda' (Williams, 2007) and an expression of a commitment towards forging closer affiliations with the West and Central Europe through a visible denunciation of the political past.

In terms of non-Lithuanian (and non-eastern European) tourist perceptions of heritage sites such as Grutas Park it is likely that without having experienced the statues and monuments in their original context, they become signifiers of something experienced as caricature (Williams, 2008). For indigenous Lithuanian visitors to the site, it is unlikely that there is any power symbolised by the 'Lenins' and 'Stalins' that they encounter, as their presence has no current influence on their day-to-day affairs. Indeed, there is a certain humour in corralling displaced monuments into a heritage spectacle and intimations of the postmodernity of dark tourism (Lennon & Foley, 2000: 5) are evidenced in such a gesture as 'anxieties over the project of modernity are introduced'.

The statues in Grutas Park are symbolic of the failure of modernity and they elicit antagonistic criticism from a broad political spectrum. They are symbolically loaded and can be farcical, gruelling, earnest or nostalgic to visitors. They are at the heart of 'anachronism' in tourism and cultural landscapes (Horne, 1984) since the meanings they give to the past are used to justify the present and belief about how things should change. In terms of the ethics of presenting such a site to the visiting public, Grutas Park has been established in a country which has in many respects come to associate museums and monuments with blunt propaganda (Williams, 2008: 7) and so the site (along with other 'edutainment' heritage sites such as the Genocide Museum in Vilnius) may be viewed by some Lithuanian communities as the final chapter in a long era of subverted cultural values and coerced political obedience. The site itself is a caricature of an entire era remembered as a time of subverted values and culture. It is in this sense a perpetuation of the ideologies which it caricatures.

To a large extent, the memorialisation of locations such as Grutas Park serve to contain the memories, experiences and power associated with a former regime. However, they lend themselves also to an 'authenticity' of the artefacts and objects housed within them, something which visitors clearly value. The museumification process has heralded the death-knell of the ideology of the oppressive regime and a triumph over its reign. The survival of the site, although contested by visitors with varying identities which are verified by the experience, is clearly vital to a number of 'activists' who are simply not prepared to allow the old oppressors to forget what happened in Lithuania at their hands. Grutas Park provides an example of an apparent western trend to continually revalue the eastern European past through the recycling and appropriating of icons of communist ideology (similar to the popularity of the ubiquitous Hammer and Sickle T-shirt and Central Committee of the Communist Party (CCCP) 'hoodies'). By devitalising the power and the threat that communism once posed by assimilating its iconography into popular culture, the triumph of West over East is reaffirmed and celebrated.

Grutas Park fits in with the emerging paradigm of dark tourism in provoking reactions to the past and in offering an example of contested heritage with a theme of human suffering. For tourism marketers and certainly for the owner of the site, issues of morality and ethical debates are the lifeblood of the operation as word spreads of the site and its multi-faceted messages. Contested narratives create the tourism 'pull factor' (the novelty) as the western visitor increasingly seeks 'experience' and ever more narrative to make a personal judgement regarding the issues that are communicated, and to judge 'truth' and 'authenticity' subjectively.

Conclusion

Tourism activity offers a rare, observable form of ethical behaviour. Tourists 'vote with their feet' and, as such, demonstrate in visiting 'dark' heritage sites that these are morally acceptable spaces to occupy. Ethical discourses linked to the production and consumption of contested heritage sites are shaped and maintained by many voices. The issue of remembering tragedy and oppression in heritage sites and, specifically, to whom we entrust memory, is at the centre of academic debate surrounding 'truth' and 'appropriate' or 'authentic' narratives broadcast by dark tourism sites. This panic among analysts is not echoed in the behaviour of the 'dark tourism' consumer who, by virtue of experiencing dark tourism sites, continues to consume.

This chapter has suggested that dark tourism, as a broad terminology for a number of heritage sites broadcasting national tragedy, displays some traits that hold appeal for the 'alternative tourist'. This is particularly the case because central to the discursive formation of 'dark tourism' is encountering 'truth' and 'reality' and the search for something new. The curiosity of people and their determination to access ever more narrative through tourism encounters has encouraged a seemingly endless supply of individualistic tourism experiences often carried out in opposition to the Other 'mass' tourist. Dark tourism fulfils some of this demand in offering topical, thought-provoking and contestable narratives that carry a message (however provocative) of education. Such heritage sites also commonly proffer messages of social responsibility (not unlike 'ecotourism' and other tourism 'niches' invested with morality).

Heritage, like ethics, is ultimately a personal affair and each individual constructs heritage based on subjective life experiences, providing anchors of personal values and stability. For tourists visiting themed tourist sites where national identities (with narratives of tragedy strong among these) are on display, it is difficult to avoid being drawn towards interpretation such as signage, guidebooks, staged spectacles and purposefully constructed tours. Yet each visitor upon encountering heritage sets the parameters for the level of engagement with the issues, and the extent to which narrative is 'morally acceptable' is similarly personalised. Presenting narratives of national tragedy to tourists is simply another way that the tourism industry exploits and commercialises 'the unique' for the 'distinguished' consumer – just another way of 'differentiating' destinations to hold greater appeal for the discerning client. These performative narratives legitimate the metaphor of the nation state as 'exotic', 'authentic' and 'dark' and ultimately attractive.

The extent to which subjective morality is profoundly traumatised (or, conversely, legitimised and vindicated) by visiting dark tourism sites depends on how far people are willing to go as tourists to accept that 'truth' is accessible by consuming heritage. Truth, as this chapter suggests, depends on a number of ethical codes that have become embedded through cultural background, religious or secular beliefs and exposure to various other cultural narratives. Tourism experiences are personal and each individual constructs a personal experience according to a personal ethic. Postmodernity has no place for such a thing as a 'universal truth' and the moral panic that comes with the production and consumption of 'dark' heritage only adds to the appeal of these sites as visitor attractions.

Notes

1. For further discussion on the selectivity of interpretation and the appeal of certain narratives over others using examples of heritage sites themed on Lithuanian Jewish and indigenous partisan atrocities, see Wight and Lennon (2007).

2. Oskar Schindler was a German industrialist credited with saving some 1200 Jews during the Holocaust. The film *Schindler's List* condenses the Holocaust into one (Americanised) narrative. As Leventhal (1995) observes of the scene with the girl in the red coat:

> The metonymic displacement of Schindler's List is most evident in Oskar Schindler's psychic investment in and the over determination of the only colour image in the entire film (apart from the coerced reconciliation of the final scenes in Israel and the earlier scenes of Schindler in Krakow), that of the little girl in the red coat.

Chapter 8

Dark Tourism and Political Ideology: Towards a Governance Model

RICHARD SHARPLEY

Introduction

In May 2006, the winners of a competition to design an international Tsunami Memorial to be constructed in Khao Lak National Park in Thailand were announced. Commemorating the victims of the catastrophic Indian Ocean tsunami of December 2004, the winning design, selected from almost 380 entrants into the competition, proposed a number of purposes for the structure – a place for commemoration, a place for contemplation and a place for education – and included a library, museum, conference rooms and restaurants as well as spaces for contemplation and remembrance. However, both the design and its location were highly controversial. Not only was concern expressed over the ecological impacts of the building both during construction and consequently as a major (dark) tourism attraction located within a fragile forest environment, but also the scale of the project and its explicit role in attracting tourists were considered insensitive to the emotions of the friends and relatives of the hundreds of thousands who lost their lives in the disaster (Phataranawik, 2006). Moreover, it was argued that the $12.5 million cost of the memorial could be better spent on meeting the needs of local people directly affected by the tsunami although, from the government's perspective, this may have been considered a small investment given the potential number of tourists the memorial would attract.

Perhaps as a result of this controversy, the Tsunami Memorial has yet to be built, although three smaller, local memorials to the victims of the disaster have been constructed in Thailand, but which do not act as 'thanatourism' attractions (Rittichainuwat, 2008). Conversely, another memorial that has attracted significant criticism, the American National World War II Memorial in Washington, DC, was completed and opened in 2004. Located on Washington's National Mall between the Washington

Figure 8.1 American National World War II Memorial, Washington, DC
Source: www.acepiltots.com (in the public domain)

Monument and the Lincoln Memorial, the memorial commemorates all Americans who served in the armed forces or on the home front during the Second World War and, as such, should have been uncontroversial (Figure 8.1). However, its location, dissecting the National Mall in a space traditionally used for public gatherings and demonstrations, has been criticised while, in particular, its 'traditional' war memorial design (two arches within a circle of pillars) has not only been described as imperialistic, authoritarian and representative of 1930s fascism (Williams, 2007: 1), but contrasts starkly with the contemporary and dramatic symbolism of the nearby Vietnam Veterans' Memorial. It is also claimed that, given the dwindling numbers of World War II veterans, political expediency in the form of appropriate legislation facilitated the rapid approval and construction of the memorial.

These two examples of memorials to human suffering, death and sacrifice differ in many respects, not least that one has yet to be constructed. Nevertheless, not only are they representative of the undoubted proliferation of such memorials, driven by an apparently increasing desire on the part of individuals, groups and even national governments to commemorate disasters, wars, atrocities, individual sacrifice (such as the memorial to a policewoman shot while on duty outside the Libyan Embassy in London in 1984 – see Figure 8.2) or other events associated with death and suffering, both recent and historical. They are also indicative of the fact that 'across many nations, public commemorations of warfare, political violence, terrorism, and discrimination have become a political flashpoint' (Williams, 2007: 1).

In other words, the innumerable memorials, museums, sites of battles or atrocities and other 'dark' places that, around the world, are constructed,

Figure 8.2 Memorial to WPC Fletcher, St. James Square, London
Source: www.en.wikipedia.org/wiki/Yvonne_Fletcher (GNU Free Documentation Licence)

maintained, restored, adapted or promoted as public presentations of death and tragedy (frequently for touristic consumption) possess both significance related to the events they commemorate and also, perhaps inevitably, a political symbolism that emanates from the manner in which those events are (re)presented, interpreted, told or, indeed, remain untold. That is, tragedies, atrocities and disasters have the potential, through their representation and commemoration, to be exploited not only for commercial gain through tourism but also to convey political messages. As a consequence, questions arise with respect to what or whose story should be told – or, as Williams (2007: 129) asks, 'who has the clearest claim to "own" the memory or interpretation of tragedy?'; who should tell the story, how it should be told or, in the extreme, whether or not it should be told at all. For example, numerous sites related to 'The Troubles' in Northern Ireland now underpin a thriving tourism industry, with famous (or infamous) areas of Belfast in particular becoming established ingredients of the tourism experience. Yet, as Ashworth and Hartmann (2005b: 13) question, does 'promoting the visiting of atrocity sites ... legitimise the atrocity or those who committed it and thus encourage more in the same or different ideological cause?'

Not all dark tourism sites or attractions, of course, suffer such political exploitation. For example, those attractions falling within the 'light' to 'lightest' categories of Stone's (2006a) dark tourism spectrum (see Chapter 1), such as 'dark fun factories', 'dark resting places' and 'dark exhibitions' are, with some exceptions, politically benign, though perhaps ethically contestable. For example, and as observed in Chapter 2, the Body Worlds exhibition, packaged as scientific endeavour, continues to stimulate considerable debate regarding the ethics and objectives of displaying human remains that have been subjected to the 'plastination' process (Walter, 2004; Whalley, 2007). Conversely, many 'darker' sites and attractions, such as those related to conflict or atrocity, are infused with political meaning and act as a focus for political debate or conflict, particularly where there may be competing claims to ownership.

It is with this latter category that this chapter is concerned. Drawing on a number of examples and short case studies, it explores the differing ways in which the development and presentation of certain dark tourism sites and attractions may be influenced or biased by an underlying political ideology – or how death and tragedy may be exploited for political ends – before going on to propose a governance approach to planning and managing such sites. Firstly, however, a brief review of the relationship between tourism and politics and, specifically, the notion of dissonance as an outcome of politically influenced dark tourism production provides a framework for the rest of the chapter.

Tourism and Politics

As a major global social and economic phenomenon, tourism is intensely political (Harrop & McMillan, 2002: 245). Moreover, the political nature and significance of tourism has long been recognised (Richter, 1983) although, according to some, this significance has not, until more recently, been reflected in the academic literature (Hall, 1994: 3). Broadly speaking, the political aspects of tourism are manifested in two ways. Firstly, given the increasing importance accorded to tourism as a vehicle of development and regeneration, the widespread social and economic consequences of tourism and its international diversity and scale, it is inevitable that the state, to a lesser or greater extent, intervenes in the practical planning, management and control of tourism (Elliott, 1997; Hall, 2000). The nature of that intervention varies enormously, from a passive, enabling role (Jeffries, 2001) to a more active, entrepreneurial role, the latter more frequently required, though not always in evidence, in less developed economies (Tosun & Jenkins, 1998). The degree and nature of intervention will also, of course, be determined by the prevailing political ideology of the state, with comparisons typically made between market-led and centrally planned economies. For example, the Thatcher–Reagan-inspired neo-liberalism of the 1980s and the subsequent focus on privatisation and the markets in many western nations contrasted starkly with the then centrally planned tourism sectors in the former eastern Europe (Buckley & Witt, 1990; Hall, 1991).

Secondly, and of greater significance in the context of this chapter, there exists what Light (2007) refers to as the 'cultural politics of tourism development' (see also Burns, 2005). That is, tourism may be exploited for political or ideological purposes, typically to affirm or emphasise cultural identity. Thus, 'the state may assume the role of marketer of cultural meanings, in which it attempts to make a statement about national identity by promoting ... [through tourism] ... selected aspects of a country's cultural patrimony' (Cano & Mysyk, 2004: 880). In other words, the state may seek to encourage specific forms of tourism in general, and the manner in which places and events are developed and interpreted as tourist attractions in particular, as a means of affirming its own cultural and political identity (Light, 2007). Moreover, the focus of such cultural mediation may, on the one hand, be 'internal' or parochial, promoting domestic tourism to places of national significance as a means of constructing and maintaining national identity (Palmer, 1999). On the other hand, nation-states frequently adopt international tourism as a vehicle for their enhancing national cultural identity and international profile or, in some cases, in an attempt to legitimise themselves within the global community. For example, the former Marcos regime in the Philippines sought international political legitimacy through tourism (Richter, 1983) while, more recently, tourism in Myanmar has been shaped by local and external political forces (Henderson, 2003).

The extent to which the political exploitation of tourism is successful (that is, the extent to which the state is able to meet its political objectives through tourism) is itself dependent on the wider political–economic context. Economic factors may require the state to subordinate ideology to the more practical and pressing need for income or foreign exchange earnings, a factor which, for example, has strongly influenced the development of tourism in Cuba since the late 1980s (Jayawardena, 2003; Sharpley & Knight, 2009). Equally, the state may be powerless to prevent the development of forms of tourism of which it disapproves or which represent the state in a way it would not wish. Thus, since the early 1990s the heritage of communism has remained a powerful attraction for visitors to countries of the former Eastern Bloc, yet this promotes a socialist past that is firmly rejected by the countries concerned (Light, 2000). Similarly, despite efforts to promote their natural and cultural attractions, a number of countries, particularly in Southeast Asia, have developed unwelcome reputations as sex-tourism destinations (Ryan & Hall, 2001).

Furthermore, and of particular relevance to this chapter, the political exploitation of dark sites and attractions may result in what has been referred to as 'dissonance' or 'dissonant heritage' (Ashworth, 1996; Tunbridge & Ashworth, 1996). According to Ashworth and Hartmann (2005c: 254), all heritage is susceptible to dissonance; however, 'the nature of human tragedy imbues ... [dissonance] ... with a capacity to amplify the effects and thus render more serious what otherwise would be dismissible as marginal or trivial'.

As introduced in Chapter 1 of this book, dissonant heritage is concerned with the way in which the past, when interpreted or represented as a tourist attraction, may, for particular groups or stakeholders, be distorted, displaced or disinherited. In other words, dissonance occurs when 'there is a lack of congruence at a particular time or place between people and the heritage with which they identify' (Ashworth & Hartman, 2005c: 253). Such a lack of congruence may occur for a number of reasons although, generally, it arises from the fact that that the heritage, the people who identify with that heritage, and the context within which the heritage and the people interact inevitably change over time. That is, for any event, for any 'past', recent or distant, there is no single story or interpretation, but new or alternative interpretations; equally, the people who identify with that past may change, or their relationship with the past may change. At the same time, there are frequently multiple stakeholders in the heritage of past events, particularly atrocities, tragedies and disasters, such stakeholders including victims, perpetrators and contemporary independent (that is, not identifying with either victims or perpetrators) visitors to heritage sites. Therefore, the particular interpretation of the past may create an 'inheritance' for one group of stakeholders, the inevitable outcome of which is the 'disinheritance' of other stakeholders. For example, there are multiple victim groups of the 9/11 attacks on the twin towers of New York's World Trade Center, including passengers and crew on the hijacked aircraft, those who perished when the towers collapsed, the relatives and friends of those who perished, members of the New York police and fire services, the citizens (or city) of New York, and America. Therefore, the interpretation and memorialisation of 9/11, particularly at Ground Zero, is likely to 'disinherit' certain groups from 'their' tragedy.

According to Ashworth and Hartmann (2005c: 254), 'this disinheritance may be unintentional, temporary, of trivial importance, limited in its effects, and concealed'. Conversely, it may be explicit, intentional and, in the broad sense of the word, politically motivated, the purpose being, among other things, to create or enhance group or national identity, to align with a particular victim group, to (re)interpret past events to meet contemporary political agendas, to erase or deny a particular past, to celebrate victory (military, political, populist) or, perhaps, simply to encourage visitation by tourists. Much, of course, depends upon the relationship between the event and those in a position to influence memorialisation or interpretation. For example, the actual naming of the Battle of Waterloo and its subsequent memorialisation was, according to Seaton (1999), designed to privilege the role of Wellington and the British rather than the allied army as a whole, creating around the battle an ideology of British power and imperialism that, arguably, remains to this day.

Ashworth and Hartmann also argue that, given the inevitability of dissonance in (dark) heritage construction and interpretation, a universal heritage (that is, a heritage with which all stakeholders may identify) is illogical and unachievable. Indeed, as the following examples imply, some degree of political exploitation and hence dissonance is the inevitable outcome of the representation and interpretation of tragedy, atrocity and death as tourism attractions. Nevertheless, as the chapter then goes on to consider, the potential exists to manage, if not extinguish, such dissonance.

Political Ideology and Dark Attractions

Such is the diversity of dark attractions, even only those that explicitly convey political or ideological messages, that a complete review of the nature of the political exploitation and representation of death and tragedy is an impossible task. Not only are such sites and attractions becoming increasingly numerous, but each must be considered within a prevailing political and cultural context which may itself be dynamic. For example, on the still politically divided island of Cyprus, inter-communal violence leading up to and following the Turkish invasion of 1974 is represented photographically in both the Greek- and Turkish-controlled sectors of the island in exhibitions open to tourists. On the southern, Greek side, Greek Cypriots, both missing and dead, are portrayed as victims of the invasion; conversely, in the self-proclaimed Turkish Republic of Northern Cyprus, those who died are in effect portrayed as 'martyrs' of a peace operation (see Lennon & Foley, 2000: 129–144). Thus, a shared tragic past is interpreted differently according to localised political ideology, yet within an island-wide context of political pressure for reunification, itself driven, in part, by the regional politics of European Union enlargement.

At the same time, some events and their associated sites or memorialisation are more susceptible to political exploitation and controversy than others. Thus, it is not surprising, perhaps, that not only are there are more memorials, museums and other markers relating to Nazi rule in Germany (1933–1945) in general, and the Holocaust in particular, than any other period in history (Hartmann, 2005), but also that they continue to generate significant debate and controversy. For example, Marcuse's (2005) detailed review of the continuing modifications to the former Dachau concentration camp near Munich in southern Germany demonstrates how both a perceived need to sanitise its history and also its redesign 'according to the representational desires of those in charge of it' (Marcuse, 2005: 145) have resulted in the needs of successive generations of visitors remaining unmet. Equally, it is not surprising that sites and memorials related to the Holocaust are undoubtedly the most 'popular' topic within the dark tourism literature, with particular attention being paid to Auschwitz as, arguably, the epitome of Holocaust-related dark tourism (see, e.g. Lennon & Foley, 2000; Tarlow, 2005; Poria, 2007).

Nevertheless, it is possible to identify a number of themes which serve as examples of the ways in which the representation for public consumption of death, disaster, atrocity and tragedy may be influenced by political ideologies. Some of these themes, such as genocide and slavery tourism, are also considered more broadly and in greater detail in subsequent chapters.

Memorialising political pasts: Eastern Europe

The collapse of communism in the eastern Europe in the late 1980s was not only one of the most significant political events in the recent history of that continent. It also provided both the opportunity and a focus for the development of tourism to the former Eastern Bloc countries, facilitated in no small measure by the rapid development of low-cost flights from western Europe. Thus, as Williams (2007: 115) observes,

> disastrous events and political failure have emerged as a key to economic revitalisation through tourism. Since the early 1990s, Western European and American tourists who have flocked in large numbers to former communist nations particularly seek out examples of unfamiliar political arrangements and living conditions.

In other words, the 'dark' political past of eastern Europe has become a tourist attraction (Hall, 1995).

However, the end of communism and the subsequent potential for tourism development based, in part, on the representation of recent political history has caused something of a dilemma for eastern European countries. Having suffered repression under both Nazi and, subsequently, communist rule, conflict may arise between the representation and memorialisation of both periods. In particular, the communist period signified, in one sense, a victory over the Nazi regime, and was widely commemorated as such, yet that communist era is now largely disowned in those countries as they seek to construct new, post-communist identities 'characterised by a democratic, pluralist, capitalist and largely Westward-looking orientation' (Light, 2000: 158). Consequently, the potential commercial benefits of exploiting, through tourism, the communist period contrasts starkly with the desire of the former communist countries to reject that history. In Romania, for example, efforts were made to extinguish all evidence of communism following the fall of Ceausescu, local people being 'more interested in practical current political and economic progress' (Williams, 2007: 115), yet that political past remains a significant draw for tourists to the country.

The inherent dilemmas of, and managerial responses to, the touristic exploitation of the communist past in eastern Europe is considered in some depth by Light (2000). Drawing on three case studies (the Berlin Wall, the *Szoborpark* or Statue Park in Budapest, Hungary, and the Casa Poporului or House of the People in Bucharest, Romania), he identifies the conflict between official policies to construct post-communist futures and the opportunities presented by tourism to 'affirm their self-image and aspirations both to themselves and to the wider world' (Light, 2000: 12). In each case, different strategies have been adopted reflecting contemporary political ideologies. In Berlin, for example, in order to confirm the city's and country's new (since 1990) unified status, small sections of the Wall have been preserved (though mostly distant from the city centre) and specific heritage sites have been developed that place the Wall firmly in the city's past. In Budapest, statues symbolic of the communist era have been relocated in a purposefully built park on the city's edge, primarily for touristic consumption but also as a political compromise between those who wished to keep the statues as a reminder of Hungary's communist past and those who sought the destruction of all symbols of that past. Conversely, in Bucharest, the political past is, in effect, denied. The House of the People, a vast building constructed by Ceausescu as a demonstration of the power of the state, is now presented to tourists as the centre of political power in contemporary Romania, with little or no reference made to its past associations. In all three cases, however, 'there has been an attempt to negate the meanings of the heritage of communism by decontextualising it' (Light, 2000: 173).

In contrast, Budapest's *Terrorháza*, or House of Terror, confronts explicitly both the Nazi and communist eras of repression and commemorates the victims of both. Opened in February 2002, it is located at No. 60 Andrássy Road, one of the city's main thoroughfares, in a building that served as the headquarters of the Nazi-affiliated Arrow Cross Party between 1940 and 1945. From 1944, when the Hungarian Nazis came to power, the basement of the building became a prison and torture centre. Following the liberation and occupation of Hungary by the Soviet Army in 1945, the building was then taken over by their secret police (the ÁVO, subsequently renamed the ÁVH, or *Államvédelmi Hatóság*), and it remained that organisation's interrogation and torture centre until the uprising of 1956. In late 2000, it was selected as the location for a 'museum of terror' and, following both internal and external reconstruction, opened to the public less than 18 months later. According to the museum's official catalogue:

> ... it does not merely contain an exhibition dedicated to the victims' memory; its appearance too conjures up the atmosphere of the place. For too long, for too many decades we have passed by this building ... knowing, sensing that its walls were hiding monstrous crimes, a sea of suffering. ... The House of Terror Museum is proof that the sacrifice for freedom is not futile. Those who fought for freedom and independence defeated the dictatorships. (Anon, 2003: 5)

It is, therefore, less a museum in the traditional sense, and more of a memorial and education centre, a warning to younger generations (Rátz, 2006: 245). It is also a major attraction, both for international tourists and Hungarian visitors, drawing over a million visits in its first three years.

According to Rátz (2006: 246), the House of Terror is 'one of the most controversial Hungarian cultural institutions, which was created by a political decision and has been the subject of fierce criticism ever since'. That controversy surrounds both the alleged political motives behind the concept and its rapid implementation and what is seen by some as a lack of balance between the representation of, on the one hand, the period under Nazi control up to 1945 and, on the other, the subsequent communist era. With regards to the museum's development, the project was pushed through by the then right-wing government of Viktor Orbán and, though not complete, was opened some six weeks before national elections. During the election campaign, Orbán emphasised the opposition socialist party's communist leanings; hence the House of Terror, with its explicit anti-communist message, was seen by some as anti-socialist propaganda. In the event, the socialists won the election and as a result were uncomfortable with the museum as a whole and with its most controversial display, the Gallery of Victimisers, in particular (Williams, 2007: 117). There, photographs of former high ranking members of both the Hungarian Nazi and communist regimes are displayed (some of the latter still alive), the museum therefore taking on an implicit role of judgement.

Equally controversial is the limited presentation of the Hungarian Holocaust, during which some 500,000 Hungarian Jews were sent to their death in Nazi concentration camps. Not only is there concern, particularly among Jews, that the display downplays the complicity of the Hungarian Arrow Cross party in this process, thereby treating Hungary as victim rather than perpetrator, but also the dominant focus on the communist era may suggest that it was somehow 'worse' than the Nazi period (Rátz, 2006: 254).

Thus, the House of Terror fulfils a number of purposes: a memorial to victims of two terrors; a museum of artefacts from those terrors; an

Figure 8.3 The House of Terror, Budapest
Source: www.blog.laurabaker.net

educative role for present and future generations; and a tourist attraction, the dramatic metal awning with the word 'Terror' cut out of it casting a shadow of the word on the ground, perhaps exploiting the building's history to enhance its appeal to visitors (Figure 8.3). To the visitor unconnected with Hungary's 20th century history, it presents a powerful (though perhaps not complete) message; to Hungarians, the 'owners' of two periods of terror, it will inevitably remain controversial.

Genocide and the politics of reconciliation

As noted above, much of the dark tourism literature focuses upon sites and memorials associated with the Holocaust; equally, much of the literature on genocide is, unsurprisingly, concerned with the Holocaust and, in particular, the proliferation of Holocaust memorials around the world (see also Chapter 11). According to Williams (2004), for example, there are now about 250 such memorials in the USA alone. The design and interpretation of Holocaust memorials tends to reflect the political and cultural contexts within which they are placed (Jansen, 2005; Krakover, 2005), yet most focus on the need for peace, learning, tolerance and reconciliation.

It would be logical to suggest that memorials to other genocides should serve similar roles – remembering those who perished, seeking reconciliation between victims and perpetrators, and 'acting as an aide to understanding events that challenge our notion of human history' (Williams, 2004: 242). However, it is evident that memorials to genocide can only contribute to reconciliation within a wider political context that promotes reconciliation rather than denial or recrimination. For example, the Nanjing Massacre Memorial Museum commemorates and documents the massacre of 300,000 Chinese people by the Japanese in 1937, yet not only does Japan continue to deny the massacre but research has shown that the event is what the majority of Chinese people continue to most closely associate with Japan (Williams, 2007: 120). Moreover, a potential tension exists between the memorialisation of genocide or mass death and its exploitation for tourism, particularly where the generation of tourist dollars may supersede local needs. Many have questioned, for example, the need for a large (and expensive) memorial, to be financed by the state government, to the victims of the 1984 Bhopal disaster in India, while local economic and medical needs of victims remain unaddressed (Williams, 2007: 113).

Such issues are evident at the Tuol Sleng and Choeung Ek memorials to the victims of the Cambodian genocide at the hands of the Khmer Rouge between 1975 and 1979. Tuol Sleng, located in the capital Phnom Penh, is a former school that became a prison and torture centre, one of 167 set up by the Khmer Rouge to interrogate and torture suspected enemies of the regime. Discovered by the Vietnamese when they entered Phnom Penh in 1979, it was opened in 1980 as a Museum of Genocide. Choeung Ek, some 10 kilometres from the capital, is one of more than 500 'killing fields' in Cambodia. It was here that the majority of prisoners from Tuol Sleng were taken to be killed and dumped in mass graves. Again opened by the Vietnamese in 1980, the Choeung Ek Genocidal Centre is dominated by a 30-metre high glass walled *stupa*, constructed in 1988, containing some 8000 skulls of victims.

The development, interpretation, tourist experience and political contributions of these sites are considered in a detailed paper by Williams (2004). However, the key issues arising from his analysis are as follows. Firstly, both sites appear relatively untouched. For example, although various displays including photographs of hundreds of victims are presented, Tuol Sleng has not been sanitised, with torture beds and other artefacts left *in situ*. Consequently, the sites may appear more 'authentic', yet tend to emphasise the instruments and methods of torture and mass killing rather than the victims themselves. Moreover, the photographs of victims remain depersonalised – no details or possessions of individual victims exist – and, as a consequence, 'the memorials offer little to support any kind of reconciliation with the past' (Williams, 2004: 247). Interestingly, in 2005 is was announced that Choeung Ek was to be privatised, a joint Cambodian–Japanese company taking on a 30-year lease on the site with the explicit intention of exploiting its tourism potential.

Secondly, the sites were discovered and opened by the Vietnamese, traditional enemies and invaders of Cambodia, presenting a complex political context for the role of the sites in memorialisation and reconciliation. The Vietnamese also employed a number of presentational techniques at Tuol Sloeng in order to liken the Khmer Rouge's genocidal activities to the Holocaust, thereby distancing their own communist politics from those of the extreme communism of the Khmer Rouge. At the same time, through opening the two sites, the Vietnamese were able to justify their invasion of Cambodia.

Thirdly, until very recently there has been a lack of evidence of any official moves towards justice and remembrance on the part of the Cambodian government, with inconsistent policies towards national reconciliation and bringing those responsible for the genocide to trial. While this may in part reflect the current political leadership's former links with the Khmer Rouge, the result is that Tuol Sloeng and Choeung Ek are likely to be more successful in contributing to earnings from international tourism than promoting peace and reconciliation.

Battlefields: A nationalist heritage?

Gallipoli in Turkey was the site of one of the bloodiest battles of World War I. Over a period of eight months during 1915, an estimated 250,000 casualties (dead and wounded) were suffered by each side before the defeated Allied Army finally retreated. It is now a much-visited battlefield tourism destination and, perhaps, one that epitomises the horror, futility and sacrifice of war. Not only do the terrain and the positions of the Turkish defenders point to the hopelessness of the task facing the allied forces, but the numerous graves (particularly one of a young British soldier who died one month before reaching his 17th birthday, the minimum legal age for enlisting) are a powerful and emotive reminder of the scale of sacrifice. However, Gallipoli is more than a place of legitimised (by war) death and suffering; like many battlefield sites, it conveys multiple stories, experiences and meanings. As Ryan (2007b: 4) observes, battlefield sites 'are the constructions of reactions to individual stories, wider social constructs and ideologies that informed our past and inform our present and future'. In short, the representation and interpretation of battlefields may convey powerful and, frequently, multiple messages. For example, despite being a major defeat for the allied forces, Gallipoli has achieved almost mythical status through the role of the Australia and New Zealand Army Corp (ANZAC) in the campaign – and subsequently as the subject of a movie – as the 'psychological birthplace' of both Australia and New Zealand as nations (Slade, 2003: 780). As Slade (2003) suggests, many young Australians and New Zealanders now visit the site to better understand who they are. At the same time, however, Gallipoli is a significant event in Turkish history. Not only was it a pivotal point between the eventual collapse of the Ottoman Empire in 1918 and the birth of modern Turkey in 1923, but Mustafa Kemal (later known as Atatürk), regarded as a hero of the defence of Gallipoli, went on to become the first President of the Republic of Turkey (Kinross, 1964).

Of course, not all battlefield sites are imbued with such political significance. As noted in Chapter 10 of this book, battlefields and sites and attractions associated with warfare more generally constitute a large, if not the largest, category of tourism attractions. Inevitably, therefore, there are numerous ways in which they are interpreted, numerous messages or, indeed, silences. Ryan (2007b: 6–8), for example, suggests four patterns of interpretation embracing two dimensions: factual–mythic and site-specific–social context. Thus, factual–site-specific focuses on objective historical interpretation, whereas mythic–site-specific suggests particular stories or political ideologies surrounding a site. Examples of the latter might include the 'story-scapes' surrounding Gettysburg (Chronis, 2005) or the narrative of revolutionary (Red) China embodied in Jinggangshan Mountain, the place from which the Long March commenced in 1934 (Huimin *et al.*, 2007). The mythic–socially contextualised category also implies a strongly politicised focus, 'where societies or ruling cliques may wish to sustain a myth about the past' (Ryan, 2007b: 8). Examples here would include the presentation/interpretation of Second World War sites in the Pacific for Japanese consumption (Cooper, 2006).

Inevitably, perhaps, the representation or interpretation of wars/battles between nations may focus on a nationalist heritage or, to put it another way, battlefields may be interpreted in such a way as to communicate a politically nationalist message. As observed earlier, this was certainly the case at the site of the Battle of Waterloo (Seaton, 1999). As a more general example, battlefields in Scotland, particularly those associated with the so-called Highland War but also including Bannockburn (where Robert the Bruce overcame the army of King Edward II in 1314), are arguably utilised as a means of creating a Scottish identity (McCrone *et al.*, 1995). Thus, Knox (2006) considers how the physical location, interpretation and tourist consumption of the 1692 Massacre of Glencoe serves to enhance a sense of identity, particularly among domestic Scottish visitors or international visitors of Scots descent, the events of Glencoe reaffirming the vision of the 'warrior-like tendencies of the native people' (Knox, 2006: 196) within the context of a wild, forbidding and romanticised landscape.

More significantly, perhaps, the battle site of Culloden has become 'a site for an authentic Scotland, operating as a signifier of and for that country' (McLean *et al.*, 2007: 234). The Battle of Culloden, fought in 1746, is widely seen as a battle between England and Scotland, won by the English, and hence an iconic event in Scottish history and in the relationship between the two nations. According to McLean *et al.* (2007), however, this is a gross over-simplification of the event which continues to feed nationalist and anti-English feeling. In fact, the battle brought to an end the Jacobite uprising, followed by Bonnie Prince Charlie's romanticised escape, yet it was the subsequent attempt to 'destroy the fabric of Highland life and economy' (McLean *et al.*, 2007: 223), not the battle itself, that is of greater significance to Scottish history. Importantly, however, the site itself is interpreted as a 'one-off' event, as indeed are many other battlefield sites around the world. That is, the significance of Culloden, both historically and in the context of the contemporary re-emergence of Scottish nationalism and Highland culture, not only lies in the events which surround it (as at Gallipoli as discussed above) but is also strongly perceived by visitors. As a consequence, there exists a degree of dissonance between the 'factual–site-specific' interpretation of Culloden and the needs of visitors seeking contemporary meaning from the site. Thus, somewhat paradoxically, the potential political message of Culloden remains under-exploited.

Slavery tourism: From roots to regrets

Tourism and slavery are, according to Dann and Seaton (2001a: 1), 'quite antithetical'. While a similar observation may be made regarding dark tourism sites and attractions more generally, it is perhaps within the context of slavery, specifically the triangular slave trade between West Africa, England and America and the Caribbean, that the contrast between the two phenomena is most marked, the inhumane capture, transport and enslavement of up to 10 million black Africans clashing starkly with the purposeful promotion of and visitation to sites associated with that slave trade (Austin, 2000). Nevertheless, and somewhat ironically, slavery is increasingly becoming the focus of heritage tourism development, particularly in certain West African nations where slavery heritage tourism (or 'Roots' tourism as it is referred to in The Gambia, reflecting the fact that Alex Haley, in his book *Roots* – subsequently a TV series – traced his slave ancestry back to the small village of Juffere on the banks of the river Gambia) has been adopted as a tourism development strategy.

Slavery tourism is a form of dark tourism in which competing ideologies, histories and heritage are perhaps most in evidence. Moreover, maybe as a consequence, the representation of the slave trade is complex and fraught with dilemmas, not least regarding the relationship between black Africa, the former colonial powers in Europe and America and the potential impact on white–black race relations more generally. As Austin (2000: 212) notes, the interpretation of the slave trade may serve to enhance racial prejudice while, increasingly, Africa and its history of slavery are considered by some to be of declining relevance to at least some sections of the African Diaspora. At the same time, the inherent irony is that a majority of visitors to slave heritage tourism sites, certainly in the USA and Britain but also to a lesser extent in Africa, are white (Beech, 2001; Dann & Seaton, 2001a).

These issues and the practical management of slavery heritage are explored in more detail in Chapter 12, while an edited volume by Dann and Seaton (2001b), *Slavery, Contested Heritage and Thanatourism*, remains the most comprehensive treatment of the inter-relationship between slavery and tourism. In the context of this chapter, however, the important point is that the political message conveyed by slavery heritage sites may not only be complex and open to misinterpretation, but there exist three distinctive contexts for the production and representation of slavery heritage, namely, the three 'points' of the triangular transatlantic slave trade, which influence the political 'flavour' of the interpretation. Thus, in West Africa, symbols of the slave trade, most notably the castles of Ghana, have been renovated and promoted as part of an attempt to develop international tourism (Essah, 2001; Richards, 2005), particularly among African-Americans who might consider a visit to one of former slave castles an important contribution to a search for their ancestral roots (Bruner, 1996). However, the representation of Africans as victims of imperial power (and the use of the 'slave castles' as symbols of that victimisation) not only ignores the role of those structures both prior to and following the slave trade era, but denies the role or complicity of Africans themselves in the slave trade.

If Africa was the victim then England was the perpetrator, inasmuch as it was the latter country that came to dominate the transatlantic slave trade and earned considerable wealth as a result. However, recognition and representation of the English role in the slave trade through the development of slavery heritage attractions has only been relatively recent although, ironically, the anti-slavery movement had been celebrated since 1906 when William Wilberforce's home in Hull was opened as a public museum (Beech, 2001). The country's first and largest permanent exhibition commemorating slavery opened in Liverpool in 1994, the principal objective of which was to dispel simplistic racial imaging of the history of slavery, thereby endowing the victims with individuality, personality and culture (Seaton, 2001), at the same time as engaging with the contemporary black population of Liverpool. Smaller exhibitions in Bristol and Lancaster have also been developed but in common with Liverpool, the true extent of the county's role in and economic benefit from the slave trade is, if not denied, played down, as is the involvement (and subsequent power and wealth) of well-known English families in the slave trade. Thus, politically, England's role in the slave trade is acknowledged and, implicitly regretted, but not fully revealed (Beech, 2001).

In contrast to the limited number of slavery heritage attractions in England, the US, more precisely the southern states of the US, are well endowed with sites or attractions related to slavery, the most common of which are plantation houses and estates. For example, research by Butler (2001) identified over 100 former plantations open as tourist attractions. According to Seaton (2001: 120), 'slavery, though a discomforting inheritance in the US ... is nevertheless acknowledged as an undeniable fact'. However, Butler (2001) found that at the great majority of planta- tions, particularly those in the Deep South, slavery was not referred to at all, the emphasis being on the architecture and grandeur of the house rather than the slave labour that enabled its construction. Similarly, research by Buzinde and Santos (2008: 484) reveals that the presentation of slavery at one site, the Hampton Plantation, is unlikely to enhance understanding of the 'critical role played by the enslaved in the foundational narrative of the plantation or, for that matter, multicultural American society' and, as a result, slavery remains an 'unresolved issue in America'. Thus, as with slavery heritage in both Africa and England, a selective interpretation of slavery is presented to visitors, an interpretation that undoubtedly dis- owns various interest groups or stakeholders from 'their' heritage.

Towards a Model of Governance

The cases discussed above are but a few examples of the many ways in which dark tourism sites and attractions may be exploited or are suscep- tible to exploitation, according to prevailing political ideologies, or to con- veying, in one form or another, particular political messages. However, they do serve to support the argument considered earlier in this chapter that all forms of heritage are susceptible to dissonance, a dissonance that might be amplified within a context of human tragedy or suffering. In each of the above examples, such dissonance can be identified, whether in the limited representation at Budapest's House of Terror of the Hungarian Holocaust and national complicity in those tragic events, the lack of recog- nition given to black Africans in the slavery heritage of America's Deep South or, perhaps, the dominance of the ANZAC 'story' within the shared tragedy of Gallipoli and the diminished focus on the stories of others.

The question then to be addressed is: is it possible to adopt an approach to managing or interpreting such dark sites or attractions that reduces the degree of dissonance, that begins to take the needs of all stakeholders into account? According to Ashworth and Hartmann (2005c), a 'universal heri- tage', or one with which all stakeholders may identify, is impossible to achieve, particularly given the often strong or sensitive positions of the owners of the multiple 'truths' of sites or representations of tragedy, atroc- ity or suffering. That is, for example, reconciliation between victims and perpetrators of genocide or equal attention accorded to victors and vanquished at battlefield sites may be an unrealistic goal. Nevertheless, it is possible to suggest a 'governance' framework within which the man- agement and interpretation of dark sites may be located.

As a starting point, and in recognition of the potential diversity of stakeholders and their interests in dark or thanatourism heritage sites, Seaton (2001) offers a model of a 'heritage force field' to suggest how conflicts or dissonance may occur between four groups with interests in a heritage development. These four groups comprise the owners or controllers of the development; the subject group (the focus or subject of the heritage narrative); host communities, or residents located in the vicinity of the development; and, visitor groups (see Figure 8.4). The size, influence and relationship between these groups may be infinitely variable, may change over time, and may often be dependent on the nature of the heritage development itself. For example, a small, local museum, established and run by a local community *for* that local community is likely to encourage harmony between the groups – indeed, there would be little distinction between the groups. Conversely, heritage sites related to the Holocaust are, perhaps inevitably, highly contentious.

Exploring ways in which the potential conflicts between heritage stakeholder groups may be addressed, Poria (2001, 2007) argues that the re-interpretation of any dark site should be based upon the formation of a new narrative for that site; that new narrative should, in turn, be based on a conceptual framework that links a particular event or occurrence to all stakeholders' feelings associated with the event (shame or pride) and degree of involvement (active or passive). Combining these allows for four groups of 'histories':

- *good active history*: past actions undertaken by 'my' social group which inspire positive feelings, such as pride;
- *good passive history*: past actions not undertaken by 'my' social group, but from which they have derived benefits;
- *bad active history*: past actions undertaken by 'my' social group which inspire negative feelings, such as shame;
- *bad passive history*: past actions not undertaken by 'my' social group, and which inspire negative feelings, such as revenge or sadness.

According to Poria (2007), bad active histories are, generally, not included in heritage interpretation, resulting in dissonance or a formally sanctioned

Figure 8.4 The heritage force field
Source: Adapted from Seaton (2001)

Figure 8.5 A model of dark heritage governance

'collective amnesia' (Timothy & Boyd, 2003). Thus, in order to address such potential dissonance or to diminish the influence of political ideology in the messages conveyed through dark heritage interpretation, new narratives should be created, embracing all four histories within a more cooperative approach to interpretation.

By combining Seaton's model of a 'heritage force field' and Poria's concept of stakeholder histories, it is possible to derive a model of governance for dark or thanatourism heritage sites. This is based upon a continual, sequential process of stakeholder identification, the determination of the histories of each stakeholder, and the negotiated or cooperative writing or re-writing of the heritage narrative for the site (Figure 8.5). Moreover, as new information or knowledge emerges, or as the political/cultural context of the site evolves, the new narrative should be reviewed or refined through the same process.

Such writing/re-writing of the narrative does not imply equal significance being given to each history. Rather, it suggests that recognition should at least be given to all the relevant histories (good and bad) of all stakeholders as a foundation for a more cooperative and inclusive approach to heritage interpretation. Thus, for example, the complicity of the Hungarian Arrow Cross party in the Hungarian Holocaust deserves more explicit acknowledgement in Budapest's *Terrorháza*; similarly, greater emphasis should be placed, perhaps, on the role of English traders (and the subsequent fortunes made) in the slave trade. Of course, the extent to which this alternative approach to dark tourism interpretation is possible is dependent on a variety of factors, not least the nature of the site itself and the power or political ideology of the owners/controllers group. In particular, the desire of governments to create a new national identity (or to deny an old identity) is likely to supersede any demand for greater recognition of all stakeholders' histories or stories. Nevertheless, it does provide a basis for encouraging harmony, reconciliation, understanding or learning (or reducing the potential for dissonance) through a more inclusive memorialisation and interpretation of dark or tragic pasts.

Part 3

Dark Tourism in Practice

Chapter 9

'It's a Bloody Guide': Fun, Fear and a Lighter Side of Dark Tourism at The Dungeon Visitor Attractions, UK

PHILIP R. STONE

> *A warning – in the Dungeon's dark catacombs it*
> *always pays to keep your wits about you.*
> *The exhibits have an unnerving habit of coming back to life …*
> Merlin Entertainments, 2009a

Introduction

Much of the dark tourism literature has, to date, focused upon sites that offer a representation of death and disaster which, in turn, may have had a profound bearing upon both individual and collective consciousness. Consequently, dark tourism which offers a greater perceived sense of 'darkness', more specifically those sites and experiences which generate moral discourse (and panic), which possess greater political and commemorative dimensions as well as having spatial and temporal affinities to the actual death/disaster event and are perhaps perceived as historically inaccurate or selective in their representation, has been increasingly scrutinised within the literature. Additionally, official tourism marketing is progressively exploiting the commercial aspects of tragic history. Indeed, a recent online poll commissioned by the Czech Tourist Board sought to discover, and thus promote, the 'top ten *darkest* places of interest' within the Czech Republic (emphasis added; Šindeláøová, 2008).

It is suggested, therefore, that those visitor sites which fall towards the 'darker' periphery of Stone's Dark Tourism Spectrum, a typology which locates dark tourism within a conceptual 'darkest–lightest' framework, have received most attention in terms of critical analysis and commentary (Stone, 2006a; see also Chapter 1). For instance, specific manifestations of *darkest* dark tourism, such as the (re)packaging of genocide for tourist consumption, have been investigated by Simic (2008) who provides a feminist narrative of the advent of 'genocide tourism' in Bosnia and Herzegovina. Meanwhile, Cole (1999b) discusses the historical perils of selling the Holocaust (also Mintz, 2001; Weissman, 2004), while Keil (2005) examines Holocaust sites and the crossing of boundaries between conceptual domains of pilgrimage, commemoration and pleasure-seeking (see also Staines, 2002; and Chapter 11).

Likewise, those *darker* sites which revolve around tragic accidents or intentional killing and which subsequently provoke dialogue with regard to commemoration politics and aesthetics or private grieving in public places have, again, received a significant amount of attention. For example, the death of Princess Diana in 1997, an event which appeared to inaugurate now familiar acts of private mourning in public spaces (Walter, 2007), generated discourse which centred on 'dark shrines' (after Stone, 2006a). Moreover, Merrin (1999) highlighted media involvement in both creating and perpetuating (dark) perceptions of temporary memorial shrines for contemporary tourism consumption. Similarly, memorial sites such as Ground Zero, the site of mass murder and carnage, and the commodification of tragedy post 9/11, most notably for political advantage and the management of collective memory, has been well documented (e.g. Bubriski, 2002; Heller, 2005; Simpson, 2006; see also Chapter 6).

Thus, while 'darkest/darker' tourism appears to have received an increasing amount of academic attention, the lighter forms of dark tourism – that is, those commercial visitor sites and attractions which recreate and commodify death, suffering and the macabre, and which are entertainment-centric – have received limited attention within the tourism literature. Therefore, the purpose of this chapter is to outline an exploratory study of a *lighter* form of dark tourism, namely The Dungeon visitor attractions which operate in the UK and Europe. In so doing, the chapter not only addresses a significant gap in the literature in terms of lighter dark tourism, but also places dark tourism entertainment within a framework of fear and psychosocial relevance to an individual's own life-world.

Lighter Dark Tourism: 'Feel the Fear, Experience the Fun'

The parameters for sites and attractions which offer a marketable reconstruction of death, suffering or the macabre are set out by Stone (2006a) in his classification of dark tourism. In particular, Stone's conceptual taxonomy suggests that 'lighter' shades of dark tourism do indeed exist and are dependent upon defining 'dark product features'. These essentially revolve around the perceived intensity of politicisation and commemoration, as well as temporal and spatial aspects of the 'death/disaster' site. In short, lighter forms of dark tourism are those commercial visitor attractions which trade on (re)created and (re)presented death and suffering, and are subsequently referred to as 'dark fun factories' (Stone, 2006a). Specifically, it is suggested that:

> A Dark Fun Factory alludes to those visitor sites, attractions and tours which predominately have an entertainment focus and commercial ethic, and which present real or fictional death and macabre events. Indeed, these types of products possess a high degree of tourism infra-structure, are purposeful and are in essence 'fun-centric'. (Stone, 2006a: 152)

The lighter side of dark tourism and the so-called dark fun factories which operate within this micro-niche (Novelli, 2005) have been examined under various guises. For example, the commodification of the supernatural and its role in constructing touristic landscapes is examined by Inglis and Holmes (2003). In particular, they observe how ghosts and other paranor-mal entities have been interpretatively recreated within a Scottish context and, specifically, they reveal shifting relationships between ghosts/ haunted spaces and dark fun factory mechanisms which have been devel-oped to stimulate the wider tourism industry. They go on to highlight the rise of 'Ghost Walk' tours in Edinburgh, where history and the supernatural meet and where 'the threat of the phantom has been turned into a promise, and the fear of the spectral has been transformed into *fun*' (emphasis in the original; Inglis & Holmes, 2003: 57; see also Mercat Tours, 2009; Scotland Now, 2006). Similarly, Bristow and Newman (2004) explore lighter forms of dark tourism and what they subsequently term 'fright tourism'. In essence, Bristow and Newman (2004: 220) suggest, albeit rather simplistically, how the ostensible notion of fright tourism 'is a natural extension of risk recre-ation.' They go on to compare both the commercialisation of the Witch Trials of 1692 in Salem, MA with the allegorical fictional incarnation of Count Dracula of Transylvania, Romania, and their respective economic and devel-opmental roles within the mainstream tourism sector.

While the examples of Edinburgh's Ghost Walk tours, the Salem Witches attractions and Dracula tourism are specific to geographical locations, and may indeed possess inherent cultural identity issues for those locations and populations (Light, 2007), more generally, *lighter dark tourism* occurs when narratives of fear and the taboo are extracted and packaged up as fun, amusement and entertainment and, ultimately, exploited for mercan-tile advantage. Consequently, the conception of fear within tourism pro-motional strategy, whereby notions of the sinister and the macabre are utilised to entice visitors, is an increasingly integral component of (dark) tourism marketing. Indeed, Neill (2001: 817), in his reflections on employ-ing fear in the promotional strategies of three urban centres, namely Belfast, Detroit and Berlin, suggests that 'fear is an inescapable dimension of the modern urban experience'. In short, visitors to tourism destinations and their attractions are offered excitement and a promise of adventure, in addition to disorientation and trepidation but also the possibility of discovering novelty. It is to these factors of excitement, novelty and trepidation that this chapter now turns within the context of a specific dark fun factory, namely The Dungeon visitor attractions. In particular, the author employs a triangulated research design to extract empirical data with regard to consumer perceptions of The Dungeon concept. Firstly, however, a brief outline of The Dungeon attraction establishes the context for the subsequent discussion of the research.

A Dark Fun Factory: The Dungeon Visitor Attraction

The Dungeon visitor attractions, as conceptual dark fun factories and as a case to illustrate lighter dark tourism, are commercial establishments which operate within the mainstream tourist attraction sector. The Dungeons are part of the Merlin Entertainments Group based in England, the second largest visitor attraction operator in the world (after Disney). Merlin Entertainments has 58 visitor attractions in 12 countries across 14 brands, served almost 33 million customers in 2007, employs up to 13,000 staff in peak season, and manages iconic UK leisure brands including the London Eye, Sea Life Centres, Madame Tussauds, Warwick Castle, Legoland and the Alton Towers Resort (Merlin Entertainments, 2009b). The Dungeon attractions are located in London, York, Edinburgh, Amsterdam and Hamburg, where 'each Dungeon offers a horror fest linked to their location – highlighting the local history's horrible bits' (Merlin Entertainments, 2009c; see also Tables 9.1–9.5). Indeed, as part of the Dungeons' marketing literature, consumers are seemingly forewarned in the visitor booklet, entitled *It's a Bloody Guide*, of the trepidations that form part of the experience:

> You are about to embark upon a journey that will take you through some of the darkest, bloodiest and most frightening times in history! On your journey you will witness some of history's most notorious and dangerous serial killers at work. You will hear the screams of the tormented, tortured souls, as unspeakable cruelty is committed. Smell the foul stench of death all around you, as plague-ravaged bodies are left in the street to rot and fester. Feel your way into the darkness as you try to escape the twists and turns of the underground labyrinth. Taste the fear, feel your hear pounding and your adrenaline pumping as you venture into your final journey on one of our terrifying rides. ... All this and more awaits you as you enter the Dungeons ... will you escape? (The Dungeons, 2008)

The Dungeon product concept is essentially built upon instilling a sense of fear, trepidation, novelty and excitement into the customer

Table 9.1 Types of exhibits, shows and rides at The London Dungeon visitor attraction with marketing descriptions

Name of exhibit, show or ride	*Marketing description*
Boat Ride to Hell	Are you afraid of the dark? Are you petrified of drowning? Do you hate the feeling of falling backwards? Face your fears with the Traitor, Boat Ride to Hell at The London Dungeon!
Extremis: Drop Ride to Doom	You have been tried and sentenced. Now you must accept your fate and let the hangman guide you to the end. A final rush of adrenaline as you plummet into the dark depths to embrace your doom!
Great Fire of London	The Great Fire of London rampaged through the City of London, turning everything in its wake to cinders. Travel back to 1666 and experience the burning reality of the fire that left 200,000 people destitute.
Jack the Ripper	The 1880s were a dangerous time for women to walk alone in London. A prolific killer frequented the dark alleys and quiet streets, preying on London's prostitutes.
Labyrinth of the Lost	One way in … but is there a way out? Experience the Labyrinth of the Lost at the London Dungeon.
Sweeney Todd	In need of a haircut? Like it or not you're going to have one … Sweeney Todd-style … and there's always a pie if you're feeling hungry!
The Great Plague	1665 – London is riddled with disease; thousands are dying in agony. Disgusting, gruesome boils, cries of panic and pain and shouts of 'bring out the dead' fill the air.

Source: The Dungeons, 2008

experience. Revolving around the 'gruesome past', The Dungeons combine live actors, shows, rides and special effects to bring life to the dead as visitors move from exhibit to exhibit through well designed rooms, each displaying a specific period of 'horrific history'; at the end of the tour, they exit into a customary gift store. Subjects that may have once been considered taboo within a museology/attraction environment, such as torture, execution, witchcraft or death, are now packaged up in The Dungeons through an amalgamation of kitsch artistic commodity

Table 9.2 Types of exhibits, shows and rides at The York Dungeon visitor attraction with marketing descriptions

Name of exhibit, show or ride	Marketing description
Dick Turpin	Discover the true story behind the world's most famous highwayman, Dick Turpin, at The York Dungeon. Find out why the infamy of this daring criminal has lasted almost 300 years.
Ghosts of York	Afraid of ghosts? You will be when you enter the Ghosts of York experience. A sense of malice and danger builds in the darkness around you before a pale, translucent figure suddenly appears!
Gorvik	The Vikings had in their ranks warriors known as Bezerkers, the most crazed and feared fighters whose frenzied nature in battle was thought to be drug induced. Learn the terrifying story of the Vikings at The York Dungeon.
Guy Fawkes	Remember, remember the 5th of November; gunpowder, treason and plot! Follow the explosive story of Guy Fawkes, from the traitorous plotting of his accomplices to destroy king and parliament through to the relentless torture after his capture.
Implements of Torture	A mischievous torturer will put the fun back into pain! Stretching your imagination with some backbreaking interactive torture treatments! You may just laugh till your head falls off!
Judgement of Sinners	This 17th-century judge knows exactly what you've been up to; the court isn't impressed and the punishments will be harsh! You could be left to languish in the rat-infested dungeon or be given a gruesomely fun task to perform ...
Labyrinth of the Lost Roman Legion	Enter the Labyrinth of the Lost at your peril! Discover the ancient fortress of Roman York and the Emperor Constantine, buried beneath York Minster.
The Black Death	The York Dungeon is host for the return of the most devastating and horrifying disease Europe has ever seen. The plague wiped out over 24 million people, almost half Europe's population at the time!

Source: The Dungeons, 2008

Table 9.3 Types of exhibits, shows and rides at The Edinburgh Dungeon visitor attraction with marketing descriptions

Name of exhibit, show or ride	*Marketing description*
Anatomy Theatre	If you are squeamish at the sight of modern surgery you will be in for a shock at the Edinburgh Dungeons' Anatomy Theatre. In the 18th century, medical and surgical schools were a catastrophic mess of unhygienic barbarism!
Mary King's Ghost	It is 1646 and an overwhelming stench hits you as you enter the mysterious Mary King's Close. You are suddenly struck by the horrific realisation that this is the resting place of abandoned plague victims.
Haunted Labyrinth	Enter the Edinburgh Dungeon's Haunted Labyrinth – a dark and terrifying maze of catacombs that stretch from beneath the Castle, under the Royal Mile and away into the eerie unknown.
Judgement of Sinners	Are you a sinner? If you are, you may be reluctant to enter the Judgement of Sinners exhibit at The Edinburgh Dungeon where torturous equipment lies in wait!
Sawney Bean	Some travellers have gone missing and rumours are flying around that the cannibal Sawney Bean has dragged them deep into his cave, but beware! Sawney has spotted some tasty flesh and is heading your way.
William Wallace	Feel the passion of Scotland's warrior hero, Sir William Wallace, as you experience the glory of victory against the English at the Battle of Stirling Bridge.

Source: The Dungeons, 2008

and playful mirth (see Figures 9.1–9.4). Nevertheless, a fundamental feature of The Dungeon concept is the ability to tap into visitor emotions (see Best, 2007), with the sense of shock, horror and revulsion and to create a *safe* congregant space where *unsafe* ideas of the taboo may be inspected close up through a morbid gaze (after Urry, 2002; also see Gurian, 2006; Cameron, 2003; and Chapter 4). Indeed, in The Dungeons' own visitor survey, customers are invited to judge personal 'terror levels' at the end of their visit, rating their overall 'scare factor' on a scale from being *terrified* to *slightly nervous* to *not being scared at all* (The Dungeons, 2009).

Table 9.4 Types of exhibits, shows and rides at The Amsterdam Dungeon visitor attraction with marketing descriptions

Name of exhibit, show or ride	Marketing description
Council of Blood	The Council of Blood at The Amsterdam Dungeon is a glimpse into 16th-century Holland and the primeval law enforcement that encased everyone's lives in fear.
Labyrinth of the Lost	The Amsterdam Dungeon challenges you with the notorious Labyrinth of the Lost. The Labyrinth twists and turns in a dizzying maze of passages. Enter at your own peril!
Reaper – Drop Ride to Doom	At the Amsterdam Dungeon the giant, robed figure, clutching his scythe, greets you and guides you into your seats for the Drop Ride to Doom! A strange power compels you to comply and take your place beside your fellow victims.
Soul Merchants De Voc	The shipping trade of the VOC in the 17th and 18th centuries involved journeys under horrendous conditions, with disease and death commonplace. Learn the true story behind the sailors' abhorrent suffering under the VOC.

Source: The Dungeons, 2008

These issues of terror and perceptions of customers as they consume The Dungeon experience are now explored in the context of a specific illustrative case, namely, The York Dungeon.

The York Dungeon: An empirical illustration of lighter dark tourism

York is a walled city located in northern England and is a major tourist destination. The city, with its rich history spanning almost 2000 years, originated in Roman times under the name of Eboracum and became associated with influential historical figures such as Constantine the Great. In 866, the Vikings captured the city and renamed it Jórvík. In later years, York became a centre for Christianity, particularly for the group of churches which comprise the Anglican Communion. The gothic York Minister, one of the largest cathedrals in Europe and itself a major tourist attraction, is the seat of the Archbishop of York, the second-highest office in the Church of England. Thus, York remains ecclesiastically important, representing one of the two provinces of the Church of England (the other being Canterbury in the south-east of the country).

Table 9.5 Types of exhibits, shows and rides at The Hamburg Dungeon visitor attraction with marketing descriptions

Name of exhibit, show or ride	*Marketing description*
Extremis: Drop Ride to Hell	You have been judged and sentenced and now must accept the consequences of your crimes and experience the brand new Extremis: Drop Ride to Hell! Your heart pounds with fear as the hooded hangman gleefully guides you into position and your end draws near. Muster all the courage you possess as you step over the trapdoor and prepare for your own hanging! There is no time to scream as you feel the floor give way; your heart leaps into your throat and you plummet sharply into the darkness below ...! Please be aware: you must be over 1.2 metres tall to experience the Extremis ride.
The Great Fire	It is 1842 and Hamburg is engulfed in a raging inferno! The Great Fire is swallowing the city with swathes of orange death, people are fleeing for their lives and thousands of firefighters are battling the flames.
Stortebeker's Execution	Stortebeker was a notorious pirate who sailed the seas in the 14th century. He and his crew of 70 comrades were caught and sentenced to death on 20 October 1400. The story of his execution has lived on through the centuries as legend.
Sturmflut 1717	In 1717 Hamburg was crippled by a powerful storm. The devastation and horrific casualties haunt the city to this day. Jump on board your boat in The Hamburg Dungeon and witness the heavens break and the ground shake as you ride the storm of 1717!
The Plague	Step into 1350 in The Hamburg Dungeon, when the Black Death reached the Hamburg gates, and experience the horror of civilization falling prey to the repugnant disease.

Source: The Dungeons, 2008

The York Dungeon (see Figure 9.5) is situated in a converted warehouse-style building close to the River Ouse in the city of York, and is approximately a 10-minute walk from the religiously emblematic York Minister. It is here that the juxtaposition of religion and the commercialisation of the

Figure 9.1 Dungeon exhibit illustrating torture by bleeding
Source: www.DBullock.com, 2008

supernatural and malevolence is most prominent. While York Minister trades on its awe-inspiring architecture and the promise of redemption and salvation through religious and moral conduct, the York Dungeon trades on its technology and creativity to represent pain, malice and immorality for contemporary consumption. By way of provocation, Webster (2006: 5), after her visit to a Dungeon attraction, states:

> ... it is not the study or reenactment of the gruesome histories that I object to, it is the glorification of evil. If we say we're followers of Christ, why do we choose to amuse ourselves with Satan's triumphs?

Figure 9.2 Dungeon exhibit showing a medieval torture method whereby a caged rat is placed on a prisoner's abdomen and hot coal is placed on top of the cage; the only way for the rat to escape the hot coal is to gnaw through the victim's stomach
Source: Sammiqueen, 2006

During the winter of 2008, the author undertook an exploratory ethnographic study at the York Dungeon, the principal purpose being to develop a deeper understanding of consumer experiences/perceptions of it as an example of a lighter dark tourism visitor attraction. The York Dungeon was chosen as a sample case principally owing to its geographical proximity. Research methods were triangulated through a series of (covert) participant observations, semi-structured interviews and a focus group. The participant observations were carried out at the York Dungeon over a two-day period by the author posing as a fee-paying customer. At the same time, a number of semi-structured interviews with actual customers and visitor attraction staff were also undertaken at the site. The focus group, facilitated by the author and audio-recorded, was subsequently carried out at the University of Central Lancashire, UK, its participants drawn from the university's undergraduate community. Each focus group member had visited at least one of the UK Dungeon attractions as a customer within the past two years. The limitations of this research are recognised, in particular the relatively small number of visitor interviews and the restricted composition of the focus group. Nevertheless, it was intended primarily as an exploratory study designed to identify themes and issues as a basis for further research, although, as

Figure 9.3 Visitor waiting to be impaled as 'part of the horror show' by real-life female actor at The London Dungeon
Source: Alexrk2, 2008

Figure 9.4 Torture method exhibit at the Dungeon Visitor Attractions
Source: Claytron, 2006

Figure 9.5 Visitors queuing outside The York Dungeon, York, UK
Source: Tomgensler, 2007

the following section reveals, a number of significant findings emerged that are of direct relevance to this chapter.

Consumer expectations and performative experiences

A number of key themes emerged from this exploratory study. Firstly, a disjunction became evident between consumers' *expectations* prior to the visit and their actual *experience* of the Dungeon attraction. During a site interview, for example, one visitor remarked:

> ... having not read anything about the tour we assumed that we were visiting a museum ... we expected a theatrical set up and for the exhibits to be of a gory nature, but we also anticipated an educative/informative visit – historically relevant to York and relating to crime and punishment. ... Had we known what we were going to, we would have definitely given it a miss. ... We were not expecting what we got! The York Dungeon is entertainment and uses York's history to scare visitors silly. (Interviews, 2008a)

The issue of visitors not fully realising or appreciating what the Dungeon product/experience entailed was also confirmed by Dungeon staff who suggested that 'a lot of customers come in thinking it is a museum, and soon discover it is not' (Interviews, 2008b). In particular, the interactiveness of the exhibits, especially the live actors, ensures that the distinction between traditional museology and a tourist attraction is apparent early in the tour.

Indeed, one of the first exhibits/shows at the York Dungeon is an actor portraying a barber surgeon – a medical practitioner common throughout Europe until the early 19th century. With exaggerated comical gestures and an embellished bloodied costume and make-up, the actor attempts to illustrate the perils of experimental anatomy in days gone by. With a plastic cadaver on his 'operating table', the actor playfully wrenches rubber intestines and a synthetic heart from his silent prop, as the visitor, now part of a shocked if not enthralled audience, gazes upon this morbid show. In an attempt to add relevance to the present day, the actor holds up a jar of leeches, used extensively in pre-modern clinical blood-letting, and delights in informing the audience that leeches are making a resurgence within 21st-century medical practice. The final act involves the actor choosing someone from the audience to conduct an 'experiment'. With nervous laughter, a visitor is chosen and taken behind a partition curtain and, with the lights dimmed to create a silhouette, the audience watches as the visitor/victim is sat upon a stool and the actor surgeon is seen to hold a hammer above his head. As the hammer falls (with sound effects) and the lights go out, the 'victim' is seemingly bludgeoned; the rest of the audience gasp and are then told to leave the room and to continue their tour. Of course, the visitor who volunteered to be part of the experiment soon rejoins the tour party, and his Dungeon experience continues (Obs, 2008).

While consumer expectations of the actual Dungeon product may be fragmented, perhaps due to a marketing mismatch, there was almost universal agreement from the focus group that the Dungeon concept was fun, comical and indeed clever, yet also artificial and built around fear and fantasy (Focus Group, 2008). In particular, one focus group respondent suggested 'the Dungeon did not have any soul; it was fake and empty' (Focus Group, 2008). This is despite the claim from Merlin Entertainments that 'as you delve into the darkest chapters of our grim and bloody past, recreated in its dreadful detail, remember: everything you experience *really happened*' (emphasis added; Merlin Entertainments, 2009a). With indications of historical ambiguity in the Dungeon's representations of the past, one respondent suggested her initial reaction to the Dungeon 'brand' was that it was going to be similar to that of 'Dungeon and Dragons', a fantasy adventure role-playing game first devised in the 1970s and subsequently the subject of television programmes and film animations. The respondent went on to note that, while she associated dragons as *unreal*, she also associated the Dungeon (visitor attraction) in a similar vein (Focus Group, 2008). Similarly, other respondents suggested the 'Dungeon' name was misleading as it implied a premise of crime and punishment, yet the actual attraction staged themes which went beyond penal codes and justice and included exhibits/shows depicting Hell, disease, anatomy and the supernatural (Focus Group, 2008; Interviews, 2008a). Another respondent, who again was initially confused about what to expect of the Dungeon attraction, stated 'essentially you have to pay your money to find out what is at the Dungeon' (Focus Group, 2008). Nevertheless, regardless of consumer prior expectations, what is clear is that the process of *heritagisation* – in this case, the conversion of macabre history into a product for consumption – has resulted in a fantastical *performative experience* for visitors, as illustrated by the barber-surgeon show described above. Consequently, performance theory and the concept of staged authenticity within tourism performances (MacCannell, 1989; Krishenblatt-Gimblett, 1997) may help to explain the dynamics of the Dungeon as a seemingly *heterotopic* tourist attraction which exists, in content terms at least, on the fringes of conventional leisure attractions and mainstream tourism. While a full critique of performative theory of interpretation (and experience) and its relationship with the lighter side of dark tourism is beyond the scope of this chapter, it is perhaps worth noting that performances and performative *ethics* involve respect, responsibility and care toward others and towards otherness (Jamal & Hill, 2002; see also White, 1991; Heidegger, 1996; and Chapter 3).

Ethical dimensions and psychosocial connections

Ethical and moral dimensions of the Dungeon experience were a second major theme of this exploratory study. When questioned about their personal involvement in the Dungeon experience, many respondents likened themselves to other visitors at the attraction and were non-judgemental about the ethical stance of fellow tourists. One respondent suggested that 'you can't judge someone, because you are in the same place as them – making a judgement on them is like making a judgement on yourself' (Focus Group, 2008). Similarly, respondents empathised with other tourists and a particular respondent stated: 'I see myself as within a pack of tourists moving around. I don't look down on them, as I'm one of them' (Focus Group, 2008).

Therefore it appears, perhaps understandably, that visitors do not wish to be seen as partaking in a 'morally suspect' tourist activity and are, perhaps, altruistic in their views of the ethical codes of Others. However, a more fundamental suggestion is that visitors to the Dungeon attraction are utilising the space and its contents moralistically and consequently making judgements about moral codes and standards within their own life-worlds (see Chapter 4 for a theoretical discussion on this). Indeed, one respondent suggested that punishment and torture methods from the past and re-created at the Dungeon 'can be accepted more, because that was the way it was; it was part and parcel of the past'. However, the respondent went on to clarify that past methods of punishment 'had no political inference, unlike what happened at Auschwitz, therefore it makes it [the Dungeon] more morally acceptable' (Focus Group, 2008). Here, a comparison is made with an episode of human history which still haunts contemporary imagination, namely, the Holocaust. Consequently, the respondent makes a *psychosocial connection* between what he gazed upon in terms of represented past torture at the Dungeon and Holocaust torture that is more recent and viewed as politically and racially motivated. In particular, the implication is that the gruesome past represented by the Dungeon is deemed as (morally) *acceptable* because that is how society was perceived to operate and thus considered as the norm. However, it becomes (morally) *unacceptable* when political dimensions are added and in this case the respondent compares 'immoral punishment' at Auschwitz with 'moral punishment' from a past penal system which is perceived as collective and thus socially sanctioned. As a result, the argument put forward in Chapter 4 that dark tourism places act as contemporary spaces to reflect, record and interpret moral concerns is supported, to an extent, by the embodied visitor/respondent who engaged with the Dungeon's representation of torture, pain and suffering and made moral connections with more recent tragic history. Additionally, perhaps, for this respondent the stratification of his own life-world is made apparent as he builds associations between past and present morality and, in doing so, a 'tension of consciousnesses' between the past, present and future is realised (after Schutz & Luckmann, 1974). This latter point, of course, requires further clarification and scrutiny in future research.

Even so, another illustration of this effervescent and emotional engagement with the Dungeon as a morally informative space is the respondents' reactions to the level of (re-created) punishment meted out in relation to the crime. Certainly, within the torture chambers at the York Dungeon, some visitors flinch when they see metal instruments designed intentionally to exact pain and death. During one observation, a female customer looked visibly sickened as an actor in the torture chamber demonstrated the 'Claw', a torture implement also known as the ungula or the 'Spanish Spider', the primary purpose of which was to inflict wounds to limbs, and in particular to mutilate the breasts of women (Obs, 2008). With this in mind, the focus group went on to suggest that present-day society would not accept punishment methods as represented by the Dungeon because 'we live in a better time' and 'we have been taught to accept that the law is right' (Focus Group, 2008). Crucially, though, while respondents recognised the evolution of society (for the better) and appreciated the nature of penal justice today, there were concerns that society could regress back to methods of punishment as represented in the Dungeon torture chambers (Focus Group, 2008). Indeed, the allegation of torture by American military forces at Guantanamo Bay in Cuba, where alleged terrorist suspects are incarcerated, was cited as a contemporary example of modern-day torture (Interviews, 2008a; see also AFX News, 2005; Leung, 2005). Again, respondents appear to make a psychosocial connection between their 'morbid gaze' at the Dungeon and an aspect of the Other, in this case alleged torture employed at Guantanamo Bay, which is deemed *relevant* to their own individual and collective life-world. In particular, respondents appear to fear the ethics of punishment methods employed in the past being resurrected to deal with modern-day crime, thus impacting (negatively) on intrinsically held morals and standards.

Mortality and relevancy to life-worlds

The issue of relevancy, especially with regard to mortality and its association to an individual's life-world, was a third major theme from this study. Specifically, the exhibit at York Dungeon which depicted the Black Death, a plague spread by rats carrying the bacillus now identified as *Yersinia pestis* which blighted much of Europe during the Middle Ages, was singled out by respondents as an event which generated most empathy. The Black Death exhibit portrays scenes of terror, loss of life, bereavement and graphic illustrations of the effects of bubonic plague on realistic life-sized mannequin models in medieval environments (Obs, 2008). Indeed, promotional material for the exhibit places the visitor within a recreated Plague environment:

> You are there, amid the horror ... you could try drastic remedies – filling your house with smoke; smearing yourself with your own excrement; or even sucking the pus from the boils on the dead and dying. Fear grips you. Are you already infected? In desperation you seek out a Plague Doctor. Like some huge crow in his full-length cloak, thick goggles and a beak stuffed with spices and herbs, he is almost as terrifying as the disease itself. The wait is a nightmare. Death is everywhere. Will the Plague Doctor pronounce you the latest victim? (The Dungeons, 2008)

Respondents stated that they consciously thought of the actual victims of the plague, albeit briefly, and their own life position during their Dungeon experience (Focus Group, 2008). Subsequently, a respondent noted how she extracted meanings of randomness and indiscrimination of the Plague and the arbitrary manner in which the disease afflicted 'ordinary' people. This respondent in particular, who was of Irish descent, linked her tourist experience of the Great Plague at the Dungeon with that of the consequences of the Irish Famine of the 1840s, which she perceived as another type of 'plague' and which, seemingly at random, affected the ordinary population. The respondent went on to suggest that, had she lived in these particular periods of history, she herself perhaps would have succumbed to a similar fate to that illustrated by the Dungeon (Focus Group, 2008). Again, in terms of relevancy to life-worlds, the respondent made a psychosocial connection between the Dungeon exhibit and her own socio-cultural environment. Importantly, however, this respondent viewed the death of Plague victims as unfair, causing 'innocent people to die who have not done anything wrong' (Focus Group, 2008), and empathised more with this exhibit as it 'de-sequesters death' and tapped into her consciousness of mortality, innocence and relevancy (Stone & Sharpley, 2008).

Interestingly, though, respondents suggested that, while the Black Death exhibit might make them consider their own mortality, especially within the context of 'ordinariness of victimhood', other displays such as the Dick Turpin exhibit did not. Indeed, Dick Turpin, the infamous horse-stealer and highwayman of 18th-century England who has since become a 'concoction of fiction, folklore and borrowed glory' (The Dungeons, 2008), was executed at The Mount, on the Knavesmire, near York's famous race-course. The York Dungeon, in its representation of Turpin's execution, now permits visitors to experience pseudo capital punishment. In a large pitch-black room, illuminated only by a dimly lit image of Turpin's hanging scaffold and noose and by the faint yet comforting glow of mandatory fire-exit signs, visitors are instructed to sit in silence on pew-like benches. As an actor performs the role of Thomas Hadfield, Turpin's hangman, the 'voice' of Turpin's ghost booms out through audio speakers and the audience are subjected to Turpin's angry ranting as he famously launches himself off the scaffolding to his death. At that precise moment of execution, and with accompanying sound-effects, the benches upon which the visitors are seated jolt and launch forward at 45 degrees, symbolically allowing the visitor to experience Turpin's hanging (Obs, 2008). However, respondents suggested that exhibits which feature particular criminal personalities who were prosecuted for misdemeanours were not relevant to their own life-world and, consequently, they did not empathise as much for their demise (Focus Group, 2008). Here, they made a distinction between innocent and ordinary people, as depicted in the Black Death exhibits, and the guilty and extraordinary 'mythical' characters such as Dick Turpin. In doing so, it is suggested that levels of 'mortality contemplation' vary substantially according to visitor psychosocial perceptions of relevancy, empathy and virtuousness.

Conclusion

This chapter has attempted to propel the debate beyond the rhetoric of 'darker' dark tourism. In doing so, the author has examined what has been termed 'lighter dark tourism' and the purposeful commodification of death, pain and suffering. In the context of a specific case example, namely the Dungeon visitor attractions, dark tourism consumption has been placed within a framework of fun, fear and psychosocial relevancy with visitors' own socio-cultural environments. Of course, it would be naïve to suggest that this research has generalisations for the wider population in terms of dark tourism consumption, meaning and experiences; owing to research design limitations, this is not the case. Nevertheless, this chapter in general, and the research described in particular, casts some light on possible future research avenues which, within a (lighter) dark tourism setting, may revolve around issues of consumer expectations, performative interpretation and experience, effervescent/emotional engagement of morality, and the degree of relevancy of interpretation/ meaning to individual and collective life-worlds. Additionally, as the issues noted above are called upon to be extracted, formalised and interrogated, future research may adopt a psychology context in its attempt to rigorously shore up the current fragility of (lighter) dark tourism research.

The Dungeon as a tourist attraction has strategically deployed taboo subjects and commercially exploited macabre and tragic history. As a result, the Dungeon attractions exist within the mainstream tourism sector as contemporaneous cultural spaces, acting as receptacles of 'highly charged' ideas and representations that appeal to mass-market demographics (Williams, 2001). Nihilistic narratives of fear, death, horror and violence at the Dungeons are celebrated and (re)created through mimesis, kitsch and pastiche representations. Cultural interplay is both encouraged and sanctioned by visitors who, depending upon the eclecticism of their own life-worlds and the perceived 'ordinariness' of the exhibited victim(s), extract appropriate meanings of morality and mortality. In turn, the Dungeon visitor attraction space not only allows for fun and entertainment at a rudimentary level but also, and perhaps more fundamentally, offers an emancipatory space for reassessment and self-reflexivity that allows for an optimistic reconfiguration of visitor outlooks and interpretive strategies. In doing so, the Dungeon and lighter shades of dark tourism perhaps favour the poetic use of shock in order to generate a rupture in audience conditioning and expectation and, despite obvious historical ambiguities, provide a deeper, more critically alert awareness of things-as-they-were (Lavine, 1991). It is on this premise of how things were and how things are now that psychosocial connections are potentially made by visitors within the Dungeon attractions, whereby gruesome moments from history are illuminated for the present day and, in turn, cast light on otherwise unseen (taboo) subjects.

Acknowledgements

The author wishes to thank the following people for their valued insights and contribution to this chapter: Olivia Newton, Sinead Renouf, Tom Richens, Lauren Semans, Nichola West, Stephanie Keith, Mark Pearson and Alysaa Nicholls.

Chapter 10

Battlefield Tourism: Bringing Organised Violence Back to Life

FRANK BALDWIN and RICHARD SHARPLEY

Introduction

Battlefields, military graves, memorials and other sites associated with warfare have attracted visitors for well over a thousand years. In the year 334, for example, Alexander the Great interrupted his invasion of Asia to visit ancient Troy and the Tomb of Achilles while, throughout history, significant battles have been commemorated in one way or another. Thus, Simonides' epigram to the Spartans at the site of the Battle of Thermopylae (480 BC), Battle Abbey and the Bayeux Tapestry, both dating back to the late 11th century and commemorating the Battle of Hastings in 1066, and the Lion Mound at Waterloo (completed in 1826) are all well known and much visited examples of battle memorials.

Over the last century, however, war-related tourism has increased significantly, reflecting both the growth of tourism more generally and also the number of wars and other military conflicts that have occurred (and continue to occur) since the early 1900s. In particular, the First World War represents a watershed in the emergence of battlefield tourism. That is, although there is evidence of earlier organised travel to battlefield sites during the latter half of the 1800s, the Battle of Waterloo being a notable example (Seaton, 1999), it was after the First World War that visits to battlefield sites – or battlefield tourism – emerged on a larger scale (Lloyd, 1998). Since then, war-related tourism has expanded dramatically, to the extent that 'the memorabilia of warfare and allied products ... probably constitutes the largest single category of tourist attractions in the world' (Smith, 1996: 248). Of course, such attractions include not only battlefields and associated on-site memorials and graveyards, but also innumerable memorials, museums and other structures and places that commemorate wars, battles and associated events or atrocities. Nevertheless, not only are battlefields, as a sub-category of the totality of warfare attractions, 'a quintessential example of that form of attraction which has been called "dark tourism" ... or "thanatourism"' (Seaton, 1999: 131), but their significance and role, both as sites of frequently large-scale 'licensed' death and atrocity and, subsequently, as tourist attractions, remains the subject of intense debate (Fyall *et al.*, 2006; Ryan, 2007a). Therefore, the purpose of this chapter is to consider, through the context of battlefields, the fundamental relationship between tourism and war and, drawing on the case of tourism to the First and Second World War battlefields of northern Europe, to explore the motives for and management of tourism to such sites.

Battlefield Tourism: An Overview

As observed above, battlefield tourism is not a new phenomenon. Historically, visits to the sites of famous battles have long been in evidence although it is only in more recent times, commensurate with the emergence of modern tourism, that tourism to battlefields, either as specifically motivated trips or as part of a holiday or tour, has become more popular and widespread. Undoubtedly, the first and most enduring example of battlefield tourism is Waterloo where, according to Seaton (1999), three sequential groups of tourists can be identified: those who witnessed the actual battle on 18 June 1815; those who visited the site in its immediate aftermath (journalists, relatives of the dead and injured, government functionaries); and 'recreational tourists' (Seaton, 1999: 136) who, to the present day, have continued to visit the site in large numbers. For the latter group, a local tourism sector soon sprang up to meet the needs of visitors, while the nascent tour-operating industry in the UK ran frequent trips to Brussels and Waterloo from the 1850s (Swinglehurst, 1974). By the early 1900s, tours were also being offered to the South African battlefields of the Boer War, with Thomas Cook, for example, organising trips to the battlefields well before the conclusion of hostilities in 1902 (Lloyd, 1998). Around the same period, legislation in the USA in 1890 enabled the establishment of National Battlefield Parks, the purpose primarily being to 'memorialise the bravery and sacrifice of those who died on them' (Hanink & Stutts, 2002), though they soon became popular tourist destinations. In particular, Gettysburg, the site in 1863 of the bloodiest battle of the American Civil War (and, subsequently, of Lincoln's famous Gettysburg Address), has long been the country's most visited battlefield site, currently attracting over 2 million tourists a year (Chronis, 2005).

Following the end of the First World War, large numbers of tourists began to visit the sites of the major battles. Indeed, the overall growth in tourism post-1918 can be explained by the fact that 'many hundreds of thousands of people, from all parts of the world, rushed to the scene of war during the years immediately following 1918 merely to satisfy a morbid curiosity' (Norvall, cited in Lloyd, 1998: 29). People travelled either on trips offered by commercial tour operators or joined pilgrimages organised by a variety of voluntary bodies, such as the YMCA or the Salvation Army. Most notably, a pilgrimage to Belgium and France organised by the British Legion in 1928 attracted over 11,000 participants and remains the largest such trip to the battlefields of the First World War. Interestingly, some 30 guidebooks to the battlefields were produced between 1919 and 1921 (Lloyd, 1998: 30), a trend that continues to this day (e.g. Seaton, 2000b; Thompson, 2004a, b).

The Second World War similarly contributed to a subsequent growth in battlefield tourism, both in Europe and elsewhere. For example, numerous battlefields or sites of conflict in the Pacific region, from Pearl Harbour to Hiroshima, continue to attract large numbers of tourists (Cooper, 2006). Equally, more recent conflicts, such as the Vietnam War, have been followed by an increase in related tourism activity (Henderson, 2000). It is now possible, for example, to visit the sites of battles between the British and Argentine forces (made famous by the almost instantaneous global coverage on television) during the Falklands conflict (www.visitorfalklands. com). Overall, battlefield tourism has become a significant sector of the tourism market, supported by a large number of dedicated tour operators and promoted by national or local tourism bodies anxious to 'cash in' on the heritage of war and battle.

A complete review of battlefield tourism is beyond the scope of this chapter (see, e.g. Ryan, 2007a). Nevertheless, a number of key issues underpin the debates surrounding the subject, collectively embraced by the distinction between battlefield 'tourism' and 'pilgrimage'. As Lloyd (1998: 20) observes, even by the late 1800s there was 'already uncertainty about the appropriateness of battlefield tourism', the commercialised or, perhaps, ghoulish (or thanatoptic) gazing upon sites of mass suffering and death contrasting with the desire of those to commemorate the fallen or to make sense of enormous sacrifice. The commercial exploitation of battlefields is satirised in the following poem, 'High Wood', written by a serviceman in 1918.

> Ladies and gentlemen, this is High Wood,
> Called by the French, Bois des Furneaux,
> The famous spot which in Nineteen-Sixteen,
> July, August and September was the scene
> Of long and bitterly contested strife,
> By reason of its High commanding site.
> Observe the effect of shell-fire in the trees
> Standing and fallen; here is wire; this trench
> For months inhabited, twelve times changed hands;
> (They soon fall in), used later as a grave.

It has been said on good authority
That in the fighting for this patch of wood
Were killed somewhere above eight thousand men,
Of whom the greater part were buried here,
This mound on which you stand being .... Madame, please,
You are requested kindly not to touch
Or take away the Company's property
As souvenirs; you'll find we have on sale
A large variety, all guaranteed.
As I was saying, all is as it was,
This is an unknown British officer,
The tunic having lately rotted off.
Please follow me – this way ..... the path, sir, please,
The ground which was secured at great expense
The Company keeps absolutely untouched,
And in that dug-out (genuine) we provide
Refreshments at a reasonable rate.
You are requested not to leave about
Paper, or ginger-beer bottles, or orange peel,
There are waste-paper baskets at the gate.

Philip Johnston

This distinction between tourism and pilgrimage gives rise to a number of questions, including: how should battlefield landscapes be interpreted: the glorification of war or the promotion of peace? How should battlefields be managed – sanitised and 'cleansed' or maintained with the detritus of war? Does the passing of time reduce the sanctity of battlefields? Can or should battlefields be promoted as symbols of national identity (Slade, 2003)? How can the sacrifice of thousands provide meaning and understanding to contemporary visitors? It is to some of these issues that this chapter now turns.

What follows is from a battlefield tour practitioner's perspective. That is, it based upon experience and observations gained from the planning and leading of tours principally to First World War battlefields, though it also draws upon research undertaken by the Royal British Legion (the UK's leading charity providing financial, social and emotional support to the ex-Service community and their families) on the experience, attitudes and intentions of visitors to battlefields, cemeteries and war memorials overseas, as well as conceptual models relevant to the visitation of battlefield sites. It explores differing motives for visiting battlefield sites within the context of the tourist–pilgrim dichotomy before highlighting implications for the management of such sites. It then concludes with a number of short case studies.

Battlefield Tours: A Practitioner's Perspective

As observed above, battlefields are arguably one of the most visited thanatourist sites. But few visitors to battlefields would happily regard themselves as 'dark tourists' or 'thanatourists'. Many would be horrified to think that academia places them in the same category as, for example, those who travel to witness the sites of disasters or visitors to sites of murder or execution, linked by a common thread of visiting places of death. Soldiers in battle are licensed to break one of society's profound rules and are potentially murderer and victim in the service of their community. We do not treat soldiers in the same way that we would other killers or their victims; we have a set of attitudes and a language to soldiers. These, in turn, have an impact on our attitudes to visits to battlefields, memorials and war graves and the business of battlefield tourism.

By way of introducing the following discussion of battlefield tourism, it is firstly interesting to note some of the findings of a survey commissioned by the Royal British Legion in 2006. Based upon a sample of 1000 respondents across the UK, this found, among other things, that:

- 28% of people had visited a battlefield or war memorial overseas.
- 34% of men and 11% of women said that they were interested in military history.
- 43% of women and 30% of men said that they were interested in family history.
- 32% of the people interested in family history and 46% of people interested in military history had visited a battlefield grave or war memorial overseas.
- Around 6% of men and 4% of women said that they definitely planned to visit an overseas battlefield; 25% of men and 20% of women said they possibly planned to make such a visit.
- No significant differences were identified between social class or regional background with respect to interest in battlefields. However, there was a difference in the experience of visiting battlefields, with 47% of adult respondents from social economic classes A and B (senior/middle management, administrative or professional) reporting that they had visited an overseas battlefield, war cemetery or war memorial compared to 27% C1, 20% C2, 17% D and 16% E. This is probably a function of greater wealth to support overseas travel.

More specific reference is made to these findings below. However, in order to consider the reasons why people visit, or may consider visiting, battlefields, it is first useful to distinguish between the two forms of visitation referred to above, namely, *pilgrimage* and *battlefield tours*.

Dictionary definitions of pilgrimage offer themes of travel for religious endeavour, spiritual comfort or enlightenment, themes which are central to debates regarding the 'spiritual dimension' of contemporary tourism (Timothy & Olsen, 2006; Sharpley, *forthcoming*). For the purpose of this chapter, however, *pilgrimage* is defined as travel to and visitation of battlefield memorials for remembrance, the focus being on the spiritual value of visiting a grave. The purpose of a battlefield *tour*, conversely, is to understand what happened and why. This too can be an act of remembrance, but through understanding what the people did and why they did it. Thus, the distinction between battlefield pilgrimage and tours is blurred in practice, although it is of course possible, on the one hand, for some pilgrims to have no interest in the history or, on the other, to visit a battlefield without any element of pilgrimage or homage to the dead.

Pilgrimage to Battlefield Sites and Grieving

One of the most powerful reasons to visit battlefields is to grieve for the dead; indeed, visiting graves and memorials to the dead is a common cultural ritual. Bushaway (1993) describes how the British language and customs of remembrance are derived from the experience of the Great War, providing us with a framework for interpreting the battlefield as a sacred place. He argues that the images and role of the battlefield as sacred ground evolved as a response to the losses and the pyrrhic nature of the victory of 1918. Table 10.1 summarises the transformation of what Bushaway refers to as the 'sustaining ideology' between the beginning of the Great War and its end. His list of concepts, or 'sustaining ideologies', recognisably reflects the language of the battlefield pilgrim and of the memorials to the fallen.

Table 10.1 The transformation of sustaining ideologies

1914	*1919*
Specific war aims	World peace
Patriotism	Supranationalism
Service/duty	Sacrifice
Heroism	Sanctification
Casualties	The Fallen/The Glorious Dead
Comradeship	Fellowship
The soldier's experiences	Christ's Crucifixion
Victory	Expiation and redemption
Battlefields	Holy or sacred ground
Defeat of Germany	Defeat of war

Source: Adapted from Bushaway (1993)

The British Legion (as it was until 1971) has been instrumental in perpetuating this particular framework, while the language of the 1928 Great Pilgrimage guide is still relevant:

> We Pilgrims are going to offer homage to the dead of the British Empire ... the great majority of whom lie buried in those beautiful cemeteries in France and Flanders. And in this act itself we shall be bringing consolation to the widows and orphans, the mother who has lost her boy, the maiden the man of her choice. Those who are not able to come themselves will learn from those who have seen, how comforting is the serene beauty of those white headstones. (Harter & Gavin, 1929)

Other countries may do things differently, although some of the themes are common. Moreover, the sentiments have much in common with Lincoln's Gettysburg address: 'We cannot dedicate – we can not consecrate – we can not hallow – this ground. The brave men, living and dead, who struggled here, have consecrated it, far above our poor power to add or detract'. The struggles of the combatants have hallowed this ground, which is sacred. The living are charged with a duty to fulfil the cause.

From experience and observation, it is evident that there are differences in the types of battlefield visitors who can be seen to visit as an act of pilgrimage and/or grieving:

Widows, veterans and immediate family

Grief is a human process and visiting a grave is important for many people to manage grief. Thus, veterans revisit to pay respects to old comrades who did not come back, while such visits may also form part of the personal healing process (Figure 10.1). For example, St Dunstan's, a Forces charity in the UK, once helped to pay for a Falklands War veteran to revisit the scene of his injury; similarly, the Medical Officer of one army unit has recommended that several post-traumatic stress disorder patients should revisit the battlefield as part of their cure. Some people, such as widows or immediate family members, may also find the revisit important and therapeutic. For example, when death in battle has ended a marriage, the visit to a grave can be significant. In some cases, widows have visited the grave of a husband they last saw 65 years ago and return looking 10 years younger or more at peace with themselves. It is also often seen as an opportunity to finish conversations that have been unsaid for a lifetime. As a more specific example, Mrs Doreen Sutherland married her husband in 1938. When her husband sailed for Africa as an officer in the Royal Artillery she was pregnant with her first son; she saw him on leave just once before he was killed in action in Italy in 1944. He never saw his youngest son. Subsequently, her sons visited their father's grave in the

Figure 10.1 Battlefield as a place of pilgrimage. Royal British Legion Pilgrimage, Mohnesee, 2008
Photo: Keith Wiseman

1960s but, at the time, suggested that Doreen might not like to visit. Forty years later, she heard from a friend that the British Government paid for war widows to visit their spouses' graves and so, at the age of 89, she went – and found the visit extremely therapeutic. She is now a keen advocate of the scheme and has since helped the Royal British Legion to promote it.

Second and third generations

It is not only immediate relatives who feel grief. In one instance on a battlefield tour (see Case Study 2), a 14-year-old schoolgirl from a small town in North Yorkshire had a name and cemetery on a piece of paper. We searched for the cemetery on a hot day. The rest of the class stayed on the coach while the guide took the girl to the grave of her great aunt's father. She traced the names of her great uncle and great aunt at the base of the gravestone: '*We will never forget you, Bert and Mabel*', and burst into tears, overcome with emotion. She was alone apart from the guide; here was someone grieving for a distant relative.

More generally, experience shows that the British public is quite capable of feeling strong emotions over the deaths of distant figures, and the graves and battlefields of the world wars are particularly powerful means of exposing that emotion.

Family history

There can be pride in knowing that you are related to a dead hero and a sense of identity from their experience and endeavour. Family history is one of the fastest growing hobbies in both Britain and America and one of the most popular search topics on the internet. As a consequence of this growing interest in genealogy, increasing numbers of people are discovering that they have relatives who fought and died in battle. The Royal British Legion research referred to above revealed that, overall, 37% of people had an interest in family history (though with a gender bias of 43% of women and 30% of men) and that a significant proportion of them had visited, or were interested in visiting, a battlefield.

Public grief and pilgrimages

As suggested earlier, battlefield pilgrimages can be defined as travelling for remembrance with the focus on the spiritual and emotional experience of visiting graves and memorials. Many countries have a tradition of organising travel to commemorate significant anniversaries of bloody battles. The Gettysburg address, for example, arguably the most powerful piece of American rhetoric, was delivered to an audience of battlefield pilgrims, while there are numerous contemporary examples of such commemoration which attract battlefield pilgrims. There is an act of Remembrance at the Menin Gate in Ypres every day, while there are regular anniversary services at the Thiepval Memorial to the Missing on the anniversary of the first day of the Somme. Battlefields may also become national symbols or part of national myths. The American ceremonies at the St. Laurent Cemetery on the bluffs above Omaha Beach, for example, are a powerful symbol of the sacrifice of the new world to save the old, while the Israeli Army pilgrimage to Masada is a symbol of national will. In 1921, King George V made a pilgrimage to the battlefields of the Great War. Over 80 years later his grand daughter, Queen Elizabeth II, visited Ypres at the centre of the 90th anniversary commemorations of the Battle of Passchendale.

Through ceremonies, religious services and pilgrimages, battlefields (or related memorials, such as the Cenotaph in London) can be public national symbols of grief. The Royal British Legion's rituals and ceremony illustrate some of the themes of public remembrance. Their Pilgrimages are led by a senior member of the organisation, the 'National Chairman's Representative'. The tour is accompanied by a Standard Bearer. The standards play a significant part in the ritual of Remembrance. Besides the symbolic salutation of the lowered standard over the grave, it also provides a photogenic visual image. These public representatives give the pilgrim visible evidence of the support of the nation's custodians of remembrance. The nation is with the pilgrim at the graveside. There is also a balance between allowing someone the privacy to visit a grave and the support of a group showing public respect.

The social dimension of pilgrimage

The act of travelling together provides a social dynamic for a visit to a battlefield. A pilgrimage is likely to be a significant family milestone, perhaps as significant as an important wedding anniversary. The setting and stimulus can also act as a trigger for family conversations that will not happen on any other occasion, and may be once-in-a-lifetime experiences. For example, a brother and sister and their families take their mother to visit the scene of her father's wartime experiences and pay respects to his fallen comrades; similarly, a veteran takes his children to show them where he was lucky to escape death. These are occasions where generations can contemplate their personal link with fate. As one nine-year-old on a tour said: 'So if great-granddad hadn't been wounded here and met great granny in England – we wouldn't be here at all.'

In a similar vein, a pilgrimage can stimulate conversations between generations that would not happen anywhere else. A daughter takes her father to visit the grave of his old station commander, a famous bomber pilot. She is a busy executive, he is a reticent quiet man. The company of a few old airmen, and a few days in each others company, means that they have an opportunity to talk. She comments at the end of the tour: 'I have learned so much about my father'.

Pilgrimage is also a social occasion or event. As considered at length in Chapter 2 of this book, death is, arguably, the modern taboo; people are uncomfortable about talking to the bereaved or about their own feelings. Yet the presence of other people in a tour visiting graves or memorials can be very comforting and therapeutic, while the experience of travelling as pilgrims can make for strong friendships; the act of travelling together enables people share experiences and to form lasting bonds. For example, some of The Royal British Legion's pilgrims to Holland have travelled together for many of the last 25 years.

Battlefield Tours

In comparison to a pilgrimage, which is rooted in some spiritual need to pay respects to the dead, a battlefield tour has the purpose of understanding what happened and why. Thus, the essence of a battlefield tour is to visit the site and to gain a greater understanding of the battle from a study of the detail of the ground over which the battle was fought. Even the closest study from books, maps and primary sources does not tell the whole picture, and so the fine detail of the ground, referred to as 'micro-terrain' by Richard Holmes (2006), can provide a key to understanding the events of a battle. For example, it is necessary to stand in the shallow re-entrant on Omaha Beach below the US cemetery at Coleville Sur Mer to understand how this provided a covered route for the US soldiers who captured the D-Day Defences on the bluffs. The ground also allows the visitor to see something of the view that the soldier may have seen although, of course, the level of battle damage, combined with the passage of time and modern development, may have changed the site to the extent that visitors are required to exercise varying degrees of imagination in their experience of the site.

There are several observable types of battlefield (tour) visitor.

Veterans

Many veterans seek to understand more about the overall campaign in which they participated. They may be vividly aware of their own experience, but seek to understand the wider picture. A guided battlefield tour may be the first time that they have understood what happened or the significance of their own role. Moreover, on occasions, veterans can provide additional information that helps historians enhance their knowledge of particular battles or events. For example, one British Army Staff College Battlefield Tour included two German veterans, Generals Hans von Luck and von Rosen. During the visit, the testimony of the veterans provided the reason why a German counterattack with very heavy Tiger tanks commanded by von Rosen was halted; they were stopped by the fire from their own anti-tank guns under the command of von Luck (Daglish, 2005). Veterans also often seek to visit during the major anniversaries, during which they meet old comrades and receive public acknowledgement and acclaim for their efforts and the sacrifices of their comrades. This can be very important to the self-esteem of people who may feel that society has forgotten their sacrifices and does not value them. Indeed, some veterans appear to install themselves for several weeks on the Normandy battlefields in locations where they can meet tourists and talk to them.

Leisure visitors

The vast majority of modern tourists at battlefields are not veterans, but individuals with a leisure interest in military history. Royal British Legion market research revealed that 34% of men and 11% of women describe themselves as 'interested in military history'. Of these, 46% indicated that they had visited a battlefield overseas, suggesting that a significant market exists among this group. This popular interest would appear to be rooted in society's fascination with the soldier and battle. The soldier is uniquely licensed to be both executioner and victim. Soldiers risk their lives for their country; it is seen as an ultimate test of manhood (Holmes, 2006).

As Dr Johnson once said, 'Every man thinks less of himself for having never been a soldier.' In the modern world, the popular active interest in battles and military history stretches well beyond the diminishing proportion of the population who serve in the armed forces. Not only is military history (both factual and 'factional', or fiction based on fact) a major publishing genre, but there also exist re-enactment groups for almost every period of military history, while war gaming is a popular hobby. Moreover, popular films such as *Saving Private Ryan*, or TV series such as *Band of Brothers* or the *Sharpe* series generate significant interest, as a specific form of movie-induced tourism, in visiting the locations for the actions portrayed.

An interest in military history can, therefore, take many forms. The majority of enthusiasts who visit battlefields may read relevant books, watch TV or films, or have played a computer game or some other war game. Others may have a wide-ranging interest in military history, while yet others may restrict their interest to particular campaigns or periods, such as the Great War or the English Civil War. A minority may have a more proactive or intensive interest, including:

- *Re-enactors or living history enthusiasts.* There are a substantial number of military history enthusiasts whose interest takes the form of dressing in the clothing and equipment of historic prototypes. Besides visiting sites themselves, re-enactors or 'Living History' groups provide a spectacle for the public and a focus for a visit to a historic site. They also enable visitors to visualise the site and obtain some (albeit sanitised) understanding of the reality of life in the period. Although many re-enactment events are not related to a specific historic battlefield, a significant number are and, paradoxically, become larger events than the original. For example, the 2008 Gettysburg re-enactment attracted an estimated 20,000–30,000 participants, far more than took part in many American Civil War engagements!
- *Collectors.* Some battlefield visitors appear motivated by the desire to 'collect' some aspect of battlefields in the same way that people collect stamps or trading cards. For example, there is one British battlefield tourist who plans to visit all British battlefields; he doesn't appear to have any particular interest in a particular period, just a self-determined goal as a focus for days out. There are also those who seek to visit the sites of Victoria Cross (the highest military honour in Britain) actions and the graves of those who have been awarded the VC. More problematically, there are, in addition, visitors who collect battlefield artefacts, often using metal detectors and, on occasion, finding and robbing graves of the war dead.
- *Preservationists.* Threats to historic battlefields, either from neglect or development, often generate interest among military history enthusiasts. In addition, the Battlefields Trust, a UK-based charity with the

aim of battlefield preservation, interpretation and education, was founded during the unsuccessful campaign to prevent a major road being built over the southern end of the Battlefield of Naseby.

Educational visits

Importantly, schools and other educational establishments organise visits to battlefields. There are several features of educational visits to battlefields that differ from more general leisure visits. Typically, educational tourists will be intending to meet certain learning objectives. A tour may also provide support for particular parts of the national curriculum, while teachers may have a personal interest in military history and seek to share that enthusiasm and interest.

It is estimated that, in the UK, around 30% of schools undertake tours to battlefields although, in recent years, the proportion of schools undertaking out-of-school activities in general has been falling, primarily due to Health and Safety regulations. Nevertheless, visiting battlefields provides an opportunity to bring history to life, allowing History students to have a greater understanding of what it might feel like to be a soldier of the time. Similarly, for the English department, a tour provides the background and context for an understanding of literature or art inspired by conflict, while Religious Studies provides a framework for visits to sites of mass slaughter in order to explore the spiritual issues and the reactions of different faiths. Travel to relevant battlefields can be an activity that provides language students with an activity on, say, a trip to France or Germany.

The experience of visiting battlefields may also provide young people with an opportunity to explore their reactions to death, perhaps reflecting the potential mediating role of dark tourism as discussed in the first section of this book. Certainly, the sight of the names on the walls of the missing, the sheer scale of the cemeteries and an understanding of what happened on the battlefield provokes some thought about mortality in almost everyone of any age.

Visits by the Armed Forces

An interesting category of battlefield visitors are members of the Armed Forces who, perhaps, view the battlefield as a future as well as a past. Soldiers have been visiting battlefields for professional study for centuries, a practice that has been documented by Peter Caddick-Addams (2007). The British Armed Forces draw distinctions between different usages of a battlefield for training and study or, more specifically, between a battlefield tour (a passive experience with a guide lecturing to the tour from a series of static locations; see Figure 10.2) and a so-called 'staff ride', which places greater emphasis on preparation, participation and learning. A staff ride might require participants to draw leadership lessons or even

Figure 10.2 A battlefield for professional study. Normandy Platoon Army Training Regiment: Pirbright Realities of War Battlefield Tour, Ypres Salient, February 2008. By the time this book is published, many of these soldiers will have served in Iraq or Afghanistan
Photo: Keith Wiseman

plan how they might tackle the same ground with modern troops. The same study without the historic content becomes a Tactical Exercise without Troops (TEWT) or a tactical planning exercise (see Figure 10.3).

Since 2001, the British Army has sent soldiers undertaking their basic training to visit battlefields of the First and Second World Wars. These tours are integrated with the vocational training for soldiers, the focus for those early in their training being on the core values of the British Army. Soldiers at a more advanced stage of training are expected to relate their military knowledge to the historic battlefield and, perhaps, relate historic lessons to their own operational battlefield experience.

There are also several non-military organisations that use battlefields as the basis for management training. Two such organisations in the UK are Business Battlefields and Corporate Battlefields, each offering management or leadership development programmes based on battlefield sites as, effectively, civilian versions of staff rides.

Peace visits

Finally, battlefield tours may be used to promote peace and reconciliation. For example, the International School for Peace Studies in Messines,

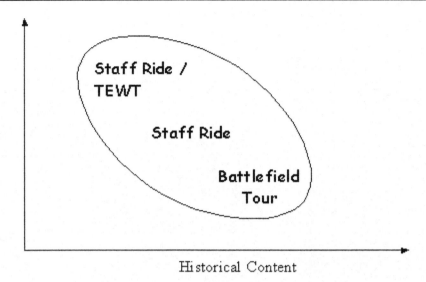

Historical Content

Figure 10.3 Staff ride – battlefield tour continuum
Source: Adapted from Caddick-Adams (2007)

Belgium, has used the surroundings of the Great War battlefields as the setting for reconciliation programmes across the sectarian divides in Northern Ireland. The School was created to exploit the potential for mutual understanding, respect for differences, and reconciliation through remembrance of the unique events of June 1917, when the traditionally opposing factions of Irish politics, namely, Catholic nationalists and Protestant unionists, fought side by side for a common cause in Mesen/ Messines, Belgium. The International School for Peace Studies offers a venue and a vision for all, in a non-threatening, peaceful setting where participants will be given the opportunity to understand first-hand the realities of brutal conflict, and where through expert facilitation they will be encouraged to engage in educational and training programmes (www. schoolforpeace.com).

Battlefield Tours: Implications

There are, then, numerous roles played by battlefields as tourist sites, from destinations for tourist-pilgrims to contemporary training grounds for military personnel. Equally, there is a significant diversity with respect to the motivations and behaviour of visitors to battlefield sites. Indeed, such is this diversity that it is difficult, if not impossible, to describe or categorise all forms of battlefield-related tourism. Nevertheless, visits to battlefield sites may be conceptualised according to different criteria.

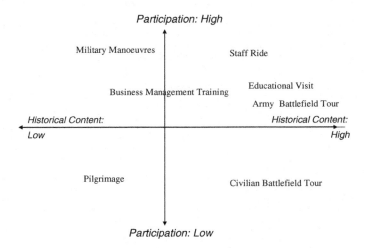

Figure 10.4 High vs. low participation battlefield visits
Source: Adapted from Caddick-Adams (2007)

Figure 10.4, for example, locates different types of battlefield on a grid according to levels of participation and historical interest.

Here the positioning of pilgrimage reflects relatively passive behaviour with little historical interest (but, as discussed above, a greater spiritual 'interest' in the meaning or manner of death), whereas an educational visit may involve greater participation based on deeper historical interest. Alternatively, Figures 10.5 and 10.6 model the two broad drivers of

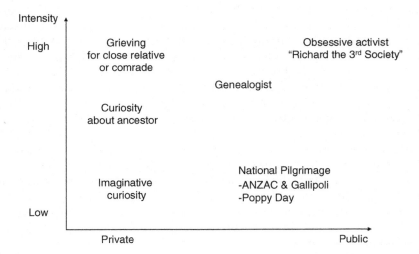

Figure 10.5 Pilgrimage, grieving and battlefield tours

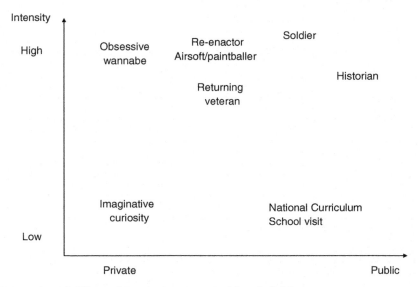

Figure 10.6 Military history interest and battlefield tours

battlefield tourism considered in this chapter, (grief/family interest and historical interest), identifying different types of activity according to levels of intensity on the vertical axis and the extent to which it is a personal or shared (public) activity on the horizontal axis.

The conceptual basis of these models may not survive rigorous analysis. However, on the one hand, not only do they reveal the breadth of activity and purpose underpinning battlefield tourism but, significantly, they also call into question the general categorisation of visits to battlefield sites as 'dark tourism'. That is, although battlefields and other sites and attractions related to war are frequently referred to collectively as 'dark tourism' sites, such a categorisation is both misleading and over-generalises the diversity of purpose and activity of visits to battlefields. Certainly, battlefield tourism as pilgrimage, focusing on achieving some spiritual meaning from visiting the graves of fallen soldiers, may be seen as a form of dark tourism, but it would be difficult and illogical to similarly label the active use of battlefield sites for management training as 'dark'. Thus, care should be taken in attaching the term 'dark tourism' to all forms of battlefield tourism.

On the other hand, the models provide a useful basis for segmenting the market for battlefield tourism businesses. The different needs and motives, for example, between a group of pilgrims and a group of battlefield tourists require different service design and different messages for customers. For example:

- The marketing strategy of a battlefield tour needs to take account of the sensitivities of different types of visitor. A battlefield tour of a

Second World War battlefield may include detailed descriptions of the nature of armoured warfare and the experience of the individual soldier. However, though of interest to the military historian, this is unlikely to be welcomed by a grieving pilgrim, who may not wish to dwell too closely on exactly what happens when a tank is hit by an armour-piercing shell. Similarly, the presence of re-enactors can be a very sensitive issue, in particular to serving soldiers or veterans.

- The design of the tour, its content, the accommodation provided and its intangible elements should, of course, take into account the differences between various types of visitors. This affects the promotional messages, nature and style of content as well as the logistics of touring.
- Destinations managers need to be able to provide services that can support a range of visitors' needs. For example, experience shows that remembrance events play a significant role in determining the popularity of First and Second World War battle sites – for example, the daily Menin Gate Ceremony in Ypres Belgium attracts hundreds of tourists every day. Thus, formal and regular commemorations may be a particularly effective marketing tool at battlefield sites.
- For those sites which attract children, including school groups, care must be taken over the way in which death is presented to them (for example, the extent to which they are exposed to harrowing images of warfare and death) and a degree of judgement is inherent in the presentation of the site; younger generations may wish to consider the meaning and relevance of wars within the context of their contemporary life and society.

Given the diverse and complex nature of battlefield tourism, it is, of course, difficult to identify more specific implications relevant to the management and presentation of all battlefield sites. Therefore, to conclude this chapter, a number of short case studies are now provided to demonstrate the complexity of issues surrounding the practice of battlefield tourism.

Conclusion: Case Studies

Case 1: Memorials and battlefields

Battlefields attract memorials. People erect memorials to the dead, to their heroes or to an image evoked by the battle. The Battlefield of Waterloo is a good example (Seaton, 1999). In the years after the battle, memorials were erected to individuals such as Colonel Alexander Gordon, one of Wellington's aides. The Dutch erected a memorial to their Crown Prince on one of the most visible parts of the battlefield, the famous Lion Mound, while the most numerous memorials are to the French. Many of these were erected many decades after the battle. For example, Victor Hugo's column and the Dying Eagle are memorials erected by a later generation of French to their Napoleonic ideals. In recent years, visitors have erected new memorials on this old battlefield, including memorials to British Regiments and artillery batteries.

Undoubtedly, memorials provide a reason for people to visit battle-fields; they provide a focus for public and private remembrance. This is particularly true of the memorials to the missing. They also provide evidence on the ground of the battle – without memorials, visitors can be disappointed. They may also possess an aesthetic quality that attracts interest. For example, the memorials to the missing by Lutyens, Blomfeld and Jaggers and the Canadian memorials at Vancouver Corner and Vimy Ridge are stunning pieces of sculpture and architecture and, hence, attractions in their own right.

However, the proliferation of memorials can make it harder to under-stand the battle itself, what happened and why. The Lion Mound at Waterloo was built from the soil on the Allied position. This resulted in lowering the ridge by some 1–2 metres and making it harder to interpret the battle. The Lutyens memorial to the Missing of the Somme was built in the centre of the German position at Thiepval, a key part of the battlefield. It is an eye-catching landmark visible for miles, a vast memorial arch set in a park of trees. However, the park and trees obstruct the view from the memorial so that it is no longer possible to appreciate the arcs of fire that the defenders faced, making it harder to understand why Thiepval was so important.

Case 2: The girl in the cemetery

A 15-year-old schoolgirl from Yorkshire visits the Somme. She has brought with her the name of a soldier and a grave reference researched by her family. It is a distant relative, her grandmother's uncle. She and her family live in North Yorkshire while the dead soldier was a Hampshire man from Portsmouth. There is an inconsistency in that the student has been told by her family that this man has no known grave, but it is clearly a reference to a plot in a cemetery.

It is a hot day and close to lunchtime by the time we find the cemetery. It is one of three with the same name and it is not until the last cemetery that we find the grave that we are looking for. The only people to leave the tour bus are the student herself, a couple of her friends, the group leader and the battlefield guide. The tour guide and the student find the grave. The others are scattered around the cemetery. The student stands at the grave – and bursts into tears. She says: 'I thought you had gone' and points to the phrase at the bottom of the grave, something like 'Dutiful Father of Fred and Rose', her grandmother's cousins.

This looked like a personal reaction. None of her friends were there so this response was not to meet some social expectation. She was not playing to the crowd. Not every young person who visits the grave of a relative has such a visible response, but it is clear that even distant relatives can provoke some deep emotions.

Case 3: Henry Compton School

Henry Compton School is a comprehensive school for boys aged 11–16 in Fulham, West London. The students are from very diverse backgrounds. In February 2007, they appeared on a television programme called Fortune TV, where good causes could bid for funding from a panel of millionaires. They wanted funding to take a party of students to visit the battlefields of the Great War and to visit the memorial to Walter Tull (the first black British outfield footballer and commissioned officer). One panellist voted against the bid after questioning the students, explaining that, in his opinion, 'none of these kids will get anything from visiting the battlefields'.

About 40 students from years 9–12 (i.e. ages 13–16) took a tour to the Western Front in March 2007. It was a very diverse group, with students from Afghan, Algerian, Cuban–Irish, Libyan, Moroccan, Nigerian, Syrian and Portuguese backgrounds. The school was originally founded as a board school in the last decade of the 19th century, and still has the Roll of Honour from the Great War; therefore, they were able to visit the graves and tell the stories about people who had walked the same school corridors and sat in the same classrooms. The tour found a local hero, Edward Dwyer, a Fulham boy who was born a few hundred yards from the school and who won the Victoria Cross in 1915. During the course of the three-day tour, we found graves, memorials or battles that provided evidence of the participation of people from the same backgrounds as all the students on the tour. The Afghans found familiar names on the Menin Gate among the solders of the (North-west) Frontier Force; the Moroccans saw the memorial to the Moroccans at Vimy Ridge and the huge number of Muslim graves in the French cemetery at Neuville St Vaast, near Arras, France. After a while, everyone wanted to know what people like them did in the Great War. We found Russian graves in Arras and the Portuguese Military Cemetery at Neuve Chappell. The guide had to explain that not every nationality fought on the Western Front but mentioned the worldwide nature of the conflict. At the Thiepval visitor centre, some of the students were attracted by the computer terminals and put their own names in the Commonwealth War Graves Commission website. The Libyan student discovered an Osman Ali, with the same tribal name, who died for Britain in the Libyan frontier force in 1941.

Case 4: Realities of war tours

It might be paradoxical to expect Army recruits to benefit from visiting the battlefields, cemeteries and memorials of the battles of the World Wars.

For example, recruits visiting Ypres will see more names on memorials and gravestones than are in the entire regular British Forces. However, the policy seems popular among army recruits and their training teams. Typically, examples from the World Wars are used to explore how the core values of the British Army apply in practice. Battlefield guides provide the historic content and the recruits' training team puts it into a contemporary context. For example, the guide talks about the concrete bunkers that the Germans used in the Ypres area in 1917 as an adjunct to trench warfare. The recruits carry out a planning exercise to think about the technology and tactics they would invent to solve the problems of attacking an entrenched enemy. The platoon staff, an experienced platoon commander and his team of NCOs, remind the recruits that fortified farm compounds in Afghanistan are not dissimilar to bunkers and comment about the way the modern army tackles the same task as that faced by Allied soldiers in World War I.

The parading at the Menin Gate is a powerful emotional moment for a group of soldiers in training; it provides a training vehicle for recruits to understand how the core values of the army are applied. Visiting historic battlefields may provide recruits with an appropriate environment to allow them to reflect on why they might want to join the army. Besides learning vocational lessons, battlefield visits also provide an opportunity for team building. Recruits seem to reflect on the emotional links that they have with the soldiers that fought in the World Wars.

Overall, the realities of war tours are part of the practical education of soldiers and are part of accredited vocational courses. The recruits have to complete workbooks which are assessed. The soldiers under training also pay a proportion of the costs of the tour. Visiting the ground is key to the qualification because the impact of the terrain – the battlefield – on battle is a key factor.

Acknowledgements

The authors are grateful to The Royal British Legion and Peter Caddick-Adams for permission to use survey results, conceptual models and other material.

Chapter 11

'Genocide Tourism'

JOHN BEECH

Introduction

The pairing of the words 'genocide' and 'tourism' may seem unlikely. Indeed, the lay person may be surprised that such an activity exists. Nevertheless, to give some idea of the potential scale of genocide tourism, it is worth noting that, by the early 1990s, some half a million tourists per year were visiting the site of the Auschwitz concentration camp and that, nowadays, the level of visitation exceeds a million visitors per year (Auschwitz-Birkenau State Museum, 2007). Rwanda, conversely, now attracts just 30,000 international tourists a year, yet not only is this a significant increase after almost a decade of negligible tourist arrivals, but also many of these tourists visit memorials to the 1994 genocide, in particular the Kigali Genocide Memorial and the Ntarama Church Memorial. Thus, this arguably most extreme form of dark tourism is a significant area of tourism, and one which deserves serious and sensitive study.

While the Holocaust may immediately spring to mind as the archetype of genocide, the definition of 'genocide' itself is problematic[1] and it is, therefore, necessary to consider first what qualifies as genocide and what falls outside a definition of genocide.

The Definition of Genocide

The term 'genocide' is a relatively recent invention. Etymologically, it is an extension of the usage of the suffix '-cide', meaning 'killing', as in 'suicide' (the killing of oneself) or 'fratricide' (the killing of one's brother). The prefix 'geno-' derives from the Latin *gens*, a race of people. It was coined by Dr Raphael Lemkin, a Polish Jew, in the 1930s, and he used it to describe the massacre of Christian Assyrians by the Iraqis (EuropaWorld, 2001). He also saw its relevance to the mass killings of Armenians by Turkey following the First World War, although whether the latter can be

defined as genocide is hotly disputed both by the current Turkish government and by Turks in general. The application of the term is thus contentious, and has been so since its first use.

In 1948, shortly after the fall of Nazi Germany, the United Nations (UN)
adopted the *Convention on the Prevention and Punishment of the Crime of
Genocide*, thus enshrining the term in the context of international law. The
immediate contextual origin of this adoption was, therefore, what is today
known as the Holocaust. While the extermination of Jews in Nazi Germany
constituted the major part of this mass killing of people, others were also
systematically killed, including the Roma (more widely known as the
Gypsies), the disabled, homosexuals and left-wing opponents of the Nazi
regime. In the original sense of the term used by Lemkin, Roma would fall
within the term genocide, but the other categories would not. The UN
definition thus became limited specifically to the mass killing of people on
racial, but not political or social, grounds. Since 1948, the Convention has
been applied in two cases: Rwanda in 1998, following the genocide in that
country in 1994, and Serbia in 2007, applied to crimes committed against
peoples in Bosnia-Herzegovina in the former state of Yugoslavia. In July
2008, a third case was started, against Omar Al Bashir, President of Sudan,
in connection with alleged atrocities committed in Darfur.

If we take a descriptive definition of genocide, that is, a definition that
includes cases which are generally termed as genocide – a crime against a
race – rather than a prescriptive definition or, in other words, one which
lays down a benchmark against which cases are judged to see whether
they qualify as genocide, then the following examples of genocide can
immediately be identified: in Turkey against Armenians (although, as
noted above, this remains contested); in Iraq against Christian Assyrians;
in Nazi Germany against Jews and Roma; in Rwanda against Tutsis; in
Bosnia-Herzegovina against Bosnians; and in Sudan against Darfuris.
Nevertheless, other contenders for qualification as genocide need to be
considered, such as the mass killing of North America's First Peoples or
First Nations, and the phenomenal loss of life of African peoples through
European/North American slavery. For this consideration we need to turn
to a pragmatic prescriptive definition.

Although definitions of genocide are not universally agreed, the
following list indicates where there is now general agreement:

- The killing is against a racial group because of their race.
- The killing is deliberate.
- The killing is systematic.

However, genocide is now often considered to embrace activities short
of killing, such as ill-treatment, both physical and mental, enforced measures of birth prevention, and the enforced removal of children (Office of
the High Commissioner for Human Rights, 1948). This latter extension of

the definition would logically demand the inclusion of the practice of slavery within genocide although, for the purposes of this book, slavery, specifically the trans-Atlantic slave trade, is not included in the definition of genocide but is explored in detail in Chapter 12 (see also Chapter 8). Certainly, the emphasis of slavery was on callous and inhumane *exploitation* of people, albeit with a cold-blooded indifference to the value of human life, rather than on the *extinction* of a race, as was the intention in, for example, the Holocaust. Nevertheless, the 'outer limits' of genocide thus remain ill-defined and contentious.

To conclude this introductory consideration of the definition of genocide, it needs to be noted that there *are* examples of what might be described as 'successful' genocide – that is, the complete extermination of a race. These include the extermination of the Guanches, the original inhabitants of the Canary Islands, and the Aboriginals of Tasmania. Neither case has, however, spawned any significant levels of tourism, no doubt to a large extent because of the extinction of the races concerned and the lack of desire on the part of the current occupants of these lands to include these extinctions as part of their heritage.

The Study of Genocide Tourism

The origins of the study of genocide tourism can be traced back to the work of John Tunbridge and Greg Ashworth and their seminal book *Dissonant Heritage* (Tunbridge & Ashworth, 1996). The book's subtitle, *The Management of the Past as a Resource in Conflict*, is revealing in that it clearly identifies the contentiousness of its subject matter. Its interpretation of 'heritage' as 'interpreted past' makes clear that the issues of whose heritage is under consideration, by whom and for what purpose, must be addressed. Their arguments are developed in three particular contexts: the heritage of atrocity in central Europe, in particular in the context of the Holocaust; the heritage of the settlers in North America; and the heritage of Southern Africa and the conflict between 'black' and 'white'.

In discussing the 'usability' of atrocity as a heritage resource in the central European context, they identify the interplay of five factors which will determine the effectiveness of heritage sites:

- The nature of the cruelty perpetrated;
- The nature of the victims;
- The nature of the perpetrators;
- The high-profile visibility of the original event;
- The survival of the record.

They also point out that there are significant difficulties in the practice of atrocity heritage interpretation. These will help, in varying degrees, our analysis in the later sections of this chapter when specific cases of

Table 11.1 Relevance of Tunbridge and Ashworth (1996) 'difficulties' applied to genocide tourism

Tunbridge and Ashworth difficulties	*Relevance to genocide tourism*
Intended and received messages	The difficulty here lies with who is sending a message to whom – typically this is the state sending a message to individuals with a very personal perspective
The event and its site	Tunbridge and Ashworth point out that sites of the events may not be particularly suitable for visitation and that a developed site at a 'non-authentic' location – the US Holocaust Memorial Museum in Washington DC, for example – may provide a good example of 'locational creativity'
Atrocity as entertainment attraction	Not particularly relevant to genocide tourism, although it is a potential danger to be watched for
The case of urban walls	Not relevant to genocide tourism
The durability of the artefacts of war	Durability is certainly relevant to visitation at the sites of concentration camps in particular, with the degree to which the original buildings have survived, and the degree to which they have been conserved, varying considerably from camp to camp
The interpretation of battlefield sites	Not particularly relevant to genocide tourism
The interpretation of city bombardment	Not particularly relevant to genocide tourism, although it is relevant in the case of the Warsaw Ghetto and Uprising
War memorials as heritage	Again, relevant at particular sites, such as the memorial to the victims of the Holocaust in Berlin
Museums of war or of peace?	Although this is relevant in the cases of genocide which occurred during civil wars, it is less appropriate as a consideration in the case of, for example, the Holocaust. A parallel consideration in this case is, however, the extent to which it is a museum of peace and reconciliation

genocide tourism practice are reviewed, and they are summarised in Table 11.1.

Tunbridge and Ashworth (1996) devote an entire section to the concentration/extermination camp as the heritage of genocide. As well as operational differences – whether the camp's use was mainly for the concentration of political opponents to the regime or for the extermination of specified groups (mainly on racial lines; that is, for Jews and Roma) – they identify the interpretation at the site as a key factor in differentiation between sites. Especially relevant to this is the post-war use of the camp site, which in some cases continued as political prison camps for dissidents against the communist regimes which replaced the Nazis. In the case of Auschwitz, they focus on the issue of identity – the victims being seen as Jews rather than as Polish Jews, or simply as Poles.

As has been noted elsewhere in this book, the work of John Lennon and Malcolm Foley (Lennon & Foley, 2000) drew the scholastic context of this evolving thread of study away from the heritage context to the tourism context. Firmly anchored at the darker end of the dark tourism spectrum (Sharpley, 2005; Stone, 2006a), their survey had a strong focus on the sites where genocide had occurred, in particular on the Nazi concentration camps, and on the sites directly associated with genocide, such as the house where the Schwansee conference was held and the (then) beginnings of the Schindler tourism phenomenon in Krakow, but also on the 'locationally creative' sites (to use the terminology of Tunbridge and Ashworth), such as, again, the US Holocaust Memorial Museum, and the Museum of Tolerance at the Simon Wiesenthal Center in Los Angeles.

Further development of the genocide tourism literature has, however, been somewhat sporadic. Although some attention has inevitably continued to be focused on Holocaust tourism in general (Ashworth, 1996; Cole, 1999b) and Auschwitz tourism in particular (Lennon & Foley, 2000; Miles, 2002; Poria, 2007 and others – see below) it remains relatively limited, whereas few studies have been made of tourism to other genocide sites, and only in more general contexts such as visitor perceptions of security (e.g. Grosspietsch, 2006). This lack of attention is, on the one hand, surprising given the scale to which tourism has grown at sites such as Auschwitz and the US Holocaust Memorial Museum, the latter attracting nearly 2 million visitors per year since its opening in 1993. On the other hand, as a research area it can be difficult or challenging – the lack of research using visitor surveys at concentration camps is not so surprising, perhaps. However, a study of the Buchenwald concentration camp site (Beech, 2000) develops the argument on contested space – contested between those who come to remember, the survivors and the relatives of those who died there, and those who come to not forget, the interested but not directly involved public, and those on educational visits. This issue is also explored in the context of battlefield sites in Chapter 10.

Marcuse adds to our understanding of the broader context in which genocide tourism happens, but his publication *Legacies of Dachau* (Marcuse, 2001) could not in any way be described as written from a tourism perspective. He has made this study of the role of Dachau with particular reference to how the process of projecting the past into the present is a contested process.

Following on from *Dissonant Heritage* (Tunbridge & Ashworth, 1996), Greg Ashworth and Rudi Hartmann return to the theme of dissonant heritage in *Horror and Human Tragedy Revisited: The Management of Sites of Atrocities for Tourism* (Ashworth & Hartmann, 2005a) which, although focusing on a sometimes broad interpretation of atrocity, devotes a significant degree of attention towards genocide tourism (specifically Holocaust tourism) and its management. Its contents include an exploration of the motives for engaging in atrocity/genocide tourism (Ashworth & Hartmann, 2005b), and a study of memorials and memorialisation of the victims of the Nazis (Hartmann, 2005). However, a major theme of the book is the dissonance resulting from the manner in which particular sites were developed as attractions rather than day-to-day management and interpretation issues.

Evidently, a variety of issues are of relevance to the study and management of genocide tourism, some of which are addressed in the literature, others of which remain under-researched. For example, the potential undoubtedly exists for genocide sites, as with dark sites more generally, to be exploited or subjected to particular interpretation for political or ideological purposes, including the promotion of peace and reconciliation. This issue is explored in Chapter 8, with a specific discussion about the extent to which the memorialisation of the Cambodian genocide at the Tuol Sleng Museum of Genocide in Phnom Penh and Choeung Ek Genocidal Centre has promoted greater national reconciliation (see below and also Williams, 2007), while others have focused specifically on the political exploitation of the Holocaust (Finklestein, 2000; Burg, 2008). It is also relevant to consider, from an ethical perspective, the way in which the victims of genocide are exploited through the creation of memorials or museums that commemorate the event. For example, the display of personal possessions of victims may add to the authenticity or poignancy of the visitor experience while attributing additional meaning to often mundane items, yet their use may be simply to elicit an emotive response from the viewer. Moreover, the anonymity of such items serves only to depersonalise the original owner/victim (Williams, 2007). Similarly, anonymous photographs, such as those at Tuol Sleng, depersonalise the victims yet, in some way, their very being is transferred through the images to innumerable visitors gazing upon them, while the use or display of the human remains of genocide victims raises a number of ethical dilemmas that deserve consideration.

More generally, an issue that also deserves attention is the practical planning and management of genocide sites or memorials that, serving three potential audiences – relatives of the victims, the perpetrators (and those related to them in some way) and 'third party' visitors unconnected to the site, event or those involved – need to satisfy different and, perhaps, competing needs. However, while mourning, reconciliation, forgiveness or repentance may underpin the motives of the first two groups, there is a lack of knowledge about the third group – tourists – and their motives, particularly when visiting the sites of more recent genocide/atrocity, such as in Cambodia, Rwanda or Bosnia. Here, not only is the memory and experience of genocide still very much a powerful element of contemporary life, but also evidence is still visible or, in the case of mass graves, still emerging. Thus, in a sense, the Armenian genocide and the Holocaust, though present in the culture of particular groups or nations, are past historical events; conversely, the three more recent genocides are still very much present, with significant implications for their exploitation and management as tourist sites (Simic, 2008).

Given the relative paucity of research into genocide tourism (other than that related to the Holocaust), the following sections consider the five major genocides that have engendered a tourism dimension, in varying degrees, in order to identify common themes or challenges (if any) in managing genocide tourism. The order in which they are considered is that of their chronological occurrence; a brief review of Holocaust tourism is included as a basis for comparison with other, less documented (in the tourism context) genocides.

Armenian genocide tourism

The present sovereign state of Armenia is just one part of the geo-cultural area that is also termed Armenia. As well as the state of Armenia, geo-cultural Armenia extends (or, at least, extended historically) across a significant part of Turkey as well as parts of Iran, Georgia and the Ukraine. During the First World War, the Armenians within the then Ottoman (Turkish) empire were seen by the (Muslim) Ottoman government as being in sympathy with their fellow Christians in the Russian empire. Consequently, between 1915 and the end of the war and then subsequently between 1920 and 1923, an estimated one and a half million Armenians perished as a result of what some see as methodical abduction, torture, starvation and massacre (www.armenian-genocide.org). The suppression of the Armenians at this time was seen by Armenian nationalists as genocide, and is recognised as such by many historians. However, the term genocide is not today accepted as a fair or accurate description of those events by the current Turkish government. The contentiousness of how events have been viewed and, in particular, whether they constituted genocide by successive Turkish governments is well summarised by Tunbridge and Ashworth (1996):

- It never happened.
- It did happen but was a general outcome of war.
- It did happen, but had a counterpart in the massacre and displacement of Turkish Muslims in the Balkans and in Russia in the period immediately before the war.

- It occurred under the Ottomans, and the current Turkish regime is therefore not to blame.
- It was in part the victims' fault, in view of their provocative and arguably treacherous activities.

It is not perhaps surprising that, in view of the sensitivity of the subject to Turks, genocide tourism does not take place within today's Turkey. However, a memorial to the events of 1915–1923, the very large Tsitsernakaberd Armenian Genocide Memorial, is located in Yerevan, the capital of today's Republic of Armenia, and similar memorials can be found in a number of other cities across the country. Moreover, reflecting the geographical spread of the Armenian diaspora, Armenian Genocide Memorials are also located in other cities around the world, including Paris, Marseilles and Bremen in Europe, and Glendale and Las Vegas in the USA. As with any significant memorial, these genocide memorials provide both a focus for those with a connection (that is, for those of Armenian extraction), at least on specific occasions, and on a much smaller scale a general tourist attraction for those 'third party' visitors without a connection to the genocide.

While the purpose of the memorial in Yerevan is simply to 'memorialise the victims' of the genocide (Armenian Genocide Memorial-Institute, 2007a), the Armenian Genocide Museum-Institute in Yerevan has two specific objectives: research and education (Armenian Genocide Memorial-Institute, 2007b). The purpose of education in particular emphasises that the tourist consumption will tend to be domestic and/or ethnic Armenians living overseas, any international visitation being welcomed but not expressly targeted.

Completed in 1967, the Memorial has been described as a 'pilgrimage site' (Armenian Genocide Memorial-Institute, 2007c). This date is important to an understanding of its intended function. Armenia was at that time a Soviet Republic and hence subject to rulers who wished to suppress local nationalism for their own political purposes. The construction of the memorial resulted from popular demonstrations in 1965 commemorating the 50th anniversary of the massacres and thus had a deeper meaning than just the commemoration of the genocide – it served as a statement of political and cultural identity, a role it still bears today, serving as a physical focal point for celebrations each 24th of February since 1967 (the genocide is generally considered to have commenced on 24 February 1915, the day when over 200 Armenian community leaders were arrested in Constantinople).

Genocide tourism cannot be described as a 'purpose of visit' for the majority of international visitors to Armenia; rather, it is blended into the cultural heritage of the country. Most tours, for example, focus generally on Armenia's natural and Christian heritage, although, because of the genocide's place in national identity, visits to the memorial and museum have become a regular part of organised visits. The image of the country that the Armenian government projects through its tourism promotion emphasises the long history of civilisation in Armenia, its Christian heritage and its richness of folk crafts (Embassy of the Republic of Armenia, 2008), but domestic private sector promotion, such as '7 Days' (2005) and international tour operator promotion, for example Audley Travel (2008), present the Memorial and the Museum as 'standard' visitor attractions to visit when in the capital. It should also be noted that, out of roughly 500,000 tourist arrivals in 2007, the great majority were people of Armenian extraction. Official figures suggest that just 58,000 visitors stayed in hotels and, of these, some 11,000 were on vacation (Arca News Agency, 2008), the inference being that many international visitors stay with friends and relatives. The genocide tourist attractions in Armenia are thus aimed more at a domestic market and the visiting Armenian diaspora to emphasise national identity. There are few visitors from Turkey (0.9% of arrivals in 2007) and so, while intended primarily to be educational, the memorial and museum are unlikely to contribute to a broader purpose of promoting peace and reconciliation.

Holocaust tourism

While it is assumed that readers will be aware of the basic details of the Holocaust, some features which are relevant in particular to genocide tourism should be noted.

The atrocities of the Holocaust were committed under the regime of the Nazis and, thus, geographically they took place not only within the borders of today's Germany but also in the lands which they occupied or within which puppet regimes were installed. These include, to the west, Belgium, Denmark, part of France, the Netherlands and Norway and, to the east, Austria, Czechoslovakia (today's Czech Republic and Slovakia), Hungary, Poland and Yugoslavia (in particular today's Croatia and Serbia). This range of countries is significant in that the subsequent histories of most of the countries in eastern Europe, and indeed part of today's Germany itself, were under communist regimes. This resulted in some cases of revisionism in the way that the sites were used (sometimes being in use as camps for political prisoners, as in the case of Buchenwald in the former East Germany) and viewed by the relevant authorities.

In general, the sites in the west were used as transit camps while the death camps were found to the east, often in the countries occupied by the Nazis rather than within the borders of Germany. To add to the potential for confusion, it should be remembered that the borders of Germany to the east, in particular with respect to Poland, were altered after World War II.

Other sites associated with the Holocaust, examples of which are open for tourist visitation, also include the slave labour camps. These range from the famous factory of Oskar Schindler in Krakow (Poland), which is memorable only for its role in the Holocaust, to Europe's largest subterranean lake at Hinterbrühl in Lower Austria where, for a short time, construction work on the Heinkel 162 jet fighter was undertaken by 2000 slave labourers housed in a Nazi concentration camp.

The scale of the Holocaust and its associated diaspora of Jews fleeing the Nazis has resulted in a number of Holocaust museums in countries which do not have sites at which atrocities actually took place. The most notable of these are the United States Holocaust Memorial Museum at Washington, DC and Yad Vashem in Jerusalem, with its associated Holocaust History Museum. While the emphasis of the latter is arguably on remembrance, although clearly with a significant aim of educating (Krakover, 2005), the former has a clear emphasis on education – the Museum reports that 90% of its visitors today are not Jewish. Other cities outside the territories of Nazi Germany which have significant Holocaust museums include Buenos Aires, Cape Town, Fukuyama, Melbourne, Montreal, London (at the Imperial War Museum), Paris and numerous cities in the USA.

Within Germany, the Memorial to the Murdered Jews of Europe was opened in Berlin in 2004 as a place for remembrance and commemoration (Foundation for the Memorial to the Murdered Jews of Europe, 2008). The sheer size of the memorial, a sculpture entitled Field of Stellae consisting of approximately 2700 stellae, or concrete slabs, and covering some 19,000 square metres on a site in the centre of Berlin, has ensured that it is difficult for any tourist visiting Berlin not to become aware of its existence. Beneath the memorial is an information centre.

A final small group of significant visitor attractions directly related to the Holocaust consists of the Anne Frank House and the Connie ten Boom Museum in the Netherlands, and the Memorials to Jewish ghettoes, notably the Memorial of the Heroes of the Warsaw Ghetto in Warsaw.

Of all the varieties of genocide tourism, Holocaust tourism is easily the most extensive. There are several reasons for this:

- There is a very large number of sites for visitation.
- The range of sites is larger than for other areas of genocide tourism.
- The sites are entirely within the western world, including the USA, and thus within relatively easy reach of potential visitors.
- Those who died were from the western world.
- The genocide was particularly systematic and took place over a longer period than any of the other genocides discussed.

So extensive are the possibilities for visitation that a guide book of the sites has been produced (Terrance, 1999), providing details of what is at each site, how to find it, and information on visitation conditions such as times of opening and charges.

Cambodian genocide tourism

In the period following the withdrawal of French colonial rule in 1953, Cambodia (then Kampuchea) suffered considerable political instability and civil strife. In early 1975, communist troops, known as the Khmer Rouge, under Pol Pot seized power and began a period of severe repression of those they considered enemies of the state in order to establish a 'new order' – a return to a 'year zero'. Religion was suppressed, agriculture collectivised and an attack on intellectuals and 'bourgeoisie' began. So excessive were these attacks that a Yale University study, the *Cambodian Genocide Program*, estimates that, in the period from 1975 to 1979, 1.7 million people, 21% of the country's population, lost their lives (Yale University Genocide Studies Program, 2008).

The Pol Pot regime was brought down following an invasion of Cambodia by Vietnamese troops in 1979, and a less extreme communist regime assumed power. In 1993, a democratic system was introduced. Since 2004, actions have been taken to bring the Khmer Rouge leaders before a United Nations tribunal, although Pol Pot himself died in 1998.

Cambodia is becoming increasingly popular as a tourist destination. Since 2000, the annual number of international tourist arrivals has more than quadrupled, from 466,000 in 2000 to over two million in 2007. The country's most famous and popular attraction is, of course, the temple complex at Angkor Wat – more than half of all international tourists visit the site – while the capital city, Phnom Penh, has a range of cultural sites which appeal to western visitors. As well as other temple sites, Cambodia also offers a number of hill and beach resorts aimed at the international tourist market. These are often packaged as part of multi-country tours to western tourists, bundled with Vietnam, Laos and/or Thailand.

The two main sites for genocide tourism visitation are the Tuol Sleng Museum of Genocide and the Cheung Ek Genocidal Centre or 'killing fields'. As also described in Chapter 8, the Tuol Sleng site was originally a school which was taken over by the Pol Pot regime as a torture and detention centre. The site has been to a large extent preserved as it was found when liberated by Vietnamese troops, enhancing the authenticity of the site. It once housed the infamous map of Cambodia made from human skulls, but this was dismantled in 2002. Those imprisoned at Tuol Sleng who did not die there under torture were transferred to the nearby Cheung Ek killing fields for extermination. Here some mass graves have been disinterred, but many remain undisturbed out of respect to the dead. There is a Buddhist memorial at the site today.

As considered in Chapter 8 and suggested by Williams (2004), Tuol Sleng and Cheung Ek are probably more successful as tourist sites than as a focus for peace and reconciliation, although their 'official' promotion as tourist attractions is objective yet muted. For example, after describing the role of Tuol Sleng as a detention and torture centre, the Cambodian tourism website states that:

> Altogether, a visit to Tuol Sleng is a profoundly depressing experience. There is something about the sheer ordinariness of the place that make it even more horrific; the suburban setting, the plain school buildings, the grassy playing area where several children kick around a ball, rusted beds, instruments of torture and wall after wall of harrowing black-and-white portraits conjure up images of humanity at its worst. Tuol Sleng is not for the squeamish. (Tourism of Cambodia, 2008)

The comments of visitors to Tuol Sleng posted on travel websites tend to reflect this description, although many find it both a depressing yet positive experience. For example, one tourist writes:

> The Tuol Sleng Museum is another sobering experience. Such a tragic, desolate place. Some people say that it's not the type of holiday they'd want, but I think that if you visit Phnom Penh, then it is a must do. It is important that people understand what happened here. We cannot pretend that these terrible things never occurred and it helps you to understand why the country is in the situation it is. To me, the visit was a show of respect. (Tina-Perth on www.virtualtourist.com, 2008)

Nevertheless, the increasing numbers of tour groups visiting both Tuol Sleng and Cheung Ek (often disturbing those wishing to contemplate the sites and their dark history in relative peace), along with the fact that the latter has been transferred to a Cambodian–Japanese consortium on a 30-year lease as a commercial tourism venture, suggests that the Cambodian genocide – and the memory of its victims – will be increasingly exploited for tourist dollars (Williams, 2004).

It is also interesting to note that the infamy of the killing fields was popularised in the west by the eponymous film of 1984, which tells the story of Dith Pran, a journalist who managed eventually to escape from Cambodia. A Cambodian Cultural Museum and Killing Field Memorial was established in Seattle by Dara Duong, another survivor of the killing fields, and its stated aims include honouring the dead, educating visitors and providing research resources. In particular, it was designed to remind the children of Cambodian immigrants to Seattle of their background.

Rwandan genocide tourism

The Rwandan genocide occurred over a relatively short period of time, between April and June of 1994. It is estimated that approximately 800,000 people were killed in just 100 days. Most of those killed were Tutsis and most of those who did the killing were Hutus. However, the conflict might be described as a rather one-sided civil war. Tensions between the two groups had been festering since the days of Belgian colonial rule and the atrocities which occurred in 1994 were triggered by the mysterious death of the Rwandan president Juvenal Habyarimana, a Hutu, in a plane crash caused by a rocket attack on 6 April 1994. The scale of death can be explained, in part, by the fact that the two ethnic groups had lived in the same areas, although they actually shared the same language and many customs. By July 1994, a Tutsi-led rebel force had captured the capital city of Kigali, a government involving members from both ethnic groups was formed and the atrocities ceased. An estimated two million Hutus fled across borders into neighbouring African countries and, although Rwanda is today largely peaceful, tensions continue in neighbouring countries, most recently in eastern Congo, because of the large number of displaced people. The role of the French government in the origins of the immediate events of 1994 is still debated (BBC News, 2004).

Although the genocide occurred very much on a local basis, particular centres of atrocity can be identified. At a site where over 250,000 victims are buried, the Kigali Genocide Memorial Centre has been established. The Centre offers not only displays on the Rwandan genocide but also of other genocides throughout the world. In addition to the mass graves, the Centre also has memorial sculptures, a Memorial Garden and a Wall of Names (Kigali Memorial Centre, 2008). Its main purpose is to act as a memorial to the victims of the genocide, though it also focuses on education:

> One of the principal reasons for the Centre's existence is to provide educational facilities. These are for a younger generation of Rwandan children some of whom may not remember the genocide, but whose lives are profoundly affected by it ... The Centre will provide programmes for school children to come and learn about, and from, the history of the genocide. (Kigali Memorial Centre, 2008)

Around the country there are a number of memorials associated with mass graves and/or sites of massacre. These include Bisesero, Murambi, Ntarama, Nyanza, Nyarabuye and Nymata. Tour operators now offer organised visits to the Kigali Memorial Centre and some of the other memorials, especially those where there is a building where a massacre occurred and which are closer to Kigali, as part of their Rwanda package. Often the genocide tourism element of a package is branded as cultural heritage, and sits alongside Rwanda's other major attraction, that is, nature tourism/trekking to view mountain gorillas in Virunga National Park.

Great efforts have been made to achieve reconciliation between the two communities. The genocide is still an event which is alive in contemporary consciousness, and visitors who ask a Rwandan whether they are a Tutsi or a Hutu will be met with the almost mantric response 'I am a Rwandan'.

Nevertheless, according to one commentator, the image of peace and reconciliation in the country is little more than a façade (Sullivan, 2008). The staff at the various visitor sites see the presence of these places as part of the catharsis needed to achieve reconciliation – see, for example, the testimony of a guide at the Murambi Genocide Memorial (Majtenyi, 2007). Another common feature of the presentations at these sites is that they should serve as a lesson to ensure that genocide should not happen again.

No research has been undertaken into the reasons for tourists wishing to visit the country's genocide sites, nor into their reactions or responses to such visits. Nevertheless, there is evidence of the significant emotional impact that visiting particular genocide sites, particularly at locations such as churches where victims sought sanctuary, may have on visitors. For example, one tourist, after visiting the school at Murambi, where 45,000 people were slaughtered, writes:

> Today, the school is a memorial to the victims of the massacre. In a number of the old classrooms, the preserved bodies of some of the victims are laid out on tables. The bodies are desiccated because of the lime used to preserve them, but their contorted bodies, and mouths open in silent screams are a horrifying testament to the events that happened here. No one was spared. In some rooms, small bodies belonging to children and infants lay on the wooden slats, mouths open in silent screams, their skulls split open from the blow of a machete or club. In some cases, bodies seem to lay in each others arms, as if seeking solace and protection from a loved one in their final moments. Occasional tuffs [sic] of hair attached to heads, and articles of clothing still adorn the bodies.
>
> You walk from room to room, a caretaker opening each door to let you view the remains inside. You are told it is ok to take photo-graphs. You do, feeling slightly sick and disgusted with yourself ... You think you should be crying. You think you should smash things. You feel you should be feeling something, anything, but instead, feel dazed. A thick numbness fills your skull as room after room is opened, and body after body is seen. (Travelpod, 2008)

Yet, while such sites may be shocking or profoundly moving for interna-tional visitors, it may be necessary to question the ethics of allowing outsiders to gaze upon the victims of an intensely national tragedy.

Bosnian genocide tourism

The break-up of the confederation which formed the Republic of Yugoslavia was rapid and bloody following the death of Tito, and is beyond the scope of this chapter for any detailed discussion – see, for example, Glenny (1996) or Little and Silber (1996). For the purposes of considering genocide tourism related to this conflict, we shall focus on the Srebrenica Massacre of 1995. While this specific episode is widely recognised as the most high-profile activity that has been termed 'genocide', wider definitions would include a series of incidents which took place during the preceding three years and are generally termed 'ethnic cleansing'.

As a result of the civil war taking place across much of the former Yugoslavia, Srebrenica found itself in June 1995 as an enclave of Bosnian Muslims surrounded by Serbian troops. In an attempt to protect these Bosnian Muslims, the United Nations declared the area immediately round and including Srebrenica a 'safe haven'. A deployment of Dutch troops from the UN peace-keeping force, UNPROFOR, was sent to the area. Facing heavy Serbian opposition, the Dutch troops, who were lightly armed as they were fulfilling a peace-keeping role, were unable to resist Serb attacks and withdrew, allowing the troops of the army of the Republika Srpska to take over the enclave. Although two NATO air strikes subsequently took place, control of the enclave remained with the Serbs. It is generally accepted that approximately 8000 Bosnian Muslims were massacred and buried in mass graves, and many of the remaining Muslims were removed from the enclave (see Simic, 2008).

A sense of peace is beginning to return to the area and tourism is now possible again. However, the awkwardness that genocide tourism can engender when events are relatively recent is clear in the following description, quoted in full from the Srebrenica webpage of the Tourism Association of the Federation of Bosnia and Herzegovina website:

> Not long ago the memorial cemetery was opened in Srebrenica. The memorial centre is a beautiful and touching place.
>
> Life may be returning to normal in Srebrenica, but the women and children who survived will continue to live their lives without their brothers, fathers, husbands and friends.
>
> Despite its tragic past, the beautiful dense forests that line the hillside or the plethora of bears and wolves that roam the wilderness to the southeast of town are certainly a sight to see.
>
> Go to Srebrenica. There are nice places to see in and around Srebrenica. The natural thermal springs, the stunning pine covered hills, and lovely villages that dot the countryside. (BH Tourism, *undated*)

This ambivalence is also reflected in the accounts written by those who have visited recently – see, for example, an account blogged on www.realtravel.com by a visitor in 2006 (Verbeek, 2006). Such ambivalence may arise, in part, from the inability of international tourists to understand or make sense of the genocide. That is, to tourists as 'outsiders' unconnected with the massacre at Srebrenica, the memorial can serve no purpose of reconciliation, while the scale of the massacre may lie beyond their comprehension.

Conclusions

It is clear that the five cases discussed above concern genocides that arose in different contexts, at sites in different continuing or successor states, on different scales and in different periods in history. In particular, the Armenian Genocide and the Holocaust may be considered historical (though still unresolved) events while, in the case of Cambodia, Rwanda and Bosnia, the genocides are still very much a part of contemporary life. The case for drawing general conclusions at the descriptive level is therefore not a compelling one.

Nevertheless, a number of variables can be identified which can serve as a basis for comparative studies or longitudinal studies. The latter are not very well represented in the literature, exceptions being Beech (2000) and Marcuse (2005). This point is important as it emphasises that these atrocity sites are evolutionary rather than static. Generally, the following apply to all genocide sites:

- History, it is said, is written by the victors, but in the case of genocide this term is inappropriate. The two alternative perspectives from which genocide is commemorated, memorialised and presented for educational purposes are typically either the *victims* (or their *diasporic descendants*) or the *political successors to the perpetrators*.
- Sites which are presented as genocide tourist attractions are the *sites where the atrocities were perpetuated, nearby sites for memorialisation*, in a few cases *directly associated sites* (the Anne Frank House for example) or *neutral but convenient sites* such as the Washington Holocaust Memorial Museum.
- The purpose of the attraction is typically a mix of *memorialisation, education* and *research resource*.
- A further variable is the degree of *revisionism* in the interpretation, a matter which is inherently contentious and difficult to be objective about.
- Sites vary in the extent to which they preach *reconciliation and forgiveness*. Few, the camp at Mauthausen being an honourable exception, attempt an *explanation* of why the atrocity occurred.

From a specific tourism perspective, the evident variations in the five cases described above also raise a number of issues that deserve further research. Firstly, it must be questioned whether it is in fact possible to sub-categorise this particular form of dark tourism collectively as 'genocide tourism'. Although the sites, museums and memorials related to each of the genocides attract visitors, the scale and composition of visitation varies significantly, as does potential reasons for visiting. For the 'historical' sites relating to the Armenian genocide and the Holocaust, it is likely that either pilgrimage or education are the dominant focus in the presentation and visitation of the sites. At the more contemporary genocide sites, it may be that tourists are drawn by the horror of the events commemorated.

Secondly, many contemporary genocide sites are, in a sense, 'live'; mass graves, human remains and personal artefacts are still being discovered while, at the national level, the events surrounding the genocide and its aftermath have yet to be fully resolved. Thus, tourists, particularly those with no personal connection to the genocide, its victims or perpetrators, may be seen as intruders in a national process of grieving, learning, memorialisation, political reconciliation and social reconstruction. This in turn suggests that although tourism may be considered an attractive source of income (as is particularly the case in Cambodia), sensitivity is required in the management of tourism at the sites both out of respect for the victims and their relatives and to ensure that any reconciliation process is not hindered or diminished by the commercial exploitation of the sites. At the same time, however, research may identify the extent to which tourism may actually contribute to the social healing process by providing a window through which a national tragedy can be shared and commemorated with the world at large.

Finally, genocide tourism provides a powerful context for exploring the production and consumption of dark tourism more generally. Many of the issues raised throughout this book, from the potential role of dark tourism in mediating between life and death to more practical ethical and interpretation issues, are of particular relevance to understanding genocide tourism. Therefore, further research into tourism related to genocide sites may contribute not only to their more effective management but also to our broader understanding of the phenomenon of dark tourism.

Note

1. For a range of definitions of 'genocide', see the Aegis Trust (2005) website at www.aegistrust.org/index.php?option=content&task=view&id=87&Itemid=118. More generally, *Holocaust and Genocide Studies* is the principal forum for scholarship on the Holocaust and other genocides. See http://hgs.oxfordjournals.org/archive/.

Chapter 12

Museums, Memorials and Plantation Houses in the Black Atlantic: Slavery and the Development of Dark Tourism

ALAN RICE

> *One of the sinister and poignant features of slavery is that it is a*
> *phantom industry that leaves scant traces;*
> *its capital lies in people, long since dead, not machinery.*
> Seaton, 2001: 117

Introduction

The history of slavery and the middle passage has been dominated by wilful amnesia and silence, particularly in the public realm. The last 20 years, however, have witnessed voices breaking though and can be seen, for example, in the success and cultural purchase of Toni Morrison's landmark book *Beloved* (1987), the inauguration of the UNESCO Slave Route project in 1993, and the opening of the first large-scale permanent exhibit dedicated to the slave trade at the Merseyside Maritime Museum, Liverpool in 1994 (superseded by the International Slavery Museum in 2007). Although none of these are conventional memorial projects, they have helped galvanise a succession of creative and memorial initiatives throughout the Northern Hemisphere to publicly acknowledge the slave trade and its consequences, making the subject of slavery key to the tourist experience in many locales. This chapter will look at such sites of public and private memory in Britain and America and discuss the cultural politics of these locations and the implications for them of the growth of tourism. Before I move on to this, however, I want to complete the Transatlantic slave triangle by briefly commenting on the implications for tourism and memorialisation where the trade began with the export of enslaved Africans from the West African coast.

West Africa: Tourism, Memorialisation and the Slave Trade

The black British writer, Caryl Philips, in his *The Atlantic Sound* (2000), describes the excesses of certain sentimentalised appropriations of African locale by African American tourists which, according to him, have far more to do with bogus emotionalism than a proper coming to terms with the past. He comments acerbically on one particularly anodyne ceremony at Elmina Castle during the Panfest festival that was undertaken by 'people of the diaspora who expect the continent to solve whatever psychological problems they possess' (Philips, 2000: 173). Philips' reservations about the appropriation of African memorial space by western-educated, black tourists is well made and is best illustrated by the fact that many local Ghanaians chafed at the emphasis in the exhibitions on the diaspora to the exclusion of local history. It is echoed in the controversy over the restoration of Cape Coast Castle and its development as a museum space in the early 1990s. African American commentators talked of the restoration as a 'whitewashing of the history associated with the slave trade' (Singleton, 1999: 156). Edward Bruner makes this point most forcefully:

> For many African-Americans, the castles are sacred ground not be desecrated. They do not want the castles to be made beautiful or to be whitewashed. They want the original stench to remain in the dungeons. A return to the slave forts for diaspora blacks is a 'necessary act of self realisation', 'for the spirits of the diaspora are somehow tied to these historic structures'. Some diaspora blacks feel that even though they are not Ghanaians, 'the castles belong to them'. (Bruner, 1996: 291)

For the African American tourists, the castles' meaning is wholly circumscribed by their function as slave forts; however, the locals see the castles as being as much about colonial and post-colonial relations in a complex historical relationship with European visitors where they at times had agency. Hence, the forts can never be just about the victims of the slave trade. These examples illustrate the malleability of meaning for such locale in a black Atlantic replete with varied interest groups. For, in a global economy, where the marketing of black memory provides mercantile opportunities for some, there is also ideological payback for others who want to interpret sites like the slave castles through a narrow nationalistic gaze. Those left out in such a marketplace of ideologies are usually the local disenfranchised Africans who do not have the economic power of the African American tourists. This is exemplified by past restrictions around Elmina Castle that banned all people 'except tourists' (Singleton, 1999: 158). The American historian Edward T. Linenthal describes how 'these West African sites are surely an extension of the African American landscape' (Linenthal, 2006: 218). The problem with such sentiment is that this emotive attachment from the African American tourist is seen as a colonising gesture by many locals whose economic and political power at a time of American economic hegemony is less than their western visitors. Tourism in such a contested political landscape brings wealth to hard-pressed economies, but at a significant cost in terms of cross-cultural empathy and understanding. As Ellie Lester Roushanzamir and Peggy J. Kreshel (2001: 183) warn, '"heritage" can be too easily converted from contested engagements with history to a commodity intentionally fabricated for a consumer audience'.

African Americans, as tourists, seek memorial sites in Africa because Africa represents a free homeland precipitating their capture as slaves, but they also seek them there because there have historically been so few for them in the USA. In 1989, Toni Morrison complained that:

> There is no place you or I can go, to think about, or not think about, to summon the presences of, or recollect the absences of slaves; nothing that reminds us of the ones who made the journey and of those who did not make it. There is no suitable memorial or plaque or wreath or wall or park or skyscraper lobby. There's no 300-foot tower. There's no small bench by the road. There is not even a tree scored, an initial I can visit, or you can visit in Charleston or Savannah or New York or Providence, or better still on the banks of the Mississippi. (Morrison, 1989: 4)

Although there is still considerable work to be done, Toni Morrison's statement is less true now than it was in the late 1980s. There is now more public acknowledgement of the slave past in the Transatlantic world than there was two decades ago and this has manifested itself in plaques, memorials and events in many sites throughout the circum-Atlantic including, for instance: the annual celebration of the International Day for the Remembrance of the Slave Trade and its Abolition in Haiti; Liverpool and, more recently, London; national memorials erected in the centre of Amsterdam (2002) and Paris (2007) and a smattering of local ones including one dedicated to the Amistad rebels in New Haven, CT (1992) and one on the quayside in Lancaster (2005); a plaque finally put up on Sullivan Island, Charleston, to commemorate the slave lives lost in the holding pens there; dedicated exhibition spaces on Transatlantic slavery in Bristol, Hull, London and Detroit; and ambitious plans for a memorial and museum on Goree Island, Senegal. These all attest to an increased level of public activity over the last decade.

However, despite this increased activity, there is not as yet a federal memorial to the slave trade in the USA, a shameful omission in a nation many of whose famous political buildings, including the Presidential abode, the White House, were erected by slave labour and where, as John Vlach has shown, 'the monumental core' of the city 'stands on slave ground' (Vlach, 2006: 69). This anomaly, this lack of federal memorialisation, is at its starkest in Philadelphia where recent discoveries by the historians Edward Lawler Jr. and Gary Nash outline how the area around Sixth and Market Streets were home not only to the first President, George Washington, but also to his slaves who lived in 'the first federally subsidised slave quarters' in the country within earshot of the Liberty Bell (Saffron, 2003). As Gary Nash says, 'Our memory of the past is often managed and manipulated. Here it is being downright murdered' (Nash, 2006: 82). There are moves afoot to make a memorial in this space on Liberty Mall to commemorate this ambivalent place of America's founding space of freedom living hand by jowl with the extremity of chattel slavery. However, as Ingrid Saffron (2003) reports, the project is dogged by 'extreme bureaucratic indifference' and is alienating the local African American population.

Such contestation over historical sites which have links to slavery are hardly new (see also Chapter 10) and some of the most iconic signs of the slave locale are the 'everyday' Plantation Houses that dominate the landscape of ex-slave societies. One example is The Wye Plantation House, Maryland.

The Wye Plantation House

The Wye Plantation House and grounds on Maryland's Eastern Shore a few miles outside Baltimore is at first sight a typical site of mythological Southern aggrandisement. The long drive leading to a large house resplendent with Georgian columns, befitting a house constructed in the late 18th century, betokens a conventionalised encounter with antebellum myths of Southern belles and martial heroism. This particular plantation's historical originality is emphasised by the orangerie a few paces behind the kitchen which is the oldest such building in North America. Opulence and conspicuous consumption are still foregrounded in the central wing of the house where Staffordshire chinaware adorns the Chippendale furniture and European seascapes festoon the walls, showing how this family, like many others in the South, used their fantastic wealth to indulge in luxurious goods imported from Europe. These rooms are preserved in aspic in the style of the 1830s, the height of power for the Lloyd family whose descendants still enjoy the luxuries of the plantation. This is no open site, turned over to the garrulous public, however, but still a private home, preserved by the riches attendant on the wealth created by a plantation that at its height had over 500 slaves working on it and at other sites around Chesapeake Bay on 13 farms containing over 10,000 acres of arable land for the cultivation of the atypical slave crop of wheat (McFeely, 1991: 14).

For the radical cultural historian, such a site of elite mythmaking would call forth a demand to look beneath the surface to the materiality that made such wealth possible, and this chapter will undertake some critiques in this direction. For as Ola Oguibe reminds us:

> ... another notable fact of the diaspora experience, namely that the tropes of (African) survival in the Americas are lodged not only in cultural retentions among the descendants of slaves, but also in the master's annals of their violation. Memory finds its anchors in unlikely crevices and interstices of history. (Oguibe, 2001: 99)

These tropes of survival are littered throughout the archive of Anglo-European history and in the archaeological detritus of plantations, grave-yards and even shipwrecks. However, for once, at the Wye Plantation we have a literate, non-elite witness to the realities behind the façade we are presented with at this troubling site: the imposing figure of that great scion of the black Atlantic, Frederick Douglass, who was born in the shadow of the Wye Plantation in 1818. He was born, Frederick Bailey, at Tuckahoe Creek, as slave of Captain Aaron Anthony, sloop captain and chief over-seer at Wye. Douglass soon joined his master on the plantation and he describes the impressive building that confronted him for the first time:

> ... above all stood the grandest building my young eyes had ever beheld, called by everyone on the plantation the great house. ... a large white wooden building with wings on three sides of it. In front extending the entire length of the building and supported by a long range of columns, was a broad portico, which gave to the Colonel's home an air of great dignity and grandeur. It was a treat to my young and gradually opening mind to behold this elaborate exhibition of wealth, power and beauty. (Douglass, 1994 [1881]: 488)

Douglass is in awe of the building, but in his recollection of his first encounter with it he is keen to show his adult awareness of how the Lloyd family are involved in a very public display of their Southern white power. This 'elaborate exhibition' is a public avowal of status that he, as a young slave, has access to only as a feast for his eyes. Douglass fills in for us the vast industry around the great house, replete with fields under cultiva-tion, barns, a windmill and numerous slave cabins to house the workers. However, as with most Southern plantations, by the 21st century all that is left are the big houses themselves, which have become eye candy for the tourists who flock to them to indulge in *Gone With the Wind* myths of an honourable South destroyed by the ravages of the American Civil War (1861–1865). As Edward T. Linenthal has discussed, plantations in the South are engaged in 'if not denial, then the transformation into some-thing benign, through a minefield of monumental memory to the "faithful slave" and the "black mammy", the *Gone With the Wind* fiction of slavery' (Linenthal, 2006: 214). This eye candy is contextualised through tours that concentrate on the fixtures and fittings of the house to the almost total exclusion of slaves that made the wealth possible, so that on average there are 'thirty-one times as many mentions of furniture at these sites than of slavery or those enslaved' (Eichstedt & Small, 2002: 109). Such 'sites engage in the work of social forgetting' with 'deep wounds and anxieties being confined to oblivion' and, thus, 'meeting the need of whites to create a vision of the nation and themselves as noble and disassociated from racialised atrocities' (Eichstedt & Small, 2002: 15). The 'symbolic annihilation' of black presence at such sites is well documented in books such as Jennifer L. Eichstedt and Stephen Small's (2002) seminal *Representations of Slavery: Race and Ideology in Southern Plantation Museums*.

The Wye Plantation is not a museum, but still a family home. However, it is a useful case study, as here almost uniquely we have a written record from a victim to juxtapose with the official history of the house. Moreover, this case study shows how the reactionary tropes associated with plantations are established in the mythology even before it became an official tourist site. The symbolic annihilation of black presence is as marked as in the most regressive plantation museum. There are significant memorials to Frederick Douglass in Rochester, New York and in Anacostia, Washington DC, where the Frederick Douglass House is a National Park Memorial site. At his birthplace, however, there is no acknowledgement of his fame. In fact, as our party, only the second ever officially organised tour of the house, was escorted around, Frederick Douglass was not mentioned once by name. If one of the international group of academics asked about him, the Lloyd descendant escorting us would refer to him in the third person as 'he' or 'him'. His fame was an obvious embarrassment to the family and the tour a necessary trial to be got through in order to appease a National Parks Service whose financial support they might need in the future. This trial was made even more excruciating for them by the presence in the party of Frederick Douglass IV, a direct descendant of Douglass himself.

Despite the lack of help from our guide in placing the slaves as central to the story of the big house and its surrounds, as Douglass scholars we had the landscape of the plantation from his autobiographies to help us. In a sense, Douglass's autobiography gave us a guerrilla memorial to set against the official amnesia about his presence. Such counter-memories are essential for the fullest interpretation of such contested sites. Thus, the smokehouse and plantation bell still extant as mentioned in Douglass's (1994 [1845]) *Narrative of the Life of an American Slave Written by Himself* authenticated the site as redolent with images from Douglass's childhood. However, the most chilling site for Douglass scholars was the Aaron Anthony House, a small cottage tucked in behind the big house where Douglass informs us he entered 'the blood stained gate, the entrance to the hell of slavery' (1994 [1845]: 18) when he witnessed the brutal whipping of Aunt Hester by Captain Anthony. This is probably one of the most famous scenes in the history of black literature and yet the house is pathetically ordinary. If any house is haunted by the presence of atrocities against slaves, this is, and yet the Lloyd family plans for it are illustrated by the builder's sign outside. The house was being modernised to serve as a retirement house for the matriarch of the family.

Pierre Nora has talked about *'lieux de memoire,* sites of memory ... moments of history, torn away from the movement of history' (Nora, 1994: 289). The Wye Plantation is such a *lieux de memoire* where the official family/ Southern historical frame is contested by a dissident memory which haunts the buildings and that transforms them from the idyllic to the horrific. As readers of Douglass look at the glories of the plantation and the bucolic sweetness of the Anthony cottage, the counter-memory of the famous African American cannot help but be imagined. Douglass describes:

> Before he commenced whipping Aunt Hester, he took her into the kitchen, and stripped her from neck to waist, leaving her neck, shoulders, and back entirely naked. He then told her to cross her hands, calling her at the same time a d----d b-----d. After crossing her hands, he tied them with a strong rope, and led her to a stool under a large hook in the joist, put in for the purpose. He made her get up on the stool, and tied her hands to the hook.... after rolling up his sleeves, he commenced to lay on the heavy cowskin, and soon the warm, red blood ... came dripping to the floor. I was so terrified and horror-stricken at the sight, that I hid myself in a closet, and dared not venture out till long after the bloody transaction. (Douglass, 1994 [1845]: 19)

The most chilling aspect of this passage is Douglass's description of a 'hook in the joist, put in for the purpose'. This foregrounds how the plantation is a punishment factory with even aspects of internal décor adapted for the torture regime. The meat hook in the kitchen of the Anthony house is transformed into a device to hang live human meat for whipping. It is only with Douglass's dissident memory that the object's evil use in slave punishment can be uncovered; without it, visitors would be unable to fully interpret the internal décor of the house and the way it inscribes a horrific history. As Peter H. Wood describes, the 'plantation' would be better classified as a 'gulag' because 'Beyond the carefully maintained elegance and cultivation of the big house' were 'privately owned slave labour camps, sanctioned by the power of the state that persisted for generations' (Linenthal, 2006: 219).

From such examples we can see that, as constituted by the Lloyd family, the plantation and its surrounds is, in Nora's words, in fact a *lieux d'oublier* where the slave presence is elided or even worse misrepresented. Even if ready for a smattering of African American history, the Wye Plantation, like most Southern historical sites is 'not ready to abandon segregated spheres of memorialisation' (Tyler-McGraw, 2006: 158). This is nowhere more apparent than in the slave burial ground which, according to the segregationist tradition, is separate from the luxuriant family plots with their elaborate tombstones behind the house. It is across a cornfield and marked by no headstones except a recent general stone placed by the contemporary Lloyd family with the moniker 'for those who served'. Often on Southern plantations, slaves are designated servants by their masters to obscure their chattel service and pretend to a choice in their servitude. Obviously the choice of words here is a deliberate misrepresentation, glorying in a faithful service that elides the forcibly enslaved position of those buried in the gravesite.

The ghostly presences at the Wye enable a counter-memory to the Lloyd family's attempt at whitewashing history. But even officially sanctioned memorials, the signs that are meant to guide tourists around the district, should be accorded a sceptical investigation in this locale. Douglass is remembered by a plaque in the township of St. Michaels, the nearest town to his birth on the Tuckahoe Creek. Erected by town commissioners and the Maryland Historical Society in 1999, the marker reads:

> Born on Tuckahoe Creek, Talbot County, raised as a slave in St. Michaels area 1833–36. Taught self to read and write, conducted clandestine schools for blacks here. Escaped North. Became noted Abolitionist orator and editor. Returned 1872 as U.S. Marshal for the District of Columbia. Also served as DC Recorder of Deeds, U.S. Minister for Haiti.

This historical marker would seem, at first glance, to be an exemplary brief biographical description of a local hero who gained national and international fame as an Abolitionist and leading black political activist after his escape from slavery in the community. However, the neighbourhood of St. Michaels was not only the venue for the illicit (under state law in the South, teaching slaves was illegal) school for his fellow slaves which Douglass bravely ran during 1835 but, more pertinently, had been the town through which he and his fellow co-conspirators had been led in chains after their failed attempt at escape in April 1836. The townspeople shouted that he should 'have the hide taken from [his] back' (Douglass, 1994 [1855]: 320) and '[O]n reaching St. Michaels', he recalls, 'we underwent a sort of examination at my master's store' (Douglass, 1855: 321). There is no hint on the plaque that St. Michaels was the location of such dramatic events in Douglass's life, events that could have led to him being arraigned and sold away South to an even more pernicious slave regime. Pivotal to his maturation and to his later escape from the institution of slavery, this first attempt is wilfully omitted from the information provided in an attempt to place the township in the best possible light.

Obviously, for the brief notation on a plaque, there must be a brevity which will leave out the extraneous, but the choice to foreground Douglass's illicit school rather than his radical act of attempting to steal

himself away from his master points to a municipal manipulation of facts
that together with the version of history told at the Lloyd plantation means
that the locations of Frederick Douglass's birth, boyhood, youth and
young manhood are replete with *lieux de memoire* which must be dialogised through the information of his autobiographies to yield their full
radical meanings.

Official History (here with a capital 'H'), and the one presented to tourists, could be characterised as grossly inadequate in its representation of
such slave experience and although Seymour Drescher (2001: 112), in talking about the interface between monuments and history, makes a good
point about the limitations of memorials when he says that 'monuments
alone will not, in themselves, stimulate a constant rethinking of the past.
That remains the task of historians', one cannot help but think that his
special pleading for historians minimises the profession's shortcomings
which arise, in part at least, from its often obsessional empiricism. The
Angolan artist Miguel Petchkovsky highlights the interface between history and memory: 'Memory is an essential attribute of the human psyche
and is therefore more personal than historical or material knowledge.
History alone cannot enrich memory, because it is systematic and sequential' (Oostindie, 2001: xxxvi). Dialogising history with other forms, such as
biography, folklore, memorials and artistic representation, helps to fill that
contested history with the memories and experiences it needs in order to
reflect a more accurate and human face, to literally 'find an anchor for
memory' (Oguibe, 2001: 100). The tour of the Wye Plantation and environs
allowed for such anchoring through a dynamic and performative counter-
narrative, a guerrilla memory, that we tourists sought from our knowledge of slavery and Douglass's biography. Pierre Nora (1994: 285)
described how, '[H]istory is perpetually suspicious of memory and its true
mission is to suppress and deny it' and, at sites like the Wye Plantation,
there is plenty of evidence to show how dissident memory is denied by
the weight of traditional historical narrative and must fight back. Opening
up such buildings and other sites for tourist visitors cannot be undertaken
without the greatest care to tell their full story which has at its centre the
African slave labour that underpinned the beauty and wealth that becomes
ugly and tainted immediately the counter-narrative is introduced. The
presence of these counter-memories, of course, accompanies the keepers
of these memories, African people in the diaspora, and it is incumbent on
heritage sites and cityscapes to include their perspectives when interpreting and memorialising the past.

Britain and the Slave Trade: Lancaster's STAMP

The British experience, like the American one, has been of amnesia
which is only recently being corrected. Paul Gilroy (1993) has described

the powerful nature of this forgetting in a British context in the following terms:

> Once the history of empire becomes a source of discomfort, shame and perplexity, its complications and ambiguities were readily set aside. Rather than work through those feelings, that unsettling history was diminished, denied and then if possible actively forgotten. The resulting silence feeds an additional catastrophe: the error of imagining that post-colonial people are only unwanted alien intruders without any substantive historical, political or cultural connections to the collective life of their fellow subjects. (Gilroy, 2004: 98)

This discussion of the legacy of empire that makes of black British people little more than 'alien intruders' in a British polity that eschews such 'unsettling history' has resonances in locations throughout Britain, but nowhere more so than in the ports which were central hubs of imperial trade, some of which now apparently show remarkably few legacies from this glorious and sordid past. For instance, there is virtually no maritime commercial activity any more on the quayside at Lancaster. The once bustling port in the north-west of England is now home to yuppie flats and strolling tourists navigating between the old Custom House building and the maritime-themed pubs. The source of Lancaster's wealth in the West Indies direct trade and the Triangular slave trade are detailed in rather outdated exhibits in the Maritime Museum which is now the function of the Custom House building, designed in 1764 by Richard Gillow. However, the city has always buried this history away somewhere in the background of its tale of civic pride through mercantile endeavour. In fact, the local oral history of Lancaster slave traders is often about how Lancaster merchants coming from the fourth largest slave port were mere gentleman amateurs in comparison to the professionals down the coast in Liverpool. Nevertheless, as Melinda Elder, in her monograph on the Lancaster Slave Trade and subsequent research describes (Elder, 1992, 1994), Lancaster traders were involved in frantic and murderous slave raids on the African coast and, indeed, were engaged in joint ventures with Liverpool merchants so that some voyages counted in the statistics as belonging to the larger port had such significant input from Lancaster merchants that many think they should be counted as Lancaster voyages (Elder, 1994: 15).

With very few black British residents and the large majority of these being of Asian origin rather than Caribbean or African, there has historically been little impetus for the city to foreground this aspect of its past. In contradistinction to Bristol and Liverpool with their large African Caribbean communities, Lancaster has never experienced a sustained political demand to atone for its history of slave trading. However, many Lancastrians feel there is a political imperative for white people to remember the trade and their ancestors' exploitation of Africans for profit and think that the best way to do this is for them to be reminded of the centrality of the trade to the history of the city as they go about their daily life therein. As long as the story of slavery in the city is mainly confined to the museum it is readily ignored, both by locals and by visitors to the city.

In the absence of a memorial, the local *Slave Trade Arts Memorial Project (STAMP)* worked with a number of artists, schools and community groups to increase public awareness of the slave trade and developed a series of commemorative exhibitions and performances from 2003 to 2006, culminating in a permanent memorial to the Africans who were transported on board Lancaster ships which was unveiled in October 2005. The committee had been formed in September 2002 at a training day, held at the Maritime Museum, for teachers addressing issues raised by the slave trade. Their frustration over the lack of any focus for remembering the victims in the town that they could share with their pupils galvanised the small group of curators, educators, local NGO representatives and community workers into forming a campaign. As an academic in the field, I became *STAMP's* academic advisor. Throughout the project, our committee was aware of the tortured history of British imperialism and the city's own contribution to some of its excesses, made worse by a wilful historical amnesia. Barnor Hesse articulates this problematic and the way forward to overcome it with a welcome articulacy:

> Part of the difficulty with the dominant cultural form of Britain is the inability or reluctance of its institutions to accept that European racism was and is a constitutive feature of British nationalism. While this remains unexamined, resistant to decolonisation in the post-colonial period, it continues to generate a myriad of resistances and challenges to its historical formations. These dislocate the narration of Britain as a serialised essence, articulating the story-lines of a nation that is diversely politicised and culturally unsettled. Residual multicultural disruptions are constituted as forms of disturbance and intrusiveness by those resurgences of meaning, arising from the imperial past. They continually put into question, particularly in unexposed places and at unforeseen times, matters deemed in hegemonic discourses to be settled, buried and apparently beyond dispute. (Hesse, 2000: 18)

I quote Hesse in full because his intervention speaks to the legacy of British cities like Lancaster and the possibilities of overcoming the straitjacket imposed by amnesia and indifference. For the committee there was much unfinished business, a colonial legacy that still informed relations and ideas in the city, which the city's involvement in the Transatlantic slave trade highlighted. However, because it had never been properly debated, there was a vacuum which we felt needed to be filled so that the link between current racism and the historical chattel slavery which had helped form the very bricks and mortar of the city could be foregrounded and exposed. Our aim was to use the memorial and other project activities as 'residual multicultural disruptions' in the city to help undermine what we might, following Paul Gilroy's adaption of Patrick Wright's phrase, call 'the morbidity of heritage' that effected not only locals' interpretation of their city but tourists as well (Gilroy, 2004: 109). We wanted to make a vibrant living response to the historical legacy of slavery and imperialism that would reawaken debate and not allow a complacent settling of the debate in favour of a monoglot British nationalism. The project was interested in embedding memorialisation about slavery in the city and intent on leaving a legacy so that the memorial statuary was not felt to be imposed from above by the elite but that the city, its residents and visitors, had ownership of the process and finally of the monument itself. However, it was felt that this ownership should be in the context of a critical take on local and national histories that did not allow them to remain 'settled, buried and apparently beyond dispute', as Hesse had warned in his prescient commentary. Lubaina Himid (2001) spoke at the public meeting which launched *STAMP* and articulated the need we all felt to honour the African dead and abused who had been loaded onto ships which had been fitted out on Lancaster's quayside and the profits from whose sale had helped build the wealth of the city:

> If you are going to honour the dead who have been ignored, suppressed or denied when in peril in the past, you must do it because as a city you want to show that you would do differently now, that you would be able to defend those people now. You will first have to acknowledge that your city would not be the city it is, without the sacrifice of those who were sold by or used by the city in the past. This city can only aspire to being truly great if it can I suppose in some way seek forgiveness. Could it be that a monument is a tangible seeking of forgiveness? (Himid, 2003)

The very notion of 'forgiveness' in the context of a historical wrong from two centuries ago was bound to provoke uneasiness in some sections of the populace and a number of local residents vented their fury, particularly when the proposal originally planned to site the Modernist monument directly in front of the Custom House on the quayside. (The monument was eventually placed above Damside slipway at the opposite end of the quay from the Custom House due to plans for new flood defences that would have complicated its erection on the original site.)

Probably the most splenetic response came after the memorial design was published in the local paper, the *Lancaster Guardian*, in December 2004. James Mackie's letter left no doubt about his disgust:

> ... to find that a green light has been given to the erection of this nonsense is just upsetting. The quay is one of the few near-perfect parts of

Lancaster that still remain and the old customs house is one of the most beautiful and interesting landmarks in the county. Who in their right minds thinks that the area will be improved by a mosaic-encrusted plinth and a vessel in the grass verge containing 20 cast iron enslaved figures? The artist's impression that you printed with the article was not very large or detailed but is quite enough to show that the proposed artwork is simply repulsive. (Mackie, 2005: 6)

Mackie was not alone in his opposition and the erroneous belief that the City Council was funding the monument added to the venom. *Guardian* reader Betty Norton wrote that a monument 'depicting misery and shame is no enhancement to the city, it will turn visitors away' (Collins, 2005: 2). However, at no point did the opposition to the monument gain any political leverage on the Council. In fact, the Council Leader Ian Barker sprang to the defence of the *STAMP* committee in response to Mackie's letter, crafting an informed and elegant response:

History is more than the sanitised version sometimes served up by the heritage industry. We are privileged to live in a historic town. An understanding of its history can teach our children and us a lot. But it won't do so if we deceive ourselves by ignoring the painful and repellent aspects of that history.

I have no doubt that some of Lancaster's prosperous slavers were outstanding men in the local community, kind and considerate to their family and neighbours and yet simultaneously capable of inflicting barbarous treatment on unknown Africans. If the Slave Trade Arts Memorial Project (STAMP) helps us reflect on that contradiction and how it could happen, it will be worthwhile. (Barker, 2005: 6)

Barker's articulate support makes the point that citizens like Mackie and Norton who worry about the disruption to the 'near-perfect' quay by the visual complications of a memorial to the victims of the slave trade and the fact that this might frighten tourists away are merely supporters of a sanitised history that the city has been complicit in for too long.

There was an awareness in the committee of the need for a different kind of engagement with the past than would normally happen in the cityscape and that this might well engage visitors in new ways that might be a boon to tourists rather than a disincentive. The subsequent creation of a textual city trail using designs and texts by local school children with the help of local artists and historians was instrumental in making this new focus on the slave past an attractive incentive for tourists to discover for themselves a hitherto hidden history while wandering the town and hopefully contributing to the city's economy (Global Link, 2006). The committee had decided early on that they should make the encounter with this past an everyday occurrence rather than a pilgrimage or part of an educational tour. This was key to moving slavery and its important lessons about human rights and injustice from the periphery to the centre of consciousness. As Lubaina Himid articulates, this is done not by the grand gesture or by shock tactics, but by everyday encounter:

> If the person pushing their buggy past the memorial isn't thinking, 'Oh dear what a pity all those people died', but is thinking or just catches a glimpse of fabric out of the corner of their eye or a sparkle of water then there's a kind of flowing imprint, visible, physical, the sound of the water or the flash of the colour that flows into their life as they go past. There's no point even in trying to place something like that in people's lives. But memory is not about that, it's about tiny moments, little flickers of recognition. I'd want people to meet at the memorial; a place where you feel there's a kind of continuum, where there's a going on, a tomorrow. It would be there to enter into the fabric of the day. (Rice, 2003: 24)

The everyday nature of the encounter with the public work of art is key to its quiet effectiveness and Himid's future-focused intervention informed Kevin Dalton Johnson, our commissioned sculptor, as he completed the designs for his *Captured Africans* memorial. The final design of the memorial uses a variety of materials, including stone, steel and acrylic, to create a multi-textured take on Lancaster's slave trade history (Figure 12.1).

The plinth is a circular stone with an inlaid mosaic of the Atlantic triangle with lines showing the movement of ships between the continents of Europe, Africa and the Americas. Above it are a series of acrylic blocks named for the goods traded, cotton, sugar, mahogany and tobacco, with wealth named at the top because it is the prime motivation and slaves named at the bottom because they are the goods upon which the whole trade depends. Inlaid in the acrylic are icons of the goods, so that for wealth at the top there are coins and notes, while for the slaves at the bottom there is a diagram based on the famous depiction of the slave ship *Brookes*. Just beneath this bottom block are small bronze casts of black slave figures which Johnson developed with young people at risk in Lancaster. He felt it was very important that at least one part of the sculpture should be created by local people who do not consider themselves artists in any professional sense. The acrylic blocks are hung by poles between a steel panel and a carved piece of local Peakamoor stone, both of which image the shapes of a ship.[1] In an interview with Johnson, I discussed how the sculpture as commissioned fits into the environment where it has been sited so that it can become part of the everyday life of the citizens of the town:

> as the public come down and round the bend, just at the top of Damside, you're looking straight at the side of the sculpture, so you're looking through the spaces in between the acrylic blocks to the water on the other side, and that's picked up again by the blue of the mosaic,

Figure 12.1 'Captured Africans' sculpture, Lancaster
Photo: Paul Farina

because it's predominantly blue, so that works really well. And the stone which is going round the outside, that once again fits with the new buildings on either side. It operates on very different levels in as much as that it suits the context of a ship in the triangle, going down the slipway, off it goes after it's just dropped its cargo off. It also fits very well with aesthetic context where it's positioned, the colours of the apartments and the buildings that are built either side, and it works perfectly with the slipway going straight into the river. Having seen it erected, I'm quite confident that it'll work on different levels, both in terms of subject matter and also aesthetically in terms of the environment in which it's been placed. (Rice, 2006)

What the memorial successfully does is to arrest the attention of citizens and tourists as they first encounter it. For instance, a woman who did not know about the town's slave past told me how, out of the corner of her eye, she caught the words *Captured Africans* on the metal side of the sculpture and was compelled towards it to find out more. What Johnson wanted to do was to make the slave trade and its history central to the stories the city told about itself, so that they could never be elided again. Exhibiting the slave trade in a public space was key to this. The public space where the memorial has been placed is on a main thoroughfare into the town, right on the quayside. The committee and the artist felt it more important that the memorial should be close to the water which enabled the trade than in the town centre where it would have been dwarfed by buildings and, in part at least, decontextualised. Away from its habitual relegation to an often tired museum gallery the subject of slavery is made central to the narrative of the city, enabling its full historical and contemporary implications to be teased out. Sue Ashworth from Lancashire County Museum Service and a founder member of the *STAMP* committee discussed how important it is to move beyond the walls of the museum and how Dalton-Johnson's sculpture had achieved this:

> We've always acknowledged the slave trade ever since the Maritime Museum first opened 20 years ago. But it was always dealt with in a very dry way that just focused on the facts, the tonnage and the products involved. We saw an opportunity to let people actually contemplate what had happened rather than just be bombarded with figures. There doesn't have to be a disparity between something that's informative but also appeals to your senses. (Collins, 2005: 2)

Ashworth underlines the importance of the memorial doing different memory work that foregrounds the emotions as well as the intellect, hence multiplying the kinds of visitors the city would attract. The contemplative aspect of the sculpture, however, is at the service of serious political goals as Dalton-Johnson has a strong message for contemporary race relations from his engagement with this tortured history.

> Well, it's just a fact that black people could be treated like that, and if it could happen then, it can happen again now. The reason why we need to have a memorial is so it isn't repeated – it operates on that level. There's also the other political level, in that I'm not trying to get my own back, but I'm turning the tables, as if to say, you're getting a taste of how that feels. Putting the slave trade almost on trial, on exhibition, in the way that it's actually being presented, and the fact that it's a black artist doing that, re-emphasises the political statement. (Rice, 2006)

His desire to put the slave trade on trial is because of its implications for race relations in the here and now. As Johnson himself says, the pedagogical aspect of the memorial is very important: 'the reason why the ships' names are there, and the actual numbers of slaves that were on those ships. They're very clear, and they're not abstracted in the way that other parts have been' (Rice, 2006). Additionally, the names of the ships' captains are listed in all their Anglo-Saxon banality. Many of them are traditional Lancashire or more widely British surnames which they might well share with their local and tourist viewers. The sculpture does not resist such uncomfortable realities; in fact, it foregrounds them to make them part of the public memory so that white Lancastrians and Britons have to acknowledge these atrocities and hopefully learn from them before moving on. At the moment, slave traders are primarily remembered as citizens of note and many were prominent in the 18th century polity, such as Thomas Hinde who became mayor of the city in 1769. Johnson's statue, in naming names, is a guerrilla memorialisation that works against traditional historiography. Such guerrilla memorialisation confronts Lancaster's citizenry and other European tourists with their past in ways that work against traditional memorial praxis which has tended toward unifying viewers, principally around sympathy with the victims. Johnson does this, but also acknowledges that the perpetrators of the historical atrocity should be remembered and marked lest Lancaster's citizens forget their ancestors' role in the trade. James E. Young has talked about the importance of such reminiscence in comments about Holocaust memorials which can be related to *Captured Africans*:

> (the) aim is not to reassure or console, but to haunt visitors with the unpleasant – uncanny – sensation of calling into consciousness that which has been previously – even happily – repressed. (Young, 2001: 194)

The repression of uncomfortable historical facts has been key to white British responses to slavery and colonialism and Johnson's 'haunting' of visitors to his memorial through the uncannily familiar names is a device he uses to counteract complacency about the historic responsibility of white Lancastrians for the trade that helped to make the city's wealth. As Johnson explains, the memorial has different resonances for black people, himself included: 'I don't feel I have to do the sculpture in order to remember, because I won't forget'. He continues:

> So myself, and many other black people, do not necessarily need something physical in order to remember, because we live it every day, and the way that we're treated brings it all back, what our ancestors went through, even though it's not the same degree. Outside of the black perspective, inside the white community, it's very easy to forget, and I think there are many people that would like to forget – there's a combination, a mixture there, and for that reason I think this is very important, just to remember the atrocity that happened to the slave because that's got to be core. (Rice, 2006)

Thus the memorial is not simply designed to honour the memory of the slaves carried on the ships but to engage with the complexities of that history, to name the perpetrators and highlight the centrality of slavery to the fiscal and cultural economy of the city and of the nation beyond as a means to move forward. As Paul Ricoeur says of such kinds of memory work: 'it is justice that turns memory into a project, and it is this same project of justice that gives the form of the future and of the imperative to the duty of memory' (Ricoeur, 2004: 88). Memorials at their most effective speak to their future contexts as much as to the past they commemorate, to a future-orientated responsibility, rather than a guilt-charged retrieval of a static past.

Ricoeur's statement is particularly pertinent in the wake of the Morecambe Bay tragedy of February 2004, where 23 ethnic Chinese cockle pickers died due to Victorian working conditions and a bonded labour regime that must to them have seemed akin to slavery. Hence, the memorial now has local contemporary resonances and can speak to modern forms of bonded labour too, showing the prescience of Himid's commentary noted earlier and how the local community in Lancaster has not only to respond the human rights struggles of the past but also to the corrupt practices of global capitalism that continues to throw up bodies on our beaches over 200 years after the Lancaster slave trade and the tragedy of countless slaves' social and actual deaths, albeit most of these on foreign shores.

Sue Flowers' installation, *One Tenth*, produced for the Lancashire Museum Service's Lancaster-based project *Abolished?*, expands the work of the memorial into the museums of the city, continuing the creative dialogue with the city's history and engaging in its own form of guerrilla memorialisation. The installation dialogises an extant museum collection replete with the evidence of the 'crime', accompanied by a rewriting of panels in the slavery gallery to reflect the latest scholarship on the Lancaster slave trade. The installation comments acerbically, specifically on the building it is housed in. An oil portrait of Dodshon Foster (1730–1792) had always been centrally displayed in Richard Gillow's (1764) Old Custom House in Lancaster, now the Maritime Museum. Flowers, though, wanted to highlight not this figure's bourgeois respectability as a Lancaster merchant whose house and warehouse adjoined the Gillow building, but his criminal involvement in the slave trade. Her installation dialogises the portrait (which is retained in its usual place in the room) by a bright, evocative African flag which dramatically remakes the building's interior, specifically by making images of Foster as a criminal and having them put behind bars in the windows. She says:

> The installation attempts to subvert our daily understanding of Lancaster and its history. Here the wealthy merchant is transformed into a man of our times and becomes trapped into the very fabric of the building. Here one man is criminalised – reframed inside a building which represented his wealth and power. A new representation of the man is created in a new portrait and a series of images have

become trapped behind the protective bars of the window frames. (Flowers & Himid, 2007)

Flowers' installation is replete with images of sugar and sugar cane to emphasise the goods which were exchanged for the slaves. At the centre of the room is a modelling of figures in a slave ship in the shape of sugar loaves. This reinterpretation of the infamous 1788 *Description of a Slave Ship* is linked directly to Foster's crime through an intentional numerological conceit, for the 55 loaves are representative of those taken on the voyages of his ship the *Barlborough* between 1752 and 1757.

> The whole of this work acts as a memorial to One Tenth of the enslaved Africans on the merchant ship the Barlborough and forms an epitaph to those who exploited then and the many more millions exploited internationally in the past and the present. (Flowers & Himid, 2007)

The enslaved Africans are shown to be commodified by a slave trade that sees them as goods to be exchanged. The abstraction of the enslaved Africans by the Middle Passage is shown at its most extreme in the 550 numbered fibre-glass sugar cubes that overflow in another section of the installation. Here, the black numbers on the white cubes are clean cut and dramatic evocations of the economism that denies humanity at the centre of the slave trade. Flowers, though, goes further, modelling Foster's head in a fibreglass that resembles sugar, dramatising the way his criminal pursuit of wealth has dehumanised him, turned him into the very commodity he selfishly pursued. As Sue Flowers says, 'the work acts as a memorial for the dead as much as an indictment of the criminal' (Flowers & Himid, 2007) and this is its strength as a site-specific work of art that speaks to the ghosts of Lancaster's slave past in the very building where much of that trade was recorded. The strength of such guerrilla memorialisation is that it is so woven into the fabric of the building that it cannot be naysayed. Successful installations like Flowers' *One Tenth* (2007) show how the heritage industry is not necessarily beholden to a conservative historiography of imperial triumph and that radical curatorial praxis can refigure a city's memorial space.

This is not always the case, however, and was illustrated most appositely when the National Maritime Museum in Greenwich sought to illustrate the central role of slavery in the success of the British Empire when the new *Empire and Trade* galleries were inaugurated in 1999. London was the second largest slave port after Liverpool, but this is generally overlooked so that tourists to the capital city have rarely had to confront the issue of the slave trade as being an issue local to the city. At the centre of the Greenwich exhibit was a tableau of a manacled black hand coming out from a hatch beneath an English lady drinking tea. It sought to illustrate how British refinement was bought at the cost of human degradation and exploitation. It proved too difficult for many British commentators to stomach and, after a series of splenetic letters to national newspapers and to the gallery itself, it was finally withdrawn. Robert Blyth, a curator at the museum, said that, although regrettable, the climb-down in the face of such pressure was not disastrous, as 'the tableau had done its job by the controversy it had generated' (Blyth, 2001). However, the effective censorship of the tableau meant that a crucial aspect of the narrative of Empire, the slave trade and its consequences had been elided so that the galleries effectively moved from being a potential *lieu de memoire*, however limited, to an actual *lieu d'oubli*. Subsequently, London's local story of slavery has been foregrounded in a new exhibition in Docklands opened in 2007. However, the debacle at Greenwich shows the politically charged nature of trying to tell the story of slavery effectively.

Remembering Slavery Through Children's Models

This difficulty in relating the story of slavery is illustrated in the Whitworth Art Gallery *Trade and Empire* Exhibition which was inaugurated as part of the 2007 commemorations of the Bicentenary of the Abolition of the Slave Trade. Here, there was a real attempt to deal with hidden histories by re-evaluating objects from the collection which had hitherto not been fully contextualised. Nothing could be more mundane than Abraham Solomon's 1845 portrait of 'Mrs Rosa Samuel and her Three Daughters', an everyday portrait of a Victorian family at ease in their place in the world. However, this family portrait belies the dark history of slavery that made the Samuel family's wealth. Rosa, the matriarch of the family, was born in 1809. She married her cousin, Ralph Henry Samuel, a prominent member of the Jewish community in Liverpool, a textile merchant who with his family also ran a successful cotton plantation in Rio de Janeiro, Brazil. The family made regular visits to their Brazilian plantation, unlike many plantation owners who were notorious absentee landowners and left their holdings entirely in the hands of often brutal overseers.

What makes their Brazilian connections so interesting is that they brought back with them the four models which were exhibited alongside the portrait (Figure 12.2). These four brightly dressed models are fascinating 'mementoes' of the Samuel family's sojourns in Brazil. They offer a unique insight into the dynamics of the slave–master relationship which have ramifications far beyond this one family's ideals and motivations. Made in the 1830s to mark Samuel's freeing of his slaves, they are brightly and ornately dressed in clothing that reflects their newly enfranchised status. We have no knowledge as to the motivation of Samuel in freeing his slaves long before emancipation in Brazil (1888). However, we can speculate that the legislation to free the slaves in the British Empire in

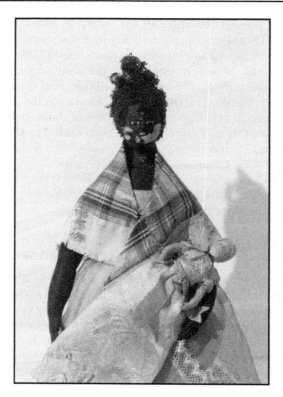

Figure 12.2 Model of freed slave
Photo: Courtesy of Whitworth Art Gallery

1833 gave him the impetus to emancipate those on his British-owned piece of soil in Latin America. The figures themselves, although individu-alised and dressed imaginatively in their market-day best, are rather crudely modelled after caricatured images of Africans and could have been influenced by the nascent blackface minstrel depictions emerging in the circum-Atlantic world in the 1830s. We can speculate that the models were played with by the daughters of the house and reminded the whole family of their Brazilian holdings when they were back in Britain. One of the female figures carries a white baby, showing how closely involved in the family's life black slave/servants were. Psychologically, they reveal the family's need for their African servants to be contained and confined in representations ordained by their master even after their actual eman-cipation. These figures are representative of the family retaining control of their docile black servants: this reflects a continuing theme in black–white relations and representations, the infantilisation of Africans through slavery, imperialism and colonialism. These objects bring with them many dilemmas for curators. Should we be preserving objects that potentially glorify a racist system that has ramifications for visitors today? As each model will take over £2000 to conserve, can such expense be justified for objects that are so tainted by their ownership and the troubled history of racial representation they exemplify? The curators wanted the exhibition to serve as a starting point for debate on these issues, but realised that the very unveiling of such troubling objects could prove problematic for many visitors.

Eventually, the very debate about the objects was used to enhance this section of the exhibition, adding labels that showed the discussion among the curators and comments from a critic of the interpretation of the objects. By doing this the curators hoped to show the open-endedness of the exhibition and the way that even their perceptions can be dialogised both internally and externally, creating a debate rather than closing it by seemingly authoritative and all-encompassing interpretations. The public comment coming from a collector of such objects critiqued the politically charged conclusions about the models:

> It is my opinion they were made in the image of the slaves on the plantation who possibly cared for the children. There is no argument they are images of slaves, but I do not think the images are racist; on the contrary, I think they were made to remind the children of the servants they were closest to.
>
> These dolls are black with red lips but remind me of African dolls I have seen for sale in West African markets made with felt, wool and cotton cloth. Dolls made by Africans, in the image of the people around them, not intended to be racist. (Anonymous Visitor, 2008)

However, as can be seen by Suandi's commentary, some of the curators were even more radically disturbed by the images. Her comments illustrate how the vigorous debate between the curators was foregrounded in the last few weeks of the show, enabling the usually private discussion to have a fully public airing.

> If it had simply been a matter of choice without hesitation, I would have chosen to place these horrendous things back into the darkest corner of the collection cupboard. They do not resemble me or any other Black person. Yet still I recognise that they are meant to be all of my people. Formed and shaped into raggedy dolls for the children of the plantation owner to drag behind them much the same way as slaves were dragged into labour.
>
> To hide the past, to conceal those parts of it which displease, hurt or offend is to collude with those who only want to speak of the past as a time of pride and glory. What civilised person is proud of how the British Empire was built?

My fellow curator was right in his decision to include them. To trap them under glass like the very specimens they are. To have them stare out at the visitor with their beady dead eyes. They represent the silence of the slave. (Suandi, 2008)

The display of such objects is charged with controversy; however, the tourist viewer is best served, not by censorship or sensationalism, but by being given access to the debate of the curators and between the curators and their public. Slavery and the racism that it spawned are replete with histories and objects that have been suppressed. Full disclosure is often painful, but is surely preferable to the saccharine narratives that are too often told. Edward T. Linenthal, in outlining the importance of slavery heritage sites in America, describes how '[C]onscientious remembrance is more than a necessary expansion of the nation's narrative. It is an act of moral engagement, a declaration that there are other American lives too long forgotten that count' (Linenthal, 2006: 224). As I hope I have illustrated in this chapter, such 'conscientious remembrance' is needed in slavery sites and in the interpretation of objects in exhibitions about slavery throughout the circum-Atlantic.

Note

1.   Images of the sculpture and an explanation of the *STAMP* project can be found at www.uclan.ac.uk/abolition.

Chapter 13

Life, Death and Dark Tourism: Future Research Directions and Concluding Comments

RICHARD SHARPLEY and PHILIP R. STONE

> *Life is not separate from death. It only looks that way.*
> Blackfoot – Native American proverb

During the writing of this book, we were fortunate to be able to take a group of our final year undergraduate students to Gunther von Hagens' Body Worlds exhibition at the Museum of Science and Industry (MOSI) in Manchester, UK. Since the first such exhibition was held in Mannheim in Germany in the winter of 1997/1998, it has proved to be highly popular – almost 780,000 people visited the first exhibition over a period of four months while, according to staff at Manchester's MOSI, the 2008 Body Worlds exhibition was not only the most popular held at the museum to date but it also attracted the highest number of people to visit an exhibition at MOSI in one day. At the same time, of course, and as discussed in a number of chapters in this book, Body Worlds has proved to be highly controversial, not least because of Gunther von Hagens himself who, through his creation of the Body Worlds exhibits and other activities such as performing a public autopsy in London in 2002, has courted praise and controversy in equal measure.

The foreword to the Body Worlds catalogue suggests two reasons for the continuing popularity of and fascination in the exhibition. Firstly, it allows people to view things never seen before; the exhibition displays the complex structure of the human body, in effect providing people with the opportunity to see inside their physical selves. Secondly, it touches on the taboo of death:

> In our society, death is repressed, blocked out, so to speak and the corpses of other people, at least, are viewed with a repulsive shudder – drilled into us through daily assaults by the same media pictures. Many people went to see the [Body Worlds] exhibition with such

expectations, and experienced that this revulsion actually decreased as they viewed the specimens, that it was lost completely and instead both amazement and a thirst for knowledge began to manifest themselves. For each visitor, this was ultimately a personal victory. (Kriz, 2007: 6)

For our students who visited the exhibition in Manchester, Body Worlds provoked contrasting emotions. For some, it did indeed prove to be a fascinating and memorable experience – a number commented that it was one of the best or most interesting exhibitions they had ever visited, an experience from which they had learnt something about themselves. For others, however, it was a depressing, unsettling and unpleasant experience. Their reaction to some of the exhibits, particularly the display of plastinated foetuses at varying stages of development, was a mixture of sadness and revulsion, and they felt that the exhibition was little more than exploitative 'edutainment'.

Not surprisingly, these differing responses were also reflected in a comprehensive book of visitor comments at the exhibition which revealed that, even within the context of a single event or attraction, many of the questions surrounding dark tourism more generally – questions which this book set out to address – are both relevant and very real in contemporary society. Certainly, the evident popularity of Body Worlds (the exhibition in Manchester, for example, was extended to meet demand) suggests a widespread interest in or fascination with life, death and mortality, but are there deeper-rooted reasons for visiting the exhibition or other dark sites? Does it permit the visitor to contemplate mortality and death (or life)? Are people drawn to Body Worlds by a ghoulish fascination or by a search for meaning? Do some dark tourism sites and attractions provide a post-visit mediation between life and death? Does the interpretation of dark sites, through specific ideological messages, kitsch displays, sanitised horror or, as in the case of Body Worlds, alleged scientific endeavour, provide a shield to the realities of death, mortality, tragedy or horror, a 'comfort blanket' against moral panics? Do visits to dark sites heighten a sense of mortality or of survival, an understanding of death or life? And, what are the ethical and management challenges surrounding the development, promotion and interpretation of dark sites and attractions, if indeed it is appropriate or accurate to label particular places or events as such?

This book has gone some way, we hope, towards answering a number of these questions but, at the same time, many chapters have identified a number of other questions and issues that deserve attention if a more complete understanding of the phenomenon of dark tourism is to be achieved. Generally, though, and as noted in the introductory chapter to this book, early academic attention on the subject was focused largely on defining and categorising dark tourism from both a supply and demand (i.e. 'thanatouristic') perspective and, by the time Lennon and Foley's book *Dark Tourism: The Attraction of Death and Disaster* was published in 2000, some significant academic work had already been undertaken into specific forms of tourism associated with death, atrocity and disaster, especially within the disciplines of museology, human geography and cultural studies. However, their book firmly established the term dark tourism in both academic and media circles and was undoubtedly influential in stimulating further research into the subject. Since then, of course, the dark tourism literature has expanded significantly, exploring and sub-categorising particular manifestations of tourism related implicitly or explicitly to death, atrocity and disaster and addressing a variety of issues concerned with the management and interpretation of dark sites. Nevertheless, research into dark tourism within a broader socio-cultural and political framework has remained limited. In particular, an implicit question within the title of Lennon and Foley's book – that is, what *is* the 'attraction of death and disaster'? – has remained largely unanswered. It is this question, and related issues, that the contributions to this book have attempted to address.

Overall, what has emerged from this book is the sense that, in some ways, 'dark tourism' is an unhelpful term. On the one hand, it undoubtedly arouses curiosity, makes good newspaper headlines – the phenomena of tourism and death/disaster are an unlikely, intriguing combination – and provides a broad framework for categorising and exploring forms of tourism that are, in some way or another, associated with death, horror, tragedy, atrocity or disaster. On the other hand, not only does it have negative connotations – the word 'dark' hinting at ghoulish interest in the macabre or, perhaps, an element of *schadenfreude* on the part of the tourist – but it is also, essentially, a label attached to the supply or production of attractions, events and experiences. That is, much of the analysis of dark tourism focuses on specific dark places or attractions, such as battlefields, cemeteries, prisons, Holocaust sites and so on. Indeed, much of the earlier research into dark tourism was concerned principally with creating, in effect, typologies of sites, attractions and activities related in one way or another with death and suffering.

However, tourism experiences in general occur at the so-called 'moment of truth', through the instantaneous production and consumption of touristic services. Thus, the overall nature of a tourism experience depends on both the characteristics of the object of consumption (the site, attraction or event) and the way it is consumed (the needs, expectations, perceptions and experience of the tourist). In other words, dark tourism experiences in particular can be described as such only if both the site and its meaning or attraction to the tourist is related in some way to the death or suffering of others. As discussed in the book, however, there exists an enormous diversity of sites and attractions that, dependent upon a variety of temporal, spatial and other factors, can be placed along a continuum or spectrum of darkness (Stone, 2006). Equally, the significance or meaning of such sites and attractions to the tourist, and the ways in which they are consumed, are also infinitely variable. Thus, the blanket categorisation of visits to places or events of, or associated with, death as 'dark tourism' simplifies and hides a multitude of meanings and purposes with respect to both their production and consumption.

In particular, and as a number of chapters in this book have demonstrated, our understanding of the relationship between tourists and dark sites remains limited. People may be drawn purposefully to such sites, perhaps seeking an opportunity to contemplate death and mortality in a society where death is sequestered and absent; conversely, a sense of ontological security may be the unexpected or unintended outcome of a visit to a dark site. Moreover, as Walter suggests in Chapter 3, the significance of dark tourism may not lie in the relationship between sites and tourists per se, but in what it might reveal more generally about the relationship between the living, the dead and society's institutions for mediating in that relationship. There is, therefore, a pressing need for empirical research into the ways in which dark sites are consumed, both in terms of tourists' motivations and experience and more generally in terms of the function of dark sites as one of many social institutions that mediate between life and death.

At the same time, and as other chapters in this book have considered, the ways in which dark sites are consumed are themselves mediated by a variety of influences, such as the broader historical, political or cultural framework within which they are located, the ideological underpinnings of the narratives they present or, more simply, the techniques by which dark places or events are interpreted or represented. Again, therefore, there is a need for research into the implications of differing narratives and different forms of interpretation on the nature and consequences of visitors' experiences at dark sites. Does, for example, the experience of 'unsanitised' genocide sites have a positive impact on visitors or does it enhance a sense of moral panic? How do differing representations impact upon different visitor groups? Is it possible to present politically and culturally 'neutral' interpretations of dark sites or is some degree of dissonance inevitable?

These, and many other questions that have emerged from this book, must remain the focus of future enquiry. However, in developing and expanding upon existing perspectives on dark tourism within broader socio-cultural and political frameworks, the book has revealed that it is a complex, emotive, multi-dimensional, politically vulnerable, and ethically and morally challenging phenomenon. There are no simple definitions of dark tourism, no simple answers to many of the questions that surround it, and no quick solutions to the challenges or dilemmas inherent in the development and promotion of dark sites. Nevertheless, as a particular theme in tourism studies (though not necessarily a specific type of tourism, for the reasons outlined above), it is not only a fascinating subject in its own right but it also represents, as with the study of tourism more generally, a powerful vehicle for exploring contemporary social life, practices and institutions. In other words, the principal benefit of studying dark tourism lies in what it reveals, or may reveal, about the relationship between life and death, the living and the dead, and the institutions or processes that mediate, either at the individual or societal level, between life and death. Indeed, as Stone concludes in Chapter 2, although the term 'dark tourism' implies a focus on death and dying, developing our understanding of the phenomenon may, ironically, tell us more about life and the living.

References

AFX News (2005) US acknowledges torture at Guantanamo. *AFX News* (24 June). On WWW at http://www.forbes.com/work/feeds/afx/2005/06/24/afx2110388. html. Accessed 9.1.09.

AHI (Association for Heritage Interpretation) (2008) At http://www.ahi.org.uk/.

Alderman, D. (2002) Writing on the Graceland wall: On the importance of author-ship in pilgrimage landscapes. *Tourism Recreation Research* 27 (2), 27–35.

Alexrk2 (2008) *London Dungeon*. On WWW at http://www.flickr.com/search/?q= dungeon&w=8487765%40N02. Accessed 14.07.09.

Anderson, B. (1991) *Imagined Communities*. London and New York: Verso.

Anon (1903) Bad elephant killed: Topsy meets quick and painless death at Coney Island. *The Commercial Advertiser* (5 Jan). On WWW at http://www. railwaybridge.co.uk/topsy.html. Accessed 12.12.08.

Anon (2003) Terrorháza: Andrássy Út 60 – House of Terror. *Official Catalogue*.

Arca News Agency (2008) Armenia tourist arrivals rise. On WWW at http://www. arka.am/eng/tourism/2008/02/04/7938.html. Accessed 12.11.08.

Ariès, P. (1974) *Western Attitudes Toward Death: From the Middle Ages to the Present*. Baltimore, MA: Johns Hopkins University Press.

Armenian Genocide Memorial-Institute (2007a) *Museum Information*. Yerevan, Armenia: Armenian Genocide Memorial-Institute. On WWW at http://www. genocide-museum.am/eng/index.php.

Armenian Genocide Memorial-Institute (2007b) *Institute Goals and Endeavors*. Yerevan, Armenia: Armenian Genocide Memorial-Institute. On WWW at http://www.genocide-museum.am/eng/index.php.

Armenian Genocide Memorial-Institute (2007c) *Description and History*. Yerevan, Armenia: Armenian Genocide Memorial-Institute. On WWW at http://www. genocide-museum.am/eng/index.php.

Armstrong, K. (2007) *The Bible. The Biography*. London: Atlantic Books.

Ashworth, G. (1996) Holocaust tourism and Jewish culture: The lessons of Kraków-Kazimierz. In M. Robinson, N. Evans and P. Callaghan (eds) *Tourism and Cultural Change* (pp. 1–12). Sunderland: Business Education Publishers.

Ashworth, G. and Hartmann, R. (2005a) *Horror and Human Tragedy Revisited: The Management of Sites of Atrocities for Tourism*. New York: Cognizant Communications Corporation.

Ashworth, G. and Hartmann, R. (2005b) Introduction: Managing atrocity for tour-ism. In G. Ashworth and R. Hartmann (eds) *Horror and Human Tragedy Revisited: The Management of Sites of Atrocities for Tourism* (pp. 1–14). New York: Cognizant Communications Corporation.

Ashworth, G. and Hartmann, R. (2005c) The management of horror and human tragedy. In G. Ashworth and R. Hartmann (eds) *Horror and Human Tragedy Revisited: The Management of Sites of Atrocities for Tourism* (pp. 253–262). New York: Cognizant Communications Corporation.

Atiyah, J. (1999) After the peace deals are signed, the gawpers arrive. *Independent on Sunday* (6 June). On WWW at http://www.kabulcaravan.com/articles_tourism09.html. Accessed 29.03.04.

Atkinson, D. (2005) Tomb raiders: Beaches and theme parks? Forget it – dark tourism is the new way to enjoy yourself. *Guardian Unlimited*. On WWW at http://travel.guardian.co.uk/darktourism/story/0,16652,1600232,00.html.

Audley Travel (2008) *Tailor-made Armenia: Places to See and Stay*. Witney: Audley Travel.

Auschwitz-Birkenau State Museum (2007) *Auschwitz Memorial – Situation as of 2007*. Oswicem, Poland: Auschwitz-Birkenau State Museum.

Austin, N. (2000) Tourism and the transatlantic slave trade: Some issues and reflections. In P. Dieke (ed.) *The Political Economy of Tourism Development in Africa* (pp. 208–216). New York: Cognizant Communication Corporation.

Avis, A. (2007) Seek, so you may find. *Turkish Daily News* (3 Nov). On WWW at http://www.turkishdailynews.com.tr/article.php?enewsid=87581. Accessed 30.7.08.

Baranauskas, E. (2002) Welcome to Grutas Park. *Bridges* 3. On WWW at http://www.javlb.org/bridges/2002/april2002/grutasx.pdf. Accessed 8.8.08.

Barboza, D. (2006) China turns out mummified bodies for displays. *New York Times* (8 Aug). On WWW at http://www.nytimes.com/2006/08/08/business/worldbusiness/08bodies.html?_r=1&adxnnl=1&oref=slogin&adxnnlx=1210612861-ZEwEXL/houmVQ+wQyvhRng.

Barker, Coun. I. (2005) Slavery is part of what we are (Letter). *Lancaster Guardian* (14 Jan), 6.

Barthes, R. (1993) *Camera Lucida*. London: Vintage.

Bauman, Z. (1989) *Modernity and the Holocaust*. Oxford: Polity.

Bauman, Z. (1993) *Postmodern Ethics*. Cambridge: Polity.

BBC (2008) Interview. *Today Programme*. BBC Radio 4 (21 Aug).

BBC News (2003) New York honours electrocuted elephant. *BBC News/Americas* (21 July). On WWW at http://news.bbc.co.uk/1/low/world/americas/3083029.stm. Accessed 12.12.08.

BBC News (2004) *Rwanda: How the Genocide Happened*. On WWW at http://news.bbc.co.uk/1/hi/world/africa/1288230.stm.

Beck, U. and Beck-Gernsheim, E. (2002) *Individualization: Individualism and its Social and Political Consequences*. London: Sage.

Becker, E. (1973) *The Denial of Death*. New York: Free Press.

Beech, J. (2000) The enigma of Holocaust sites as tourist attractions – the case of Buchenwald. *Managing Leisure* 5, 29–41.

Beech, J. (2001) The marketing of slavery heritage in the United Kingdom. In G. Dann and A. Seaton (eds) *Slavery, Contested Heritage and Thantourism* (pp. 85–105). Binghampton, NY: Haworth Hospitality Press.

Beesley, L. (2004) The management of emotion in tourism research settings. *Tourism Management* 26 (2), 261–275.

Bell, C. (2004) *Grace Darling: Heroine of the Farne Islands*. Bamburgh: Darling Books.

Beloff, H. (2007) Immortality work: Photographs as memento mori. In M. Mitchell (ed.) *Remember Me* (pp. 179–192). London: Routledge.

Bennett, G. and Round, S. (1997) Death in folklore: A selective listing from the Journal of the Folklore Society. *Mortality* 2, 221–238.

Berger, P. (1967) *The Sacred Canopy: Elements of a Sociological Theory of Religion.* New York: Doubleday.

Berlant, L. (1999) The subject of true feeling: Pain, privacy, and politics. In A. Sarat and T. Kearns (eds) *Cultural Pluralism, Identity Politics and the Law* (pp. 49–84). Ann Arbor, MI: University of Michigan Press.

Best, M. (2007) Norfolk Island: Thanatourism, history and visitor emotions. *Shima: The International Journal of Research into Island Cultures* 1 (2), 30–48.

Best, S. and Kellner, D. (2001) *The Postmodern Adventure.* London: Routledge.

BH Tourism (undated) *Srebrenica.* Tourism Association of the Federation of Bosnia and Herzegovina. On WWW at http://www.bhtourism.ba/eng.

Bilgrami, A. (2005) Interpreting a distinction. In H. Bhaba and W. Mitchell (eds) *Edward Said: Continuing the Conversation* (pp. 26–35). Chicago, IL: University of Chicago Press.

Blair, J. (2002) Tragedy turns to tourism at Ground Zero. *The New York Times* (29 June). On WWW at http://www.theage.com.au/articles/2002/06/28/10238646 57451.html. Accessed 31.7.08.

Blom, T. (2000) Morbid tourism: A postmodern market niche with an example from Althorp. *Norwegian Journal of Geography* 54 (1), 29–36.

Bly, L. (2003) Disaster strikes, tourists follow. *USA Today.* On WWW at http://www.usatoday.com/travel/vacations/destinations/.../2002-08-30-disaster-tourism.html.

Blyth, R. (2001) *Tour of Empire and Trade Galleries* (10 Mar). London: National Maritime Museum, Greenwich.

Bocock, R. (1993) *Consumption.* London: Routledge.

Boorstin, D. (1964) *The Image: A Guide to Pseudo-Events in America.* New York: Harper & Row.

Boskovic, A. (2007) *The Other in Anthropology and Cultural Studies.* On WWW at http://www.gape.prg/sasa/lecture201.htm. Accessed 25.7.08.

Bougle, C. (1926) *The Evolution of Values* (H. Sellars, trans.). New York: Henry Holt.

Bowlby, J. (1979) *The Making and Breaking of Affectional Bonds.* London: Tavistock.

Bristow, R. and Newman, M. (2004) Myth vs. fact: An exploration of fright tourism. *Proceedings of the 2004 Northeastern Recreation Research Symposium* (pp. 215–221). Westfield, MA: Westfield State College.

Brotherston, G. (1979) *Image of the New World: The American Continent Portrayed in Native Texts.* London: Thames and Hudson.

Bruner, E. (1996) Tourism in Ghana: The representation of slavery and the return of the black diaspora. *American Anthropologist* 98 (2), 290–304.

Bryant, C.D. (1989) Thanatological Crime: Some conceptual notes on offenses against the dead as a neglected form of deviant behaviour. Paper presented at the World Congress of Victimology, Acapulco.

Bryant, C. and Shoemaker, D. (1997) Death and the dead for fun (and profit): Thanatological entertainment as popular culture. Conference Paper, Southern Sociological Society, Atlanta, GA.

Bubriski, K. (2002) *Pilgrimage: Looking at Ground Zero.* New York: Powerhouse Books.

Buckley, P. and Witt, S. (1990) Tourism in the centrally-planned economies of Europe. *Annals of Tourism Research* 17 (1), 7–18.

Bunyan, N. (2003) Paralysed man pays £40 to die legally. *Daily Telegraph* (21 Jan).

Burg, A. (2008) *The Holocaust is Over: We Must Rise from its Ashes.* Basingstoke: Palgrave MacMillan.

Burns, P. (2005) Social identities, globalisation and the cultural politics of tourism. In W. Theobald (ed.) *Global Tourism* (3rd edn) (pp. 391–405). Oxford: Butterworth-Heinemann.

Burns, L. (2007) Gunther von Hagens' Body Worlds: Selling beautiful education. *The American Journal of Bioethics* 7 (4), 12–23.

Butcher, J. (2003) *The Moralisation of Tourism: Sun Sand ... And Saving the World.* London: Routledge.

Butler, D. (2001) Whitewashing plantations: The commodification of a slave-free antebellum south. In G. Dann and A. Seaton (eds) *Slavery, Contested Heritage and Thanatourism* (pp. 163–175). Binghampton, NY: Haworth.

Bushaway, R. (1993) Name upon name: The Great War and Remembrance. In R. Porter (ed.) *Myths of the English* (pp. 136–167). Cambridge: Polity Press.

Buzinde, C. and Santos, C. (2008) Representations of slavery. *Annals of Tourism Research* 35 (2), 469–488.

Byock, I. (2002) The meaning and value of death. *Journal of Palliative Medicine* 5, 279–288.

Cable News Network (2001) *Lithuanian Opens Soviet Theme Park.* On WWW at http://edition.cnn.com/2001/WORLD/europe/04/03/grutas.theme/. Accessed 1.8.08.

Caddick-Adams, P. (2007) Footsteps across time: The evolution, use and relevance of battlefield visits to the British Armed Forces. Unpublished PhD thesis, Cranfield University.

Cahoone, L. (1996) *From Modernism to Postmodernism: An Anthology.* Cambridge, MA: Blackwell.

Caillois, R. (1950) *L'homme et Le Sacre.* Paris: Gallimard.

Calinescu, M. (1987) *Five Faces of Modernity: Modernism, Avant-garde, Decadence, Kitsch, Postmodernism.* Durham, NC: Duke University Press.

Cameron, F. (2003) Transcending fear – engaging emotions and opinion – a case for museums in the 21st century. *Open Museum Journal (New Museum Developments & the Culture Wars)* 6. On WWW at http://archive.amol.org.au/omj/abstract. asp?ID=28. Accessed 11.1.09.

Cameron, D. (2008) David Cameron attacks UK 'moral neutrality': Full text of speech given in Glasgow. *The Daily Telegraph* (7 July). On WWW at http://www. telegraph.co.uk/news/newstopics/politics/conservative/2263705/David-Cameron-attacks-UK-'moral-neutrality'---full-text.html. Accessed 4.8.08.

Cannell, F. (ed.) (2007) *The Anthropology of Christianity.* Durham, NC: Duke University Press.

Cano, L. and Mysyk, A. (2004) Cultural tourism, the State and the Day of the Dead. *Annals of Tourism Research* 31 (4), 879–898.

Carlson, J. (2008) Edison vs. elephant on Coney Island. *Gothamist* (4 Jan). On WWW at http://gothamist.com/2008/01/04/edison_vs_eleph.php#comments. Accessed 12.12.08.

Carroll, L. (1865) The Mock Turtle's Story. In *Alice's Adventures in Wonderland* (Ch. 9). London: MacMillan.

Cheong, S. and Miller, M.L. (2000) Power and tourism: A Foucauldian observation. *Annals of Tourism Research* 27 (2), 371–390.

Chhabra, D., Healy, R. and Sills, E. (2003) Staged authenticity and heritage tourism. *Annals of Tourism Research* 30 (3), 702–719.

Christian, W. (1971) *Person and God in a Spanish Valley.* New York: Seminar Press.

Chronis, A. (2005) Coconstructing heritage at the Gettysburg storyscape. *Annals of Tourism Research* 32 (2), 386–406.

Clayson, A. (1997) *Death Disks: Mortality in the Popular Song.* London: Sanctuary.

Claytron (2006) *London Dungeon.* On WWW at http://www.flickr.com/search/?q= dungeon&w=87836984%40N00. Accessed 14.07.09.

Cohen, E. (1988) Authenticity and commoditization in tourism. *Annals of Tourism Research* 15 (3), 371–386.

Cole, T. (1999a) *Images of the Holocaust: The Myth of the 'Shoah Business'*. London: Gerald Duckworth.
Cole, T. (1999b) *Selling the Holocaust. From Auschwitz to Schindler: How History is Bought, Packaged, and Sold*. New York: Routledge.
Collins, R. (1988) The Durkheimian tradition in conflict sociology. In J.C. Alexander (ed.) *Durkheimian Sociology: Cultural Studies*. Cambridge: Cambridge University Press.
Collins, P. (2005) Lancaster faces up to its shameful past. *Lancaster Guardian* (28 Oct, p. 2).
Coombes, A.E. (2003) *History after Apartheid: Visual Culture and Public Memory in a Democratic South Africa*. Durham, NC: Duke University Press.
Cooper, M. (2006) The Pacific War battlefields: Tourist attractions or war memorials? *International Journal of Tourism Research* 8 (3), 213–222.
Crane, A. and Matten, D. (2007) *Business Ethics* (2nd edn). Oxford: Oxford University Press.
Cresswell, H. (1988) *The Story of Grace Darling*. London: Puffin Books.
Cresswell, T. (2004) *A Short Introduction to Place*. Oxford: Blackwell.
Crohn, D. (2007) 'Dark tourism' persists at Ground Zero, even as it makes some New Yorkers queasy. *New York Press*. On WWW at http://nypress.com/20/33/news&columns/feature4.cfm. Accessed 1.11.07.
Cross, G.S. and Walton, J.K. (2005) *The Playful Crowd: Pleasure Places in the Twentieth Century*. New York: Columbia University Press.
Curll, J. (2000) *The Victorian Celebration of Death*. Stroud, Gloucestershire: Sutton Publishing.
Daglish, I. (2005) *Operation Goodwood: Attack by Three British Armoured Divisions*. Battleground Europe Series. Barnsley: Pen & Sword Books.
Dann, G. (1994) Tourism: The nostalgia industry of the future. In W. Theobald (ed.) *Global Tourism: The Next Decade* (pp. 55–67). Oxford: Butterworth-Heinemann.
Dann, G. (1998) The dark side of tourism. *Etudes et Rapports, Série L, Sociology/Psychology/Philosophy/Anthropology* (Vol. 14). Aix-en-Provence: Centre International de Recherches et d'Etudes Touristiques.
Dann, G. and Seaton, A. (eds) (2001a) *Slavery, Contested Heritage and Thanatourism*. Binghampton, HY: Haworth Hospitality Press.
Dann, G. and Seaton, A. (eds) (2001b) *Slavery, Contested Heritage and Thanatourism* (pp. 1–29). Binghampton, NY: Haworth Hospitality Press.
Dark Destinations (2007) At http://www.thecabinet.com/darkdestinations/index.php?sub_id=dark_destinations.
David, L. (1993) *Man-made Catastrophes*. London: Headline.
Davies, D. (1996) Imagination playing with death: A review of the Exhibition Midden in Het Leven Staan Wij in de Dood. *Mortality* 1, 323–326.
Davies, D. (1997) *Death, Ritual and Belief*. London: Cassell.
Davies, D. (2000) *The Mormon Culture of Salvation*. Aldershot: Ashgate.
DBullock.com (2008) *London Dungeon: Bled by Troopsmen*. On WWW at http://www.flickr.com/photos/dbullock/3096151840/in/set-72157610748595617/. Accessed 14.07.09.
de Botton, A. (2002) *The Art of Travel*. London: Penguin Books.
Dery, M. (1999) Shoah Business: Tourists eating sandwiches in a concentration camp. *Scope* (8 Nov). On WWW at http://www.gettingit.com/article/298. Accessed 30.7.08.
Desmond, J. (1999) *Staging Tourism: Bodies on Display from Waikiki to Sea World*. Chicago, IL: University of Chicago Press.
DeSpelder, L. and Strickland, A. (2002) *The Last Dance: Encountering Death and Dying* (6th edn). New York: McGraw-Hill.

Digance, J. (2003) Pilgrimage at contested sites. *Annals of Tourism Research* 30 (1), 143–159.

Douglass, F. (1994 [1845]) Narrative of the life of an American slave, written by himself. In H.L. Gates (ed.) *Autobiographies* (pp. 1–102). New York: Library of America (original work published 1845).

Douglass, F. (1994 [1855]) My bondage and my freedom. In H.L. Gates (ed.) *Autobiographies* (pp. 103–452). New York: Library of America (original work published 1855).

Douglass, F. (1994 [1881]) Life and times. In H.L. Gates and H. Louis (eds) *Autobiographies* (pp. 453–1054). New York: Library of America (original work published 1881).

Drake, D. (2007) The will: Inheritance distribution and feuding families. In M. Mitchell (ed.) *Remember Me* (pp. 89–102). London: Routledge.

Drescher, S. (2001) Commemorating slavery and abolition in the United States of America. In G. Oostindie (ed.) *Facing up to the Past: Perspectives on the Commemoration of Slavery from Africa, the Americas and Europe* (pp. 109–112). Kingston, Jamaica: Ian Randle Publishers.

Dumont, R. and Foss, D. (1972) The *American View of Death: Acceptance or Denial?* Cambridge, MA: Schenkman.

Durkheim, E. (1958) *Professional Ethics and Civic Morals*. Glencoe, IL: Free Press.

Durkheim, E. (1984 [1893]) *The Division of Labour in Society*. London: MacMillan (original work published in 1893).

Durkheim, E. (2001 [1912]) *The Elementary Forms of Religious Life* (C. Cosman, trans.). Oxford: Oxford University Press (original work published in 1912).

Durkin, K. (2003) Death, dying and the dead in popular culture. In C. Bryant (ed.) *The Handbook of Death and Dying* (pp. 43–49). New York: Sage.

Eccleston, R. (2008) Pope says 'spiritual desert' is spreading. *Times Online* (20 July). On WWW at http://www.timesonline.co.uk/tol/comment/faith/article4367131. ece. Accessed 4.8.08.

Edensor, T. (1998) *Tourists at the Taj: Performance and Meaning at a Symbolic Site*. London: Routledge.

Eichstedt, J.L. and Small, S. (2002) *Representations of Slavery: Race and Ideology in Southern Plantation Museums*. Washington, DC: Smithsonian Books.

Elder, M. (1994) *Lancaster and the African Slave Trade*. Local Studies No. 14 (revised edn, 15). Lancaster: Lancaster City Museums.

Eliade, M. (1959) *The Sacred and Profane: The Nature of Religion*. New York: Harcourt Brace.

Elias, N. (1985) *The Loneliness of Dying*. Oxford: Blackwell.

Elliott, J. (1997) *Tourism: Politics and Public Sector Management*. London: Routledge.

Elsworth, C. (2008) Hotel Alcatraz to open as perfect gateway. *Daily Telegraph* (16 June), 15.

Embassy of the Republic of Armenia (2008) *Armenia – A Cradle of Civilization*. Washington, DC: Embassy of the Republic of Armenia.

Essah, P. (2001) Slavery, heritage and tourism in Ghana. In G. Dann and A. Seaton (eds) *Slavery, Contested Heritage and Thanatourism* (pp. 31–49). Binghampton, NY: Haworth Hospitality Press.

Europaworld (2001) *Raphael Lemkin*. On WWW at www.europaworld.org/issue40/raphaellemkin22601.htm.

Express India (2005) Dark tourism is the rage of 2005. *Press Trust of India*. On WWW at http://www.expressindia.com/fullstory.php?newsid=47480.

Feldman, J. (2008) *Above the Death Pits, Beneath the Flag: Youth Voyages to Poland and the Performance of Israeli National Identity*. Oxford: Berghahn.

Fennell, D. (2006) *Tourism Ethics*. Clevedon: Channel View Publications.

Finkelstein, N. (2000) *The Holocaust Industry*. London: Verso.

Flowers, S. (2007) *One Tenth*. Installation as part of the *Abolished?* Exhibition. Lancaster City Museums (July–Oct).

Flowers, S. and Himid, L. (2007) *Abolished?* Unpublished exhibition catalogue. Lancaster: Lancashire Museums.

Focus Group (2008) Focus Group transcript – The York Dungeon (8 Dec). York Dungeon Project, University of Central Lancashire, UK.

Foley, M. and Lennon, J. (1996a) Editorial: Heart of darkness. *International Journal of Heritage Studies* 2 (4), 195–197.

Foley, M. and Lennon, J. (1996b) JFK and dark tourism: A fascination with assassination. *International Journal of Heritage Studies* 2 (4), 198–211.

Forman, W. (1969) *The Exotic White Man*. London: Weidenfeld and Nicolson.

Foundation for the Memorial to the Murdered Jews of Europe (2008) *Memorial to the Murdered Jews of Europe*. Berlin: Foundation for the Memorial to the Murdered Jews of Europe.

Francis, D., Kellaher, L. and Neophytou, G. (2005) *The Secret Cemetery*. Oxford: Berg.

Freud, S. (1984) Mourning and melancholia. In S. Freud (ed.) *On Metapsychology* (Vol. 11, pp. 251–267). London: Pelican Freud Library (original work published 1917).

Friends of Scotland (2006) Currency of the Dead. *Scotland Now*, 2. On WWW at http://www.friendsofscotland.gov.uk/scotlandnow/currency-of-the-dead.html.

Furedi, F. (2005) *Politics of Fear: Beyond Left and Right*. London: Continuum.

Furst, L. (1969) *Romanticism*. London: Methuen.

Fyall, A., Prideaux, B. and Timothy, D. (2006) Editorial – War and tourism: An introduction. *International Journal of Tourism Research* 8 (3), 153–155.

Gallagher, T. (2003) *Fire at Sea: The Mysterious Tragedy of the Morro Castle* (reprint edn). The New York: Lyons Press.

Gardiner, M. (1996) Foucault, ethics and dialogue. *History of the Human Sciences* 9 (3), 27–46.

Garfinkel, H. (1967) *Studies in Ethnomethodology*. Englewood Cliffs, NJ: Prentice Hall.

Garrett, L. (2008) Important icons or lurid fatal attractions: Where do we draw the line over visiting sites of death, atrocities? *The Star*. On WWW at http://thestar.com/printArticle/465173. Accessed 8.10.08.

Gerfen, K. (2006) Reinventing nature: Mountains of remembrance. *Architect Magazine* (1 July). On WWW at http://www.architectmagazine.com/industry-news.asp?sectionID=1013&articleID=384852.

Gibbon, L.G. (1946) *Sunset Song*. London: Hutchinson.

Giddens, A. (1990) *The Consequences of Modernity*. Cambridge: Polity.

Giddens, A. (1991) *Modernity and Self Identity*. Cambridge: Polity.

Giddens, A. (1994a) *Beyond Left and Right*. Cambridge: Polity.

Giddens, A. (1994b) Living in a post-traditional society. In U. Beck, A. Giddens and S. Lash (eds) *Reflexive Modernization*. Cambridge: Polity.

Gilroy, P. (1993) *The Black Atlantic: Modernity and Double Consciousness*. London: Verso.

Gilroy, P. (2004) *After Empire: Melancholia or Convivial Culture*. Abingdon: Routledge.

Gittings, C. (1984) *Death, Burial and the Individual in Early Modern England*. London, Croom Helm.

Glenny, M. (1996) *The Fall of Yugoslavia*. London: Penguin.

Global Link (2006) *Lancaster Slave Trade Town Trail*. Lancaster: Lancaster Maritime Museum.

Gorer, G. (1955) The pornography of death. *Encounter* (Oct).

Gorer, G. (1965) *Death, Grief, and Mourning in Contemporary Britain*. London: Cresset.

Goss, J. (2004) The Souvenir: Conceptualising the object(s) of tourist consumption. In A.A. Lew, C.M. Hall and A.M. Williams (eds) *A Companion to Tourism* (pp. 327–336). Oxford: Blackwell.

Graham, E.T. (2007) The danger of Durkheim: Ambiguity in the theory of social effervescence. *Religion* 37, 26–38.

Grant, L. (2006) Manufacturing history. *New Statesman, Arts and Culture* (14 Aug).

Grosspietsch, M. (2006) Perceived and projected images of Rwanda: Visitor and international tour operator perspectives. *Tourism Management* 27 (2), 225–234.

Gurian, E.H. (2006) A savings bank for the soul: About institutions of memory and congregant spaces. In E.H. Gurian (ed.) *Civilizing the Museum: The Collected Writings of Elaine Heumann Gurian* (pp. 88–96). New York: Routledge.

Habermas, J. (1990) *Moral Consciousness and Communicative Action*. Cambridge, MA: MIT Press.

Habermas, J. (2003) *The Future of Human Nature*. Cambridge: Polity Press.

Hafferty, F. (1991) *Into the Valley*. New Haven: Yale University Press.

Hall, D. (1991) *Tourism and Economic Development in Eastern Europe and the Soviet Union*. London: Bellhaven Press.

Hall, C.M. (1994) *Tourism and Politics: Policy, Power and Place*. Chichester: John Wiley.

Hall, D. (1995) Tourism change in Central and Eastern Europe. In A. Montanari and A. Williams (eds) *European Tourism: Regions, Space and Restructuring* (pp. 221–244). Chichester: John Wiley.

Hall, S. (ed.) (1997) *Representation: Cultural Representations and Signifying Practices*. London: Sage; Open University Press.

Hall, C.M. (2000) *Tourism Planning: Policies, Processes and Relationships*. Harlow: Pearson Education.

Halley, G. (2004) Grief tourists lap up other people's pain. *The Sunday Independent (Ireland)* (14 Mar).

Halman, L. (1996) Individualism in individualized society? Results from the European Values Surveys. *International Journal of Comparative Sociology* 37 (3–4), 195–214.

Halsted, J. (1965) *Romanticism. Definition, Explanation, and Evaluation*. Boston, MA: D.C. Heath.

Hanink, D. and Stutts, M. (2002) Spatial demand for national battlefield parks. *Annals of Tourism Research* 29 (3), 707–719.

Harman, G. (1975) Moral relativism defended. *The Philosophical Review* 84 (1), 3–22.

Harrison, R.P. (2003) *The Dominion of the Dead*. Chicago, IL: Chicago University Press.

Harrop, K. and McMillan, J. (2002) Government, governance and tourism. In R. Sharpley (ed.) *The Tourism Business: An Introduction* (pp. 243–262). Sunderland: Business Education Publishers.

Hart, B., Sainsbury, P. and Short, S. (1998) Whose dying? A sociological critique of the 'good' death. *Mortality* 3, 65–77.

Harter, J. and Gavin, L. (1929) *The Story of an Epic Pilgrimage*. London: British Legion.

Hartmann, R. (2005) Holocaust memorials without Holocaust survivors: The management of museums and memorials to the victims of Nazi Germany in 21st century Europe. In G. Ashworth and R. Hartmann (eds) *Horror and Human Tragedy Revisited: The Management of Sites of Atrocities for Tourism* (pp. 89–107). New York: Cognizant Communications Corporation.

Hawthorn, J. (1994) *A Concise Glossary of Contemporary Literary Theory* (2nd edn). London: Edward Arnold.

Hawton, N. (2004) Tourists flock to Bosnia war tours. *BBC News* (11 June). On WWW at http://news.bbc.co.uk/1/hi/world/europe/3797549.stm. Accessed 31.7.08.

Heck, G. and Deigaard, L. (2003) *Topsy the Elephant Memorial.* Coney Island Museum, New York. On WWW at http://www.coneyisland.com/museum.shtml. Accessed 16.07.09.

Hede, A.M. (2008) Anzac ceremonies may have an element of dark tourism. *New Zealand News.* On WWW at http://www.nznewsuk.co.uk/news/?ID=11221.

Heelas, P. and Woodhead, L. (2005) *The Spiritual Revolution: Why Religion is Giving Way to Spirituality.* Oxford: Blackwell.

Hegeman, S. (2000) Haunted by mass culture. *American Literary History* 12, 298–317.

Heidegger, M. (1996) *Being and Time* (J. Stambaugh, trans.). Albany, NY: State University of New York Press.

Heller, D. (ed.) (2005) *The Selling of 9/11: How a National Tragedy Became a Commodity.* New York: Palgrave MacMillan.

Helm, T. (2008) David Cameron vows to mend 'broken society'. *The Daily Telegraph* (25 July 2008). On WWW at http://www.telegraph.co.uk/news/uknews/1561265/David-Cameron-vows-to-mend-'broken-society'.html. Accessed 4.8.08.

Henderson, J. (2000) War as a tourist attraction: The case of Vietnam. *International Journal of Tourism Research* 2 (3), 269–280.

Henderson, J. (2003) The politics of tourism in Myanmar. *Current Issues in Tourism* 6 (2), 97–117.

Hesse, B. (2000) *Unsettled Multiculturalisms: Diasporas, Entanglements, Transruptions.* London: Zed Books.

Hewison, R. (1987) *The Heritage Industry: Britain in a Climate of Decline.* London: Methuen.

Hewison, R. (1989) Heritage: An interpretation. In D. Uzzell (ed.) *Heritage Interpretation* (Vol. I, pp. 15–23). London: Bellhaven Press.

Hewitt, D. and Osbourne, R. (1995) *Crime and the Media: The Post Modern Spectacle.* London: Pluto Press.

Hicks, B. (2006) *When the Dancing Stopped: The Real Story of the Morro Castle Disaster and its Deadly Wake.* New York: Free Press.

Himid, L. (2001) Revenge: A Masque in five tableaux. *Transatlantic Slave Sites Tour* (6 Mar). Lancaster: University of Central Lancashire.

Himid, L. (2003) Monument talk. Presentation at the Slave Trade Arts Memorial Project Launch (15 Nov). Lancaster: Dukes Theatre.

Hollinshead, K. (1999) Tourism as public culture: Horne's ideological commentary on the legerdemain of tourism. *International Journal of Tourism Research.* 1, 267–292.

Holmes, R. (2006) Address to The Battlefields Trust Conference. London: National Army Musuem.

Holt, D. (1995) How consumers consume: A typology of consumption practices. *Journal of Consumer Research* 22 (June), 1–16.

Hope, C. (2004) Gulag just the ticket for Russian tourists. *The Age.com.* On WWW at http://www.theage.com.au/articles/2004/07/04/1088879370907.html. Accessed 12.12.08.

Horne, D. (1984) *The Great Museum: The Re-Presentation of History.* London: Pluto Press.

Howard, P. (2003) *Heritage: Management, Interpretation, Identity.* London: Continuum.

Howarth, G. (2000) Dismantling the boundaries between life and death. *Mortality* 5, 127–138.

Howarth, G. (2007a) *Death and Dying: A Sociological Introduction.* Cambridge: Polity Press.

Howarth, G. (2007b) The rebirth of death: Continuing relationships with the dead. In M. Mitchell (ed.) *Remember Me* (pp. 19–34). London: Routledge.

Huimin, G., Ryan, C. and Zhang, W. (2007) Jinggangshan Mountain: A paradigm of China's Red Tourism. In C. Ryan (ed.) *Battlefield Tourism: History, Place and Interpretation* (pp. 59–65). Oxford: Elsevier.

Hurley, M. and Trimarco, J. (2004) Morality and merchandise: Vendors, visitors and police at New York City's Ground Zero. *Critique of Anthropology* 24 (1), 51–78.

Hyun-Sook, K. (2006) Educating in a post-conventional society. *Religious Education*, Fall. On WWW at http://findarticles.com/p/articles/mi_qa3783/is_200610/ai_n17194917?tag=artBody;col1. Accessed 4.8.08.

Inglis, D. and Holmes, M. (2003) Highland and other haunts: Ghosts in Scottish tourism. *Annals of Tourism Research* 30 (1), 50–63.

Institute for Plastination (2008) Gunther Von Hagens' Body Worlds exhibitions mark 25th million visitor milestone (5 May). On WWW at newsletter@plastination.com

Interviews (2008a) *Research Interviews Transcripts – York Dungeon Visitors* (4 Dec). York Dungeon Project, University of Central Lancashire.

Interviews (2008b) *Research Interviews Transcripts – York Dungeon Staff* (4 Dec). York Dungeon Project, University of Central Lancashire.

Jafari, J. (ed.) (2000) *Encyclopedia of Tourism*. London: Routledge.

Jamal, T. and Hill, S. (2002) The home and the world: (Post)touristic spaces of (in)authenticity? In G. Dann (ed.) *The Tourist as a Metaphor of the Social World* (pp. 77–107). Wallingford: CABI Publishing.

Jansen, O. (2005) Trauma revisited: The Holocaust memorial in Berlin. In G. Ashworth and R. Hartmann (eds) *Horror and Human Tragedy Revisited: The Management of Sites of Atrocities for Tourism* (pp. 163–179). New York: Cognizant Communications Corporation.

Jayawardena, C. (2003) Revolution to revolution: Why is tourism booming in Cuba? *International Journal of Contemporary Hospitality Management* 15 (1), 52–58.

Jeffries, D. (2001) *Governments and Tourism*. Oxford: Butterworth-Heinemann.

Jenkins, O. (2003) Photography and travel brochures: The circle of representation. *Tourism Geographies* 5 (3), 205–328.

Jorgensen-Earp, C. and Lanzilotti, L. (1998) Public memory and private grief: The construction of shrines at sites of public tragedy. *Quarterly Journal of Speech* 84, 150–170.

Kampschror, B. (2006) War tourists fight to see Bosnia's past: Officials, worried that the wounds of the 1992–95 war are too fresh, dissuade those eager to learn about it. *The Christian Science Monitor* (16 Feb). On WWW at http://www.csmonitor.com/2006/0216/p07s02-woeu.html. Accessed 31.7.08.

Kearl, M. (1989) *Endings: A Sociology of Death and Dying*. New York: Oxford University Press.

Keil, C. (2005) Sightseeing in the mansions of the dead. *Social & Cultural Geography* 6 (4), 479–494.

Kennedy, V. (2000) *Edward Said: A Critical Introduction*. Cambridge: Polity Press.

Kershaw, I. (2003) The thing about Hitler. *The Guardian* (29 Jan). On WWW at http://www.guardian.co.uk/education/2003/jan/29/highereducation.germany. Accessed 27.10.08.

Khawaja, I. (2007) Essentialism, consistency and Islam: A critique of Edward Said's 'Orientalism'. In E. Karsh (ed.) *Postcolonial Theory and the Arab–Israeli Conflict*. New York: Routledge.

Kierkegaard, S. (1944) *The Concept of Dread*. London: MacMillan.

Kigali Memorial Centre (2008) At www.kigalimemorialcentre.org/old/index.html.

King, A. (1998) *Memorials of the Great War in Britain: The Symbolism and Politics of Remembrance*. Oxford: Berg.

Kinross, L. (1964) *Atatürk: The Rebirth of a Nation*. London: Weidenfeld and Nicolson.

Kiwi-Lomo (2008) IMG 7565. On WWW at http://www.flickr.com/photos/kiwi-lomo/2551161403/in/set-72157604684526971/. Accessed 16.07.09.

Klass, D., Silverman, P. and Nickman, S. (eds) (1996) *Continuing Bonds: New Understandings of Grief*. Bristol, PA and London: Taylor & Francis.

Knox, D. (2006) The sacralised landscapes of Glencoe: From massacre to mass tourism, and back again. *International Journal of Tourism Research* 8 (3), 185–197.

Krakover, S. (2005) Attitudes of Israeli visitors towards the Holocaust Remembrance Site of Yad Vashem. In G. Ashworth and R. Hartmann (eds) *Horror and Human Tragedy Revisited: The Management of Sites of Atrocities for Tourism* (pp. 108–117). New York: Cognizant Communications Corporation.

Krishenblatt-Gimblett, B. (1997) *Destination Cultures: Tourism, Museums and Heritage*. Berkeley, CA: University of California Press.

Kriz, W. (2007) Foreword. In G. von Hagens and A. Whalley (eds) *Body Worlds – The Anatomical Exhibition of Real Human Bodies Catalogue*. Heidelberg: Institute for Plastination.

Lantermann, E. (2007) Korperwelten as seen by visitors: Visitor survey report from the first Exhibition in Europe. In G. von Hagens and A. Whalley (eds) *Body Worlds – The Anatomical Exhibition of Real Human Bodies Catalogue* (pp. 303–311). Heidelberg: Institute for Plastination.

Lasch, C. (1991) *The Culture of Narcissism*. New York: Norton.

Lavine, S.D. (1991) Museum practices. In S.D. Lavine and I. Karp (eds) *Exhibiting Cultures: The Poetics and Politics of Museum Display* (pp. 151–158). Washington, DC: Smithsonian Institution Press.

Leahy, H. (2008) Under the skin. *Museum Practice Online* 43 (Autumn), 36–40.

Lee, R. (2002) Modernity, death, and the self: Disenchantment of death and symbols of bereavement. *Illness, Crisis and Loss* 10, 91–107.

Lee, R. (2004) Death at the crossroad: From modern to postmortem consciousness. *Illness, Crisis and Loss* 12, 155–170.

Lee, R. (2006) Reinventing modernity: Reflexive modernization vs. liquid modernity vs. multiple modernities. *European Journal of Social Theory* 9, 355–368.

Leming, M. and Dickinson, G. (2002) *Understanding Death, Dying and Bereavement* (5th edn). New York: Harcourt College.

Lennon, J. (2005) Journeys in understanding: What is dark tourism? *The Sunday Observer* (23 Oct). On WWW at http://www.guardian.co.uk/travel/2005/oct/23/darktourism.observerescapesection. Accessed 30.7.08.

Lennon, J. and Foley, M. (2000) *Dark Tourism: The Attraction of Death and Disaster*. London: Continuum.

Lennon, J. and Smith, H. (2003) A tale of two camps: Contrasting approaches to interpretation and commemoration in the sites at Terezin and Lety, Czech Republic. *Tourism Recreation Research* 29 (1), 15–25.

Leung, R. (2005) Torture, cover-up at Gitmo? *CBS News* (1 May). On WWW at http://www.cbsnews.com/stories/2005/04/28/60minutes/main691602.shtml. Accessed 9.1.09.

Leventhal, R.S. (1995) *Romancing the Holocaust, or Hollywood and Horror: Steven Spielberg's Schindler's List*. On WWW at http://www2.iath.virginia.edu/holocaust/schinlist.html.

Light, D. (2000) Gazing on communism: Heritage tourism and post-communist identities in Germany, Hungary and Romania. *Tourism Geographies* 2 (2), 157–176.

Light, D. (2007) Dracula tourism in Romania: Cultural identity and the state. *Annals of Tourism Research* 34 (3), 746–765.

Linenthal, E.T. (2006) Epilogue: Reflections. In J.O. Horton and L.E. Horton (eds) *Slavery and Public History: The Tough Stuff of American History* (pp. 213–224). New York: The New Press.

Lisle, D. (2004) Gazing at Ground Zero: Tourism, voyeurism and spectacle. *Journal for Cultural Research* 8 (1), 3–21.

Little, A. and Silber, L. (1996) *The Death of Yugoslavia*. London: Penguin.

Littlewood, J. (1993) The denial of death and rites of passage in contemporary societies. In D. Clarke (ed.) *The Sociology of Death* (pp. 69–84). Oxford: Blackwell.

Lloyd, D. (1998) *Battlefield Tourism: Pilgrimage and the Commemoration of the Great War in Britain, Australia and Canada, 1919–1939*. Oxford: Berg.

Lonely Planet (2007) *Blue List: The Best in Travel 2007* (2nd edn). On WWW at http://www.lonelyplanet.com.

Lowenthal, D. (1975) Past time, present place: Landscape and memory. *Geographical Review* 65, 1–36.

Lury, C. (1996) *Consumer Culture*. Cambridge: Polity Press.

Lyotard, J. (1979) *The Postmodern Condition: A Report of Knowledge*. Manchester: Manchester University Press.

Lyotard, J. (1991) *The Inhuman: Reflections on Time*. Stanford, CA: Stanford University Press.

MacCannell, D. (1973) Staged authenticity: Arrangements of social space in tourist settings. *American Journal of Sociology* 79, 589–603.

MacCannell, D. (1989) *The Tourist: A New Theory of the Leisure Class* (2nd edn). New York: Schocken Books.

Mackie, J. (2005) Why be slaves to our past? (Letter). *Lancaster Guardian* (7 Jan), 6.

Maffesoli, M. (1991) The ethic of aesthetics. *Theory, Culture and Society* 8, 7–20.

Majtenyi, C. (2007) *Memorial Honors Victims of 1994 Rwandan Genocide*. Washington, DC: Voice of America. On WWW at http://www.voanews.com/english/archive/2007-07/2007-07-12-voa40.cfm?CFID=65160239&CFTOKEN=42758408.

Mannino, J. (1997) *Grieving Days, Healing Days*. Boston, MA: Allyn & Bacon.

Marcel, J. (2004) Death makes a holiday. *The American Reporter* (21 Jan), 10, 2273.

Marcuse, H. (2001) *Legacies of Dachau: The Uses and Abuses of a Concentration Camp 1933–2001*. Cambridge: Cambridge University Press.

Marcuse, H. (2005) Reshaping Dachau for visitors: 1933–2000. In G. Ashworth and R. Hartmann (eds) *Horror and Human Tragedy Revisited: The Management of Sites of Atrocities for Tourism* (pp. 118–148). New York: Cognizant Communications Corporation.

Marwit, S.J. and Klass, D. (1995). Grief and the role of the inner representation of the deceased. *Omega* 30, 283–298.

Masters, B. (2003) A study in evil. *The Daily Mail*, England (20 Dec).

McCrone, D., Morris, A. and Kiely, R. (1995) *Scotland – The Brand. The Making of Scottish Heritage*. Edinburgh: Edinburgh University Press.

McFeely, W.S. (1991) *Frederick Douglass*. New York: W.W. Norton.

McGregor, S. (2003) *Post Modernism, Consumerism and a Culture of Peace*. On WWW at http://www.kon.org/archives/forum/13-2/mcgregor.pdf. Accessed 8.8.08.

McIlwain, C. (2005) *When Death Goes Pop: Death, Media and the Remaking of Community*. New York: Peter Lang.

McLean, F., Garden, M. and Urquhart, G. (2007) Romanticising tragedy: Culloden battle site in Scotland. In C. Ryan (ed.) *Battlefield Tourism: History, Place and Interpretation* (pp. 221–234). Oxford: Elsevier.

Meethan, K. (2004) To stand in the shoes of my ancestors: Tourism and genealogy. In T. Coles and D. Timothy (eds) *Tourism Diasporas and Space* (pp. 139–150). London: Routledge.

Mellor, P. (1993) Death in high modernity: The contemporary presence and absence of death. In D. Clarke (ed.) *The Sociology of Death* (pp. 11–30). Oxford: Blackwell.

Mellor, P. and Shilling, C. (1993) Modernity, self-identity and the sequestration of death. *Sociology* 27, 411–431.

Mercat Tours (2009) *Ghost-Hunter Trail.* Edinburgh: Mercat Tours. On WWW at http://www.mercattours.com/ghosthunter-trail.asp. Accessed 5.1.09.

Merlin Entertainments (2009a) *The York Dungeon: It's a Bloody Guide.* Dorset: Merlin Entertainments Group. On WWW at www.thedungeons.com. Accessed 2.1.09.

Merlin Entertainments (2009b) *Annual Review 2007.* Dorset: Merlin Entertainments Group. On WWW at http://www.merlinentertainments.biz/media/1960702479. pdf. Accessed 6.1.09.

Merlin Entertainments (2009c) *Our Brands: The Dungeons.* Dorset: Merlin Entertainments Group. On WWW at http://www.merlinentertainments.biz/en/brands/dungeons.aspx. Accessed 6.1.09.

Merrin, W. (1999) Crash, bang, wallop! What a picture! The death of Diana and the media. *Mortality* 4, 41–62.

Meštrović, S. (1991) *The Coming Fin de Siècle: An Application of Durkheim's Sociology to Modernity and Postmodernity.* London: Routledge.

Meštrović, S. (1993) *The Barbarian Temperament.* London: Routledge.

Meštrović, S. (1997) *Postemotional Society.* London: Sage.

Metcalf, P. and Huntingdon, R. (1991) *Celebrations of Death: The Anthropology of Mortuary Ritual.* Cambridge: Cambridge University Press.

Miles, W. (2002) Auschwitz: Museum interpretation and darker tourism. *Annals of Tourism Research* 29 (4), 1175–1178.

Miller, D. (1987) *Material Culture and Mass Consumption.* Oxford: Blackwell.

Mintz, A.L. (2001) *Popular Culture and the Shaping of Holocaust Memory in America.* Washington, DC: Washington University Press.

Mitchell, M. (ed.) (2007) *Remember Me: Constructing Immortality.* London: Routledge.

Moe, N. (2002) *View from Vesuvius.* California: University of California Press.

Moeller, M. (2005) Battlefield tourism in South Africa with special reference to Isandlwana and Rorke's Drift KwaZulu-Natal. Unpublished MPhil thesis, Faculty of Economic and Management Sciences, University of Pretoria.

Morgan, N. and Pritchard, A. (2005) On souvenirs and metonymy: Narratives of memory, metaphor and materiality. *Tourist Studies* 5 (1), 29–53.

Morley, J. (1971) *Death, Heaven and the Victorians.* London: Studio Vista.

Morrison, T. (1987) *Beloved.* New York: Plume.

Morrison, T. (1989) A bench by the road. *The World* 3 (1), 4–5 and 37–41.

Mortimer, L. (2001) We are the dance: Cinema, death and the imaginary in the thought of Edgar Morin. *Thesis Eleven* 64, 77–95.

Moscardo, G. and Ballantyne, R. (2008) Interpretation and attractions. In A. Fyall, B. Garrod, A. Leask and S. Wanhill (eds) *Managing Visitor Attractions: New Directions* (pp. 237–252). Oxford: Butterworth-Heinemann.

Munt, I. (1994) The 'other' postmodern tourism: Culture, travel and the new middle classes. *Theory, Culture and Society* 11 (3), 101–123.

Mutantrfog (2005) St. Peter's Fence – WTC Shrine. On WWW at http://www. flickr.com/photos/mutantfrog/27750518/. Accessed 16.07.09.

Muzaini, H., Teo, P. and Yeoh, B. (2007) Intimations of postmodernity in dark tourism: The fate of history at Fort Siloso, Singapore. *Journal of Tourism and Cultural Change* 5 (1), 28–45.

Nash, C. (2002) Genealogical identities. *Environment & Planning D: Society & Space* 20, 27–52.

Nash, G.B. (2006) For whom will the Liberty Bell toll? From controversy to cooperation. In J.O. Horton and L.E. Horton (eds) *Slavery and Public History: The Tough Stuff of American History* (pp. 75–102). New York: The New Press.

Neill, W. (2001) Marketing the urban experience: Reflections on the place of fear in the promotional strategies of Belfast, Detroit and Berlin. *Urban Studies* 38 (5–6), 815–828.

Nietzsche, F.W. (1996 [1878]) *Human, All Too Human: A Book for Free Spirits* (M. Faber and S. Lehmann, trans.) (p. 146). Lincoln, NE: University of Nebraska Press (original work published 1878).

Nora, P. (1994) Between memory and history: Les lieux de memoire. In G. Fabre and R. O'Meally (eds) *History and Memory in African American Culture* (pp. 284–300). Oxford: Oxford University Press.

Novelli, M. (ed.) (2005) *Niche Tourism: Contemporary Issues, Trends and Cases*. Oxford: Elsevier.

Obs (2008) *Participant Observation Notes – The York Dungeon* (3–4 Dec). The York Dungeon Project. Lancaster: University of Central Lancashire.

Office of the High Commissioners for Human Rights (1948) *Convention on the Prevention and Punishment of the Crime of Homicide*. Geneva: UNHCR.

Oguibe, O. (2001) Slavery and the diaspora imagination. In G. Oostindie (ed.) *Facing up to the Past: Perspectives on the Commemoration of Slavery from Africa, the Americas and Europe* (pp. 95–101). Kingston, Jamaica: Ian Randle Publishers.

Olalquiaga, C. (1998) *The Artificial Kingdom: A Treasure of the Kitsch Experience*. New York: Pantheon.

Olick, J. (1999) Collective memory: The two cultures. *Sociological Theory* 17 (3), 333–348.

Olsen, K. (2002) Authenticity as a concept in tourism research: The social organisation of the experience of authenticity. *Tourist Studies* 2 (2), 159–182.

O'Neill, S. (2002) Flood of tourists worsens pain. *Daily Telegraph* (27 Aug).

Oostindie, G. (ed.) (2001) *Facing up to the Past: Perspectives on the Commemoration of Slavery from Africa, the Americas and Europe*. Kingston, Jamaica: Ian Randle Publishers.

O'Rourke, P. (1988) *Holidays in Hell*. London: Picador.

Orwell, G. (1949) *Nineteen Eighty-Four*. London: Secker and Warburg.

Osborn, A. (2006) Club Gulag: Tourists are offered prison camp experience. *The Independent*, UK. On WWW at http://www.independent.co.uk/news/world/europe/club-gulag-tourists-are-offered-prison-camp-experience-410476.html. Accessed 12.12.08.

Ottewell, D. (2008) Bishop blasts 'body snatch' show. *Manchester Evening News*. On WWW at http://www.manchestereveningnews.co.uk/news/s/1035155_bishop_blasts_body_snatch_show.

Oviedo, L. (2005) Whom to blame for the charge of secularization? *Zygon* 40 (2), 351–361.

Palmer, C. (1999) Tourism and symbols of identity. *Tourism Management* 20 (3), 313–321.

Pearce, P. and Moscardo, G. (1986) The concept of authenticity in tourist settings. *Australian and New Zealand Journal of Sociology* 22 (1), 121–132.

Pelton, R. (2003) *The World's Most Dangerous Places* (5th edn). London: Harper Resource.

Phataranawik, P. (2006) Do we really need a tsunami memorial? *The Nation* (20 May). On WWW at http://nationmultimedia.com/2006/05/20/opinion/opinion_30004474.php. Accessed 1.5.08.

Philips, C. (2000) *The Atlantic Sound*. London: Faber.

Poria, Y. (2001) The show must not go on. *Tourism and Hospitality Research* 3 (2), 115–119.

Poria, Y. (2007) Establishing co-operation between Israel and Poland to save Auschwitz Concentration camp: Globalising the responsibility for the Massacre. *International Journal of Tourism Policy* 1 (1), 45–57.

Preece, T. and Price, G. (2005) Motivations of participants in dark tourism: A case study of Port Arthur, Tasmania, Australia. In C. Ryan, S. Page and M. Aicken (eds) *Taking Tourism to the Limit: Issues, Concepts and Managerial Perspectives* (pp. 191–198). Oxford: Elsevier.

Pretes, M. (1995) Postmodern tourism: The Santa Claus industry. *Annals of Tourism Research* 22 (1), 1–15.

Pullella, P. and Perry, M. (2008) Pope warns youth of 'spiritual desert'. *Reuters* (20 July). On WWW at http://www.reuters.com/article/topNews/idUSSP128909 20080720?feedType=RSS&feedName=topNews. Accessed 4.08.08.

Rátz, T. (2006) Interpretation in the House of Terror, Budapest. In M. Smith and M. Robinson (eds) *Cultural Tourism in a Changing World: Politics, Participation and (Re)presentation* (pp. 244–256). Clevedon: Channel View Publications.

Read, A. (ed.) (1996) *The Fact of Blackness: Frantz Fanon and Visual Representation*. London: Institute of Contemporary Arts and Seattle: Bay Press.

Reader, I. (2003) Review of 'Dark Tourism: The Attraction of Death and Disaster'. On WWW at http://cult-media.com/issue2/Rreade.htm.

Reader, I. (2007) Pilgrimage growth in the modern world: Meanings and implications. *Religion* 37, 210–229.

Reid, T. (1998) Dianaland – Shrine, memorial, money machine. *The Washington Post* (11 July).

Rice, A. (2003) Exploring inside the invisible: An interview with Lubaina Himid. *Wasafiri* 40 (Winter), 24.

Rice, A. (2006) Interview with Kevin Dalton-Johnson, Aug 2005 and Feb 2006. Unpublished manuscript.

Richards, S. (2005) Performing family: Cultural tourism to Ghana's slave castles. In G. Ashworth and R. Hartmann (eds) *Horror and Human Tragedy Revisited: The Management of Sites of Atrocities for Tourism* (pp. 224–232). New York: Cognizant Communications Corporation.

Richter, L. (1983) Tourism, politics and political science: A case of not so benign neglect. *Annals of Tourism Research* 10 (3), 313–335.

Ricoeur, P. (2004) *Memory, History and Forgetting* (K. Bramley and D. Pellauer, trans.). Chicago, IL: University of Chicago Press.

Rittichainuwat, B. (2008) Responding to disaster: Thai and Scandinavian tourists' motivations to visit Phuket, Thailand. *Journal of Travel Research* 46, 422–432.

Robinson, M. (2005) Foreword. In M. Novelli (ed.) *Niche Tourism: Contemporary Issues, Trends and Cases*. Oxford: Butterworth-Heinemann.

Rojek, C. (1993) *Ways of Escape*. Basingstoke: MacMillan.

Rojek, C. (1997) Indexing, dragging and the social construction of tourist sights. In C. Rojek and J. Urry (eds) *Touring Cultures: Transformations of Travel and Theory* (pp. 52–74). London: Routledge.

Roushanzamir, E. and Kreshel, P. (2001) Gloria and Anthony visit a plantation: History into heritage at 'Laura: A Creole Plantation'. In G. Dann and A. Seaton (eds) *Slavery, Contested Heritage and Thanotourism* (pp. 107–129). New York: Haworth Press.

Rowe, M. (2007) Intrepid travelers break new ground. *Daily Telegraph* (20 Oct), T8.

Ryan, C. (ed.) (2007a) *Battlefield Tourism*. Oxford: Elsevier.

Ryan, C. (2007b) Introduction. In C. Ryan (ed.) *Battlefield Tourism: History, Place and Interpretation* (pp. 1–10). Oxford: Elsevier.

Ryan, C. and Aicken, M. (2005) *Indigenous Tourism: The Commodification and Management of Culture*. Oxford: Elsevier.

Ryan, C. and Hall, C.M. (2001) *Sex Tourism: Marginal People and Liminalities*. London: Routledge.

Ryan, C. and Kohli, R. (2006) The buried village, New Zealand: An example of dark tourism? *Asia Pacific Journal of Tourism Research* 11 (3), 211–226.

Saffron, I. (2003) Changing skyline: Slave memorial could let city stand out. But design risks sending wrong message. *Philadelphia Inquiry* (14 Feb). On WWW at http://www.ushistory.org/presidentshouse/news/inq021403.htm. Accessed 18.2.05.

Said, E. (1975) *Beginnings: Intention and Method*. New York: Basic Books.

Said, E. (1978) *Orientalism: Western Conceptions of the Orient*. London: Routledge and Kegan Paul.

Sammiqueen (2006) *York Dungeon to the Max*. On WWW at http://www.flickr.com/search/?q=dungeon&w=24293902%40N00. Accessed 14.07.09.

Sargent, E. (2008) Curator, Wellcome Institute: Personal communication.

Sayre, J. (2001) The use of aberrant medical humour by psychiatric unit staff. *Issues in Mental Health Nursing* 22, 669–689.

Schelsky, H. (1965) *Auf der Suche nach Wirklichkeit*. Düsseldorf: E. Diedrichs.

Schneider, J. (1998) *Italy's 'Southern Question': Orientalism in One Country*. Oxford and New York: Berg Publishers.

Schulte-Sasse, L. (2006) Advise and consent: On the Americanization of Body Worlds. *BioSocieties* (1), 369–384.

Schuman, H., Akiyama, H. and Knauper, B. (1998) Collective memories of Germans and Japanese about the past half-century. *Memory* 6 (4), 427–454.

Schutz, M. (2006) Chernobyl. *Lonely Planet* (Oct). On WWW at http://www.lonelyplanet.com/travelstories/article/chernobyl_1006/. Accessed 31.7.08.

Schutz, A. and Luckmann, T. (1974) *Structures of the Life-World* (R.M. Zaner and H.T. Englehardt Jr, trans.). London: Heinemann.

Schwartz, B. and Schuman, H. (2000) History, commemoration, and belief: Abraham Lincoln in American memory, 1945–2001. *American Sociological Review* 70 (2), 183–203.

Scotland Now (2006) Currency of the dead. *Scotland Now* 2 (June). On WWW at http://www.friendsofscotland.gov.uk/scotlandnow/issue-02/sports/currency-of-the-dead.html. Accessed 5.1.09.

Seabrook, J. (2007) The living dead of capitalism. *Race & Class* 49, 19–32.

Sears, J. (1989) *Sacred Places. American Tourist Attractions in the Nineteenth Century*. Oxford: Oxford University Press.

Seaton, A. (1996) Guided by the dark: From thanatopsis to thanatourism. *International Journal of Heritage Studies* 2 (4), 234–244.

Seaton, A. (1999) War and thanatourism: Waterloo 1815–1914. *Annals of Tourism Research* 26 (1), 130–158.

Seaton, A. (2001) Sources of slavery – destinations of slavery: The silences and disclosures of slavery heritage in the UK and US. In G. Dann and A. Seaton (eds) *Slavery, Contested Heritage and Thantourism* (pp. 107–129). Binghampton, NY: Haworth.

Seaton, A. (2002) Thanatourism's final frontiers? Visits to cemeteries, churchyards and funerary sites as sacred and secular pilgrimage. *Tourism Recreation Research* 27 (2), 73–82.

Seaton, A. (forthcoming) *From Ampulla to Althorp: Death and Tourism in History*. London: London Books.

Seaton, A. and Lennon, J. (2004) Moral panics, ulterior motives and alterior desires: Thanatourism in the early 21st century. In T. Singh (ed.) *New Horizons in Tourism: Strange Experiences and Stranger Practices* (pp. 63–82). Wallingford: CABI Publishing.

Selznick, P. (1992) *The Moral Commonwealth*. Berkley, CA: University of California Press.

Shackley, M. (2001a) Potential futures for Robben Island: Shrine, museum or theme park? *International Journal of Heritage Studies* 7 (4), 355–363.

Shackley, M. (2001b) *Managing Sacred Sites*. London: Thomson.

Sharpley, R. (2005) Travels to the edge of darkness: Towards a typology of dark tourism. In C. Ryan, S. Page and M. Aicken (eds) *Taking Tourism to the Limit: Issues, Concepts and Managerial Perspectives* (pp. 215–226). London: Elsevier.

Sharpley, R. (2008) *Tourism, Tourists and Society* (4th edn). Huntingdon: Elm Publications.

Sharpley, R. (forthcoming) Tourism, religion and spirituality. In M. Robinson and T. Jamal (eds) *Sage Handbook of Tourism Studies*. London: Sage Publications.

Sharpley, R. and Knight, M. (2009) Tourism and the state in Cuba: From the past to the future. *International Journal of Tourism Research* 11 (3), 241–254.

Sharpley, R. and Sundaram, P. (2005) Tourism: A sacred journey? The case of Ashram Tourism, India. *International Journal of Tourism Research* 7, 161–171.

Shilling, C. (1993) *The Body and Social Theory*. London: Sage.

Shilling, C. (2005) Embodiment, emotions and the foundations of social order: Durkheim's enduring contribution. In J. Alexander and P. Smith (eds) *The Cambridge Companion to Durkheim* (pp. 211–238). Cambridge: Cambridge University Press.

Shilling, C. and Mellor, P. (1998) Durkheim, morality and modernity: Collective effervescence, Homo Duplex and the sources of moral action. *The British Journal of Sociology*, 49 (2), 193–209.

Siegenthaler, P. (2002) Hiroshima and Nagasaki in Japanese guidebooks. *Annals of Tourism Research* 29 (4), 1111–1137.

Silver, I. (1993) Marketing authenticity in Third World countries. *Annals of Tourism Research* 20 (2), 302–318.

Simic, O. (2008) A tour to a site of genocide: Mothers, bones and borders. *Journal of International Women's Studies* 9 (3), 320–330.

Simpson, D. (2006) *9/11: The Culture of Commemoration*. Chicago, IL: University of Chicago Press.

Šindeláøová, L. (2008) Terezín: The darkest places of interest in the Czech Republic. *4Hoteliers: Hospitality, Hotel & Travel News* (8 Nov). On WWW at http://www.4hoteliers.com/4hots_fshw.php?mwi=3491. Accessed 5.1.09.

Singer, P. (1994) *Ethics*. Oxford: Oxford University Press.

Singleton, T. (1999) The slave trade remembered on the former Gold and Slave Coasts. In S. Frey and B. Wood (eds) *From Slavery to Emancipation in the Atlantic World* (pp. 150–169). London: Frank Cass.

Skolnick, J. and Gordon, P. (2005) Editor's introduction: Secularization and disenchantment. *New German Critique* 94, 3–17.

Slade, P. (2003) Gallipoli thanatourism. *Annals of Tourism Research* 3 (4), 779–794.

Slyomovics, S. (1998) *The Object of Memory: Arab and Jew Narrate the Palestinian Village*. Philadelphia, PA: University of Pennsylvania Press.

Smart, B. (1996) Facing the body – Goffman, Levinas and the subject of ethics. *Body and Society* 2 (2), 67–78.

Smith, V. (1996) War and its attractions. In A. Pizam and Y. Mansfeld (eds) *Tourism Crime, and International Security Issues* (pp. 247–264). Chichester: John Wiley.

Smith, V. (1998) War and tourism: An American ethnography. *Annals of Tourism Research* 25 (1), 202–227.

Smith, N. and Croy, G. (2005) Presentation of dark tourism: Te Wairoa, the buried village. In C. Ryan, S. Page and M. Aicken (eds) *Taking Tourism to the Limit: Issues, Concepts and Managerial Perspectives* (pp. 199–213). Oxford: Elsevier.

Staines, D. (2002) Auschwitz and the camera. *Mortality* 7 (1), 13–32.

Starck, N. (2006) *Life after Death: The art of the obituary.* Melbourne: Melbourne University Press.

Stephenson, M. (2002) Travelling to the ancestral homelands: The aspirations and experiences of a UK Caribbean community. *Current Issues in Tourism* 5 (5), 378–425.

Stivers, R. (1994) *The Culture of Cynicism.* Cambridge: Blackwell.

Stivers, R. (1996) Towards a sociology of morality. *International Journal of Sociology and Social Policy* 16 (1–2), 1–14.

Stone, P. (2005a) Dark tourism: An old concept in a new world. *Tourism (London)* IV (25), 20.

Stone, P. (2005b) Consuming dark tourism: A call for research. *Review of Tourism Research* 3 (5), 109–117. On WWW at http://ertr.tamu.ed/appliedresearch.cfm?articleid=90.

Stone, P. (2006a) A dark tourism spectrum: Towards a typology of death and macabre related tourist sites, attractions and exhibitions. *Tourism: An Interdisciplinary International Journal* 54 (2), 145–160.

Stone, P. (2006b) Review: KZ – a feature length documentary by Rex Bloomstein. *The Dark Tourism Forum* (Nov). On WWW at http://www.dark-tourism.org.uk. Accessed 30.7.08.

Stone, P. (2007) Dark tourism: The ethics of exploiting tragedy. *Travel Weekly* (Apr).

Stone, P. and Sharpley, R. (2008) Consuming dark tourism: A thanatological perspective. *Annals of Tourism Research* 35 (2), 574–595.

Strange, C. and Kempa, M. (2003) Shades of dark tourism: Alcatraz and Robben Island. *Annals of Tourism Research* 30 (2), 386–403.

Sturken, M. (2007) *Tourists of History: Memory, Kitsch, and Consumerism from Oklahoma City to Ground Zero.* Durham, NC and London: Duke University Press.

SuAndi (2008) *Label for Brazilian models.* Trade and Empire: Remembering Slavery Exhibition, Whitworth Gallery, Manchester.

Sullivan, A. (2008) Rwanda: A nation with a dark past and tenuous future. *The McGill Tribune.* On WWW at http://media.www.mcgilltribune.com/media/storage/paper234/news/2008/09/09/Features/Rwanda.A.Nation.With.A.Dark.Past.And.Tenuous.Future-3420352.shtml.

Svenstorm (2008) New York, New York. On WWW at http://www.flickr.com/photos/svenstorm/2896933927/. Accessed 16.07.09.

Swarbrooke, J. (2001) *The Development and Management of Visitor Attractions* (2nd edn). Oxford: Butterworth-Heinemann.

Swinglehurst, E. (1974) *The Romantic Journey: The Story of Thomas Cook and Victorian Travel.* London: Pica Editorial.

Tanas, S. (2004) The cemetery as a part of the geography of tourism. *Turyzm* 14 (2).

Tanas, S. (2006) The meaning of death space in cultural tourism. *Turyzm* 16 (2), 145–151.

Tanas, S. (2008a) The perception of death in cultural tourism. *Turyzm* 18 (1), 51–63.

Tanas, S. (2008b) *Przestrzen Turystyczna Tmentarzy Wstep do Tanatoturystyki.* Lodz: Wydawnictwo Uniwersytetu Lodzkiego.

Tarlow, P. (2005) Dark tourism: The appealing 'dark' side of tourism and more. In M. Novelli (ed.) *Niche Tourism: Contemporary Issues, Trends and Cases* (pp. 47–57). Oxford: Elsevier.

Taylor, J.V. (1963) *The Primal Vision*. London: SCM.

Taylor, J. (2001) Authenticity and sincerity in tourism. *Annals of Tourism Research* 28 (1), 7–26.

Tercier, J. (2005) *The Contemporary Deathbed: The Ultimate Rush*. Basingstoke: Palgrave MacMillan.

Terrance, M. (1999) *Concentration Camps: A Traveler's Guide to World War II Sites*. Parkland: Universal Publishers.

Tester, K. (1995) *The Inhuman Condition*. London: Routledge.

The Dungeons (2008) *The Dungeons: Visitor Guide*. Dorset: Merlin Entertainments Group.

The Dungeons (2009) *The York Dungeon: Visitor Survey*. Dorset: Merlin Entertainments Group.

Thompson, C. (2004a) *The 25 Best World War II Sites: European Theater*. San Francisco, CA: Greenline Publications.

Thompson, C. (2004b) *The 25 Best World War II Sites: Pacific Theater*. San Francisco, CA: Greenline Publications.

Thorson, J. (1993) Did you ever see a hearse go by? Some thoughts on gallows humor. *Journal of American Culture* 16, 17–24.

Tilden, F. (1977) *Interpreting our Heritage* (3rd edn). Chapel Hill, NC: University of North Carolina Press.

Timothy, D. (1997) Tourism and the personal heritage experience. *Annals of Tourism Research* 24 (3), 751–754.

Timothy, D. and Boyd, S. (2003) *Heritage Tourism*. Harlow: Prentice Hall.

Timothy, D. and Olsen, D. (eds) (2006) *Tourism, Religion and Spiritual Journeys*. Abingdon: Routledge.

Tina-Perth (2008) *Tual Sleng Museum*. On WWW at http://www.virtualtourist.com/travel/Asia/Cambodia/Phnom_Penh-1194372/Things_To_Do-Phnom_Penh-Tuol_Sleng_Museum-BR-1.html. Accessed 12.11.08.

Tomgensler (2007) *York Dungeon*. On WWW at http://www.flickr.com/search/?q=york%20dungeon&w=93359333%40N00. Accessed 14.07.09.

Torgovnick, M. (1990) *Gone Primitive. Savage Intellects, Modern Lives*. Chicago, IL: University of Chicago Press.

Tosun, C. and Jenkins, C. (1998) The evolution of tourism planning in Third-World countries: A critique. *Progress in Tourism and Hospitality Research* 4 (2), 101–114.

Tourism of Cambodia (2008) *Tuol Sleng Museum*. On WWW at www.tourismcambodia.com/Attractions/toulsleng/index.asp.

Travelpod (2008) *Genocide Tourism – The Memorials, Rwanda*. On WWW at www.travelpod.com/travel-blog-entries/djchurch/rtw-2006andon/1180344240/tpod.html.

Trend, D. (2003) Merchants of death: Media violence and American Empire. *Harvard Educational Review* 73, 285–308.

Tunbridge, J. (2005) Penal colonies and tourism with reference to Robben Island, South Africa: Commodifying the heritage of atrocity? In G. Ashworth and R. Hartmann (eds) *Horror and Human Tragedy Revisited: The Management of Sites of Atrocities for Tourism* (pp. 19–40). New York: Cognizant Communications Corporation.

Tunbridge, J. and Ashworth, G. (1996) *Dissonant Heritage: Managing the Past as a Resource in Conflict*. Chichester: John Wiley.

Turner, B. (1991) *Religion and Social Theory*. London: Sage Publications.

Tyler-Mcgraw, M. (2006) Southern comfort levels: Race, heritage tourism and the Civil War in Richmond. In J.O. Horton and L.E. Horton (eds) *Slavery and Public History: The Tough Stuff of American History* (pp. 151–168). New York: The New Press.

Urry, J. (2002) *The Tourist Gaze* (2nd edn). London: Sage.

Uzzell, D. (1989a) Introduction: The natural and built environment. In D. Uzzell (ed.) *Heritage Interpretation* (Vol. I): *The Natural and Built Environment* (pp. 1–14). London: Bellhaven Press.

Uzell, D. (1989b) The hot interpretation of war and conflict. In D. Uzell (ed.) *Heritage Interpretation* (Vol. I): *The Natural and Built Environment* (pp. 33–47). London: Bellhaven Press.

Uzzell, D. (1998) Interpreting our heritage: A theoretical interpretation. In D. Uzzell and R. Ballantyne (eds) *Contemporary Issues in Heritage and Environmental Interpretation* (pp. 11–25). London: The Stationery Office.

Uzzell, D. and Ballantyne, R. (1998) Heritage that hurts: Interpretation in a postmodern world. In D. Uzzell and R. Ballantyne (eds) *Contemporary Issues in Heritage and Environmental Interpretation* (pp. 152–171). London: The Stationery Office.

Valentine, C. (2008) *Bereavement Narratives: Continuing Bonds in the 21st Century*. London: Routledge.

Vanderbilt, T. (2003) City lore: They didn't forget. *The New York Times* (13 July). On WWW at http://query.nytimes.com/gst/fullpage.html?res=9D05E4D61 E3DF930A25754C0A9659C8B63&sec=&spon=&pagewanted=all. Accessed 12.12.08.

Vega, C. (2002) Fast trade at ground zero. *The Press Democrat*. On WWW at http://nl.newsbank.com.

Verbeek, R. (2006) Remembering Srebrenica. *Realtravel.com*. On WWW at http://realtravel.com/srebrenica-journals-j1829420.html.

Vlach, J.M. (2006) The last great taboo subject: Exhibiting slavery at the Library of Congress. In J.O. Horton and L.E. Horton (eds) *Slavery and Public History: The Tough Stuff of American History* (pp. 57–74). New York: The New Press.

vom Lehn, D. (2006) The body as interactive display: Examining bodies in a public exhibition. *Sociology of Health & Illness* 28 (2), 223–251.

Wagner-Pacifici, R. and Schwartz, B. (1991) The Vietnam Veterans Memorial: Commemorating a difficult past. *American Journal of Sociology* 97, 376–420.

Wall, I. (2004) Postcard from hell. *The Guardian* (18 Oct). On WWW at http://www.guardian.co.uk/nuclear/article/0,2763,1329885,00.html. Accessed 31.7.08.

Walter, T. (1984) Death as recreation: Armchair mountaineering. *Leisure Studies* 3 (1) (Jan).

Walter, T. (1991) Modern death: Taboo or not taboo? *Sociology* 25, 293–310.

Walter, T. (1992) Angelic choirs: On the non-secularisation of choral music. *The Musical Times* (June), 78–81.

Walter, T. (1993) War grave pilgrimage. In I. Reader and T. Walter (eds) *Pilgrimage in Popular Culture* (pp. 63–91). Basingstoke: MacMillan.

Walter, T. (1994) *The Revival of Death*. London: Routledge.

Walter, T. (1999) *On Bereavement: The Culture of Grief*. Buckingham: Open University Press and Philadelphia, PA: Taylor & Francis.

Walter, T. (2004) Body Worlds: Clinical detachment or anatomical awe? *Sociology of Health & Illness* 26 (4), 464–488.

Walter, T. (2005) Mediator deathwork. *Death Studies* 29 (5), 383–412.

Walter, T. (2006) Disaster, modernity, and the media. In K. Garces-Foley (ed.) *Death and Religion in a Changing World* (pp. 265–282). Armonk, NY: M.E. Sharpe.

Walter, T. (2007) The new public mourning: Genuine grief or crocodile tears? In M. Stroebe *et al.* (eds) *Handbook of Bereavement Research and Practice: 21st Century Perspectives.* Washington, DC: American Psychological Association Press.

Walter, T., Pickering, M. and Littlewood, J. (1995) Death in the news: The public invigilation of private emotion. *Sociology* 29 (4), 579–596.

Wang, N. (1999) Rethinking authenticity in tourism experience. *Annals of Tourism Research* 26 (2), 349–370.

Warraq, I. (2007) *Defending the West. A critique of Edward Said's Orientalism.* Amherst, NY: Prometheus Books.

Wass, H., Miller, D. and Redditt, C. (1991) Adolescents and destructive themes in rock music: A follow-up. *Omega* 23, 199–206.

Weber, M. (1948) Science as a vocation. In H. Gerth and C. Mills (eds) *From Max Weber.* London: Routledge.

Webster, K. (2006) Laughing at history's gore: The London Dungeon. *Minds in the Making: An e-Collection from Calvin College.* Grand Rapids, MI: Calvin College.

Weissman, G. (2004) *Fantasies of Witnessing: Postwar Efforts to Experience the Holocaust.* New York: Cornell University Press.

West, P. (2004) *Conspicuous Compassion: Why Sometimes it Really is Cruel to be Kind.* London: Civitas.

Whalley, A. (2007) Body Worlds through the eyes of its visitors. In G. von Hagens and A. Whalley (eds) *Body Worlds – The Anatomical Exhibition of Real Human Bodies Catalogue* (pp. 299–303). Heidelberg: Institute for Plastination.

White, S. (1991) *Political Theory and Postmodernism.* Cambridge: University of Cambridge Press.

Whitworth Art Gallery (2008) *Four Models of Freed Slaves, 1834–36, Brazilian maker, Mixed Media.* Label accompanying Brazilian models, 'Trade and Empire: Remembering Slavery', inserted April 2008. Whitworth Art Gallery, Manchester.

Wight, A.C. (2006) Philosophical and methodological praxes in dark tourism: Controversy, contention and the evolving paradigm. *Journal of Vacation Marketing* 12 (2), 119–129.

Wight, A.C. (2008) Re-engineering 'authenticity': Tourism encounters with cuisine in rural Great Britain. In L. Rubin (ed.) *Food, Eating and Culture: A Cross-Disciplinary Feast* (pp. 153–165). Jefferson, NC: McFarland Press.

Wight, A.C. and Lennon, J. (2007) Selective interpretation and eclectic human heritage in Lithuania. *Tourism Management* 28 (2), 519–529.

Wight, C. and Lennon, J. (2004) Towards an understanding of visitor perceptions of 'dark' attractions: The case of the Imperial War Museum of the North, Manchester. *Journal of Hospitality and Tourism* 2, 105–122.

Williams, C. (2001) Beyond good and evil? The taboo in the contemporary museum: Strategies for negotiation and representation. *Open Museum Journal (The Taboo),* 4. On WWW at http://archive.amol.org.au/omj/abstract.asp?ID=12. Accessed 11.1.09.

Williams, P. (2004) Witnessing genocide: Vigilance and remembrance at Tuol Sleng and Choeng Ek. *Holocaust and Genocide Studies* 18 (2), 234–255.

Williams, P. (2007) *Memorial Museums: The Global Rush to Commemorate Atrocities.* Oxford: Berg.

Williams, P. (2008) *The Afterlife of Communist Statuary: Hungary's Szoborpark and Lithuania's Grutas Park.* St. Andrews: University of St. Andrews, Forum for Modern Language Studies.

Willmott, H. (2000) Death. So what? Sociology, sequestration and emancipation. *The Sociological Review* 4, 649–665.

Wilson, J.Z. (2008) *Prison: Cultural Memory and Dark Tourism.* New York: Peter Lang.

Winkel, H. (2001) A postmodern culture of grief? On individualization of mourning in Germany. *Mortality* 6, 65–79.

Woodthorpe, K. (2007) Bodies in the cemetery. Paper presented at the 8th International Conference on the Social Context of Death, Dying & Disposal. Bath, UK.

Xie, P. and Wall, G. (2008) Authenticating ethnic tourist attractions. In A. Fyall, B. Garrod, A. Leask and S. Wanhill (eds) *Managing Visitor Attractions: New Directions* (pp. 132–147). Oxford: Butterworth-Heinemann.

Yale University Genocide Studies Program (2008) *Cambodian Genocide Program.* New Haven, CT: Yale University.

Young, J. (2001) Daniel Liebeskind's Jewish Museum in Berlin: The uncanny arts of memorial architecture. In B. Zelizer *Visual Culture and the Holocaust* (p. 194). London: Athlone Press.

Yuill, S. (2003) Dark tourism: Understanding visitor motivation at sites of death and disaster. MSc thesis, Texas A & M University.

Zimonjic, V. (2006) Sarajevo reveals its war wounds for tourist cash. *The Independent* (2 May). On WWW at http://findarticles.com/p/articles/mi_qn4158/is_20060502/ai_n16214567. Accessed 31.7.08.

Index

Absent death: 30, 32, 36, 37
Alcatraz: 20, 90, 112
Anzac: 35, 157, 161
Atrocity heritage/sites: 12, 95, 148, 209, 212, 219, 222
Atrocity tourism: 10, 12, 13, 59
Auschwitz: 15,20, 35, 44, 52, 56, 58, 69, 87, 130, 131, 137, 142, 181, 182, 207, 211
Authenticity: 21, 111, 112, 113, 115-7, 125, 132, 134, 136, 137, 142, 181, 212, 217

Bannockburn: 158
Belfast: 147, 169
Black Death: 172, 183-4
Black Spots: 13
Body Worlds: 5, 23, 24, 25, 32, 48, 49, 51, 86, 104, 106, 148, 247, 248
Boer War: 47, 87, 187
Boorstin, Daniel: 4, 115, 116
Bosnia: 58, 168, 208, 213, 220-1
Bracketing (of death): 28, 32, 36
British Empire and Commonwealth Museum: 105
Buchenwald: 211, 215

Cambodia: 15, 19, 156, 157, 212, 213, 217-8
Ceausescu: 153
Chernobyl: 59
Cobain, Kurt: 94
Collective effervescence: 60, 63, 64, 67, 71, 72, 125
Comfort culture: 120, 126
Continuum of intensity: 15, 16
Corporate Social Responsibility (CSR): 131-2
Cuba: 3, 149, 182
Culloden: 44, 85, 158, 159
Cyprus: 151

Dachau: 152, 211
Dallas: 10, 27, 56
Darling, Grace: 109-11
Diana, Princess: 9, 18, 44, 54, 56, 57, 90, 122, 168
Diaspora, African: 159
Dicing with death: 10, 11
Disney World: 140
Dissonance/dissonant heritage: 8, 12, 13, 130, 134, 137, 138, 148, 150, 151, 159, 161, 162, 163, 209, 212

Douglass, Frederick: 228-32
Dracula: 10, 169
Dread: 28, 31, 32, 33, 36, 37
Dream factory: 129
Dungeon, York: 69, 125, 172, 174-84
Dunnotar Castle: 47
Durkheim, Emile: 60, 63, 64, 66, 68, 70

Edutainment: 48, 49, 50, 111, 135, 141, 248
Elmina Castle: 225
Ethics, tourism: 133
Experience economy: 134

Farne Islands: 109-11
Flight 93 Tours: 5, 20
Fort Siloso, Singapore: 13
Frank, Anne (House of): 52, 54, 137, 216, 222
Fright tourism: 10, 169
Fun factory, dark: 21, 148, 169, 170

Gallipoli: 15, 35, 92, 97, 157-8, 159, 161
Gambia, The: 159
Genealogy: 42, 43, 46, 47, 50, 51, 54, 194
Genocide: 6, 15, 21, 136, 138, 140, 141, 152, 155, 156, 157, 161, 167, 168, 207-23
Gettysburg: 58, 158, 187, 192, 194, 197
Ghosts/ghost walks: 84, 86, 94, 169, 172, 173, 242
Gladiatorial games: 4
Glencoe: 85, 158
Graves/graveyards: 7, 10, 13, 15, 16, 20, 26, 35, 39, 43, 45, 46, 50, 85, 88, 156, 157, 186, 190, 191, 193, 194-5, 197, 201, 205, 213, 217, 219, 221, 228
Grief tourism: 5, 10, 57
Ground Zero: 5, 8, 10, 15, 50, 53, 54, 58, 59, 64, 67, 70, 121, 125, 126, 150, 168
Grutas Park, Lithuania: 129, 138-42

Heritage Force Field: 97-101
Highgate Cemetery: 87
Hiroshima: 132, 188
Holocaust: 7, 8, 10, 17, 46, 49, 52, 53, 56, 58, 87, 100, 132, 135, 137, 148, 152, 157, 161, 162, 163, 168, 172, 215-217
Holocaust Memorial Museum: 20, 132, 137, 211, 222
Hot interpretation: 12
Houses of horror: 7, 11, 35

Individualisation: 60
International School for Peace Studies: 199, 200

Japan: 8, 45, 49, 50, 51, 132, 156, 158

Khmer Rouge: 156, 157, 217
Kigaliu Genocide Memorial Museum: 207, 219
Kitsch: 113, 120-8, 171
Kwai Bridge: 17
KwaZulu: 96

Lithuania: 13, 112, 129, 138, 139, 140, 141, 142
Lockerbie: 13

MacCannell, Dean: 116
Medicalisation: 30, 31, 32
Memento mori: 23, 42, 48-9, 51
Menin Gate: 194, 203, 205, 206
Morbid tourism: 10, 13
Mormon: 41-2
Morrison, Jim: 94
Morro Castle, SS: 3, 4, 13
Mortality moments: 26, 34, 37
Mourning sickness: 6, 57
Myanmar: 149

Neutralisation, social (of death): 32, 37
Nostalgia: 11, 41, 113, 121, 123, 127, 128

Old Gaol, Melbourne: 90
Omaha Beach: 56, 194, 196
Ontological security: 27-29, 30, 32, 33, 37, 53, 250
Orientalism: 77, 80
Other, The: 76-8
Otherness (of death): 83, 84

Panic, moral: 58, 63, 70, 71, 113, 138, 140, 143, 248
Pearl Harbour: 50, 188
Pere La Chaise: 88, 96
Philippines: 149
Pilgrimage: 4, 7, 13, 16, 18, 41, 47, 54, 62, 84, 135, 168, 188, 189, 191-5, 201, 202, 215, 222, 237
Plague: 184, 170, 181, 182
Politics (of tourism): 148-51
Pompeii: 15, 86, 95
Presley, Elvis: 10, 13, 18, 96
Prison tourism: 10, 15, 20, 112, 140, 153, 156

Robben Island: 20, 96
Roots tourism: 159
Romanticism: 81, 84
Royal British Legion: 188, 189, 190, 192, 193, 194, 196
Rwanda: 6, 207, 208, 213, 228-30

Sacred space: 85, 96, 97, 99
Sarajevo: 18, 58
Schadenfreude: 11, 17, 38, 249
Schindler, Oskar: 12, 136, 144, 211, 216
Sealed Knot: 111
Secular/secularism: 16, 27, 40, 60, 70, 71, 82, 83, 116, 143
Sensation tourism: 13, 15
Sequestration (of death): 27, 29, 30, 31, 32, 40, 72
Slave Trade Arts Memorial Project: 234
Soham, Cambridgeshire: 5, 57, 90
Souvenirs: 14, 15, 111, 121, 125, 135, 136
Spectrum, dark tourism: 20-2, 138, 167, 201, 250
Srebrenica: 221
Sport and War Exhibition: 91-93

Taboo (of death): 24, 25, 26, 28, 52, 169, 171, 185, 195, 247
Taj Mahal: 17, 44
Terrorhaza, Budapest: 132, 153
Te Wairoa (buried village): 14
Thomas Cook: 133, 187
Tilden, Freeman: 113-4
Tribute WTC Visitor Centre: 64, 66, 67
Tuol Sleng/Choeung Ek: 156, 212, 217, 218
Turpin, Dick: 172, 184
Tussauds (Madame): 90, 95, 96, 170
Twin Towers: 50, 59, 122, 123, 150

Vietnam: 18, 49, 52, 54, 56, 97, 146, 156, 157, 188, 217
Vilna Gaon Jewish Museum: 138
Vilnius: 112, 138, 141
Von Hagens, Gunther: 23, 48, 104, 106, 242
Voyeurism: 17, 70

Waterloo (Battle of): 5, 15, 97, 151, 158, 186, 187, 203
Wellcome Trust: 101
Westminster Abbey: 87
Wilberforce, William: 160
Worlds Trade Centre: 5, 59, 123, 150

Yad Vashem: 216

CPSIA information can be obtained
at www.ICGtesting.com
Printed in the USA
BVOW06s0005071216
470008BV00004B/4/P